MAX-PLANCK-INSTITUT
FÜR AUSLÄNDISCHES ÖFFENTLICHES RECHT
UND VÖLKERRECHT

Beiträge zum ausländischen öffentlichen Recht und Völkerrecht

Begründet von Viktor Bruns

Herausgegeben von
Armin von Bogdandy · Anne Peters

Band 275

Aydin Atilgan

Global Constitutionalism

A Socio-legal Perspective

Springer

ISSN 0172-4770 ISSN 2197-7135 (electronic)
Beiträge zum ausländischen öffentlichen Recht und Völkerrecht

ISBN 978-3-662-55646-7 ISBN 978-3-662-55647-4 (eBook)
https://doi.org/10.1007/978-3-662-55647-4

Library of Congress Control Number: 2017951868

Springer

Printed on acid-free paper

This Springer imprint is published by Springer Nature
The registered company is Springer-Verlag GmbH Germany
The registered company address is: Heidelberger Platz 3, 14197 Berlin, Germany

Acknowledgments

This book is a slightly edited version of my PhD thesis that I achieved at the Albrecht Mendelssohn Bartholdy Graduate School of Law of the University of Hamburg. First and foremost, I wish to thank my supervisors, Prof. Dr. Stefan Oeter and Prof. Dr. Karl-Heinz Ladeur for their great support. Prof. Dr. Ladeur was always quite supportive and patient, and his immense knowledge has always illuminated my way. Prof. Dr. Oeter was very encouraging and cooperative at all steps of this project, and I was very lucky to have such an open-minded and wise supervisor. I should note that writing this dissertation under their supervision has left a great impact on me, and this inquiry could not have been achieved without their valuable contributions and mentorships.

Apart from my supervisors, my sincere thanks go to Prof. Dr. Andreas Fischer-Lescano, Prof. Dr. David Nelken, and Prof. Dr. Chris Thornhill. They hosted me in their institutes, dealt with my research problems, and they had a significant role in the construction of my intellectual world. I am also grateful to Prof. Dr. Hauke Brunkhorst for him handling my questions and giving me the chance to discuss various points of my research in his colloquiums. Furthermore, I must express my thanks to Prof. Dr. Turgut Tarhanli and Prof. Dr. Mithat Sancar for their encouragement and insightful contributions at the earlier phase of this project; and also to Prof. Dr. Anne Peters and Prof. Dr. Armin von Bogdandy, the editors of the book series "Beiträge zum ausländischen öffentichen Recht und Völkerrecht."

A profound compensation of this project has been that I got to know wonderful people during my research in various cities and countries. Their amazing cooperation and sincere help have been engraved into my memory: Thank you to the Family Wischnath, Bojan Gavrilovic, Marco and Corina Johns, Wiebke Greeff, Burak Nisanci and Jörg Kitlinski. Your thoughtfulness and friendships were key to overcome many difficulties.

The most special acknowledgments go to my family. I am grateful to my father for all his support to this day; he has always been there for me whenever I needed him. Finally, I wish to thank my dearly beloved ones, Eylem and Maya, who have always provided me with an unending inspiration. This book is, above all, the product of their patience. Their love was and will always be my greatest support and source of inspiration.

Aydin Atilgan

Contents

1 Introduction 1

2 International Law, Globalization, and Transformation 7
2.1 International Law and Globalization 7
2.1.1 Globalization, Sovereignty and Changing Structures 9
2.1.1.1 Rise of Network Society 10
2.1.1.2 Erosion of Sovereignty 15
2.1.2 Challenges of Globalization towards International Law 20
2.1.2.1 Dimension of Transformation: From Westphalian towards Post-Westphalian 20
2.1.2.1.1 New Law for a New World 20
2.1.2.1.2 From "Law of Cooperation" towards "Law of Integration" 23
2.1.2.2 Expansion of International Community 29
2.1.2.2.1 International Organizations and Non-Governmental Organizations (NGOs) . 29
2.1.2.2.2 Individuals and Impact of Human Rights . . . 35
2.1.2.3 A New Normative Framework 38
2.1.2.4 Fragmentation and International Law 43
2.1.2.4.1 Increasing Differentiation and Fragmentation 43
2.1.2.4.2 New Spaces, Regimes and Jurisdictional Rules 47
2.1.2.5 Blurring Borderline Between Public and Private Law . 49
2.1.2.6 Paradigm Shifts 51
2.1.2.6.1 Earlier Shifts: International Community 52
2.1.2.6.2 Post-War Shifts 55
2.2 Responses to the Transformation: An Inquiry for a New Paradigm? . . 58
2.2.1 The Rise of the Idea of Global Law 59
2.2.2 Global Law and Constructivism 62
2.2.3 A Global Public Order? A Genealogy of Pluralism, Administrative Law and Constitutionalism 64

2.2.3.1 Global Legal Pluralism 65
2.2.3.2 Global Administrative Law 66
2.2.3.3 Global Constitutionalism 69

3 Constitutionalism in Global Context: A Developing Discourse 73
3.1 Mapping Global Constitutionalism Theories 74
3.1.1 Global Constitutionalist Theories: Assumption of an Ongoing Constitutionalization Process 75
3.1.1.1 Holistic Approaches: World State, Cosmopolitanism, Universalism 75
3.1.1.1.1 Cosmopolitanism and "the World State" . . . 75
3.1.1.1.1.1 Kantian Tradition and Cosmopolitanism 76
3.1.1.1.1.2 The Idea of "World State" 81
3.1.1.1.2 The UN Charter as a Constitution 86
3.1.1.1.3 Constitutionalization of the WTO 91
3.1.1.2 Micro-Constitutionalization 94
3.1.1.2.1 World Society and Constitutions as Structural Couplings of Law and Politics . . . 94
3.1.1.2.2 Teubner and Fischer-Lescano: Constitutional Fragments 98
3.1.1.3 Compensatory Constitutionalism 103
3.1.2 Global Constitutionalism as a "Noetic" Idea 106
3.2 Viability of Global Constitutionalism 108
3.2.1 Responses and Challenges to Global Constitutionalism 109
3.2.1.1 "Unrealistic" Perspective of Global Constitutionalism 109
3.2.1.2 "Flaws" of Global Constitutionalism 111
3.2.2 Interrogation for Viability of Global Constitutionalism 115
3.2.2.1 Commonalities of Global Constitutionalism Theories 115
3.2.2.2 What Does the Global Constitutionalism Discourse Lack? 116

4 Meaning of Contemporary Constitution 121
4.1 Key Concepts 121
4.1.1 The Main Idea of Contemporary Constitution and Constitutionalism 121
4.1.1.1 Historical Development of Modern Constitution and Constitutionalism 127
4.1.1.1.1 Pre-modern Developments 127
4.1.1.1.2 Rise of Modern Constitutionalism 132
4.1.1.2 Identification of Constitution: Discursive Facts 136
4.1.1.2.1 Traditional Idea of Constitution: Analytical Interpretation of Constitution 138

4.1.1.2.2 *Constitutions in Context: The Dichotomy of Political Constitution and Legal Constitution* 142
4.1.1.2.2.1 Legal Constitution 145
4.1.1.2.2.1.1 Theoretical Background. 145
4.1.1.2.2.1.2 German Basic Law (Grundgesetz) as a Legal Constitution 150
4.1.1.2.2.2 Political Constitution 153
4.1.1.2.2.2.1 Theoretical Background. 153
4.1.1.2.2.2.2 The Human Rights Act and the British Constitution 161
4.1.1.2.2.3 Contextual Identity of Constitution 166
4.2 Contemporary Constitutionalism and Globalization 172
4.2.1 Relationship and Communication Between Constitutions . . . 172
4.2.1.1 Migration of Constitutions and Contemporary Constitution as a Mobile Phenomenon 172
4.2.1.2 Contemporary Constitution and Transconstitutionalism 178
4.2.2 Changing Framework of Legitimacy 181
4.2.2.1 Transformation of Constituent Power. 181
4.2.2.2 Contemporary Constitution as Increasingly a Rights-based Concept 185
4.2.3 Contemporary Constitutionalism and Integration 186
4.2.3.1 Integrative Power of Modern Constitutions 186
4.2.3.2 Changing Face of Integrative Function. 189
4.2.4 Meaning of Contemporary Constitution 194
4.2.4.1 A Deviation or a Continuance of Modern Constitution?. 194
4.2.4.2 Typology Problem. 195
4.2.4.3 A New Paradigm to Explain Diversity and Relativity of Constitutions. 198

5 Contemporary Constitution and the Cultural Paradigm 209
5.1 Constitution as a Cultural Phenomenon. 209
5.1.1 Cultural Paradigm and the Concept of Constitutional Culture 209
5.1.2 Constitutional Culture as a Reflection of Political and Civic Culture 212
5.1.2.1 Constitutional Culture as a Political Culture 212

5.1.2.2 Constitutional Cultures Between Political Decisions and Social Discourses: Theory of Richard Münch ... 216
5.1.3 Constitutional Culture as a Variation of Legal Culture 218
5.1.3.1 The Idea of Legal Culture 218
5.1.3.2 Constitutional Culture as Legal Culture 223
5.2 Reflections on Constitutional Culture 228
5.2.1 Constitutional Cultures in Territorial Basis 228
5.2.1.1 The British Constitutional Culture 229
5.2.1.2 The German Constitutional Culture 231
5.2.1.3 The American Constitutional Culture 233
5.2.2 Constitutional Culture in Context: Case of Human Rights ... 235
5.2.3 Cultural Identity of Constitution 240

6 Contemporary Constitutionalism to Understand Global Constitutionalism 243
6.1 Global Constitutionalism and the Narrower Meaning of Constitution 243
6.1.1 Global Constitutionalism from the Point of 'Achieved Constitutions of the Past' 243
6.1.2 Some Further Aspects of Modern Constitutionalism: Integration, Unity, Separation of Powers 246
6.1.3 Fragmented Global Order: A Proto-Constitutional Order? ... 250
6.2 Global Constitutionalism from the Point of the Cultural Paradigm .. 251
6.2.1 Prospects for a Global Constitutional Culture 252
6.2.1.1 Global Constitutional Culture as a Global Legal Culture 253
6.2.1.1.1 Global Internal Legal Culture 254
6.2.1.1.2 Global External Legal Culture 259
6.2.1.2 Global Constitutional Culture as a Global Political Culture 268
6.2.1.2.1 Post-Westphalian Values and Consensus .. 269
6.2.1.2.2 Global Constitutional Culture and Legitimacy 274
6.2.1.2.3 A Global Rule of Law? 275
6.2.2 Global Constitutionalism and Constitutional Culture 281
6.3 Prospects for the Future of Global Constitutionalism 284
6.3.1 Global Constitutionalism as a Matter of Transconstitutional Relations 285
6.3.2 Global Constitution as a Metonym 289

7 Conclusion 293

Bibliography 299

Chapter 1
Introduction

Globalism is currently a buzzword explaining many phenomena as well as law and state. While some social facts, such as economics and politics are very frequently dealt with in the context of globalism, the law still evokes local meanings and is not at the core of globalization studies. On the other hand, it has not been immune to the impacts of globalization, and it has gained new meanings by increasing transnational relations.

It goes without saying that international law is currently understood by legal professionals quite differently than by their former colleagues that practiced law in the early twentieth century. In the age of increasing economic and political globalization, it is evident that we cannot interpret international law like de Vattel, Grotius, or lawyers involved in the Lotus ruling of the PCIJ. On the other hand, in the face of the turbulences of globalization and the end of the Cold War, attempts to identify the new world order have not yet come to an end. In this context, various candidate paradigms appear to vary in a broad range depending on different backgrounds of their proceeding fields to illuminate the transformation of international law.

One of these responses to paradigm inquiries in international law is global constitutionalism. It goes without saying that the idea of a global constitution is deemed to be utopia-like by many, since international relations are viewed as anarchic or as an arena for power struggles. Above all, the international legal order has not seen a formally promulgated constitution yet. Therefore, we could say that global constitutionalism is a discourse about a discursive constitution. In this case, we could ask, to what extent could this discourse have viability, given the recent developments in international law and constitutional law?

Global constitutionalism is currently represented by various ideas, or better to say, by various schools. I shall touch upon the most notable of them in this text. These ideas vary as a result of their distinct approaches to international law, the international community, and the idea of constitution. At this point, it is of note that

A. Atilgan, *Global Constitutionalism*, Beiträge zum ausländischen öffentlichen Recht und Völkerrecht, https://doi.org/10.1007/978-3-662-55647-4_1

this research does not have an ambition to reflect in particular any of them, in other words, favour one of them. Moreover, this research does not proceed from any presumption that a constitutionalization process is ongoing in the global realm. Likewise, this research does not stick to any presumption that a constitutionalization in the global realm would be desirable. On the other side, as will be demonstrated below, due to the diverse ideas in this realm, global constitutionalism cannot be allocated to one of these ideas in particular. Instead, this research considers global constitutionalism an umbrella term to identify these integrationist approaches in international law that adhere to a constitutional language. In this sense, global constitutionalism should be regarded as a discourse containing various ideas that underpin and challenge themselves at the same time.

As done in this text, global constitutionalism is likely to be considered as akin to other global law approaches, global legal pluralism and global administrative law, on the ground that a base of a global legal order is common for these strands. With a view to understanding the very idea of global constitutionalism, it is a must to have a grasp of the evolution of international law and the making of international law; and the changing structures of relevant categories, such as statehood, international relations, and so on. While dealing with this transformation in international law, what comes to the fore is mostly the changing structure of the state practice in international law and new norm making processes in particular to the context of the aftermath processes of the WWII and globalization, from the second half of the twentieth century to this day.[1] Global constitutionalism, in this sense, is of an intimate relationship with the changing nature of international law.

However, a striking point in the global constitutionalism debate is the discursive structure of the constitution reflected in this discourse with diverse backgrounds. The idea of the contemporary constitution was also exposed to various impacts of globalization, and under these circumstances, the concept of the constitution came along with new issues regarding its identity. In this regard, the main strategic drive of this research will be finding an answer to what extent global constitutionalism deals with the contemporary idea of the constitution.

While examining the viability of the idea of the global constitution for the international legal order, I shall be pursuing an interdisciplinary methodology. Global constitutionalism has to do with public international law and constitutional law discourses. The intersection point of these two discourses also reflects a ground for societal discourses. This issue brings a dichotomy of norms and facts into play. That is to say, how far normative developments of international law find their factual correspondents in the society is another actual problem to be sorted out. This is a longstanding problem of the sociology of constitutions as well. This is so, because as Thornhill states, the question of "which internal forces cause societies to produce constitutions and constitutional rights" has still not been answered comprehensively, and furthermore, "the founding sociological attempt to enable modern

[1] Paul Schiff Berman, "From International Law to Law and Globalization" (University of Connecticut School of Law Articles and Working Papers, Paper 23, 2005, http://lsr.nellco.org/uconn_wps/23), last visit 11.07.2013.

societies internally to comprehend their articulated normative structure has not been concluded."[2] At this point, global constitutionalism can be regarded as an output of the development of modern constitutionalism. As such, global constitutionalism is related to the societal dynamics of modern constitutionalism, and such a sociological perspective also needs to be developed to deal with the fundamental questions of global constitutionalism. To address this question evidently requires employing basic tools of a sociological perspective, such as "the social structure," "the social stratification," and "the social function."[3] Against this background, Raymond Wacks argues that a sociological account of law relies on three fundamental claims:

> that we cannot truly grasp the meaning of law except as a "social phenomenon," that an analysis of legal concepts provides only a partial explanation of "law in action," and that law is merely one form of social control.[4]

These all will help to construct the fundamental claims of this research. On the other hand, the weakness of normative tools in the global constitutionalism discourse brings discursive tools into prominence. As a consequence, global constitutionalism is viewed as a rather theoretical matter. Therefore, it is defined as an "academic artefact,"[5] a "forum,"[6] a "discourse"[7] or an "intellectual movement"[8] by some scholars.

The striking point is that global constitutionalism concerns transnational relations, instead of those which are traditionally regarded as subjects of general international law or domestic laws. Transnational level embraces these levels, but it goes further. We are most likely to call this approach a "global socio-legal perspective." In Darian-Smith's words, a global socio-legal perspective means "adopting a 'global imaginary' that destabilizes our modern and linear understandings of what law is, where law appears, and how law works."[9] This standpoint unveils a holistic

---

[2] Christopher J. A. Thornhill, *A Sociology of Constitutions: Constitutions and State Legitimacy in Historical-sociological Perspective* (Cambridge: Cambridge University Press, 2011), 6.

[3] Raymond Wacks, *Understanding Jurisprudence: An Introduction to Legal Theory* (Oxford: Oxford University Press, 2009), 163.

[4] Ibid., 162.

[5] Antje Wiener, "Global Constitutionalism: Mapping an Emerging Field" (Paper presented at the Conference "Constitutionalism in a New Key? Cosmopolitan, Pluralist and Public Reason-Oriented," WZB and Humboldt University, Berlin, 28-29 January 2011, http://cosmopolis.wzb.eu/content/programs/conkey_Wiener_Mapping-Field.pdf), last visit 10.01.2014.

[6] Christine E.J. Schwöbel, *Global Constitutionalism in International Legal Perspective* (Leiden: Nijhoff, 2011), 148.

[7] Anne Peters, "The Merits of Global Constitutionalism," *Indiana Journal of Global Legal Studies* 16, no. 2 (2009): 397.

[8] Anne Peters, "Fragmentation and Constitutionalization," in *The Oxford Handbook of the Theory of International Law*, ed. Anne Orford and Florian Hoffmann (Oxford: Oxford University Press, 2016), 1015.

[9] Eve Darian-Smith, *Laws and Societies in Global Contexts: Contemporary Approaches* (Cambridge: Cambridge University Press, 2013), 13.

approach toward law that deals with global phenomena in view of broader links of law to societal facts. In other words, I shall not adhere to mere normative processes of international law and constitutional law, but I shall seek a way to blend these two discourses by drawing on newly emerging socio-legal discourses regarding global matters and constitution.

For this purpose, in the first chapter, I shall unveil the new conditions in the international legal order led by globalization. The main claim is that these new conditions set the ground for the global constitutionalism discourse, and as a matter of fact, this discourse appears to fill a gap to identify a new rationality of the contemporary world. In other words, global constitutionalism is an attempt to establish a new paradigm in international law that is led by the great global turmoils and burgeoning complex relations which came to light beginning from the aftermath of the World War II.

However, this discourse hosts some different views on international law and international relations. In the second chapter, the global constitutionalism discourse will be considered in two respects. First, this discourse will be mapped, and contributions to this discourse will be categorized regarding their understanding of constitutionalization. The prominent contributions from the legal scholarship will be introduced. Following that, the issue of the viability of this discourse will come to the fore, and I shall examine the viability of the idea of global constitutionalism regarding some parameters. The idea of global constitutionalism has been responded in various ways within the legal scholarship, and we will take a glance at the challenges to this idea first. The meaning of contemporary constitutionalism will be central to this interrogation. In other words, to what extent the global constitutionalism discourse can reflect the contemporary constitutionalism will be viewed as the key issue in the interrogation of the viability of this discourse.

From this point forth, the third chapter will aim at unfolding the meaning of the contemporary constitution. For this purpose, I shall deal with contemporary discursive facts regarding constitutions besides historical developments and the traditional idea of constitution. Further on, we will proceed from the fact that constitutional law, like international law, has undergone serious transformations led by globalization, and this gave rise to a number of implications. Against this background, the text will set forth that contemporary constitutionalism requires these implications to be taken into consideration in order to depict the whole framework.

In parallel with the search for a socio-legal inquiry of contemporary constitutionalism, I shall draw on the cultural paradigm to understand contemporary constitutionalism, and the fourth chapter will be dedicated to this purpose. The cultural paradigm is still underdeveloped in constitutional law. However some significant academic works have appeared in this field recently, and they will also guide this research to an understanding of the truth of contemporary constitutionalism.

As I aim at drawing a framework for contemporary constitutionalism through conventional sources of the constitutional theory and the cultural paradigm, I shall utilize this framework in the fifth chapter in order to interrogate the viability and the truth of global constitutionalism. In other words, the global constitutionalist discourse will be examined through the contemporary idea of constitution; and its compliance with the truth of contemporary constitutionalism will be viewed as crucial for the viability of this discourse. I shall also propose a reconstruction of the discourse of global constitutionalism in accordance with the main findings from the unveiled facts of contemporary constitutionalism.

Chapter 2
International Law, Globalization, and Transformation

2.1 International Law and Globalization

According to an increasingly strengthening idea in the international law scholarship, traditional institutions and instruments of international law are now far from meeting the needs and challenges of our day, and they need to be reformed or replaced by new ones.[1] This is also true for national laws. Domestic legal systems suffer from various obstacles in implementing jurisdiction over entities that operate beyond national borders.[2] On the other side, public law and international law have already been in a transformative process through new norms, new forms and new actors. The catalyst of both challenges and transformation arises as a common phenomenon: globalization. Globalization, as Sands argues, goes hand in hand with three other phenomena of our era, namely technological innovations, democratization, and privatization.[3]

In the relationship between international law and globalization, a prominent issue is the changing structure of the state practice and new norm making processes as a continuance of the aftermath of the World War II, say, from the beginning of the second half of the twentieth century to this day.[4] In this regard, global constitutionalism -the main issue of this research- is one of the responses to the changing nature of international law.

---

[1] Anne-Marie Slaughter, *A New World Order* (Princeton: Princeton University Press, 2004), 8.

[2] Alan Boyle and Christin Chinkin, *The Making of International Law* (Oxford: Oxford University Press, 2007), 21.

[3] Philippe Sands, "Turtles and Torturers: The Transformation of International Law (Pinochet and Shrimp/Turtle cases)," *New York University Journal of International Law and Politics* 33, no. 2 (2001): 527-559.

[4] Paul Schiff Berman, "From International Law to Law and Globalization" (University of Connecticut School of Law Articles and Working Papers, Paper 23, 2005, http://lsr.nellco.org/uconn_wps/23), last visit 11.07.2013.

A. Atilgan, *Global Constitutionalism*, Beiträge zum ausländischen öffentlichen Recht und Völkerrecht, https://doi.org/10.1007/978-3-662-55647-4_2

In the traditional understanding of international law by the earlier generations of scholars, international law consists of international conventions among and between states, international customs, general principles of law, "judicial decisions and the teachings of the most highly qualified publicists of the various nations, as subsidiary means" as mentioned under Article 38(1) of the Statute of the International Court of Justice;[5] and also activities of international organizations, such as the United Nations.[6] Two core principles guided this order: "First, law was deemed to reside only in the acts of official, state-sanctioned entities. Second, law was seen as an exclusive function of state sovereignty."[7] The idea of the transformation of international law is basically rooted in the rejection of these principles. At this point, two new developments undermining these principles rise from different actors in international law, and transnationalization of law became quite influential over scholars who focused on the changing framework of international law.[8]

Given the transformations and challenges at stake, some legal scholars examined and criticized the narrow focus of international legal scholarship. In this regard, for example, in his very stimulating academic works, Paul Schiff Berman states that the current framework of international law remains incapable of depicting the development and operation of norms beyond national borders. Thus, it needs a new framework, by drawing on cross-border norm development at the intersection of conflict of laws, civil procedure, Cyberlaw, comparative law, the cultural analysis of law, and traditional international law. He suggests dealing with international law within a new and a broader framework of "law and globalization" to grasp the multifaceted nature of law.[9] In another relevant work, Bederman puts challenges to the traditional international law that arose in the age of globalism into four categories: Diversity, Permeability, Legitimacy, and Exceptionalism.[10] In the face of these challenges, he suggests a new descriptive reading of public international law as well.

Below, dynamics of this transformation and challenges to the traditional understanding of international law will be elucidated, and thereby this transformative process will be depicted. The main goal of this chapter is to reveal the challenges

---

[5] Statute of the International Court of Justice, 26 June 1945, http://www.icj-cij.org/documents/?p1=4&p2=2, last visit 14.06.2015.

[6] Berman, "From International Law," 487.

[7] Ibid., 487.

[8] Ibid., 489. As a matter of fact, transnational space is based on its own logic, independent from international law, and it appears as a third layer of "social pattern-reproduction" in addition to modern statehood and feudal structures in the evolution process of modern states. This means that the transnational realm developed hand in hand with the modern statehood, instead of a model of "zero-sum relationship." Poul Kjaer, *Constitutionalism in the Global Realm: A Sociological Approach* (London: Routledge, 2014), 1-2, 32. What is meant by "transnationalization of law" here is indeed to be seen as a continuance of this relationship, not a self-evident development in international relations.

[9] Berman, "From International Law," 490.

[10] David J. Bederman, *Globalization and International Law* (New York: Palgrave Macmillan, 2008).

from new forms of relationships and societal facts for international law, and thus to examine what makes the traditional form of international law dysfunctional for meeting the pressing needs of this era. Globalization and transformation of international law have so far been discussed in different perspectives.[11] Accordingly, various responses to this process have arisen from the international law scholarship. In the second part of this chapter, these responses will be introduced, and finally, the linkage between the transformative process in international law and the idea of constitutionalism will be discussed.

2.1.1 *Globalization, Sovereignty and Changing Structures*

Globalization is indeed not a new fact of life. Environmental and demographic forms of globalization are the oldest ones beginning with the flow of human species hundreds of thousands years ago.[12] An economic globalization was also observed in the nineteenth century.[13] Keohane and Nye advance the claim that what makes the difference in current globalization is its "thickness," that is to say, the intensity of globalization.[14] In other words, current globalization that has strong technological and communicative aspects is much more intense than in the era of the Silk Road.

Globalization is defined in various ways. Globalization basically means an increase of globalism that "is a state of the world involving networks of interdependence at multicontinental distances."[15] That is to say, globalization and globalism have to do with multiple relationships, not with single connections. Furthermore,

---

[11] However, it is of note that academic works that explain this transformation aggregately are rare, since the studies on law and globalization rather concern some contextual issues. For most remarkable ones: Ibid.; Philip Alston, "The Myopia of the Handmaidens: International Lawyers and Globalization," *European Journal of International Law* 3 (1997): 435-448. Rafael Domingo, *The New Global Law* (Cambridge: Cambridge University Press, 2010). Frédéric Mégret, "Globalization," *Max Planck Encyclopedia of Public International Law*, last updated: February 2009, http://opil.ouplaw.com/view/10.1093/law:epil/9780199231690/law-9780199231690-e939?prd=EPIL, last visit 19.06.2014. Berman, "From International Law." Shavana Musa and Eefie de Voider, "Interview with Professor Neil Walker- Global Law: Another Case of the Emperor's Clothes?," in *Reflections on Global Law*, ed. Shavana Musa and Eefje de Volder (Leiden: Brill, 2013), 3-20. Charlotte Ku, *International Law, International Relations and Global Governance* (London: Routledge, 2012). Andrew Halpin and Volker Roeben, ed., *Theorizing the Global Legal Order* (Oxford: Hart Publishing, 2009). Sands, "Turtles and Torturers."

[12] Robert O. Keohane and Joseph S. Nye Jr., "Introduction," in *Governance in a Globalizing World*, ed. Joseph S. Nye and John D. Donahue (Cambridge: Visions of Governance for the 21st Century, 2000), 3.

[13] Ibid.

[14] Ibid., 7.

[15] Ibid., 2.

they refer to multicontinental relationships and networks, in addition to the regional ones.[16] As a continuous process, globalization is the diminution of distances on a large scale.[17] The current use of globalization terminology mainly reflects a major shift in global trends that seeks a less statist view in the aftermath of the Cold War, as of the 1990s.[18] This change has had many impacts on economics, politics, environment, etc., as well as law. At this point, legal transplantations- i. e. migration of rules between countries, or better to say, between different legal systems,- are one aspect of these impacts on law, as well as on the growing transnational face of law.

From a more critical point of view, globalization is also likely to be described as "a dominant trend toward integration in an economistic era of late Westphalian geopolitics, or more fundamentally as signalling the birth of a planetary structure that is dominated by market force."[19] Accordingly, it is misleading to consider globalization as a term concerning "homogenization," "equity," or "universality."[20] The same issue also arises about the character of recently emerging forms of law, and in particular international law. The impacts of globalization on international law are controversial, and there are various responses from legal scholarship to this phenomenon. Before discussing the outcomes of this transformation, to have a look at some macro facts is necessary.

2.1.1.1 Rise of Network Society

The contemporary society features a stratified normative structure of a global system, some of whose levels remain within the national borders, whereas some others extend beyond the national domains.[21] Moreover, globalization has resulted in a cardinal transformation of the operation of the states regarding transgovernmental relations; or in other words, it gave rise to the "disaggregation of the state" in conducting international relations, as put forward by Anne-Marie Slaughter.[22] This idea mainly argues that the concept of the unitary state in fact consists of a fiction; and various networking bodies have become its principal operational actors. The networks appear as the main transmission bodies of communication in transgovernmental relations as well as economic and cultural relations. A noticeable point is that networks do not resemble other social groupings. A network is more than a "densified grouping of negotiated relationships among stable subjects," and it is

---

[16] Ibid.

[17] Ibid., 2.

[18] Richard A. Falk, *The Declining World Order: America's Imperial Geopolitics* (New York: Routledge, 2004), 17.

[19] Ibid., 18.

[20] Keohane and Nye, "Introduction," 3.

[21] Chris Thornhill, "Rights and Constituent Power in the Global Constitution," *International Journal of Law in Context* 10 (2014): 384.

[22] Slaughter, *A New World Order*, 12.

continuously constituted within a dynamic process in which it is constructed while reintegrating its nodes and its relationships by itself.[23] The contemporary literature on networks regards them as the types of a new territoriality, and therefore they can be depicted as "inchoate geographies."[24]

Networks are the semi-formal hybrid bodies of transgovernmental and social relations, and they are the key actors of the state disaggregation mentioned above.[25] Networks that have more loosened structures than traditional bureaucratic organizations superseded the traditional actors in the management of these kind of relationships to a certain extent.[26] Against this background, they became the "new relational rationality" of the contemporary world.[27] The transformation of institutionalism in international law into the emergence of governmental and non-governmental networks went hand in hand with a number of societal issues. The idea of transgovernmental networks between states was first introduced by Nye and Keohane, as these networks are "sets of direct interactions among sub-units of different governments that are not controlled or closely guided by the policies of the cabinets or chief executives of those governments."[28] Nye and Keohane state that beginning with the Bretton Woods Conference of 1944, the key governance regimes, such as GATT, NATO, or IMF have operated in a club-like model.[29] This model led to more confidentiality, but also to more interdependence on the other hand.[30]

---

[23] Karl-Heinz Ladeur, "Towards a Legal Theory of Supranationality: The Viability of Network Concept," *European Law Journal* 3, no. 1 (1997): 47-48.

[24] Saskia Sassen, "Neither Global Nor National: Novel Assemblages of Territory, Authority and Rights," in *Laws and Societies in Global Contexts: Contemporary Approaches*, ed. Eve Darian-Smith (Cambridge: Cambridge University Press, 2013), 25.

[25] The concept of "network" focused here is articulated in different forms by some scholars: Such as "Global Assemblages" (Saskia Sassen), "Self-contained Regimes" (Gunther Teubner). However, this does not mean that the interpretation of this fact by these scholars is entirely the same, and they trigger the same points. Above all, the network concept of Slaughter is somewhat confined to the transgovernmental networks that stem from the disaggregation of state. In other examples, the concept of network is employed to explain social, cultural, economic and political relations between different novel forms of relationships within a broader span. Sassen, "Neither Global Nor National," 23-28; Andreas Fischer-Lescano and Gunther Teubner, "Regime-collisions: The Vain Search for Legal Unity in the Fragmentation of Global Law," *Michigan Journal of International Law* 25, no. 4 (2004): 999-1046.

[26] Joseph S. Nye and David Welch, *Küresel Catisma ve Isbirligini Anlamak*, trans. Renan Akman, (Istanbul: Is Bankasi Kültür Yayinlari, 2010), 406.

[27] Karl-Heinz Ladeur, "Globalization and Public Governance – A Contradiction?," in *Public Governance in the Age of Globalization*, ed. Karl-Heinz Ladeur (Aldershot: Ashgate 2004), 1-24.

[28] Robert O. Keohane and Joseph S. Nye, "Transgovernmental Relations and International Organizations," *World Politics: A Quarterly Journal of International Relations* 27, no. 1 (1974): 39, 43.

[29] Keohane and Nye, "Introduction," 26.

[30] Ibid., 26.

An increased number of networks has been observed over time as a part of the transformation of governmental administrations to new modes of governance.[31] This process goes along with the emergence of the global governance in decentered forms which have resulted in the development of a society of networks.[32] On the other hand, these new forms of governance are capable of constituting normative orders. Yet, these forms are not highly specialized, that is to say, they are without much internal differentiation; and they are "reducing normative orders to somewhat elementary utilities."[33] However, their normative power is strong enough to subdue the states.[34] They arise beyond conventional alliances or treaty partners. Since specialization and regulation are both outcomes of the modern industrialized society; the number of networks of regulators with specialised experts increases day by day, and networks are gaining more and more importance on regulatory matters in international relations.[35] Transgovernmental networks may be found within international organizations, or they appear as networks developed within a framework of an agreement done by presidents of states, or as national networks which develop spontaneously and outside any formal framework.[36] The main functions of networks are to exchange information, to take roles in enforcement of regulations, and to harmonize different laws of nations.[37]

Anne-Marie Slaughter also draws attention to the developing networks between national and transnational courts. As stated by her, what is behind this fact is that global economy leads to a global litigation. This occurs in both formal and informal ways. Judges from especially supreme or constitutional courts gather, discuss, and exchange their opinions; they refer to the rulings of other courts for their own decisions. An interaction through an informal or semi-formal cooperation between national and transnational courts is ongoing in this dimension.[38] Slaughter opines that this interaction leads to an "integrated global justice system" which is of two characteristics:

> (1) litigants move relatively freely across borders, carrying their disputes with them and choosing a particular national forum subject to judicial review of that choice; and (2) judges defer to or reject their foreign counterparts for reasons of efficiency, fairness, or the "ends of justice" rather than of sovereign prerogatives.[39]

---

[31] Berman, "From International Law," 502.

[32] Ladeur, "Globalization and Public Governance," 5.

[33] Sassen, "Neither Global Nor National," 24.

[34] Ibid., 24.

[35] Slaughter, *A New World Order*, 39.

[36] Ibid., 45.

[37] Ibid., 51.

[38] Ibid., 65 ff.; Christian Walter, "International Law in a Process of Constitutionalization," in *New Perspectives on the Divide Between National and International Law*, ed. Janne Nijman and Andre Nollkaemper (Oxford: Oxford University Press, 2007), 200.

[39] Ibid., 91.

In addition to the transgovernmental regulatory networks, in international relations, it is worth to mention the networks of civil society, such as networks on environment, public health, business, and networks of judges or diaspora communities as significant actors on global matters.[40] Networks have also incarnated in the form of illegal networks, such as Al-Qaeda, or as other global networks of human trafficking, drugs, money laundering, etc. In addition, co-operation and collaboration between firms is based on rather "spontaneously generated flexible ways" within the globalization process, instead of the formerly established ways of cooperation between the states. This is a bottom-up coordination, rather than top-down, which is performed through the networks of inter-relationships.[41]

The networks do not have much in common with former systems of the past. They are hybrid and experimental. They cannot be grasped via a state-centric perspective since they rely on the plurality of different legal orders.[42] The societal transformation is at the core of this development.[43] In the operational processes of these networks, law is also subject to a transformational process, where public and private actors become permeable.[44]

Moreover, different networks may constitute further networks, or to put it differently, "networks of networks," which are made up of innovative organizational relationships between networks.[45] The reflexive nature of these networks fairly differs from the former normative systems.[46] This transformation in operation of the public power results in the transformation of the relationship of the state and legal practice. It has been argued that the heterarchical structure of networking relations has eroding effects on the traditional, hierarchical concept of law as well as on the integrative features of the states.[47]

Furthermore, this decentralised and heterarchical structure reshaped international law by creating a plurality of hybrid legal orders, that require new meta-rules of collision norms by reason of the overlapping operations and colliding norms of these bodies. The striking point is that the rise of networks and the fragmented structure of the global realms, which arises as a concomitant to the operation of networks,

---

[40] Berman, "From International Law," 503.

[41] Ladeur, "Globalization and Public Governance," 5.

[42] Karl-Heinz Ladeur, "The State in International Law" (Comparative Research in Law & Political Economy Research Paper No. 27, 2010, http://digitalcommons.osgoode.yorku.ca/cgi/viewcontent.cgi?article=1094&context=clpe), 5, last visit 21.04.2013. Fischer-Lescano and Teubner, "Regime-Collisions," 999-1046.

[43] Ladeur, "State in International Law," 15.

[44] Ibid., 16.

[45] Slaughter, *A New World Order*, 50.

[46] Ladeur, "State in International Law," 4.

[47] Karl-Heinz Ladeur, "The Theory of Autopoiesis as an Approach to a Better Understanding of Postmodern Law- From the Hierarchy of Norms to the Heterarchy of Changing Patterns of Legal Inter-relationships" (EUI Working Paper Law no. 99/3, 1999, http://cadmus.eui.eu/bitstream/id/943/law99_3.pdf), 34-35, last visit 13.04.2014.

have a pivotal role in shaping debates over the changing nature of the international legal order. The issue of the society of global networks has a lot to do with the global constitutionalism as well as some further discourses regarding integration and interdependence in international law. In this regard, global networks have both constituent and deconstructing roles in the discourse of global constitutionalism, as will be mentioned in the details further.[48]

Despite the fact that networks are immensely important in understanding global governance in the age of globalization; it is of note that they are also fairly controversial since they lead to a reduction of the transparency of transgovernmental relations, and as such they create handicaps for accountability.[49] However, these networks lay the foundations of the contemporary global legal order,[50] and they are regarded as the most efficient dynamics of the emerging system.

To grasp the reality of the international legal system, Berman suggests that "studies of the international legal order, (…), must address the interplay of a wide variety of normative commitments and law-giving entities."[51] According to this view, societal dynamics of international law which depict how law is produced and operated beyond formal governmental actions must be first analysed so as to grasp the reality. However, this is not very easy on the normative basis, due to the growing indistinction of public and private law in the transnational practice.[52] On the other side, the transformed relations of the global realm towards a constitutionalization still lack a theory of normativity.[53]

In an account of 1965, it was rightly articulated that the international community would at the furthest be depicted as a "*gesellschaft type of society.*" As such it was different from an integrated and organized society which was subject to the "statal law," as the main subject of this so-called community was sovereign states.[54] The current scholarship of international law approves that actors of this field have become varied and the sovereign state is no longer perceived as a monolithic body as it has undergone a disaggregation process. In terms of constitutions, the state-centered constitutionalism has lost its power, since independent regulatory agencies and governmental networks have become more decisive over constitutional issues that transcend the scope and eligibility of national constitutions.[55]

---

[48] See in general, Fischer-Lescano and Teubner, "Regime-collisions," 1005-1006.

[49] Berman, "From International Law," 503.

[50] Slaughter, *A New World Order*, 69.

[51] Berman, "From International Law," 511.

[52] Ladeur, "State in International Law," 16.

[53] Antje Wiener, "Constitutionalism Unbound: A Practice Approach to Normativity" (Paper presented at 'Practice, Ethics and Normativity' at the Annual Millennium Conference 'Out Of The Ivory Tower - Weaving the Theories and Practice of International Relations, London School of Economics & Political Science, London, 22-23 October 2011, http://ssrn.com/abstract=2103049 or http://dx.doi.org/10.2139/ssrn.2103049), 3, last visit 11.04.2014.

[54] J. G. Starke, "Elements of the Sociology of International Law," *Australian Year Book of International Law* 1 (1965): 121.

[55] Andrea Hamann and Hélène Ruiz Fabri, "Transnational Networks and Constitutionalism," *International Journal of Constitutional Law* 6, no. 3-4 (2008): 484.

All in all, an expectation of globalization to unify law does not seem realistic given the fragmented structure of the global realm and the nature of the emerging relational rationality. As a matter of fact, the monolithic image of globalization is illusionary. This is true for further fields also, as Zygmunt Bauman points out a crucial texture of globalization, "[g]lobalization divides as much as it unites; it divides as it unites – the causes of division being identical with those which promote the uniformity of globe."[56] Therefore, it should be emphasized that, as this chapter broadly deals with, the main fact that is accompanied with political globalization is the fragmentation of the global domain. The same is true of the global legal order. That is to say, in contrast to the expectations for a globalized legal order, i. e. a legal unification, the fragmented operation of law in the global realm impeded a parallel development with the political globalization.[57]

It is also noteworthy that some scholars mitigate the foundational role of networks in global society. For example, Grimm does not concur with those who highlight the role of informal global networks on legislative processes. From his point of view, their impacts over the legislative activities are found only in the preliminary stages, and this does not amount to an influence from pressure groups.[58]

The rise of the network society and the new relational rationality has had far-reaching effects on the contemporary international law scholarship. It is evident that this new relational rationality had the greatest impact on the traditional concept of sovereignty.[59] In other words, this profound shift in international relations engendered a debate on the character of state sovereignty, as some argued that the disaggregated form of the state practice generated a new form of sovereignty, namely a "disaggregated sovereignty." This development has been considered relevant with the fact that the current law making processes pursue a "network model" instead of the traditional "pyramidal model."[60] This issue is an immensely important component of the debate on the erosion of sovereignty.

2.1.1.2 Erosion of Sovereignty

State sovereignty is a timeworn concept that originates from the feudal power relationships, and in the modern sense, it has first appeared in the writings of Jean Bodin and Thomas Hobbes.[61] It constituted one of the essential characteristics of

---

[56] Zygmunt Bauman, *Globalization: The Human Consequences* (New York: Columbia University Press, 1998), 2.

[57] Ladeur, "State in International Law," 18.

[58] Dieter Grimm, "The Constitution in the Process of Denationalization," *Constellations* 12, no. 4 (2005): 454.

[59] Berman, "From International Law," 527.

[60] Hamann and Fabri, "Transnational Networks," 483.

[61] Friedrich Kratochwil, "Leaving Sovereignty Behind? An Inquiry into the Politics of Post-Modernity," in *Legality and Legitimacy in Global Affairs*, ed. Richard Falk, Mark Juergensmeyer and Vesselin Popovski (New York: Oxford University Press, 2012), 127-148.

states in the Westphalian order, and referred to "the *ascription of a status* to an actor based on mutual recognition."[62] In addition, sovereignty granted three fundamental features to the modern state: "internal coherence, external independence, and supremacy of law."[63] Of these features, external independence means the claim of sovereignty against any power beyond the domestic territory, and it is also known as "sovereignty in international law" or "independence."[64] In the traditional sense, sovereignty in international law means that states are only bound by norms that they agree to obey. This understanding of "unrestrained sovereignty" was best reflected in the Lotus ruling of the Permanent Court of International Justice that stated,

> International law governs relations between independent States. The rules of law binding upon States therefore emanate from their own free will as expressed in conventions or by usages generally accepted as expressing principles of law and established in order to regulate the relations between these co-existing independent communities or with a view to the achievement of common aims. Restrictions upon the independence of States cannot therefore be presumed.[65]

This understanding of sovereignty was to be abandoned to a great extent in the aftermath of World War II. In this regard, particularly due to the foundation of the UN and the EC, a fundamental shift in the definition of the concept of sovereignty took place. The UN Charter introduced a new term, "sovereign equality" under Article 2(1): "[the UN] is based on the principle of the sovereign equality of all its Members."[66] As seen from the drafting process of the UN Charter, the combination of these two words, "sovereign" and "equality" had a special meaning:

> In this combination, sovereignty was meant to exclude the legal superiority of any state over another, but not a greater role played by the international community vis-à-vis *all* its members. The new term proved to be an accurate description of a development characterizing the international legal order in the age of League of Nations and, in particular, the UN (…).[67]

In other words, the main intention here was to demonstrate that the traditional understanding of the sovereignty was useless in the new era. In other words, the idea of the alleged eternal freedom of states was superseded by the idea of a sovereignty

---

[62] Ibid., 134, emphasis belongs to the original text.

[63] Martin Loughlin, "Ten Tenets of Sovereignty," in *Sovereignty in Transition: Essays in European Law*, ed. Neil Walker (Oxford: Hart Publishing, 2006), 59.

[64] Bardo Fassbender, "Sovereignty and Constitutionalism in International Law," in *Sovereignty in Transition: Essays in European Law*, ed. Neil Walker (Oxford: Hart Publishing, 2006), 116.

[65] The Case of the S.S. Lotus, (France v. Turkey), PCIJ, Series A, No. 10 (1927), para. 18, cited by Fassbender, "Sovereignty and Constitutionalism," 117.

[66] The UN Charter, 26 June 1945, https://treaties.un.org/doc/publication/ctc/uncharter.pdf, last visit 11.12.2014.

[67] Fassbender, "Sovereignty and Constitutionalism," 128.

restricted by an international community. The abolition of the *jus ad bellum* under the UN Charter is likely to be held as a major example. As Fassbender affirms, the ban on the use of force under the UN Charter refers to a prerequisite for enjoyment of sovereign equality rather than a restriction on sovereignty.[68]

Beyond these institutional developments in international law, globalization and new relational forms introduced by it have also had deep impacts on the fate of the concept of sovereignty. The globalization of legal and economic matters resulted in the traditional public international law and private international law no longer being able to respond to the new issues posed by globalization.[69] At the heart of this problem is the rise and challenge of the "governance" against governments through some new hybrid actors that replace the traditional ones in many areas.[70] The globalized political and economic relations unveiled the fact that the single and independent modern law of the sovereign nation states was an exaggeration of legal positivists, and this sort of construction of a legal order no longer responds to the new relational facts and needs.[71] As will be mentioned in the details below, the increasing indistinctness between public and private international law has also arisen as an undermining factor for the traditional understanding of sovereignty.

In short, state sovereignty has acquired a new meaning, particularly in the twentieth century. In this respect, sovereignty no longer marks an absolute and unlimited freedom of action for states, as once noted by Hans Kelsen, as "[s]overeignty of the States, as subjects of international law, is the legal authority of the States under the authority of international law."[72] Among contemporary international relations and law literature, a strong idea appeared that globalization and new forms of global governance have largely eroded state sovereignty; and also sovereignty is no longer a useful term to identify the contemporary state.[73] Some observers argue that, the traditional sovereignty principle of the Westphalian system has already become obsolete, and it needs to be discussed within the framework of a "post-sovereign"

---

[68] Ibid.

[69] Karl-Heinz Ladeur, "Ein Recht der Netzwerke für die Weltgesellschaft oder Konstitutionalisierung der Völkergemeinschaft,“ *Archiv des Völkerrechts* 49 (2011): 251.

[70] Global governance is a term that is completely different from the world government. Governance is simply "the processes and institutions, both formal and informal, that guide and restrain the collective activities of a group." Governance is not only conducted by governments and international organizations, but it also includes private firms and non-governmental organizations, in some cases without a governmental authority. Keohane and Nye, "Introduction," 12-19.

[71] Ladeur, "Legal Theory of Supranationality," 44.

[72] Hans Kelsen, "The Principle of Sovereign Equality of States as a Basis for International Organization," *Yale Law Journal* 53 (1944): 207-208, cited by Bardo Fassbender, "The United Nations Charter as Constitution of the International Community," *Columbia Journal of Transnational Law* 36, no. 3 (1998): 582.

[73] Kratochwil, "Leaving Sovereignty Behind?," 127. For an opposite view, Loughlin, "Ten Tenets of Sovereignty."

world.[74] Having considered the changing characteristics of the recent state practice, Kratochwil draws attention to the newly emerging communal character of sovereignty. That is to say, the new form of the concept of sovereignty concerns participation in international organizations, instead of single judgments.[75] This new form of sovereignty was constituted by "inter-state" and "intra-state" norms, particularly by virtue of the recent impacts of human rights law.[76] As a supporting idea, it has also been advanced to show that through increasing networking activities in the global realm, national borders and political geography lost their traditional roles to a certain extent, and this weakens the territorial sovereignty.[77] Furthermore, in a more extreme vein, Linda Bosniak states that nation states are no longer necessary since the concept of citizenship is now theoretically viable without nation states.[78] In international relations literature, the idea of the erosion of sovereignty has been referred to either underline impacts of increasing cooperation and institutionalization or to reflect the "going alone strategy" of USA to international relations, in particular in the aftermath of September 11.[79]

Beyond academic works, the dissolution of the traditional state sovereignty has also been an issue discussed by the international tribunals. As a striking example, the International Criminal Tribunal for the Former Yugoslavia (ICTY) in the Tadic case stated that:

> [d]ating back to a period when sovereignty stood as a sacrosanct and unassailable attribute of statehood, this concept recently has suffered progressive erosion at the hands of the more liberal forces at work in the democratic societies.[80]

The impacts of globalization on the nature of international law vary. These impacts are mostly discussed within the framework of the sovereignty of nation states. It is widely conceded by contemporary academic works that nation states dysfunction to some extent in a globalized world, and a paradigm shift is necessary or has already occurred.[81] One salient fact is that the emergence of distinct global markets has transcended governance capabilities of nation states and this has led to the birth of various global regulation regimes. As it is commonly articulated, "governance"

---

[74] Kratochwil, "Leaving Sovereignty Behind?," 127.

[75] Ibid., 135.

[76] Milena Sterio, "The Evolution of International Law," *Boston College International and Comparative Law Review* 31, no. 2 (2008): 231.

[77] Ladeur, "Globalization and Public Governance," 11.

[78] Linda Bosniak, "Citizenship Denationalized," *Indiana Journal of Global Legal Studies* 7 (2000): 491, cited by Russel Menyhart, "Changing Identities and Changing Law: Possibilities for a Global Legal Culture," *Indiana Journal of Global Legal Studies* 10 (2003): 173.

[79] Kratochwil, "Leaving Sovereignty Behind?," 135.

[80] Prosecutor v. Dusko Tadic a/k/a "Dule," ICTY IT-94-1-AR7, 22.10.1995, para. 55, http://www.icty.org/x/cases/tadic/acdec/en/51002.htm, last visit 20.03.2012.

[81] Christine E.J. Schwöbel, *Global Constitutionalism in International Legal Perspective* (Leiden: Nijhoff, 2011), 82.

replaced "government." This process was not only confined to markets but also related to science, culture, technology, health, the military, transport, tourism, sport, politics, law and welfare, as it gave rise to various autonomous global systems.[82] In terms of legal formation, globalization marks a deformalization and pluralization.[83] As a paradoxical feature, it requires decentralization as well as regulation at the same time.[84]

Beyond these impacts of globalization, some new developments in the traditional Westphalian structure of public international law also came into play in the transformation process of sovereignty. A very remarkable development is the introduction of the principle of "responsibility to protect" that was adopted in 2005 by the United Nations.[85] The adoption of this principle granted the UN a new role to intervene in nation states by use of force under certain conditions, and it was first exercised with the intervention in Haiti. This principle made human rights and public accountability a core component of state responsibility, and thus, it underpinned a fundamental shift in the major dynamics of the Westphalian state order.

As a matter of fact, the traditional idea of sovereignty has been contested since the early twentieth century. From this day on, sovereignty was on the target of burgeoning pluralist political ideas that sought to replace it with the concept of "polyarchism."[86] These endeavours to abandon sovereignty continued to the present day, and in particular, it has been a very remarkable, contested issue in the course of globalization.

On the other hand, it is of note that sovereignty proved that it is a highly adaptable concept, as it succeeded in surviving under different challenging conditions.[87] In spite of the growing erosion in the age of globalism, one can hardly regard state sovereignty as an entirely meaningless concept at the present time. In other words, the Westphalian sovereign state retains its existence along with the new forms of international relationships.[88] This is likely to be depicted as "the untamed side of the sovereignty."[89] Furthermore, globalization can hardly be viewed as the ground for a chaotic process that results in the dissolution of public order.[90] Globalization is rather characterised by a "transnational" form that bypasses the state and the previous forms of international relations, in particular in terms of the world economy.[91]

---

[82] See in general, Fischer-Lescano and Teubner, "Regime-collisions."

[83] Ladeur, "Ein Recht der Netzwerke," 252.

[84] Slaughter, *A New World Order*, 8.

[85] Kratochwil, "Leaving Sovereignty Behind?," 136.

[86] Loughlin, "Ten Tenets of Sovereignty," 55.

[87] Fassbender, "Sovereignty and Constitutionalism," 115.

[88] Ladeur, "Globalization and Public Governance," 11-12.

[89] Fassbender, "Sovereignty and Constitutionalism," 140.

[90] Ladeur, "Globalization and Public Governance," 1; Peer Zumbansen, "Transnational Law," in *Elgar Encyclopedia of Comparative Law*, ed. Jan M. Smits (Cheltenham: Edward Elgar, 2006), 740 ff.

[91] Ladeur, "Globalization and Public Governance," 5.

The concept of state sovereignty has not been entirely marginalized within this form, as it is required to preserve public order. Therefore, a major conclusion of this interrogation is that states have not been stripped from their traditional characteristics, yet they rather engaged in a new operational framework.[92]

2.1.2 *Challenges of Globalization towards International Law*

In the age of globalization, studies regarding the transformation of international law and seeking its reconstruction under new terms refer to several common symptoms of this transformation. These symptoms should be read as the causes of dysfunction of international law in traditional terms. In other words, they appear as the challenges of globalization to the conventional understanding of international law within the legal scholarship. As a matter of fact, the transformation in international law is considered within a greater framework, namely the Post-Westphalian order of international relations that supplants the traditional understanding of international relations that originated from the Peace of Westphalia among the European states in 1648. The Post-Westphalian transformation overlaps the globalization era to a large extent, and globalization is more likely to be perceived as a ground for the Post-Westphalian turn. In other words, globalization comes along with some challenges for the traditional understanding and institutions of general international law, and with a response to these challenges that rises in the form of a Post-Westphalian order. This interaction will be elucidated in this section.

2.1.2.1 Dimension of Transformation: From Westphalian towards Post-Westphalian

2.1.2.1.1 New Law for a New World

International law has undergone a serious transformation during the twentieth century, which resulted in a new structure that involved new agencies other than the nation states. It is evident that the new institutional architecture of the post-war process and globalization, along with the end of the Cold War were the most notable factors of this change. Although there were some attempts to read international law as the law of a unified legal order in the period between the two world wars by some western scholars, such as Georges Scelle and Alfred Verdross, the rise of the Cold War period is likely to be viewed as a certain breakdown of these ideas. In the aftermath of World War II, the normative strength of international law was broadly disdained by some scholars in view of the inability of international law and international institutions to prevent the brutalities of World War II.[93] This disdain had to

[92] Slaughter, *A New World Order*, 31.

[93] Ku, *International Law*, 21.

do with the ascendance of the realist paradigm within the field of international relations in a certain degree. The sense of rejection of international law in this period was sharpened by harsh criticism of inter-war international law projects that did not comply with the reality of the international relations by some scholars, such as Hans Morgenthau and E. H. Carr.[94] Nevertheless, the twentieth century also saw a significant institutionalization movement, the end of the Cold War and also the increase of globalism that revived the belief in a coherent system of international law and an international community.[95]

Currently, many international law scholars agree on the realization of a transformation process in international law, and on a need to reformulate the framework of international law. As a matter of fact, public international law had never been a static field, and a transformational progress had always been in question. What the current ongoing transformation implies is commonly explained as a transformation from the "Westphalian" order of international law towards a "Post-Westphalian" one. In a nutshell, the traditional Westphalian order of international relations was constructed upon the legal principles of the equality of states, the immunity of sovereigns and the doctrine of non-intervention on others' domestic affairs.[96] In the Westphalian system, there was no higher authority over individual states, and as it was stated in the Lotus ruling of the Permanent Court of International Justice, "states cannot be bound without their consent."[97] Global governance emerged within this framework as "one of facilitating the relations among sovereigns and sovereign states."[98]

Due to the growing cross-border relations, this scheme began to change in particular in the late nineteenth and twentieth centuries. In the long run, the central attention of the international system turned to "human values" from "state values."[99] Further, Sands argues that transformations in the field of general international law could be perceived as a continuum of *jus gentium*.[100] Globalization has come to the fore as an alternative term to replace the Westphalian order, as it challenges the Westphalian order in many terms. However, the concept of globalization was found "vague and uncrystallized" by Falk, on account of the increasing American hegemony as a global empire.[101] That is to say, globalization was an inadequate and inapt concept to understand this development. At this juncture, although globalization has significant roles in the transformation of the Westphalian order, the concept of "Post-Westphalian order" has become a more common term in portraying the continuance and disengagement of the newly emerging structures in international relations.

---

[94] Ibid., 21-28.

[95] Schwöbel, *Global Constitutionalism*, 97.

[96] Falk, *Declining World Order*.

[97] The Case of the SS Lotus (France v. Turkey), cited by Ku, *International Law*, 160.

[98] Ku, *International Law*, 162.

[99] Ibid., 162.

[100] Sands, "Turtles and Torturers," 536.

[101] Falk, *Declining World Order*, 13.

A number of reasons can be found behind such a preference of this concept. First of all, the rise of new social and political facts and structures does not imply the elimination of old ones. The state had been the most central factor in the Westphalian order, and it has still been so in the new era. On the other hand, the state is not the only determinant and the only element of the Westphalian order. In the course of a Westphalian order of international relations, various societal forces were also influential over this structure, such as "war, social forces, civilizational and religious energies, and inequalities of power/wealth." To be more clear, the primary characteristics of the Westphalian order were,

> primacy of the territorial state as political actor on a global level, the centrality of international warfare, the autonomy of the sovereign state to govern affairs within recognized international boundaries, the generalized tolerance of "human wrongs" committed within the scope of sovereign authority, the special leadership role in geopolitics claimed by and assigned to leading state(s), the weakness of the rule of law, and the absence of strong institutions of regional and global governance.[102]

These Westphalian dynamics are still alive to a great extent in the new era, and globalization has not been capable of transforming or abolishing them thoroughly. That is to say, old and new dynamics coexisted at the same time in this new scheme. Therefore, it is evident that a Post-Westphalian order of international relations has not been established yet, in spite of a strong pressure for a transformation of the international realm in this dimension.[103] This led to the coexistence of the Westphalian and the Post-Westphalian orders. For example, the veto power of five permanent members of the UN Security Council still reflects the Westphalian reality.[104] G-7 summits are likely to be held up as an example that reflects such a mixed structure, since these summits are in substance networking activities, despite the fact that the governmental relations and power relations are at the core thereof. Against this background, the Post-Westphalian reconstruction of the world order is to be considered feeble in many terms. Nevertheless, successful achievements of the Post-Westphalian mindset should not be underestimated. The European experience of regionalism is a good example in this sense in consideration of a broad range of developments from a well-established human rights protection system to the mobility of labour or a prosperous peace system.[105] It has been argued that this was a result of globalization and the fragmentation of the newly arising state structures particularly in Europe, which develop a special sensitivity to the differences as a part of a greater universalism.[106] In this respect, some scholars point to the revolutionary aspects of this transformation in the political communities where the

---

[102] Ibid.

[103] Ibid.

[104] Ibid.

[105] Ibid., 38.

[106] Andrew Linklater, *The Transformation of Political Community: Ethical Foundations of the Post-Westphalian Era* (Columbia SC: University of South Carolina Press, 1998), 8.

Post-Westphalian transformation has been accomplished, since societies no longer confront each other as their geopolitical rivals.[107] Seen in this light, new institutional frameworks of the Post-Westphalian order have an ethical function of enlarging the dialogical community of the world politics.[108] Moreover, in particular by virtue of globalization, a globalized *force majeure* gave rise to a legal sense of obligation for states, and this became quite influential over states to comply with international law. Sterio explains the psychological motivation of this legal sense for states in the contemporary international relations by stating:

> [states] have to envision the impacted state, as well as non-state actors; they have to calculate whether any of their international legal obligations under the myriad of international treaties they may be party to will be triggered; and they have to fear any grievances that may be asserted against them in a variety of possible jurisdictions.[109]

2.1.2.1.2 From "Law of Cooperation" towards "Law of Integration"

As explained above, the idea of a "Post-Westphalian transformation" does not suffice to depict the contemporary framework of international law, on the ground that a thorough transformation has not occurred yet. Therefore the new framework of international law marks an "inchoate order." The most striking feature of this new order is the bypassed central role of nation states to a certain extent. Under the new relational rationality, in which new agencies and mutual obligations proliferate, identification of new relational forms arises as a meaningful question. The new relational reality of the global realm also challenges traditional realist views on the nature of international law. Kjaer highlights that the traditional realist perspectives of international relations, which regard the global realm as a domain of anarchy and power politics, are unacceptable from a sociological standpoint. In contrast to such realist views, according to him, a striking aspect of the world order is stability and high level of order, despite various financial crises, armed conflicts, ecological catastrophes and so on.[110] This high level of the order could be understood as a consequence of a trend towards integration in the global domain. This trend, which spawns more coherence and affinity in this domain, also marks the new inchoate order of global law. It has also for so long been debated among public international law scholars that recent developments in international society, in particular under the influence of globalization and developments in the aftermath of World War II, entail enlarging the focus of public international law, since public international scholarship has already shown an inability to illuminate the truth of the international legal order through traditional methods. This idea has given rise to a new scholarship that

[107] Ibid.

[108] Ibid., 7.

[109] Sterio, "Evolution of International Law," 245.

[110] Kjaer, *Constitutionalism in Global Realm*, 72.

leaves behind the traditional views that focus on only normative frameworks of the law of nation states and the law among nation states.[111]

Inquiries for a reliable pattern for a peaceful coexistence of states had commenced much before the current discourse of global constitutionalism. Samuel von Pufendorf (1632–1694), Abbé de Saint Pierre (1658–1743), and Kant, who wrote "Perpetual Peace: A Philosophical Sketch" (1795), were the most notable authors who suggested such a coexistence through a confederational or federational basis.[112] Among them, Kant's piece particularly remained much more influential over the contemporary integrationist ideas.

The Post-WWII era, which was marked by increasing institutionalization, increasing codification, increasing competence of the judiciary, and thus increasing the limitation of freewill of states, was described as a transformation from "law of coordination to law of cooperation" in the earlier period of the transformative process in question.[113] This change indeed implied an immense progress in the history of international relations, in contrast to the ideas of Thomas Hobbes, articulated in Leviathan in 1651, that states by no means can overcome the perpetual war conditions because of their independence, although individuals could achieve this through a social contract.[114] Beyond doubt, the most important development was the foundation of the United Nations in the aftermath of World War II in this context. That it was enacted in the form of a charter was not by accident, that is to say, it pursued a special purpose:

> A charter has the character of a law, presupposing a hierarchical relationship of rulers and ruled. (…) A law is an instrument of vertical integration, as distinct from a covenant which is a form of horizontal integration of the participating entities.[115]

In this respect, the legal functions of the UN Charter largely differed from the Covenant of the League of Nations.[116] As will be touched on in the details in the next chapter, such character of the UN Charter constitutes the core of a debate on the emergence of a global normative order.[117] Moreover, some other developments in treaty law are of importance. The Vienna Convention on the Law of Treaties of 1969 introduced some foundational norms for treaty law. In particular, Article 53 of this Convention is noteworthy, as it introduced *jus cogens* rules that invalidate norms conflicting with them, and thereby constitute superior rules for the international legal order. Furthermore, the United Nations Convention on the Law of the Sea of

---

[111] Berman, "From International Law," 487.

[112] Ulrich K. Preuß, "Equality of States – Its Meaning in a Constitutionalised Global Order," *Chicago Journal of International Law* 9, no.1 (2008-2009): 36.

[113] Preuß, "Equality of States," 34.

[114] Ibid., 36; Fassbender, "United Nations Charter."

[115] Preuß, "Equality of States," 38.

[116] Ibid.

[117] Fassbender, "United Nations Charter."

1982 is to be noted as an example of an international convention that was drafted as a globally overarching law.

Beyond this progress of the normative framework of the international legal order, the growing institutionalization has been a crucial aspect of the trend towards a law of integration in the global realm. Furthermore, as a supranational legal system, the European Union demonstrated that the constitution could be thought in a context beyond nation states, despite the attempts for a supranational constitution ending up with a fiasco. Even to a lesser extent, the establishment of the World Trade Union, which also appears in the centre of the global constitutionalization debate, is noteworthy.

Apart from these, one of the most striking transformative facts in international law in the twentieth century is the changing character of jurisdiction. The jurisdiction was earlier perceived as a fact depending on a sovereign power within a defined territory, and it acquired an extra-territorial form by virtue of the increased number of international courts in the twentieth century. This development came along with the development of the concept of universal jurisdiction, in particular in the field of human rights.[118] It is also of note that the international legal order responded to the catastrophes of the twentieth century by establishing ad hoc courts, such as the International Criminal Tribunal for the former Yugoslavia (ICTY) and the International Criminal Tribunal for Rwanda (ICTR), and finally the International Criminal Court (ICC) against genocides and crimes against humanity. The trend in expanding the scope of the jurisdiction of international criminal courts also gave rise to the recognition of some new types of crimes against humanity, such as genocide and war crimes.[119] The rise of human rights protection through international and regional organizations and courts was a notable development of the twentieth century, and this movement succeeded to a large extent, in particular regarding the operation of the Council of Europe (CoE) and implementation of the European Convention on Human Rights (ECHR). The success of transnational human rights protection was a consequence of a rhetorical persuasion, treaty codification, and various forms of soft law that reshaped the international consensus over time.[120] Zangl draws attention to two major reasons for increasing judicialization in international adjudication. First, judicialization strengthens adjudication procedures, "because it is more difficult to prevent their invocation and their rulings." In addition, judicial procedures "convey more dignity" and this eases justifying decisions or outcomes in public.[121] Therefore, it is evident that judicialization has had practical outputs for adjudicatory processes and has been preferred largely by many international or transnational entities.

These courts and their founding statutes have not been able to establish a full-fledged global protection system yet, as many countries are not party to these

[118] Sterio, "Evolution of International Law," 222.

[119] Ibid., 238.

[120] Paul Schiff Berman, "A Pluralist Approach to International Law," *The Yale Journal of International Law* 3, no. 2 (2007): 304.

[121] Bernhard Zangl, "Is There an Emerging International Rule of Law?," in *Transformations of the State*, ed. Stephan Leibfried and Michael Zürn (New York: Cambridge University Press, 2005), 88.

statutes or have not ratified them. However, the current achievement has been considered as an evidence of the increasing cooperation and integration between states and the solidarity against human rights conflicts.

The progressive and reconstructing interpretations and activisms of international courts have left profound impacts on the identification of the nature of the international legal order. Some contributions to the discourse of global law and global constitutionalism placed a particular emphasis on some of these court rulings that referred to the growing integration in the global realm.

These rulings were rather from transnational human rights courts. In the Loizidou case, the European Court of Human Rights (ECtHR) identifies the European Convention on Human Rights as "a constitutional instrument of European public order."[122] The Court also repeated this view in some other cases. For example, in the Bosphorus ruling, having referred to the Loizidou case, the Court noted that ECHR is the "'constitutional instrument of European public order' in the field of human rights."[123] One striking point is that the Court never employed this term until the 1990s, and since then it has referred to such constitutional quality of the convention very rarely.[124] A recent example is the Al-Dulimi decision of the ECtHR. A striking point of this judgment is that three judges discuss the idea of global constitutionalism through the constitutionalization processes of the UN and the ECHR systems in their concurring opinion.[125] It is also noteworthy that they identified the ECtHR as "the European Constitutional Court."[126] Nevertheless, the Court has always been careful and prudent in using the term of constitution, and it never advanced a claim that the convention is "completely constitutional."[127]

Some rulings of the International Court of Justice (ICJ) were also discussed in the context of the constitutional features of *jus cogens* and *erga omnes* norms. The Barcelona Traction case is noteworthy, by reason of its special emphasis on "communitarian" interpretation of obligations arising in the international community. In this ruling, it was stated that,

> In particular, an essential distinction should be drawn between the obligations of a State towards the international community as a whole, and those arising vis-à-vis another State

---

[122] Loizidou v. Turkey, Judgment (Preliminary Objection), 15318/89 (23.03.1995), para. 75, http://hudoc.echr.coe.int/sites/eng/pages/search.aspx?i=001-57920, last visit 01.11.2013.

[123] Bosphorus Hava Yolları Turizm ve Ticaret Anonim Şirketi v. Ireland, Judgment (Merits), Grand Chamber, 45036/98 (30.06.2005), para. 156, http://hudoc.echr.coe.int/sites/eng/pages/search.aspx?i=001-69564, last visit 29.10.2013.

[124] Ed Bates, *The Evolution of the European Convention on Human Rights: From Its Inception to the Creation of a Permanent Court of Human Rights* (Oxford: Oxford University Press, 2010), 153.

[125] Al-Dulimi and Montana Management Inc. v. Switzerland, 5809/08, Concurring Opinion Of Judge Pinto De Albuquerque, Joined By Judges Hajiyev, Pejchal and Dedov (21.06.2016), para. 7 ff., http://hudoc.echr.coe.int/eng?i=001-164515, last visit 12.03.2017.

[126] Ibid., para. 60.

[127] Bates, *Evolution of European Convention*, 153.

> in the field of diplomatic protection. By their very nature the former are the concern of all States. In view of the importance of the rights involved, all States can be held to have a legal interest in their protection; they are obligations erga omnes.[128]

Following that, the Court indicates the sources of these obligations. According to the ICJ, they can derive from the outlawing of acts of aggression, and of genocide, the principles and rules concerning the basic rights of the human person, including protection from slavery and racial discrimination.[129] The Court acts in accordance with natural law, and argues that those which are not found in positive law documents are conferred by from "universal or quasi-universal international instruments."

Having referred to Article 103 of the UN Charter, in the Lockerbie case, the ICJ underlined the supremacy of the UN Security Council decisions over the Montreal Convention.[130] Furthermore, the Court of First Instance of the European Communities (CFI) identified *jus cogens* norms in a constitutional framework in the Kadi and Yusuf cases. In both of these rulings of 2005, the Court argued limits of its own jurisdiction regarding bindingness of the Security Council decisions, and it noted that *jus cogens* norms empower the Court to examine these decisions, given the peremptory character of these norms:

> None the less, the Court is empowered to check, indirectly, the lawfulness of the resolutions of the Security Council in question with regard to jus cogens, understood as a body of higher rules of public international law binding on all subjects of international law, including the bodies of the United Nations, and from which no derogation is possible.[131] Following that, the Court states that the Security Council resolutions would have no binding effect if they do not comply with *jus cogens* norms.[132]

---

[128] Barcelona Traction, Light and Power Company, Limited, (Belgium v. Spain), ICJ 3, 32 (05.02.1970), para. 33, http://www.icj-cij.org/docket/index.php?p1=3&p2=3&case=50&p3=4, last visit, 25.09.2013.

[129] Ibid., para. 34.

[130] Questions of Interpretation and Application of the 1971 Montreal Convention Arising from the Aerial Incident at Lockerbie (Libyan Arab Jamahiriya v. United States of America), Provisional Measures, Order, ICJ Reports 1992 (14.03.1992), para. 42,130 http://www.icj-cij.org/docket/index.php?sum=460&code=lus&p1=3&p2=3&case=89&k=82&p3=5, last visit 19.09.2013.

[131] Ahmed Ali Yusuf and Al Barakaat International Foundation v. Council of the European Union and Commission of the European Communities, Judgment of the CFI, 306/01 (21.09.2005), para. 277, http://curia.europa.eu/juris/showPdf.jsf?text=&docid=59905&pageIndex=0&doclang=en&mode=lst&dir=&occ=first&part=1&cid=590169, last visit 25.09.2013. Yassin Abdullah Kadi v. Council of the European Union and Commission of the European Communities, Judgment of the CFI, 315/01 (21.09.2005), para. 226, http://curia.europa.eu/juris/showPdf.jsf?text=&docid=59906&pageIndex=0&doclang=en&mode=lst&dir=&occ=first&part=1&cid=596999, last visit 25.09.2013.

[132] Ahmed Ali Yusuf and Al Barakaat International Foundation v. Council of the European Union and Commission of the European Communities, para. 281.

In these cases, the CFI pursued the idea that there is an intrinsic relationship between human rights and the concept of *jus cogens,* and thus the Court regarded *jus cogens* norms as creating a sort of public order.[133]

The constitutional approach of the International Criminal Tribunal for the former Yugoslavia to international law in the Tadic case is also noteworthy. While arguing limits of the power of the Security Council, the ICTY notes that,

> The Security Council is an organ of an international organization, established by a treaty which serves as a constitutional framework for that organization. The Security Council is thus subjected to certain constitutional limitations, however broad its powers under the constitution may be. Those powers cannot, in any case, go beyond the limits of the jurisdiction of the Organization at large, not to mention other specific limitations or those which may derive from the internal division of power within the Organization.[134]

Thereby the ICTY drew attention to the constitutional framework of the UN Charter. Further, it highlights that the power of the Security Council is subject to a certain limitation, and limits of this limitation are as broad as a state whose power is restricted by a constitution to a certain extent.

Another significant aspect of the expanding competence of international courts and tribunals concerns their common attitude to maintain the unity of international law by referring to decisions of each other.[135] Berman draws attention to the changing roles of international courts by emphasizing that courts are currently more inclined to "apply international norms transnationally, to engage in a transnational judicial dialogue, and even to adopt conceptions of universal jurisdiction."[136] This incline implies their constant approach to international law in favour of the international community. This issue also relates to the increasing networking between courts as mentioned earlier.

As seen, an integrationist approach to international law has become a salient feature of the Post-Westphalian turn. International and transnational courts sought the coherence of an international legal order in many remarkable cases, and left behind a number of rulings that can underpin the scholarly ideas on a legal integration within the international community. On the other hand, it is of note that, in spite of these integrationist readings of international law by international courts, international and transnational judiciary has not concurred on a common approach to the nature of international law. As a matter of fact, this is mostly regarded as a serious challenge of globalization to the conventional understanding of international law. The fragmentation of international law and its impacts on international jurisdiction will be dealt with more in details below.

---

[133] Andrea Bianchi, "Human Rights and the Magic of Jus Cogens," *European Journal of International Law* 19, no. 3 (2008), 491-499.

[134] Prosecutor v. Dusko Tadic, para. 28.

[135] Andreas L. Paulus, "International Legal System as a Constitution," in *Ruling the World?: Constitutionalism, International Law, and Global Governance*, ed. Jeffrey L. Dunoff and Joel P. Trachtman (Cambridge: Cambridge University Press, 2009), 86.

[136] Berman, "From International Law," 489.

2.1.2.2 Expansion of International Community

International law traditionally regarded states as the only agencies.[137] Insufficiency of states in the new relational rationality of international relations led to the enlargement of the international community through various new agencies in norm making. These new agencies are individuals, NGOs, corporations as well as some hybrid agencies in the form of networks that stem from either disaggregation of states or complex relationships between various actors. Accordingly, the international community gained a new complex form through these agencies. That is to say, the meaning of the international community is now rather shaped by the context of its use.[138] This change poses one of the most prominent challenges in the globalization age towards the conventional use of general international law.

2.1.2.2.1 International Organizations and Non-Governmental Organizations (NGOs)

The evolution of international organizations provides valuable hints regarding Post-Westphalian transformation in international law. The Congress of Vienna of 1815 and the Hague Conference of 1899, as predecessors of some contemporary organizations, have left behind a structural legacy which can still be observed in the structure of current international organizations. The former one represents a model where a smaller council of significant powers gathers, while the latter holds universal participation as central.[139] This has been viewed as a legacy of the Westphalian order.[140] The UN and G-20 reflect these models in many respects. However, different forms of organizations have arisen in parallel with various needs of the international community over time. Transnational and supranational bodies, as well as some hybrid models, are to be held up as major examples. Furthermore, the development of international organizations spawned new ones, and this led to a fact that most of the current international organizations have been established by other international organizations, not by treaties among states as in the classical model.[141] For example, The Food and Agriculture Organization spawned European Commission on Agriculture and twenty other organizations, and states have been represented only by a passive assent through their membership to the parent organizations in this kind of organizations.[142] A major consequence of this transformation is that states and traditional treaty law have no longer a monopoly over the creation of international organizations.[143]

---

[137] Sterio, *Evolution of International Law*, 216.

[138] Ku, *International Law*, 45.

[139] Ibid., 46.

[140] Ibid.

[141] Ibid., 51.

[142] Ibid.

[143] Ibid.

International organizations have superseded some of the authorities of states in international relations since they gained a new function to "break the traditional mould of being simply forums for inter-State negotiation or mere harmonization of national regulatory strategies via the glacial process of treaty negotiation and implementation."[144] Seen in this light, international organizations currently have a fundamental function in reconstructing relational rationality of international relations, and this gives rise to the aforementioned increasing erosion of the state sovereignty. Within the contemporary framework international organizations carry out various functions: "to frame issues, set agendas, legitimize action, and coordinate behaviour through an accepted framework, script, or general principles."[145] To entitle them "public international organizations" reflects a realistic depiction in this sense.[146] In addition, these organizations also have a legitimating function for the actions that would not be accepted, if they were only performed by states. This is true particularly in the use of force, on the ground that authorization by the UN recently became a form of legitimacy to gain public support for the use of force and to build alliances.[147] In this respect, the following words highlight such function of the UN explicitly:

> [T]he world organization has come to be regarded, and used, as a dispenser of politically significant approval and disapproval of the claims, policies, and actions of states, including, but going far beyond, their claims to status as independent members of the international system.[148]

Despite the opposite views that argue that international organizations operate only as agencies of states, they are increasingly enjoying a certain autonomy. The words of Dag Hammarskjöld, the Second Secretary-General of the UN in 1955, confirm this opinion:

> It has rightly been said that the United Nations is what the Member nations make it. But it may likewise be said that, within the limits set by government action and government cooperation, much depends on what the Secretariat makes it.[149]

The rise of international organizations, in particular in the twentieth century, had significant impacts on the nature of law-making in international law, in particular regarding treaty-making. In the current situation, as most of the treaties are concluded by international organizations, such as UN, WTO, ILO etc., Alvarez depicts

---

144 Bederman, *Globalization and International Law*, 174.

145 Ku, *International Law*, 109.

146 Bederman, *Globalization and International Law*, 174.

147 Ku, *International Law*, 116.

148 Inis L. Claude, Jr., "Collective Legitimization as a Political Function of the United Nations," *International Organization* 20 (1966): 367, cited by Ibid., 110.

149 Dag Hammarskjöld, "International Cooperation within the United Nations," in *Dag Hammarskjöld: Servant Peace*, ed. Wilder Foote (New York: Harper and Row, 1962), 93 cited by Ibid., 111.

these institutions as "virtual treaty machines." He states that treaty making is currently performed by basically following these steps: 1) Treaty-making conferences of international organizations 2) Expert treaty-making bodies 3) "Managerial forms of treaty making" (or "treaty making with strings attached," basically ILO model).[150] According to him, this development in international law has had some practical consequences for treaty making, and they are essential to understand the nature of globalization. First of all, different actors came into play by using international organizations as venues for treaty making, and thus less powerful states, NGOs and other stakeholders held a better position in treaty making. As a matter of fact, this decreased the importance of the role of states in treaty making. In addition, the main characteristics of an international organization as a "treaty venue" become decisive on the fate of procedures. Thereby the will of a single power is restricted by a collective one. International organizations also function as bearers of vast information on a specific matter. All in all, within such a framework, treaty negotiations can be held much more easily and quickly: "Treaty negotiations are, in short, more likely when they can take advantage of organizational venues whose 'sunk costs' have already been absorbed by their members."[151]

As a notable example of these organizations, the WTO comes to the fore, as it is a prominent subject of the debates on global law and globalization. The reason for this is that the categories of public and private, and the levels of supranational/regional and international are fairly intertwined within the framework of the WTO, and therefore the borderline between law and governance is quite blurred.[152] The WTO presents an innovative, and at the same time a controversial governance design. The WTO succeeds the diplomacy-based General Agreement on Tariffs and Trade (GATT), and it has generated a semi-autonomous regime that has its own administrative, legislative and judicial procedures.[153] On the other hand, it performs in accordance with general international law unless a WTO rule does not allow this. It also resembles other international organizations in terms of everyday activities, the decision-making system and so on.[154] Not only does it undertake the trade negotiations between member states but it also plays a significant role in the enforcement of agreements.[155] It deals with a broad range of trade issues from the liberalization of trade to intellectual property rights. The decision makers of the WTO are the representatives of national trade ministries. The negotiating sessions have recently become open to the public and the NGOs. On the other hand, the dispute settlement

---

[150] Jose E. Alvarez, "The New Treaty Makers," in *International Law: Classic and Contemporary Readings*, ed. Charlotte Ku and Paul F. Diehl, 3rd ed. (Boulder, Colo: Lynne Rienner Publishers, 2009), 102-104.

[151] Ibid., 106-112.

[152] Panagiotis Delimatsis, "A Global Law Perspective of the WTO," in *Reflections on Global Law*. ed. Shavana Musa and Eefje de Volder (Leiden: Brill, 2013), 156.

[153] Ibid., 154.

[154] Ibid., 154.

[155] Bederman, *Globalization and International Law*, 174.

system of the WTO is the hallmark of this organization. The dispute settlement system is deemed to have a disproportionate power compared to the political bodies of the WTO: "breaking with the conventional role of international tribunals; it is seen as wielding greater *relative judicial power*, and acting more as an *independent source of normativity*."[156] The dispute settlement system of the WTO performs through panels and the Appellate Body. The WTO is fundamentally an inter-state organization, and actors other than states do not have a right to access to this system. However, the private sector and the NGOs can issue *amicus curiae* briefs.[157] In short, the development of the WTO is deemed to be a significant paradigm shift in trade regulation since it provided a combination of the regulation of various trade dynamics. In this regard, its legal system and organizational structure reflect the shift of the regulatory power from public to private law on trade issues, and from national to international due to the increased economic globalization.[158] On the other hand, the WTO accommodates a high tension on the structural basis, between its state-centred mentality and the stateless nature of commercial transactions. This structure is also very central to the debate on the increasing erosion of state sovereignty, in particular, due to the operation of its dispute settlement system.[159]

The new roles of international organizations have been contested in terms of their operational frameworks. The very expert-oriented and closed-circuit nature of these organizations leads to the disputes concerning accountability, transparency, and legitimacy. Organizations like the WTO, the World Bank and the IMF very often face criticism over these issues.[160] This problem also reflects one of the dark points of global governance. However, as Bederman argues, this is not to be viewed as a commonality of all global governance bodies. In this regard, these institutions commenced as the instruments of the nation-state politics, and they "need time to adjust to the new conditions of a globalized world."[161] In this framework, institutions such as the European Court of Human Rights and the United Nations High Commisioner for Refugees seem to have overcome this problem, as they serve to democratic principles, and have also achieved transparency and accountability in transitional processes.[162]

It is of note that, as a non-state agency, the role of Non-Governmental Organizations (NGOs) in international law is increasing.[163] Currently, a broad range of NGOs

---

[156] Tomer Broude, "International Judicial Bodies as Sources of Normativity: The WTO Dispute Settlement System in Comparative Context," in *Governance and International Legal Theory*, ed. F. Dekker and Wouter G. Werner. (Leiden: Springer Science+Business Media, B.V., 2004), 238; emphasis belongs to the original text.

[157] Jan Klabbers, *International Law* (Cambridge: Cambridge University Press, 2013), 274.

[158] Delimatsis, "A Global Law Perspective," 153-155.

[159] Ibid., 156-158.

[160] Bederman, *Globalization and International Law*, 174.

[161] Ibid., 175.

[162] Ibid., 176.

[163] According to general estimates, today over 30.000 NGOs are in operation. Ku, *International Law*, 122.

are performing within the framework of international law, and they perform many main and complementary works along with other subjects of international law. States and international organizations obtain information and further support from these bodies regarding a broad range of social and political issues.[164] They can have significant impacts on law-making processes "by offering draft agreements, preparing position papers, monitoring, filing friend of the court amicus briefs, and even through limited direct participation in international proceedings."[165] Furthermore, they represent a political impulse in an organized way to "call attention to their concerns, raise awareness of an issue, and promote change."[166] Their well favored position in the global realm stems from their flexibility, ability to meet specific needs and effectiveness in maintaining public support.[167] The NGOs are also recognized within the framework of the UN (e.g. UN Charter Article 71). Their existence is quite necessary for the developing countries that lack resources and expertise to participate in policy making, as well as the development of human rights, women's rights, peace protection, worker protection, and so on. The pioneership of Amnesty International to the Torture Convention of 1984 can be held up as a remarkable example.[168] Another good example is the role of NGO lobbying efforts in drafting the Convention on the Elimination of Discrimination Against Women (CEDAW).[169] In addition, transnational networks can be built by NGOs or be subject to their participation in some cases. A notable example of the NGO networking is the Coalition for an International Criminal Court that became very effective in drafting the Statute of the International Criminal Court.[170] However, legitimacy and transparency issues come to the fore also from the international NGOs in many cases.[171]

A very remarkable transformation in the relational rationality of globalization was mentioned above under Sect. 2.1.1.2. At the cost of repetition, the globalization era has seen a kind of deconstruction of the idealized form of international relations through the emergence of a network society. A new hybrid form of networks dominates transgovernmental relations and global governance, and they also appear as self-contained regimes. At this stage, international law faces another challenge from such re-structuration of international relations. There are some linked issues with this development. The re-identification of law between these entities arises as a cardinal issue. As will be elucidated at various points of this chapter, this re-identification faces serious issues, on the ground that public and private law has become permeable in many respects, and this relational rationality has mostly been based on a heterarchy

[164] Klabbers, *International Law*, 89.

[165] Ku, *International Law*, 123.

[166] Ibid.,120.

[167] Ibid., 121.

[168] Ibid., 123-124.

[169] Alvarez, "New Treaty Makers," 109.

[170] Ku, *International Law*, 124.

[171] Bederman, *Globalization and International Law*, 175.

instead of a hierarchy, which provides an inconvenience for applying traditional forms of law. Consequently, in the current stage of globalism, the domestic and the international domains are engaged in a very intense and complex relationship on the ground that states and international organizations become closely dependent on each other in carrying out their functions.[172] Within this framework, effective regulation and governance require flexibility and adaptability, and the current formation of institutionalization and normative structuration aims at achieving these requirements.[173]

All in all, as it is the main concern of this section, it is no longer possible to advance the claim that international law merely consists of a framework that reflects the will of states through traditional diplomatic instruments.[174] International law is currently performed rather via a horizontal organization scheme. However, how to re-define the central point of international relations is still a controversial issue since the newly emerging structures, such as networks, are indefinite in many terms. In a point of view that still gives significant credit for states, Ku argues that this horizontal scheme is a consequence of states being in search of allies to advance their interests. Thus, they join forces either with each other, or with sub-national components of states, NGOs, private enterprises, or international organizations "to shape and to carry out their obligations."[175]

On the other hand, it seems that this idea is not acclaimed by pluralist approaches to international law. For instance, Berman concludes in the following way, in view of serious changes of actors playing roles in the construction of international law:

> (…) we need to think of international law as a global interplay of plural voices, many of which are not associated with the state, and that we need to focus on how norms articulated by a wide variety of communities end up having important impact in actual practice, regardless of the degree of coercive power those communities wield. (…) This new scholarship, I have argued elsewhere, begins to turn the focus of inquiry from "international law" –traditionally conceived as state-to-state interactions – to "law and globalization" a more multivalent study.[176]

In other words, Berman emphasizes that international law is no longer a monolithic entity as it was assumed earlier, but a collection of interests, by referring to the proliferation of the new role players in international relations. Increasingly complex structures of international organizations and contributions of new agencies, notably the NGOs, are the most remarkable factors that affect this situation. On the other hand, another sort of agency that arose within this framework is "individuals." It is worth dealing with this under another sub-title, as it is also strictly related to international human rights that marked a significant shift on the character of international law.

---

[172] Ku, *International Law*, 99.

[173] Ibid., 99.

[174] Ladeur, "Ein Recht der Netzwerke," 255; also see Christian Tomuschat, "Obligations Arising for States Without or Against Their Will," *Recueil des Cours* 241, no. 4 (1993): 199.

[175] Ku, *International Law*, 100.

[176] Berman, "A Pluralist Approach," 308-311.

2.1.2.2.2 Individuals and Impact of Human Rights

Under the framework of the Westphalian order, individuals were considered only as citizens of states, and thus they were regarded as only objects of international law, not bearers of rights and obligations.[177] This began to change towards the end of the nineteenth century by virtue of an international movement and a number of conferences to end the slave trade.[178] The involvement of individuals as the new subjects of international law also became a prominent development in international law particularly via the rise of the international human rights movement in the aftermath of World War II. In this regard, the adoption of the Universal Declaration of Human Rights of 1948 was a breakthrough.[179] In the age of globalization, the rise and consolidation of individual rights had a curtailing effect on the state behaviour and sovereignty. This also affected expectations of individuals from states to a great extent. That is to say, individuals expected more protection from international law as a shield against states, because of its influence on everyday life. This protection has been provided by a broad range of norms of international human rights, international labour law, or international tax law.[180] After all, the international human rights movement transformed the eighteenth century liberalism into the communitarianism by commitments of the welfare states.[181]

Furthermore, in the current framework of international law, the indigenous people are also considered as independent subjects of international law since they are in a special position in terms of their claims on native lands. This can appear as a distinctive problem with various aspects, such as environmental protection and intellectual properties.[182]

On the other hand, beginning with the Nuremberg Trials, individual responsibility has become a pertinent part of the issue of the statehood in international law. A remarkable development in this field is the establishment of the International Criminal Court (ICC). Nevertheless, in view of the tension between USA and the foundational process of the International Criminal Court in particular, it is still doubtful that individual responsibility has become an established principle of international law.[183]

The aftermath of World War II, which saw enormous violations of human rights, was a turning point for the development of human rights law. The international protection of human rights was found necessary in order to prevent a recurrence of such brutal atrocities and crimes against humanity. In this regard, the establishment of the

[177] Klabbers, *International Law*, 106.

[178] Ibid., 108.

[179] Ibid., 109.

[180] Sterio, "Evolution of International Law," 252.

[181] Louis Henkin, "A New Birth of Constitutionalism: Genetic Influences and Genetic Defects," *Cardozo Law Review* 14, no. 3-2 (1992 – 1993): 542.

[182] Klabbers, *International Law*, 89.

[183] Ladeur, "Ein Recht der Netzwerke," 248.

United Nations marks "[i]nternationalization of human rights and humanization of international law" as a great step for the international protection of human rights.[184] It also denotes a normative model that was followed by a number of international treaties, such as the Universal Declaration of Human Rights, Genocide Convention, Convention on the Elimination of All Forms of Racial Discrimination, and so on. The process that commenced after the adoption of the UN Charter led to a "normative consolidation of international human rights law."[185] However, this development did not mean that the UN Charter introduced a full-fledged protection of human rights. Instead, the UN Charter was purposefully drafted to be weak since drafters were not in a position to give strong commitments in this field by allowing for a Bill of Rights in the text as they had gross social problems regarding human rights violations at that time. For example, the racial discrimination was *de jure* in force in the USA. The USSR still had Gulags, and the UK and France still had colonies.[186] This period was followed by the institution-building process that began in the late 1960s through the emergence of universal and regional treaty-based institutions. The UN Human Rights Committee, Committee on the Elimination of Racial Discrimination, the European Court of Human Rights, Inter-American Commission and Court of Human Rights came into being during this period. This process was succeeded by the emergence of special mechanisms to protect human rights within the special competence of some organizations, such as UNESCO and ILO.[187] However, it is of note that institutionalization in the human rights field has been effective since the late 1980s, as the Cold War was a hindrance to the efficacy of these institutions.[188] The impact of the end of the Cold War on human rights issues is likely to be seen in the fourth paragraph of the Vienna Declaration on Human Rights of 1993, which reads as follows: "the promotion and protection of all human rights is a legitimate concern of the international community."[189] This post-Cold War declaration is also of importance since it promulgates the universal character of human rights without rejecting the relativity of cultures, as it is stated in the fifth paragraph of the Declaration:

> All human rights are universal, indivisible and interdependent and interrelated. The international community must treat human rights globally in a fair and equal manner, on the same footing, and with the same emphasis. While the significance of national and regional particularities and various historical, cultural and religious backgrounds must be borne in mind, it is the duty of States, regardless of their political, economic and cultural systems, to promote and protect all human rights and fundamental freedoms.[190]

[184] Thomas Buergenthal, "The Normative and Institutional Evolution of International Human Rights," *Human Rights Quarterly* 19 (1997): 703.

[185] Ibid., 705.

[186] Ibid., 706.

[187] Ibid., 711.

[188] Ibid., 712.

[189] Ibid., 713.

[190] Vienna Declaration and Programme of Action, adopted by the World Conference on Human Rights in Vienna, 25.06.1993, http://www.ohchr.org/EN/ProfessionalInterest/Pages/Vienna.aspx, last visit 10.07.2015.

This paragraph seems to have considered that a more inclusive language was necessary to specify universal duties for states. Furthermore, the content of the Vienna Declaration reflects a profound transformation and progress in the mindset that dominates the international human rights protection, compared with the substance of the Universal Declaration of Human Rights of 1948 regarding the division between international law and domestic law that remained in favour of the oppressive governments in many cases.[191]

Moreover, it is of note that the emergence of these institutions also became the ground for the rise and growing significance of non-governmental human rights organizations.[192] There are a number of reasons for the increased institutionalization in the field of human rights. Of these reasons, the end of the colonial period and a search for a common stance against the apartheid were remarkable. In this regard, the UN mechanisms were deemed to be the major instruments of the struggle against the apartheid. An alliance with the UN opened the way towards further coalitions for other international human rights issues.[193] On the other hand, the increasing consciousness on social causes of human rights violations that stem from poverty, corruption, diseases, lack of educational resources, etc. has led to a high demand for international cooperation.[194] This fact means that social causes behind the human rights violations require further interventions that exceed the power of nation states in terms of human and financial resources, and international cooperation remains the only way of dealing with many of these violations. In the field of human rights, an effective struggle against the impunity for breaches of human rights required some other novelties to international law, such as the adoption of the accountability of individuals and the establishment of criminal tribunals like the ICTY, ICTR, and finally, the ICC. This development came about as a necessity on the ground that some individuals could benefit from the domestic impunity in many cases, although their states were convicted before international courts. Therefore, the accountability of individuals before international tribunals has arisen as a result of this necessity, in other words, a requirement of an effective struggle against impunity in cases regarding grave violation of human rights. Furthermore, transnational institutionalization has arisen as an effective way of promoting, monitoring, and implementing many human rights norms.[195]

As a result of these developments in the field of human rights, some scholars argue that the field of human rights is no longer a separate branch that is governed in principle by general international law, but rather it marks a philosophy that is increasingly becoming determinant on international law.[196] Accordingly, it is also

---

[191] Buergenthal, "International Human Rights," 723.

[192] Ibid., 711.

[193] Ibid., 712.

[194] Ibid., 715.

[195] Sterio, "Evolution of International Law," 229.

[196] Hugh Thirlway, *The Sources of International Law*, 1st ed. (Oxford: Oxford University Press, 2014), 175.

suggested that general international law can be considered as one of the sources of human rights obligations of states.[197] This opinion grants priority to human rights against international law, as it reconstructs international law on a moral ground. Nevertheless, this point is still quite controversial in the contemporary international law literature, and some public international law scholars that focus on the state practice seek the source of bindingness of human rights norms in customary law or general principles of law through positivist perspectives.[198]

All in all, the legal and factual basis for a national and international division has vanished in terms of human rights issues. However, this does not mean that a global consensus has arisen on the protection mechanisms of human rights. The firm opposition from USA against the International Criminal Court, the impunity for crimes committed in Guantanamo, and the weak construction of regional human rights organizations other than the Council of Europe can be held up as notable examples. There is still a lot to do for further transnational institutionalization on human rights. However, the Council of Europe and the European Court of Human Rights come into prominence as the most remarkable and fruitful normative projects in this field along with transnational human rights activism. Therefore, they are mostly viewed as good models for inchoate institutionalization in this area as they left a strong impact on the understanding of norms in international law.

2.1.2.3 A New Normative Framework

International customs and treaties are the primary sources of international law in the traditional understanding of public international law. As very often referred, they are officially recognized as the main sources of international law under Article 38(1)(b) of the Statute of the International Court of Justice. However, Post-Westphalian transformation and globalization had significant impacts on the leading position of these two sources in many respects. International law that is conducted among states through customs and treaties reflects just a theoretically idealized world. Due to the development of global governance, it no longer fits the reality of international relations.[199] On the other hand, this does not imply the complete dysfunction of these normative sources. The greater part of international law still consists of *jus dispositivum*, where the consent of state parties is crucial for enforcement.[200] What I underline here is rather increasing loss of function of these sources to meet the needs of the international community, and the rise of different regulatory instruments so as to achieve this requirement.

---

[197] Ibid.

[198] Bruno Simma and Philip Alston, "The Sources of Human Rights Law: Custom, Jus Cogens and General Principles," *Australian Yearbook of International Law* 12 (1988-9): 82. For a counter argument: Thirlway, *Sources of International Law*, 180-181.

[199] Klabbers, *International Law*, 37.

[200] Thirlway, *Sources of International Law*, 35.

As mentioned in sect. 2.1.1.2, states mostly enter into relations through transgovernmental networks which consist of hybrid formal and informal bodies, but not only through diplomatic bodies, as envisioned in the traditional doctrine of sources of international law.[201] In this sense, governance is depicted as "network governance."[202] Furthermore, large multinational companies and many NGOs take initiatives in international relations in setting standards, thus in doing so, they exercise authority as well.[203]

International custom is defined as "evidence of a general practice accepted as law" in Article 38(1)(b) of the Statute of the ICJ. Beyond this very broad definition, the ICJ determined the meaning of the term in various rulings. The response from the states to these general practices has been very central to these findings:

> (…) actions by States 'not only must amount to a settled practice, but they must also be such, or be carried out in such a way, as to be evidence of a belief that this practice is rendered obligatory by the existence of the rule of law requiring it. The need for such a belief, i. e., the existence of a subjective element, is implicit in the very notion of the *opinio iuris sive necessitatis.*[204]

In this regard, the role of *opinio iuris* is very central to the Court's definitions in some other rulings as well.[205] In addition, international customs emerge spontaneously, and the source of their binding character is controversial in legal theory, where various opinions are found on this matter.[206]

Moreover, the relevance of customary law with Post-Westphalian transformation under conditions of globalization is debatable. The slow and cumbersome emergence of customs as well as them being subject to a "political hijacking" are problematic in this regard.[207] Furthermore, reliance of customs on state practice grants it a conservative character.[208] International customs suffer from an epistemological uncertainty that makes the meta-law in a custom creation unknown.[209] At this point,

---

[201] Slaughter, *A New World Order.*

[202] Klabbers, *International Law*, 38.

[203] For example, as a standard setting body, Basel Committee is one of the most notable ones. Ibid., 37.

[204] North Sea Continental Shelf Cases (Federal Republic of Germany v. Denmark; Federal Republic of Germany v. Netherlands), Merits, ICJ Rep 3, (1969) cited by Tullio Treves, "Customary International Law," Max Planck Encyclopedia of International Law, 2006, 17, http://opil.ouplaw.com/view/10.1093/law:epil/9780199231690/law-9780199231690-e1393?prd=EPIL, last visit 14.11.2014.

[205] Ibid., 17.

[206] Ibid., 4-6.

[207] Boyle and Chinkin, *Making of International Law* 21.

[208] Ibid., 21.

[209] Jörg Kammerhofer, *Uncertainty in International Law: A Kelsenian Perspective* (London: Routledge, 2011), 60.

the meaning of state practice appears as controversial, and it gives rise to relatively contrary theories.[210]

Koskenniemmi argues that the doctrine of customary law is indeterminate, since it is circular as it considers state behaviour as the evidence of *opinio juris*, and in return, *opinio juris* as the evidence of state behaviour.[211] Beyond the unclarity of the concept of *opinio juris*, the question of when an act binds a state comes to the fore. The precondition of *opinio juris* is the state consent for creation of a custom. However, the extent and indication of consent are ambiguous.[212] What is more, it is evident that the conventional understanding of the free will of states as it was articulated in Lotus ruling of the PCIL as "[t]he rules of law binding upon States therefore emanate from their own free will"[213] should be found obsolete in an age of globalization and high interdependence.[214] In this respect, to what extent a custom is to be regarded as a general norm in international law arises as a major question. Furthermore, the unclarity of the making of customs is very problematic on the ground that increasing cooperation and interdependence and new relational forms of globalization require more clear and predictable forms of regulation.

All in all, international customs are viewed as non-reliable normative sources of international law, and in addition, the doctrine of customary law is not able to respond to the current normative requirements of the international community for the reasons mentioned above.

As referred to in the above section briefly, public international law had to respond to the new developments and forms of cooperation between states regarding normative instruments as well. The emanation of new institutions, mostly by the initiative of international organizations rendered the role of traditional law largely unnecessary as the role of states became largely secondary through the operations of these institutions.[215] That is not to say that treaties have lost their functions completely in this field, but it is an indication of the eradication of the primary role of treaties in international law.

On the other hand, a similar situation on treaty law should be noted. As a major step towards a Post-Westphalian order, the rise of peremptory norms, or in other words *jus cogens,* in treaty law was vital. The cornerstone provision introducing peremptory norms, Article 53 of the Vienna Convention on the Law of Treaties reads as follows: "A treaty is void if, at the time of its conclusion, it conflicts with

---

[210] Ibid., 62 ff.

[211] Martti Koskenniemmi, *From Apology to Utopia: The Structure of International Legal Argument; With a New Epilogue* (Cambridge: Cambridge University Press, 2005), 437.

[212] Kammerhofer, *Uncertainty in International Law*, 77.

[213] Ibid.

[214] Tomuschat, "Obligations Arising for States." Further, Koh argues that interaction in transnational legal process is the most remarkable ground for states to obey international law. Harold Hongju Koh, "The 1994 Roscoe Pound Lecture: Transnational Legal Process," *Nebraska Law Review* 75, no. 1 (1996): 203.

[215] Ku, *International Law*, 51.

a peremptory norm of general international law."[216] In this respect, the increased number of *jus cogens* norms in international law can be seen as a significant step in restricting state will in treaty law. Nevertheless, *jus cogens* is still a controversial issue in terms of the source of these peremptory norms.[217]

A striking example of a deviation from the traditional manner of treaty law is human rights treaties. The norms included by these treaties are relatively different from traditional international legal norms. In the framework of traditional international law,

> State A may not do certain things to State B, State C, or any other State. Conversely, States B, C, or any other state may not do the same thing to State A. States A, B, and C, however, may do whatever they wish within their own borders.[218]

The new human rights norms gave rise to a significant shift in this field. A noteworthy example is the Torture Convention of 1984.[219] In Article 2 of this convention, it is stated that,

> 1. Each State Party shall take effective legislative, administrative, judicial or other measures to prevent acts of torture in any territory under its jurisdiction.
> 2. No exceptional circumstances whatsoever, whether a state of war or a threat of war, internal political instability or any other public emergency, may be invoked as a justification of torture. (…).

As viewed in this Article, the regulation is not limited to the behaviour of a state. These kind of norms can regulate a state's behaviour against its own citizens and residents within its borders, and a state is under the obligation of justifying this behaviour before other state parties.[220] Furthermore, these new sorts of human rights instruments mostly include norms concerning universal jurisdiction.[221] The Genocide Convention of 1948 can also be held up as an example at this point.[222] On the other hand, these treaties impose some duties on states (to give effect to the provisions of the present Convention …), and this is to be viewed as a characteristic of

---

[216] Vienna Convention on the Law of Treaties, 23.05.1969, http://legal.un.org/ilc/texts/instruments/english/conventions/1_1_1969.pdf, last visit 11.09.2012.

[217] Thirlway, *Sources of International Law*, 35.

[218] Sterio, "Evolution of International Law," 227.

[219] Multilateral Convention Against Torture and Other Cruel, Inhuman or Degrading Treatment or Punishment, 10.12.1984 (hereafter Torture Convention), https://treaties.un.org/doc/Publication/UNTS/Volume%201465/volume-1465-I-24841-English.pdf, last visit 27.11.2012.

[220] Sterio, "Evolution of International Law," 227.

[221] e.g. Torture Convention, Articles 5-7.

[222] Convention on the Prevention and Punishment of the Crime of Genocide. adopted by the General Assembly of the United Nations, 09.12.1948, (hereafter Genocide Convention) https://treaties.un.org/doc/Publication/UNTS/Volume%2078/volume-78-I-1021-English.pdf, last visit 29.12.2012.

contemporary human right norms.[223] In this context, Article 5 of this Convention reads as follows:

> The Contracting Parties undertake to enact, in accordance with their respective Constitutions, the necessary legislation to give effect to the provisions of the present Convention and, in particular, to provide effective penalties for persons guilty of genocide or of any of the other acts enumerated in article III.

In this regard, some human rights norms play a similar role as domestic law, and thus a significant function of these norms is a limitation of state sovereignty.[224]

The Post-Westphalian turn in international law has seen new forms of regulations in parallel with the needs of governance. Depending upon the expansion of the international community by new agencies, new forms became necessary along with the new frameworks that are more overarching. Increased cross-border activities required a more practical and operable normative framework through regulatory activities of international organizations' governance bodies. The most remarkable outcome of this process is the emergence of networks as "self-contained regimes."[225] These regimes are considered as part of general international law. However, due to their innovative and hybrid character, whether or not they spawn new sorts of norms other than formally recognized by Article 38 of the ICJ, arises as a pressing question.[226]

As indicated in the previous section, human rights have appeared as an actual example of this problem. In the current stage of the development of human rights, to explain the ground of bindingness of international human rights norms through traditional sources of international law does not seem very plausible.[227] In this regard, although it is technically not a binding instrument and has the power of a recommendation as a General Assembly resolution, the Universal Declaration of Human Rights has had enormous effects on the development of human rights.[228] As demonstrated in the previous section, human rights currently appear as an issue where the national and international borders have become blurred. In addition to that, the International Court of Justice held "humanitarian considerations" as sources of law that can generate legal rights and obligations in some of its rulings, although the Court has not developed a coherent approach so far.[229]

---

[223] Sterio, "Evolution of International Law," 229.

[224] Ibid., 230.

[225] See above Section 2.1.1.2. For a counter argument about "self-contained regimes": *Fragmentation of International Law: Difficulties Arising from the Diversification and Expansion of International Law: Report of the Study Group of the International Law Commission*, Finalized by Martti Koskenniemi, (Geneva: International Law Commission, Fifty-eighth session, 1 May-9 June and 3 July-11 August 2006) (hereafter ILC Report), para. 5,225 http://daccess-dds-ny.un.org/doc/UNDOC/LTD/G06/610/77/PDF/G0661077.pdf?OpenElement, last visit 16.07.2014.

[226] Thirlway, *Sources of International Law*, 174.

[227] Ibid., 175-184.

[228] Klabbers, *International Law*, 109.

[229] e.g. Corfu Channel Case, Thirlway, *Sources of International Law*, 185-189.

In this new framework, the major function of new normative instruments became standardization and regulation.[230] The operation of international organizations gives rise to the "socialization" of the member states when states begin to conform to certain behaviours over time due to the long-standing interaction.[231] The codes and standards created by these organizations can have the same legal effects as treaties in terms of obligations. For instance, recommendations of the International Atomic Energy Agency are quite functional on the ground that they

> enable a complex regulatory system to function smoothly without mandatory reliance on a cumbersome treaty-making or amending process while still allowing the option of (re) negotiating a treaty when consensus is available.[232]

Within this framework, the position of soft laws is also noteworthy. Most of the regulatory instruments of international organizations consist of formally non-binding recommendations, in that they are mostly not equipped with the authority to take binding decisions.[233] It has been argued that many soft law norms can have a binding character to various degrees. Klabbers advances the claim that the term "soft law" is misleading and unhelpful in this sense.[234] According to him, the traditional doctrine of sources is not realistic, since international law lacks an objective criterion to distinguish what law is. It is not possible to explain, for example the efficiency of standards developed by the Basel Committee by the traditional doctrine of sources, and also recognition of the bindingness of some soft law norms by international courts.[235] In addition, there is a recent trend in international law that replaces "law making" with the doctrine of sources that is considered as a consequence of these facts.[236]

Furthermore, as touched upon in this chapter, blurring of the borderline between public and private law in transnational governance should also be seen as another major factor for the inquiry of new regulatory instruments.

2.1.2.4 Fragmentation and International Law

2.1.2.4.1 Increasing Differentiation and Fragmentation

Although the idea of a unified legal order and a legal community has left marks on the theory of international law, this idea has also seen a notable challenge from those who pointed to the influence of the fragmentation in international law. The

---

[230] Ku, *International Law*, 151.

[231] Ibid., 152.

[232] Barry Kellman, "Protection of Nuclear Materials," in *Commitment and Compliance*, ed. Dinah Shelton, (Oxford: Oxford University Press, 2003), 487, cited by Ibid., 153.

[233] Klabbers, *International Law*, 38.

[234] Ibid., 38.

[235] Ibid., 38.

[236] Ibid., 40.

fragmentation of the international legal order arose as a matter of the after-Cold-War-era, as many new international organizations and tribunals proliferated in this period.[237] The report concerning the fragmentation of international law of the International Law Commission in 2006, which was led and finalized by Martti Koskenniemmi, has been a salient reference point to the debate on fragmentation in international law.[238]

The report mainly addresses the remarks on the fragmented structure of the international legal order that stems from an increasing differentiation:

> What once appeared to be governed by "general international law" has become the field of operation for such specialist systems as "trade law," "human rights law," "environmental law," "law of the sea," "European law" and even such exotic and highly specialized knowledges as "investment law" or "international refugee law" etc. – each possessing their own principles and institutions.[239]

According to this report, there are a number of reasons of fragmentation in the international legal order. Indeed, as the report agrees, international law had always had a fragmented character, since diverse national legal systems created an incoherent form. Accordingly, it places great emphasis to the transformation from a world fragmented into the states towards a world fragmented into specialized regimes. Moreover, the international legal order has no common general legislative body, and the increasing functional differentiation resulted in an autonomization of legal institutions and spheres of legal practice. This development has come about as a direct consequence of globalization. General international law has undergone a transformation, and as a result of this transformation, it has become a field of various specialized systems, such as trade law, human rights law, environmental law, law of the sea, etc. The newly emerging actors, in particular networks, have become quite influential in the formation of these systems.[240] Consequently, the loss of an overarching perspective on the law was accompanied by conflicts between rules or rule systems. The self-contained regimes that arose within this process impede a coherent framework of international law.[241] These new rule systems have no clear relationship with each other, and normative conflicts between them

> do not arise as technical "mistakes" that could be "avoided" by a more sophisticated way of legal reasoning. New rules and legal regimes emerge as responses to new preferences, and sometimes out of conscious effort to deviate from preferences as they existed under old regimes.[242]

---

[237] Anne Peters, "Fragmentation and Constitutionalization," in *The Oxford Handbook of the Theory of International Law*, ed. Anne Orford and Florian Hoffmann (Oxford: Oxford University Press, 2016), 1012.

[238] ILC Report.

[239] Ibid., para. 8.

[240] Ibid., para. 245.

[241] Ibid., para. 10-17.

[242] Ibid., para. 245.

It is a heterarchical order. The relevant hierarchies exist only within particular fields. This spontaneous and unhierarchical nature of international law gives rise to endemic normative conflicts.[243] The noteworthy point is that fragmentation does not make law redundant in international relations, and it operates by drawing on the conventional methods of public international law. The crucial point underlined by this report is that in order to comprehend the operation of international law rightfully, a particular emphasis must be placed on the "collision of norms and regimes and the rules, methods and techniques for dealing with such collisions."[244]

The fragmentation in international law is a result of increasing differentiation via transnational bodies. The major problem regarding this fragmented order is that general international law does not provide a basis for understanding this structure, and it does not have the necessary instruments to meet the needs of this field.[245] In this regard, the differentiation in global society comes along with new forms of governance. A remarkable example of this development is the operation of the Internet Corporation for Assigned Names and Numbers (ICANN). ICANN is a US based non-profit organization, and in technical terms, it basically "coordinates the Internet Assigned Numbers Authority (IANA) functions, which are key technical services critical to the continued operations of the Internet's underlying address book, the Domain Name System (DNS)" and provides "one global internet" by means of this coordination.[246] It creates

> a form of international governance [that] has an atypical character in as much as it originates out of spontaneous co-operation among a network of people who have a number of common interests and have set up a sort of "community."[247]

The ICANN operates through a "bottom-up" and "consensus-driven" model that includes public and private sector along with technical experts as the stakeholders of its operation. In this respect, the ICANN's community consists of

> registries, registrars, Internet Service Providers (ISPs), intellectual property advocates, commercial and business interests, non-commercial and non-profit interests, representation from more than 100 governments, and a global array of individual Internet users.[248]

---

[243] Ibid., para. 246.

[244] Ibid., para. 249.

[245] Lars Viellechner, "Verfassung als Chiffre," *Zeitschrift für ausländisches öffentliches Recht und Völkerrecht* 1 (2015): 248.

[246] The official website of ICANN, https://www.icann.org/resources/pages/welcome-2012-02-25-en, last visit 18.06.2015.

[247] Karl-Heinz Ladeur, "ICANN and the Illusion of a Community Based Internet: Comments on Jochen von Bernstorff," in *Transnational Governance and Constitutionalism*, ed. Christian Joerges, Inger-Johanne Sand and Gunther Teubner (Portland: Hart Publishing, 2004), 283.

[248] The official website of ICANN.

Its main goal has been shown as maximizing benefits of the Internet for the international community.[249] The establishment of the ICANN was also supported by the US government, on the ground that the government expected it to work faster and more practically than a governmental body in dealing with rapidly increasing issues of internet domain names.[250] As a dispute settlement system, the ICANN has developed the Uniform Domain Name Dispute Resolution Policy (UDRP), and it operates as an alternative to national judicial bodies. The UDRP may involve private and governmental actors at once. The procedure is primarily held online. A time and cost-efficient dispute resolution system has been adopted. That is to say; it prescribes a very quick resolution of disputes and an affordable application mechanism that is also supposed to be good for small-business owners.[251]

On the other hand, in case of the ICANN, conventional instruments of public international law remain insufficient to sort out some specific problems with this field. In particular, the ICANN suffers a democratic legitimation problem, for the reason that it has not developed a satisfactory democratic election process that is overarching for all users of the internet.[252] It is evident that under the current structure of international law, given its bottom-up structure, international organizations are not capable of presenting a solution to this problem.[253] As an alternative dispute resolution system, the UDRP also reflects an actor in a pluralist order, where a heterarchy between other actors appears instead of a hierarchical system that requires the priority of different elements of a system.[254]

Beyond the increasing differentiation in the global realm, "conflicting interpretations of international law" are also to be considered as a ground for fragmentation.[255] One remarkable example is the rejection of the effective control rule of the ICJ by the Appeals Chamber of the International Criminal Tribunal for the Former Yugoslavia. In the Tadic Case, the Appeals Chamber of the ICTY rejected this rule that first appeared in the Nicaragua ruling of the ICJ,[256] where the court concluded that USA could not be considered accountable for its actions in a territory which was not under its effective control. The Appeals Chamber of the ICTY refused to comply with this rule of the ICJ. In both of these cases, the issue was the ascription of actions and responsibilities of individuals to States, which was indeed an open-ended problem. However, the Appeals Chamber of the ICTY did not find the

[249] Luke A. Walker, "ICANN's Uniform Domain Name Dispute Resolution Policy," *Berkeley Technology Law Journal* 15 (2000): 303, 307.

[250] Keohane and Nye, "Introduction," 24.

[251] Walker, "ICANN's Uniform Domain Name," 300.

[252] Ladeur, "ICANN and Illusion," 283.

[253] Ibid., 284.

[254] Viellechner, "Verfassung als Chiffre," 248.

[255] Ku, *International Law*, 32.

[256] Military and Paramilitary Activities in and Against Nicaragua (Nicaragua v. United States of America), Merits, Judgment, ICJ Reports (1986), http://www.icj-cij.org/docket/?sum=367&p1=3&p2=3&case=70&p3=5, last visit 29.10.2012.

conclusion of the ICJ in the Nicaragua case persuasive, on the ground that the ICJ required the efficient control of a territory for the state responsibility:

> The requirement of international law for the attribution to States of acts performed by private individuals is that the State exercises control over the individuals. The degree of control may, however, vary according to the factual circumstances of each case. The Appeals Chamber fails to see why in each and every circumstance international law should require a high threshold for the test of control.[257]

Further, the Court asserted that the rule upheld by the ICJ was at variance with the international judicial and state practice, where a lower degree of control was sought in the acts of military or paramilitary groups.[258] In view of these facts, the Appeals Chamber did not apply the effective control test originated from the Nicaragua case to the case at issue.

The fragmentation of international law has been regarded as a major challenge by the academic inquiries that seek unity in the international legal order. This challenge has been expressed by a number of scholars so far.[259] These accounts have briefly stated that an inquiry for a unified legal order that is supposed to be a ground for a constitutionalization is not realistic since this fragmented order promises only the escalation of fragmentation. This debate will be handled in detail in the second chapter.

2.1.2.4.2 New Spaces, Regimes and Jurisdictional Rules

In the Post-Westphalian phase of international relations and law, due to increasing transactions beyond national borders, a pressing question has arisen regarding legal jurisdiction. In traditional international law, the question of jurisdiction was analysed by referring to physical locations. However, this reference currently dysfunctions to some extent since physical locations lose importance increasingly, and international legal scholars need a new reference for new jurisdictional rules.[260] The activities and entities having no local presence are at the core of this problem. The economic actions through internet communication and globalization set the ground for these new forms of governance, and these forms arise independently of the physical geography to a certain degree. In addition, non-state entities claim their judicial authority by producing their own norms in case of a broad range of legal issues. This is likely to be seen as a deadlock of the Westphalian nation-state system

---

[257] The Prosecutor v. Duško Tadic, para. 117.

[258] Ibid., para.124-145.

[259] Fischer-Lescano and Teubner, "Regime-Collisions." Martti Koskenniemmi, "The Fate of Public International Law: Between Technique and Politics," *The Modern Law Review* 70, no. 1 (2007): 1-30.

[260] Berman, "From International Law," 530.

that dysfunctions or fails to respond to the various needs of the international system. This scheme has to do with

> extraterritorial content regulations, trademark rules, taxation schemes, and criminal investigations regarding internet transactions, to controversies surrounding universal and transnational criminal jurisdiction for human rights violations, to arguments about the legitimacy of various international tribunals.[261]

Under these circumstances, these new forms of norm production require rethinking about the new ways of delimiting the scope of legal jurisdiction and developing hybrid jurisdictional, or choice-of-law models instead of adhering to the former models that are rather based on the geographical forms.[262]

Moreover, as will be mentioned under various sections in this chapter, the fragmented structure of international law generates another problem of the jurisdictional rules. In contemporary international law, many cases include complex substances, and they may concern different norms of various regimes at the same time. For instance, a case may have to do with trade law, as well as human rights or environmental law. The WTO Appellate Body held such cases that are very well known in the literature of international law.[263] Due to various substantial dimensions of a case, it may concern procedural norms of different regimes. However, the fragmented structure of international legal order –in terms of disconnectedness of the fragmented entities- is the greatest hindrance for harmonization of different rules of different regimes. Another potential, and indeed more actual problem is overlapping norms and rulings of different regimes. Furthermore, a case may be held by different tribunals of different regimes at the same time, for instance by a human rights court and a dispute settlement body of a trade regime. In this regard, it evidently becomes a gross threat against the (aimed) objective coherence of law and international law.

This issue was also underlined in the Report of the International Law Commission on Fragmentation of International Law, as mentioned earlier. According to this report, one serious problem about overlapping jurisdictional rules appeared in the case of the environmental effects of MOX Plant Nuclear Facility in the UK. The possible environmental effects of this facility were subject to three different procedures before three separate institutions:

> an Arbitral Tribunal set up under Annex VII of the United Nations Convention on the Law of the Sea (UNCLOS), the compulsory dispute settlement procedure under the Convention on the Protection of the Marine Environment of the North-East Atlantic (OSPAR Convention) as well as under the European Community and Euratom Treaties within the European Court of Justice (ECJ).[264]

---

[261] Ibid., 532.

[262] Ibid.

[263] Ernst-Ulrich Petersmann, "Multilevel Trade Governance in the WTO Requires Multilevel Constitutionalism," in *Constitutionalism, Multilevel Trade, Governance and International Economic Law*, ed. Christian Joerges and Ernst-Ulrich Petersmann (Oxford: Hart Publishing, 2011), 31 ff.

[264] ILC Report, para. 10.

That is to say, there were three overlapping jurisdictional norms for one case, namely the "(universal) rules of the UNCLOS, the (regional) rules of the OSPAR Convention, and the (regional) rules of EC/EURATOM" that address the same facts.[265] This situation gave rise to the question of which should have been decisive: "the law of the sea, about (possible) pollution of the North Sea, or about inter-EC relationships?"[266] As the Report emphasized, the normative structure of current international law has not produced a satisfying answer to this problem so far. In this regard, this problem also threatens "objectives of legal certainty and the equality of legal subjects."[267]

2.1.2.5 Blurring Borderline Between Public and Private Law

Another challenging issue for international law scholars is the increasingly blurring borders between public and private law. Indeed, as some scholars point out, private law has never been "private," as the state has always stood behind the enforcement or creation of private law norms, and the enforcement of these norms aims to achieve public goals.[268] This process has a lot to do with the changing and expanding nature of public international law. For instance, under the new framework of international organizations, various private bodies, corporations, labour unions, and NGOs take part in the operation of these organizations.[269] As emphasized before, international law is currently far from its traditional formation where states and public bodies were the only subjects of law. That is to say, under new circumstances of the international legal order; conflicts of law, business transactions, and private and non-state actors became a growing issue within the public international law discourse.[270] As a consequence of this development, a sort of a private authority has appeared in global governance, which arose particularly in the fields of trade agreements, rating agencies, product safety, standardization and *lex mercatoria*.[271]

A remarkable issue at this point is the creation of new cross-border regimes and regulation concerning certain fields, some commercial entities and international transactions that involve them. For example, the UN Convention on the International Sale of Goods (CISG) includes a number of default rules that contracting parties refer to if their international sale contract does not prescribe any rule on

---

[265] Ibid.

[266] Ibid.

[267] Ibid., para. 12.

[268] Berman, "From International Law," 520.

[269] Ku, *International Law*, 48.

[270] Berman, "From International Law," 520.

[271] Peer Zumbansen, "Carving Out Typologies and Accounting for Differences Across Systems: Towards a Methodology of Transnational Constitutionalism," in *The Oxford Handbook of Comparative Constitutional Law*, ed. Michel Rosenfeld and Andras Sajo (Oxford: Oxford University Press, 2012), 82.

certain matters. The contracting parties can bypass any nation-state law, and instead, they can opt for a sort of *lex mercatoria* for their transactions.[272]

At this juncture, the role of the WTO and its Appellate Tribunal, as well as other trade courts that developed through free trade agreements in creating a common trade law, is striking. In general terms, rulings of these courts challenge the state sovereignty and override domestic court decisions, and they may involve some environmental and labour NGOs that are becoming increasingly active within the new framework of the WTO.[273] Furthermore, private investors have the right to bring an action against the regulatory decisions of a NAFTA member in another free trade panel framework.[274] These and other similar mechanisms of the free trade panels create and enforce norms that bear characteristics of public law norms, and as such, they reflect an increasingly blurring distinction between "private" and "public" in international law.[275]

These new cross-border regulatory norms were involved by treaties that were negotiated between states, however they also reflect private commercial interests. Sterio explains this new form of mixed relationship by arguing that "in today's inter-connected world, globalization has dictated a harmonization of substantive rules in specific fields. This harmonization supersedes national rules and undermines the traditional concept of state sovereignty."[276]

As to the traditional roles in traditional international law, commercial relations are no longer conducted only between public bodies. Commercial relations have developed into a mixed structure of public parties and foreign investors:

> This public/private merger in the field of cross-border commercial law epitomizes the entire shift of international law from a body of law governing inter-state relations, to a complex web of regulations concluded between state and non-state actors and governing private entity-state relations.[277]

This issue also has to do with the evolution of the role of contracts in public law and the network society.[278] The public contracts no longer reflect only a decision of an administrative body. In other words, commercial agreements are no longer negotiated and concluded only by states. Instead, they also involve private parties as direct contracting partners.[279] Within a framework in which a network society arose, the role and character of public contracts changed fundamentally.[280] The rise of direct

---

[272] Sterio, "Evolution of International Law," 240.

[273] Berman, "From International Law," 521.

[274] Ibid., 522.

[275] Ibid., 523.

[276] Sterio, "Evolution of International Law," 240.

[277] Ibid., 240.

[278] Karl-Heinz Ladeur, "The Role of Contracts and Networks in Public Governance: The Importance of the 'Social Epistemology' of Decision Making," *Indiana Journal ofGlobal Legal Studies* 14, no. 2 (2007): 329-351.

[279] Sterio, "Evolution of International Law," 242.

[280] Ladeur, "Role of Contracts," 331.

transnational cooperation between governmental bodies instead of the traditional international cooperation is a leading factor in this development, and this new structure can also involve private parties. According to Ladeur, this relates to a further evolution of the cognitive infrastructure of postmodern societies. The rationale of the new formation of contracts has been explained by him as follows:

> Contracts are a form of public-private coordination in conditions that are characterized by a rise of the experimental design of projects and of the operation on the basis of a cognitive infrastructure that is dominated by fragmented networks of interrelationships that find their repercussion in border-spanning "epistemic communities" of people generating knowledge in a project-like form of cooperation.[281]

All in all, the traditional distinction between public-private law has also been strongly challenged by the new relational rationality of globalization where cooperation through public-private networking appeared in a new rationality. This transformation also challenged the traditional meanings of legal instruments. In addition, the hidden impacts of private parties in norm-making in international law should be taken into consideration as a significant part of this transformation. In this regard, the lobbying activities of private investors on their national governments come to the fore in the processes of negotiations over bilateral agreements. Despite the fact that bilateral agreements reflect the traditional form of international law, according to Sterio, "they signal a shift in the type of actors present on the international scene" and they demonstrate that "non-state actors have gained an important seat in the world of international relations."[282] Furthermore, state interests and trade-offs are no longer only subject matters of treaties, but they may also include rights and liabilities of private parties.[283] These above-mentioned facts should be considered as the profound impacts of globalization over the nature of international relations and international law.

2.1.2.6 Paradigm Shifts

The changing perceptions of the nature of international law have a lot to do with the changing paradigms in the international legal scholarship. As stressed before in this chapter, the twentieth century has seen a great transformation of the historical Westphalian system of international law. For instance, The UN Charter reflects the paradigm shift in international law in various terms. At the beginning, it was a strong evidence of a turn of the traditional state-centred Westphalian system, in terms of the inclusion of "the principle of equal rights and self-determination of peoples" and "respect for human rights" by the UN Charter.[284]

---

[281] Ibid., 331.

[282] Sterio, "Evolution of International Law," 242.

[283] Ibid., 243.

[284] Petersmann, "Multilevel Trade Governance," 18.

Furthermore, two of the most significant turning points of the twentieth century were the elimination of the Cold War, and the emergence of a market-oriented global integration that has also given a powerful inspiration to many scholars for the establishment of a new liberal international order that is based on constitutionalist and democratic principles.[285] These developments were also the breaking points of proceeding for the queries for new paradigms in international law.

2.1.2.6.1 Earlier Shifts: International Community

Beyond doubt, the primitive development of the international legal theory that paved the way for various theories of integration was the adoption of the idea of the international community. In particular, in the aftermath of the global catastrophes of the twentieth century, the assumption of the unity of a legal community via the proliferated international organizations became manifest. This was also evident in the academic works of some notable scholars of this era. This idea arose in the form of the homogeneity of the legal community, and this framework has been a prominent basis for the "integrationist" ideas.[286]

The ideas of Georges Scelle, who was a universalist, came out of the confrontations of World War I and II.[287] Scelle rejected some dominant and well-established ideas on the character of international law. For example, "heterogeneity of states," "states' sacred egoism" or "anarchic" character of international law were far from his thought.[288] According to Scelle, law and international law emerge out of the social reality that is identified by solidarity, not out of the will of states. Normative treaties of international law exist for the expression of international solidarity requirements. He also argued for the unity of international and national law and universality of law, which would be regarded as an extreme form of monism, so to speak.[289] All societies make their laws due to the same fundamental process since the law originates from the social reality. In this process, only procedures differ. He prescribes an infinite plurality of legal systems within an overarching order:

> An individual is a citizen of his state and of his town, and is a member of his church, of his sports club, and of the universal community; he is therefore subject to several legal orders which are interlaced and superimposed. The "law of people" is thus hierarchically structured.[290]

---

[285] Ernst-Ulrich Petersmann, "Constitutionalism andInternational Organizations," *Northwestern Journal of International Law & Business* 17 (1996-1997): 398.

[286] Schwöbel, *Global Constitutionalism*, 96.

[287] Hubert Thierry, "The European Tradition in International Law: The Thought of Georges Scelle," *European Journal of International Law* 1 (1990): 194.

[288] Ibid., 205-206.

[289] Ibid., 198-199.

[290] Ibid., 200.

The idea that a universal legal system ecumenically governs national laws is very central to the thought of Scelle. Therefore, he rejects the notion of state sovereignty. Instead, individuals are in the heart of this legal system. He also considers it inevitable that the increasing solidarity will culminate in world federalism in the future. However, this federalism does not require an institutional basis. According to Scelle, the international community is a form of "normative federalism," given the hierarchy of norms mentioned above.[291] Departing from these points, he also envisioned a constitution for the international community. In this regard, Scelle opines that:

> Every intersocietal collectivity, including the universal community of the "law of people" rests, like the best integrated collectivities, and notably state collectivities, on a body of constitutive rules essential for their existence, for their longevity, and for their progress.[292]

From Scelle's point of view, the laws regarding law-making, adjudication and enforcement have generated constitutional laws of the international society. Furthermore, he enumerated some kinds of freedoms which are to be glorified by the "common conscience and experience" of universal law. These freedoms were the right to live, the struggle against war, international asylum and humanitarian intervention, the right to physical freedom, the struggle against slavery, the right to freely choose one's nationality, the right to economic liberty, the right to religious freedom, and freedom of language and education.[293]

At this point, it is of note that newly emerging ideas on the character of international law mentioned here have never been unrivalled or entirely dominant. As Andreas L. Paulus underlines, whereas international law scholars of the interwar period, such as Hersch Lauterpacht, strived to formulate the unity of the international legal system, this period was also marked by the famous Lotus ruling of the PCIJ, which regarded state sovereignty as the crucial element of the international law. There were also some legal scholars, such as HLA Hart, who were not convinced by the idea that international law is a true legal system.[294]

The debate on the existence of an international community also concerns a question about how this community is governed. Christian Tomuschat, who was in favor of interpreting the international law as a community legal order argued for a constitutional system. He advanced the claim that the international legal order was essentially not only determined by the will of states, and that their will was also confronted by some other facts. According to him, every governance system is operated through law-making, administration and adjudication. This is also true of the international community, and at this point, the question is whether or not the international community is regulated by a constitution: "[T]he international community can indeed be conceived of as a legal entity, governed by a constitution."[295] The

[291] Ibid., 205.

[292] Georges Scelle, *Précis de droit des gens*, Vol. I (1932), cited by Ibid., 201.

[293] Ibid.

[294] The Case of the SS Lotus (France v. Turkey), cited by Paulus, "International Legal System," 73-74.

[295] Tomuschat, "Obligations Arising for States," 195, 236.

core element of this constitutional framework is the sovereign equality of states.[296] That is to say, the states are still considered as the main actors of this legal order. However, the international community is a community of values that are enshrined by the international obligations of *erga omnes* and *jus cogens*. The states can retain their legitimacy as long as they adopt and respect the fundamental obligations of the international legal community.[297] In this regard, he views the international community as a group of human beings that functions as "social substractum" of international law, which in a sense substitutes the function of people in domestic law. On the other hand, this does not mean that he counts this function as a source of democratic legitimacy. In other words, international law does not have its own sources of democratic legitimacy. According to Tomuschat, sources of democracy can merely be found in the domestic domain.[298] This sort of an understanding of international law broadly reflects the universalist tradition in international relations that was mainly represented by Kant, Grotius and some Spanish scholastics.[299]

Another salient point is that the common traditional assumption that constitutions cannot exist beyond domestic legal systems has changed. The idea that a constitution can survive beyond the borders of nation states had come about in the post-war periods of the twentieth century. One of the earliest contributions to this field belongs to Alfred Verdross, who wrote in the aftermath of World War I. Alfred Verdross, who wrote the book "Die Verfassung der Völkerrechtsgemeinschaft" (The Constitution of the International Legal Community) in 1926, was a monist. That is to say, he assumed the unity of international and national law. In his view, the constitution of the international legal community consists of fundamental principles of international law which determined its sources, subject, execution and jurisdictional issues.[300] Afterwards, he pointed to the UN Charter as the constitution of the international order in a normative sense in an account written together with Bruno Simma.[301] That is to say, they held the UN Charter as a set of norms which is in a higher position than other norms. After these two scholars, this idea was also going to be advanced by Bardo Fassbender, a German scholar, whose works are found at the heart of the discourse of global constitutionalism. A common point of these scholars is the idea that there is not a generally agreed framework of the constitution.[302] According to those who argue that constitution is not tied to a state,

---

[296] Ibid., 292.

[297] Christian Tomuschat, "International Law: Ensuring the Survival of Mankind on the Eve of a New Century, General Course on Public International Law," in *Recueil des Cours* 10, no. 25 (1999): 75-76, cited by Armin von Bogdandy, "Constitutionalism in International Law: Comment on a Proposal from Germany," *Harvard International Law Journal* 47, no.1 (2006): 235.

[298] Ibid., 236.

[299] Ibid., 237.

[300] Fassbender, "United Nations Charter," 541.

[301] Alfred Verdross and Bruno Simma, *Universelles Völkerrecht: Theorie und Praxis*, 1976, cited by Ibid., 542.

[302] Ibid., 569.

constitutions are rather providers of a framework for a legal order of a society.[303] Accordingly, the existence of a constitution does in fact have to do only with the existence of a legal order. In short, these institutionalist and normativist views of global constitutionalism could be viewed as a peak point in the evolution of the idea of the international community.

2.1.2.6.2 Post-War Shifts

Koh identifies the aftermath of World War II as the heyday of international law:

> In the main, those who designed the post-war international system were lawyers who believed in the rule of law, not power, in international affairs and in the willingness of states to cooperate within international, institutional and constitutional frameworks.[304]

Furthermore, according to him, these postwar developments in international law have proved Louis Henkin to a great extent, who claims that "almost all nations observe almost all principles of international law almost all of the time."[305]

Beyond doubt, it was much easier to interpret the character of international law in the pre-World War II period. The formation of international relations was much more stable,[306] and as articulated in the Lotus doctrine, it had a primitive form, compared to post-WWII developments. Inquiries in search of a paradigm to understand this era involved various dimensions. The international legal order was depicted as an anarchic system by some. On the other hand, as mentioned above, new paradigm alternatives appeared, which described the dimension of new law towards the rule of law and integration.[307]

Nye and Welch argue that despite the fact that the regulating principle of the international realm is anarchic, the system itself is not chaotic; and it is well ordered to a certain extent, as global interactive relations mostly demonstrate us.[308] Furthermore, neorealists and game theorists still refuse the hierarchy and the functional differentiation between any coherent elements of international relations as well as the existence of any meta-norms of international law.[309]

---

[303] Schwöbel, *Global Constitutionalism*, 90.

[304] Koh, "1994 Roscoe Pound Lecture," 191.

[305] Ibid., 194.

[306] Rutti G. Teitel, "Humanity's Law: Rule of Law for the New Global Politics," *Cornell International Law Journal* 35, no. 2 (2002): 357.

[307] For inquiries for an emerging international rule of law as a new paradigm of international law: Ibid., and also Winston P. Nagan and Garry Jacobs, "New Paradigm for Global Rule of Law," *Cadmus* 1, no. 4 (2012): 130-146.

[308] Nye and Welch, *Küresel Catisma*, 62.

[309] Alec Stone-Sweet, "What is a Supranational Constitution? An Essay in International Relations Theory," *The Review of Politics* 56, no. 3 (1994): 451.

According to Nye and Welch, globalization refers to the interdependent networks across the world, but it does not imply universality.[310] The level of mutual interdependence and integration vary in different territories. For example, realist theories seem to be proved in the Middle Eastern politics whereas relationships between USA and Canada, or France and Germany comply with theories on current mutual interdependence in global matters.[311]

The shift in world politics from bipolar to multipolar could indeed be considered a challenge to the neo-realist understanding of international relations.[312] In a sense, the so-called anarchy of international relations does not simply mean disorder; instead, it denotes the absence of a centralized government. According to Sweet, this cannot be viewed as a hindrance against integrationist ideas as well as the constitutionalization of this order.[313]

When the changing paradigms of the twentieth century are considered, the New Haven School has to be mentioned as well in terms of its impacts on the development of the theory of public international law. The New Haven School, which was developed in particular by Professors Myres S. McDougal and Harold D. Lasswell, introduced a policy-oriented perspective on international law and confronted analytical approaches by referring to the sociological jurisprudence and American realists. The New Haven School mainly "adapts the analytical methods of the social sciences to the prescriptive purposes of the law."[314] The New Haven School places a special emphasis on perceiving the relationship between law and the entire social process of the world community.[315] It deemed international law as being a tool for generating a "world public order."[316] The New Haven School also created a theory that viewed individuals as primary actors of law making along with a perspective associated with the natural law.[317] In this regard, they refused the state centred views of realists and positivists that ignored other actors' roles in lawmaking.[318] In this sense, Berman argues that the New Haven School pursued an approach of a sort of

---

310 Nye and Welch, *Küresel Catisma*, 342.

311 Ibid., 368.

312 Stone-Sweet, "Supranational Constitution," 458.

313 Ibid., 469.

314 W. Michael Reisman, Siegfried Wiessner and Andrew R. Willard, "The New Haven School: A Brief Introduction," *Yale Journal of International Law* 32 (2007): 576.

315 Fassbender, "United Nations Charter," 545.

316 Myres S. McDougal and W. Michael Reisman, "International Law in Policy-oriented Perspective," in *The Structure and Process of International Law: Essays in Legal Philosophy, Doctrine and Theory*, ed. R. St. J. Macdonald and Douglas M. Johnston (The Hague: Nijhoff, 1983), 103.

317 W. Michael Reisman, "The View from the New Haven School of International Law," (Faculty Scholarship Series. Paper 867, 1992, http://digitalcommons.law.yale.edu/fss_papers/867/), last visit 09.08.2014.

318 Berman, "A Pluralist Approach," 301.

"living law," which was developed by Eugene Ehrlich to depict the reality of law beyond the state based official law, and as a component of rules of the social life.[319]

Given these contributions, the development of the New Haven School marks a novelty in the international legal theory. Although it has not been counted as a global constitutionalist approach and even though it did not take part in this debate; the New Haven School is of capital importance, as it inspired other progressive approaches in international law against the traditional analytical schools. Against this background, Fassbender noted that the debate on global constitutionalism can be perceived only by those who have a norm-oriented perspective, and the New Haven School established a theoretical basis that is particularly in parallel with global constitutionalists.[320] Furthermore, the era following that of the New Haven School has also seen law and economics, critical legal studies, postmodernism and feminism as further progressive contributions to the international legal scholarship.[321]

The issue of changing paradigms should also be discussed in the context of the constructivistapproach to international law. In particular, contemporary ideas on global law have been contrived through constructivist approaches, and constructivism in this sense is an important aspect of this matter.

From a critical point of view, paradigmatic transitions in the legal field are also likely to be read as the crisis of modern law. De Sousa Santos discusses transformation in the mainstream paradigms of the twentieth century in terms of the three pillars of modernity: emancipation, regulation and science. Against this background, what characterizes the transformation in the socio-cultural condition of this century is the "collapse of the pillar of emancipation into the pillar of regulation" in which modern science and modern law played key roles.[322] This development came about in a process that modern emancipation was reduced into "the cognitive-instrumental rationality of science" (hyperscientificization), and that modern regulation was reduced into the principle of market (hypermarketization).[323] This means that law has lost its emancipatory ideals of enlightenment, and it is still in search of a way out of the crisis through changing paradigms. In the case of international law, contemporary responses to globalization from the legal scholarship are to be understood from that perspective as well. The great crises of the modernity, such as the Holocaust, the World Wars, genocides, crimes against humanity, etc. also reflected paradigmatic crises of international law, and this fact proves that the Westphalian construction of international law failed tragically.[324] A Post-Westphalian reconstruction and ongoing attempts to reconstruct international law can be perceived as an endeavour to overcome the never-ending vicious cycle of this crisis.

[319] Ibid., 306.

[320] Fassbender, "United Nations Charter," 551.

[321] Koh, "1994 Roscoe Pound Lecture," 191.

[322] Boaventura de Sousa Santos, *Toward a New Legal Common Sense: Law, Globalization, and Emancipation* (London: Butterworths, 1995), 7.

[323] Ibid., 8.

[324] Falk, *Declining World Order*.

Consequently, it is of note that globalization and new relational rationalities of public governance have given rise to the new quests for a new paradigm to understand transformation in international law.[325] A new overarching framework has been sought to comprehend these developments. That is to say, traditional forms of state law and state-centric international law are not flexible enough to meet the needs of the dynamic relationships of globalization. New relational forms bring new spontaneous forms of law, and this is to be read as an evolutionary step of new forms of societal norms that transcend official legal systems.[326] As a matter of fact, this concerns an inchoate and unclear development that has still not given rise to a well-established theory of law. At this juncture, David Kennedy states that:

> we know very little, in fact, about the structure of global society. How is public power exercised, where are the levers, who are the authorities, and how do they relate to one another?[327]

However, this does not mean that contemporary international law lacks any queries that dig out the reality of global society. In the following section, responses from the contemporary international law scholarship to build up an idea of "global law" will be introduced briefly. Global law appears at this point as one of these queries that attempt to give a meaning to the emerging facts in question.

2.2 Responses to the Transformation: An Inquiry for a New Paradigm?

As emphasized in the previous section, the traditional instruments of public international law are no longer able to respond to the recent developments spawned by globalization in particular. The current fragmented form of the legal sphere beyond states arises as a significant obstacle to thinking of international law within a framework of certain contours. What is more, this situation gives rise to the loss of an overall perspective on the law.[328] Accordingly, the international law scholarship needs to gain a new framework in order to understand the new relational rationality of the global realm. The debate on a global law is one of the responses to this necessity. Contributions to these debates have not hitherto provided a consensus on the quality of this new order. This debate is more likely to be read as an inquiry for a new paradigm to create a new perspective for approaching international law. Such contributions, as will be touched upon below, target the fragmented structure of

[325] Ladeur, "Globalization and Public Governance," 6.

[326] Ibid., 6.

[327] David Kennedy, "The Mystery of Global Governance," in *Ruling the World: Constitutionalism, International Law, and Global Governance*, ed. Joel Trachtman and Jeff Dunoff (Cambridge: Cambridge University Press, 2009), 37.

[328] Ku, *International Law*, 33.

international law and aim at reconstructing this multipartite structure to draw a new framework for the international legal order.

2.2.1 The Rise of the Idea of Global Law

As demonstrated in this chapter, international law has undergone a serious transformation following WWII particularly. The greatest pressure for the change has come from the globalization process. Globalization has come along with a new relational rationality, and this rationality undermined traditional forms that were central to the traditional understanding of international law. Under current circumstances, international law cannot be regarded as the law of states through diplomatic relations, since the new hybrid, experimental and amorphous elements of communication across borders have appeared and have begun to dominate the new relational rationality. The most prominent impact of this was the changing character of sovereignty. Due to this shift, the traditional understanding of general international law has lost a very key pillar of its foundation, that is to say, sovereignty (or sovereign equality) of states. When it is considered along with the new face of institutionalization and legalization in the international community, states can hardly be seen as the only power and will holder of international relations, as it was earlier declared in the Lotus ruling of the PCIJ. Institutions have continuously proliferated in the global realm, and they superseded many of the powers of states. They also contributed to further shifts in legalization and judicialization. The globalization era saw new normative instruments as well as new judicial bodies in international law. New agencies generated a new law, and this made the conventional distinctions between public and private law complicated. However, this new formation of law in the global realm did not appear in a unified and consistent shape. The fragmentation marked this transformative form, and as a matter of fact, it has become the most significant and challenging texture of this new term in identifying the new character of law. There is no doubt that all these developments came about for certain reasons that caused a change in the positions of states in this realm. There are various ideas on this matter, all of which rely on strong arguments. One prominent idea is the new individual-oriented face of the international community, while some others prefer to refer to the changing needs of capitalism and market forces.

In the previous part of this chapter, the main goal was to demonstrate how the new contemporary developments of the global world are incompatible with the framework of the traditional international law. As Walker argues, not only international law, but also other relevant categories, such as supranational law and transnational law cannot promise an adequate framework to overarch the new reality of the global realm.[329] Having considered the transformative outcomes mentioned in this chapter and the inadequacy of general international law to respond to the needs

[329] Musa and De Voider, "Neil Walker," 6-7.

of the international community, some scholars argued that international law must give way to a global law.[330] Although there have been several attempts at identifying a global law for the global realm, this concept still reflects an imperfection since contours of this underdeveloped field cannot be determined very easily.

According to Rafael Domingo, global law, or in his words, the "law of humanity" alternatively, can be viewed as a "law to become," that is to say, not an established legal order.[331] From this point of view, the global legal order is not an attempt to eliminate local, national and supranational orders, but rather it seeks to harmonize them without invoking state sovereignty, and by playing a complementary and auxiliary role for local systems.[332] As it is the law of humanity, human rights should be at the centre of global law.[333]

On the other hand, Neil Walker constructs global law based on transformative features of law in the global realm, in a manner which is closer to the purposes of this text. In his point of view, global law has two sets of meanings. The first one is "globally extensive law" (or global level law or planetary law) that means "an idea of law that extends across globe."[334] In other words, this idea of global law can be seen as an overarching concept for the legal relations of the current international society. Walker gives examples of *jus gentium* and the "universal code of legality" concept of Klaus Günther as main references to his idea, but he does not draw any clear-cut contours. The second meaning of global law refers to "a new paradigm of thought":

> Global law isn't something we can find which will carve its way through everything else and shows how everything relates to each other. (…) there is partly a reference to these global level laws, but also to the intricacies of relationships to other things.[335]

There are also some other scholarly attempts to define and explain global law in a more contextual sense. For instance, one contribution highlights that the participation of private parties in regulatory matters is a foundational element of global law. In this respect, global law is

> an attempt to describe a growing decrease of the role of the State in regulatory matter, coupled with a frenetic increase of the regulatory activity of private parties at the transnational level, stemming from the globalization of economic activity.[336]

Moreover, some sceptical approaches on this debate should also not be ignored. Among them, William Twining proceeds from the idea that interdependence is a relative matter. In this regard, he argues that speaking of a transformation of human

---

330 Domingo, *New Global Law*, 98.

331 Ibid., 121.

332 Ibid., 122.

333 Ibid., 142.

334 Musa and De Voider, "Neil Walker," 7.

335 Ibid., 8.

336 Delimatsis, "A Global Law Perspective," 154.

rights and public international law into a global law is an exaggeration in view of many processes referred to as "global" operating at various sub-global assemblances. These attempts blur borders between the aspirations and the reality.[337] This being the case, Sassen points to the central role of the state to secure the global economic system through central banks, legislatures, ministries of finance and other government sectors, for the purpose of the examination of the position of the state in the globalization process.[338] This gives rise to a task for researchers to seek the global inside the national, partially at the least.[339] On the other hand, Twining still finds it helpful to construct a global perspective to law in some terms. Such a global perspective involves seeing the world as a whole and "setting accounts of particular phenomena in the context of broad geographical pictures and long historical time-frames," that is to say, setting a broad context for particular legal issues without any assumption of unification and convergence.[340] As a matter of fact, Twining argues that this has always been a deficiency of jurisprudence where legal scholars mostly thought within the framework of national boundaries of European and Anglo-American countries. Nonetheless, the recent works of a number of new generation scholars of legal theory endeavour to overcome this deficiency.[341] These endeavours also give rise to a "global perspective" to law.[342] Against this background, global law should not only cover the matter of an extensive law but also various legal systems that are subject to interaction and diffusion. Legal transplantations and legal diffusion among various legal systems are important subject matters of contemporary comparative law. It is of note that these facts do not necessarily lead to convergence, harmonization, or unification of legal systems.[343]

A very striking common feature of these attempts to construct a global law is that they mitigate (but do not exclude entirely) the role of the state in the making of law. The construction of a non-state law is not a novelty for legal theory. It was also subject to the works of earlier socio-legal scholars of the twentieth century, such as Eugene Ehrlich, who pointed out the law created outside the formal state law through his theory of "living law."[344] The theory of Ehrlich was a critique of legal positivism which he challenged by reason of its narrowness and negligence of the

[337] William Twining, "Implications of 'Globalisation' for Law as a Discipline," in *Theorizing the Global Legal Order*, ed. Andrew Halpin and Volker Roeben, (Oxford: Hart Publishing, 2009), 41. Also for a similar argumentation: Sassen, "Neither Global Nor National," 36.

[338] Sassen, "Neither Global Nor National," 36.

[339] Ibid., 37.

[340] Twining, "Implications of Globalisation," 41.

[341] Twining mentions a range of legal scholars who developed globally oriented approaches while drawing on classical jurisprudence at the same time, such as Tamanaha, Pogge, Singer, Glenn, Santos. Ibid., 45.

[342] For a global socio-legal perspective: Eve Darian-Smith, *Laws and Societies in Global Contexts: Contemporary Approaches* (Cambridge: Cambridge University Press, 2013), 12.

[343] Twining, "Implications of 'Globalisation," 52.

[344] Eugen Ehrlich, *Grundlegung der Soziologie des Rechts* (Berlin: Duncker&Humblot, 1989).

law produced in everyday life by various social actors. However, although Ehrlich created a very inspiring and illuminating theory in many terms, particularly generating a good ground to examine the legal positivist ideas; his theory was mainly devised for polemic purposes, and thus its suitability for a further legal research remained quite dubious.[345] In this regard, attempts to construct a "global law" face the same risk of being confined to polemical purposes. That is to say, a polemic level is not enough to prove that "global law" is law. On the other hand, the global law debate is not restricted by this debate, and in a more contextual basis, has been discussed in interdisciplinary stages as well. These stages are represented in the debates regarding global legal pluralism, global administrative law and global constitutionalism. The most distinctive features of these debates from the construction of global law are that these debates are in search of any linkage between the developments in the global realm and the traditional understanding of law. In other words, they seek a continuum of the traditional perception of law in new formations. Therefore, as will be mentioned below, they can be considered as inquiries for a new paradigm in law. In doing so, they reflect the relationship and relevance between international law and globalization on a more plausible ground.

2.2.2 *Global Law and Constructivism*

It is a salient fact that the constructivist methodology in international relations theory and public international law has an important role in the birth and maintenance of a global law debate. The role of constructivism comes to the fore in understanding the main difference between two approaches to global law, which was mentioned in the previous section. In this sense, the creation of a global legal order that is defined beyond the conventional borders of international law is likely to be considered as a product of this methodology. As some scholars strictly underline it, global legal order is a constructivist project.[346] Accordingly, global constitutionalism too, in this respect, is a result of constructivist efforts in the public international realm.[347]

In parallel with what was mentioned above, Wiener advances the claim that global constitutionalism does not presuppose the existence of a constitution. Referring to Weiler, she deems constitutionalism in a transnational context to be an academic artefact that reflects practices of the jurisprudence and academic discourse. Against this background, constitutionalism relates to an interdisciplinary research with a particular focus: "[Constitutionalism] merely presupposes the interplay between social and institutional practices to which claims to legality, legitimacy

---

345 Roger Cotterrell, *The Sociology of Law: An Introduction* (London: Butterworths, 1984).

346 Stefan Oeter, "Theorizing Global Legal Order - An Institutionalist Perspective," in *Theorizing the Global Legal Order*, ed. Andrew Halpin and Volker Roeben (Oxford: Hart Publishing, 2009), 81.

347 Koskenniemi, "Fate of Public International Law," 19.

and democracy are key."[348] This approach rather underlines that constitutionalism is to be reconstructed through a discourse in the international realm. There is no doubt that some other scholars have shared this idea. It was also introduced as a constructive political project by Falk, Johansen and Kim from a different perspective:

> Global constitutionalism is here defined broadly and synergistically as a set of transnational norms, rules, procedures, and institutions designed to guide a transformative politics dedicated to the realization of world order values both within and between three systems of intersecting politics in an interdependent world.[349]

As a rival of rationalist approaches,[350] constructivism has a deep and vigorous background in international relations theory and law. In this sense, the constructivist influence involves a broad range of scholars from Durkheim and Weber to Habermas and Giddens.[351] The rise of constructivism occurred as a result of exploring, in particular, the role of social facts and social practices in the construction of world politics.[352] That is to say, constructivists do not concur with realists about the fact that interests of states are formed independently of the societal factors. At that point, in particular, a Giddensian influence over international relations theoreticians is striking: "All social structures, presumably including legal structures, 'are inseparable from the reasons and self-understandings that agents bring to their actions'."[353] Further, constructivism arose as a counter movement of neorealism and neoliberalism that were also introduced as rational approaches to international relations.[354] The constructivist turn, in particular, came about within a conjuncture when the Cold War collapsed, and this development led to an existential crisis for realist and neo-realist scholars.[355] In this sense, the common purpose of constructivists was "to bring in the social to an undersocialised discipline."[356] To achieve this aim, they deal

[348] Antje Wiener, "Global Constitutionalism: Mapping an Emerging Field" (Paper presented at the Conference "Constitutionalism in a New Key? Cosmopolitan, Pluralist and Public Reason-Oriented," WZB and Humboldt University, Berlin, 28-29 January 2011, http://cosmopolis.wzb.eu/content/programs/ conkey_Wiener_Mapping-Field.pdf), last visit 10.01.2014.

[349] Richard A. Falk, Robert C. Johansen and Samuel S. Kim, "Global Constitutionalism and World Order," in *The Constitutional Foundations of World Peace*, ed. Richard A. Falk, Robert C. Johansen and Samuel S. Kim (Albany, NY: State University of New York Press, 1993), 9.

[350] Oeter, "Theorizing Global Legal Order," 81.

[351] Jutta Brunnee and Stephen J. Toope, "International Law and Constructivism: Elements of an Interactional Theory of International Law," *Columbia Journal of Transnational Law* 39 (2000-2001): 26.

[352] Antje Wiener, "Constructivism: The Limits of Bridging Gaps," *Journal of International Relations and Development* 6, no. 3 (2003): 252.

[353] Alexander Wendt, "The Agent-Structure Problem in International Relations Theory," *International Organization* 41 (1987): 335, 359, cited by Brunnee and Toope, "International Law and Constructivism," 27.

[354] Wiener, "Constructivism," 252.

[355] Brunnee and Toope, "International Law and Constructivism," 20.

[356] Wiener, "Constructivism," 257.

with "the influence of epistemic communities, issue networks, intergovernmental organizations, and norms and ideas more generally" in order to understand how social structures build "shared understandings," by staying away from "hegemonic explanatory claims."[357] Furthermore, rhetorical activities of actors in a system are crucial in the construction of law: "law is constructed through rhetorical activity producing increasingly influential mutual expectations or shared understandings of actors."[358]

The constructivist understanding of law makes it possible to measure the existence of law through the influence created by law, instead of doing so through any formal tests of validity in normative systems. This leads to an insight that construction of a legal system is never complete; so that international lawyers can overcome some theoretical constraints, such as the sources of law.[359] A constructivist model is likely to be very functional in explaining

> why specific actors (or specific groups of actors) act in a specific way, support specific legal rules (or try to evade them), make use of certain arrangements, and not of other (…)[360]

As mentioned above, global law is counted as a constructivist and a prescriptive project along with "real international law." Real international law, in this sense, is a

> very provisional and fragmentary body of legal rules and standards imposed upon the "society of states" during the 20th century (…) far from being consistent, does not embody a plausible idea of justice and bears some rather disquieting features.[361]

Under these circumstances, it is evident that without a constructivist outlook and through realist or rationalist theories, it would not be possible to argue on a global ground for such an inchoate process.

2.2.3 A Global Public Order? A Genealogy of Pluralism, Administrative Law and Constitutionalism

The legal scholarship concerning global law spawned three major strands of thought based upon the probes for the emergence of a global legal order. As will be mentioned below, these strands are likely to be considered as akin to each other, since they are in search of a common sense of public order by digging out transformational developments in the international legal order. In addition, they are likely to be seen as rival theories as they read the same facts from different perspectives by

---

357 Brunnee and Toope, "International Law and Constructivism," 30-31.

358 Ibid., 48.

359 Instead, for example, as Fuller suggests, "internal morality of law" would be employed to measure legitimacy of law, Ibid., 65-66-70.

360 Oeter, "Theorizing Global Legal Order," 65.

361 Ibid. 81.

employing different vocabularies. Three discourses at the core of the global law, namely global legal pluralism, global administrative law and global constitutionalism, generate an "alternative intimation of the law of the future."[362] Against this background, these three debates reflect an inquiry for a new paradigm for a new realm of law whose shifting contours have not become clear yet.

2.2.3.1 Global Legal Pluralism

The very idea of legal pluralism has to do with co-existing normative systems,[363] and the emergence of these systems had deep impacts on the traditional understanding of international law. The studies of pluralism originate from the discipline of anthropology, and they proceed from the fact that people may affiliate with multiple groups, and hence consider themselves to be bound by the norms of multiple groups. Given the multifaceted role of law that goes beyond formal law creating institutions, legal pluralism has become a prominent focus point among international law scholars.[364] In terms of the international law discourse, multiple norm-producing groups may appear as governmental or non-governmental networks or regimes, international organizations, ethnic or religious groups and institutions, international courts, etc., that is to say, a broad range of non-state groupings. The recent legal pluralist studies define the idea of a legal system by including non-official forms of norm-making, in other words, as: "(…) nonstate communities assert lawmaking power through more informal networks and organizations and through the slow accretion of social custom itself."[365] That is to say, legal pluralists reject the requirement for a formal authority or a coercive power to enforce and make binding norms in a legal order. As a corollary, this results in a rejection of the idea of nation states as the only norm-producing power.[366]

Moreover, the increasing differentiation in international law matters fairly for legal pluralism studies. As mentioned above, in the section regarding paradigm shifts in international law, the International Law Commission Report on Fragmentation of International Law that was finalized by Martti Koskenniemmi, generates a very remarkable source for the pluralist approach. As it was concluded in the report, international law is no longer to be perceived as general international law, since it has fragmented into many sub-branches, such as environmental law, trade law, human rights law, etc. by virtue of the increasing differentiation.[367] In addition,

---

[362] Delimatsis, "A Global Law Perspective," 155.

[363] Sally Engle Merry, "Legal Pluralism," in *The Globalization on International Law*, ed. Paul Schiff Berman (Aldershot: Ashgate, 2005), 30.

[364] Berman, "From International Law," 507.

[365] Ibid., 508.

[366] Ibid., 511.

[367] ILC Report, para. 8.

in the report, it was concluded that the fragmentation steers international law to the direction of legal pluralism.[368]

In view of the overlapping existence of various legal orders, legal pluralists suggest exploring by which norms communities feel themselves bound. This exploration requires drawing a distinction between *law in books* and *law in action,* which was a major subject matter of classical socio-legal scholars, notably Roscoe Pound.[369] Contemporary scholars that aim at approaching international law from a legal pluralist perspective, such as Paul Schiff Berman, reject the idea of the impossibility of a legal enforcement in the international legal order; and instead, suggest studying the degree to which international norms may have binding effects on communities.[370] From this point of view, even national courts can hold the same perspective in dealing with transnational issues:

> For example, in choosing the substantive legal norms to apply to a transnational dispute, a court might take into account the fact that the parties have distant community affiliation or are citizens of countries with conflicting laws and therefore seek to blend a variety of transnational norms.[371]

2.2.3.2 Global Administrative Law

Global administrative law is a concept that was coined by Benedict Kingsbury. He predicates his concept on the recently formed structure of international relations at the beginning of the twenty-first century. In this sense, global administrative law is "comprising the legal rules, principles, and institutional norms applicable to processes of 'administration' undertaken in ways that implicate more than purely intra-State structures of legal and political authority."[372] This view draws on the legacy of international administrative law, which is, borrowing from a 1935 definition by Paul Negulesco, "a branch of public law that, examining the legal phenomena which together constitute international administration, seeks to discover and specify the norms that govern this administration and to systematize them."[373] At the same time, it includes some activities of national administrations by emphasizing their transnational context. In this respect, they underline that global administrative law is

---

[368] Ibid., para. 492.

[369] Roscoe Pound, "Law in Books and Law in Action," *American Law Review* 44 (1910): 12-36.

[370] Berman, "From International Law," 539.

[371] Ibid. 540.

[372] Benedict Kingsbury and Megan Donaldson, "Global Administrative Law," *Max Planck Encyclopedia of Public International Law*, last updated: April 2011, para. 1, http://opil.ouplaw.com/view/10.1093/law:epil/9780199231690/law-9780199231690-e948?rskey=jtGmdz&result=1&prd=EPIL, last visit 10.05.2015.

[373] Benedict Kingsbury, Nico Krisch and Richard B. Stewart, "The Emergence of Global Administrative Law," *Law and Contemporary Problems* 68, no. 3/4 (2005): 28.

not to be understood as a sub-branch of general international law. On the other side, Kingsbury and other proponents of global administrative law are sceptical of analogies between national and global administrative law, since they argue that both rely on different constructive dynamics and that global administrative law is of a multi-level character.[374]

Kingsbury highlights the imperfection of global law under the framework of global administrative law:

> Institutional differentiation is less complete, roles are not clearly assigned, hierarchies are not highly specified, and bright lines do not exist between the spheres of administration and legislation or between administrative and constitutional principles and review authorities.[375]

At this point, studies on global administrative law also focus on what is lacking in global administrative law.[376] In addition, the administration in global governance reflects a highly decentralized one.[377]

According to Kingsbury, demands for transparency, consultation, participation, reasoned decisions, and review mechanisms to promote accountability are very central to the evolution of current regulatory structures. The normative responses to these demands from the global governance bear an administrative law character.[378] In this regard, administrative law can be distinguished from legislative actions through treaties, and adjudication through dispute settlement mechanisms, although global administrative law has legislative and adjudicatory elements.[379] In consequence, the administrative action includes "rulemaking, adjudications, and other decisions that are neither treaty-making nor simple dispute settlements between parties."[380]

In other words, the proponents of global administrative law focus on the administrative character of transnational regimes:

> Global administrative bodies include formal intergovernmental regulatory bodies, informal intergovernmental regulatory networks and coordination arrangements, national regulatory bodies operating with reference to an international intergovernmental regime, hybrid public-private regulatory bodies, and some private regulatory bodies exercising transnational governance functions of particular public significance.[381]

These bodies can overlap or, in some cases, unite. They reconstruct administrative law at the global level by referring to basic characteristics of domestic administrative

---

[374] Ibid.

[375] Kingsbury and Donaldson, "Global Administrative Law," para. 2.

[376] Kingsbury, Krisch and Stewart, "Emergence of Global Administrative Law," 27.

[377] Ibid., 15. Benedict Kingsbury, "The Concept of 'Law' in Global Administrative Law," *The European Journal of International Law* 20, no.1 (2009): 25.

[378] Kingsbury, "The Concept of 'Law'," 25.

[379] For example, WTO Dispute Settlement Body also performs some regulatory functions, Kingsbury, Krisch and Stewart, "Emergence of Global Administrative Law," 17.

[380] Ibid., 17.

[381] Ibid.

law. Further, they argue that national administrative laws increasingly lose their abilities to govern some issues, such as environmental protection, banking and financial regulation, law enforcement, telecommunications, trade in products and services, intellectual property, labor standards, and cross-border movements of populations. Therefore transnational administrative bodies gain subsidiary roles in these fields.[382]

The subjects of global administrative law reflect the new agencies of international law that arose in the Post-Westphalian phase of this field. That is to say, these subjects are states, individuals, corporations, NGOs, and some other collectivities, such as regulatory networks. All of these generate a global administrative space.[383]

Beyond the institutionalization processes in global administrative law, this field has also been home to some basic procedural and substantive legal principles of its own. According to Kingsbury et al., the fragmented form of global institutions and the limited form of current knowledge about this field are not to be seen as obstacles to the emergence of these principles.[384] As a matter of fact, these principles have been introduced only as "candidates." They infer these principles from various judicial and administrative experiences observed in different administrative bodies. Some of these principles are the procedural participation by larger parties (e.g. individuals, NGOs), the decisional transparency and the access to information. Other principles that stemmed from domestic law are the "reasoned decision" and the "judicial review." They were followed by some Substantive Standards: "Proportionality, Means-Ends Rationality, Avoidance of Unnecessarily Restrictive Means, Legitimate Expectations." Further, these scholars point to two sorts of "exceptions" in global law: one is the mitigation of immunities that are found in traditional international law, and the second relates to the special accountability regimes applied to some fields, such as Central Banks and security matters. In the context of global law, these exceptions should be reconstructed.[385]

All in all, global administrative law is a constructivist effort to an understanding of global law. The proponents of this view stress the inadequacy of the traditional understanding of general international law as well as global legal pluralists and global constitutionalists do. Global administrative law features administrative law character of international and transnational regulatory bodies, and it seeks to reconstruct a new normative structure that is not linked to general international law. This reconstruction primarily aims at meeting needs and demands for democratic principles in the global realm.[386] However, its proponents admit that the positive political theory of global administrative law has hitherto remained underdeveloped.[387]

[382] Ibid., 16; Kingsbury and Donaldson, "Global Administrative Law," para. 10.

[383] Kingsbury, Krisch and Stewart, "Emergence of Global Administrative Law," 23-27.

[384] Ibid., 37.

[385] Ibid., 37-42.

[386] Ibid., 48.

[387] Ibid., 61.

2.2.3.3 Global Constitutionalism

Global constitutionalism, the main research object of this project, is one of the responses given to the transformative period in international law. In that vein, Neves defines global constitutionalism as a "paradigmatic theoretical tendency."[388] Global constitutionalism is in search of a coherent and hierarchical global legal system, and thus it reflects an opposition of legal pluralism that stands for "disorder of normative orders."[389] In other words, as Koskenniemmi argues, it is an alternative to legal pluralism in reading global developments.[390]

At this point, it is of note that there are also some approaches that adopt the idea of co-existence of various constitutional systems that are found in a plurality of normative orders and do not claim superiority over each other. This view is called "constitutional pluralism."[391] Furthermore, neither global constitutionalism nor legal pluralism is represented only by one school, and instead, they are represented by various schools with contradictory views.[392] On the other side, developments and facts that give rise to a global constitutionalism debate are also read in different ways through the lens of "global administrative law," without appealing to any constitutional vocabulary.[393] A major difference of global constitutionalism from global administrative law is that global constitutionalism deals with substantial issues of global law whereas global administrative law deals with rather procedural matters.[394] On the other hand, the identification of global and transnational assemblages arises as a distinguishing point between global constitutionalism and global administrative law. These bodies, either in formal, informal or hybrid forms, are counted as administrative institutions that carry out functions within the framework of global administrative law for the latter; whereas they are somewhat bearers of a meta-law from the perspective of global constitutionalism. However, in some cases these functions may overlap. For instance, as will be discussed in the details in the second chapter, according to the idea of "compensatory constitutionalism"[395] transnational and global assemblages in question have a corresponding function with national laws that cannot respond to the needs of globalization, as the proponents of global administrative law argue this in a similar manner. However, for this perspective of

---

388 Marcelo Neves, *Transconstitutionalism*, trans. Kevin Mundy (Oxford and Portland Oregon: Hart Publishing, 2013), 56.

389 Viellechner, "Verfassung als Chiffre," 236.

390 Koskenniemi, "Fate of Public International Law," 20.

391 Viellechner, "Verfassung als Chiffre," 237.

392 Ibid.

393 Ladeur, "Ein Recht der Netzwerke." Nico Krisch, *Beyond Constitutionalism: The Pluralist Structure of Postnational Law* (Oxford: Oxford University Press, 2010).

394 Kingsbury and Donaldson, "Global Administrative Law," para. 3.

395 Anne Peters, "Compensatory Constitutionalism: The Fundamental Function and Potential of Fundamental International Norms and Structures," *Leiden Journal of International Law* 19 (2006): 579-410.

global constitutionalism, the relationship between the national and the transnational is between two meta-laws; and due to the dimension of the corresponding action, transnational law has a meta effect over national law. On the other hand, the proponents of global administrative law reject the idea of a global constitutionalization on the ground that constitutionalism requires a coherence which is missing in the global order. In this regard, global administrative law, unlike domestic administrative law, emerges without a constitutional framework. According to these scholars, a global constitutionalism can at most be in *statu nascendi*.[396]

In this text, only different contributions to global constitutionalism will be discussed, and they will be elaborated by mapping this field in the next chapter. Despite the diversity of contributions to the global constitutionalism debate, it is still plausible to identify some common features thereof.[397]

The responses of global constitutionalist contributions to the issues regarding transformation of international law vary. As to the sovereignty, global constitutionalism considers this concept in its transformative meaning. As mentioned above, some scholars point to the constructive role of sovereignty for the international community.[398] This means that the new concept of sovereignty, or "equal sovereignty" is a tamed form of traditional sovereignty and it has a certain role in the construction of the constitution of the international community. Referring to the definition of Kelsen, Bardo Fassbender states that "[s]overeign equality is the legal authority and autonomy of a state as defined and guaranteed by the constitution of the international community."[399] From this point of view, rights granted to the states by the UN Charter and international law are to be considered as "sovereign rights" of states under a constitution, and these rights are given by virtue of the sovereign equality. These are mainly "the legal protection of a state's autonomy as a space of self-determination" and "rights ensuring a state's equal membership in the international community."[400]

Universality and the objective supremacy of human rights as shared values of humankind are also basic reference points for global constitutionalist ideas. Fundamental rights can be found as pre-existing values of a given order. Against this background, the protection of individual rights is a key theme of global constitutionalism. Global constitutionalists, in this regard, reflect a sort of natural law approach. The recognition of the Universal Declaration of Human Rights by almost every state and its impacts on many domestic constitutions have also been prominent developments that are employed to underpin most of global constitutionalism theories by asserting that they gave birth to some of the global constitutional norms. In this regard, human rights reflect the ideal normative language for global

[396] Kingsbury and Donaldson, "Global Administrative Law," para. 57. Also see, Krisch, *Beyond Constitutionalism.*

[397] Schwöbel, *Global Constitutionalism.*

[398] Fassbender, "Sovereignty and Constitutionalism," 128.

[399] Ibid., 131, emphasis belongs to the original text.

[400] Ibid., 131-132.

constitutionalism.[401] On the other hand, it is also crucial to note the debate on human rights that focuses on the potentially destructive effects of universal human rights values over the diversity of local values and cultures.[402] At this point, relativism rises as an alternative to the universalist approaches. The rise of this challenge has to do with the desirability of enactment of values of a global political order.

Having considered a number of formal and informal developments, Wiener put forward the "enhanced constitutional quality" of the international order. According to her, the "enhanced constitutional quality" relates to the recent pluralist transformation of the international realm.[403] The developments that lead to this transformation range from the transformation in the character of treaty law to the newly emerged social practices of international interaction, the legal-cross referencing, blogging, etc.

In consequence, global constitutionalism is akin to global legal pluralism and global administrative law, although it is contrary to them in building a global law as an alternative to general international law. On the other hand, the global constitutionalism debate has seen various contributions from various scholars with different backgrounds, and this gave rise to different understandings of global constitutionalism. Therefore, a study on global constitutionalism inevitably needs the mapping of these contributions. On the other hand, global constitutionalist readings of international law commonly propound that the international legal community is a legal community which is governed by rules and principles and not only by power.[404] Furthermore, global constitutionalist theories advocate non-state constitutional law, and it is an attempt to "de-mystify the state and the state constitution."[405]

As mentioned, there are various theories in legal scholarship which claim that a constitutionalization is in process in the international domain, or that international legal order is, in any event, a constitutional order. Each of these theories suggests a different outlook on the matter and a different definition of global constitutionalism. On the other side, in a general view, it is hard to find a coherent and common theoretical framework of the matter through these theories. That is to say, what global constitutionalism deals with may also vary by reason of the research object of these theories.

Given the diversity of concerning theories and purposes of this project, global constitutionalism can be defined as an umbrella term that overarches these theories by seeking a constitutionalization beyond the national level. Furthermore, the conception of global constitutionalization resembles domestic constitutionalization to some extent in terms of the characterization of the transitional process; since they are of common features, as both concern a "general restructuring movement"

---

[401] Schwöbel, *Global Constitutionalism*, 118.

[402] Ibid., 118.

[403] Wiener, "Global Constitutionalism," 11.

[404] Peters, "Compensatory Constitutionalism," 586.

[405] Anne Peters, "Conclusions," in *The Constitutionalization of International Law*, ed. Jan Klabbers, Anne Peters and Geir Ulfstein (Oxford: Oxford University Press, 2009), 344.

and concepts of liberty, equality, and also fundamental rights and solutions for governmental issues.[406] Moreover, this coincides with some recent developments in the transnational realm, where constitutionalization is a matter of discussion, and which are supposed to undermine the comprehensiveness of modern domestic constitutions.[407]

[406] Loughlin, "Ten Tenets of Sovereignty," 69.

[407] Ibid.

Chapter 3
Constitutionalism in Global Context: A Developing Discourse

Global constitutionalism is an umbrella term that is employed to frame the diverse activities beyond the national domain.[1] Despite the diversity of different understandings of global constitutionalism, in general terms, it has been defined as follows:

> Global constitutionalism is an academic and political agenda that identifies and advocates for the application of constitutionalist principles in the international legal sphere in order to improve the effectiveness and the fairness of the international legal order.[2]

Although the concept of global constitutionalism evokes an idea of the legal unity in the international realm, global constitutionalist theories vary, and many of them do not even deal with such unification ideas.[3] In this regard, the fragmentation of international legal order is more central to these theories. For instance, some of them regard constitutionalization and fragmentation in international law as "mutually constitutive."[4] Nevertheless, this discourse particularly draws on the constitutional

---

[1] Christine E.J. Schwöbel, *Global Constitutionalism in International Legal Perspective* (Leiden: Nijhoff, 2011), 1. For other scholars suggesting a similar definition: Jeffrey L. Dunoff and Joel P. Trachtman, "A Functional Approach to Global Constitutionalism" (Harvard Public Law Working Paper no. 08-57, 2008, http://ssrn.com/abstract=1311983), 21, last visit 19.04.2015.

[2] Anne Peters, "The Merits of Global Constitutionalism," *Indiana Journal of Global Legal Studies* 16, no. 2 (2009): 397.

[3] Stefan Oeter, "Regime Collisions from a Perspective of Global Constitutionalism," in *Contested Regime Collisions: Norm Fragmentation in World Society*, ed. Kerstin Blome et al. (Cambridge: Cambridge University Press, 2016), 22.

[4] Anne Peters, "Fragmentation and Constitutionalization," in *The Oxford Handbook of the Theory of International Law*, ed. Anne Orford and Florian Hoffmann (Oxford: Oxford University Press, 2016), 1020.

A. Atilgan, *Global Constitutionalism*, Beiträge zum ausländischen öffentlichen Recht und Völkerrecht, https://doi.org/10.1007/978-3-662-55647-4_3

vocabulary. However, there is no concrete constitution that exists beyond the national sphere, and therefore any inquiry about its "possibility," "desirability" or "necessity" always remains controversial.[5] It is also of note that most of the debate on a constitutionalization is constructed through an academic discourse. Thus, in accordance with the above mentioned definition, the idea of "global constitutionalization" can be defined in this way:

> Global constitutionalization refers to the continuing, but not linear, process of the gradual emergence and deliberate creation of constitutionalist elements in the international legal order by political and judicial actors, bolstered by an academic discourse in which these elements are identified and further developed.[6]

A number of theories regarding global constitutionalism and constitutionalization have already arisen in the academic world. These theories mostly reflect different understandings of global constitutionalism, and different approaches to constitutional and international law as well. Below, the reader will find a mapping of these studies. At this point, it is noteworthy that this research does not aim at pursuing one of these theories, but it triggers examining to what an extent they reflect the "truth" of contemporary constitutionalism instead.

In doing so, this research will examine whether or not the international community has undergone a constitutionalization process. Under this chapter, the prominent contributions to this debate, and the facts and conceptions that they employ to prove their premises shall be found.

The section below will concentrate on the background of global constitutionalist ideas that mostly reflect outlooks from the discipline of public international law. Evidently, global constitutionalism is mostly occupied with ideas from public international law and its theory. Thus, a great deal of hitherto contributions to this field mostly come from this discipline. Accordingly, the question of how different approaches understand international law is quite central to the structuration of global constitutionalism.

3.1 Mapping Global Constitutionalism Theories

In the literature of global constitutionalism, there already are a number of studies mapping global constitutionalism theories.[7] This text will draw on these works at some points. However, this text will build a different mapping scheme. In this

[5] Lars Viellechner, "Verfassung als Chiffre," *Zeitschrift für ausländisches öffentliches Recht und Völkerrecht* 1 (2015): 237.

[6] Peters, "Merits of Global Constitutionalism," 397.

[7] For example: Schwöbel, *Global Constitutionalism.* Antje Wiener, "Global Constitutionalism: Mapping an Emerging Field" (Paper presented at the Conference "Constitutionalism in a New Key? Cosmopolitan, Pluralist and Public Reason-Oriented," WZB and

respect, the text will deal with global constitutionalist theories in two distinctive categories. The first one is a group of theories that assume an ongoing or a foreseeable process of constitutionalization in the global realm. This means that this category involves both descriptive and normative approaches to global constitutionalism. The second category consists of theories that reject the viability and existence of such a constitutionalization process, and that nevertheless give credit to an idea of global constitutionalism in a noetic form.

Furthermore, it is of note that all contributions to the global constitutionalism debate argue for an international legal community. Against this background, global constitutionalism is constructed around liberal values, and thus some scholars aptly state that this debate is of a liberal character.[8] On the other side, they mostly reflect an interdisciplinary outlook that leads to the blending of various disciplines.[9]

3.1.1 Global Constitutionalist Theories: Assumption of an Ongoing Constitutionalization Process

3.1.1.1 Holistic Approaches: World State, Cosmopolitanism, Universalism

The holistic approaches in the global constitutionalism discourse share an integrationist understanding of international law. The most notable examples are the World State debate, cosmopolitanist contributions and some other approaches that interpret some institutionalization and legalization developments in international law as a constitutionalization process.

3.1.1.1.1 Cosmopolitanism and "the World State"

The concepts of cosmopolitanism and the world state refer to very similar facts and situations indeed. They are even employed as interchangeable terms from time to

Humboldt University, Berlin, 28-29 January 2011, http://cosmopolis.wzb.eu/content/programs/ conkey_Wiener_Mapping-Field.pdf), last visit 10.01.2014. Poul Kjaer, *Constitutionalism in the Global Realm: A Sociological Approach* (London: Routledge, 2014), 6-7. Stefan Oeter, "Global Constitutionalism: Fundamental Norms, Contestation and the Emergence of Constitutional Quality," in *Peace Through Law: Reflections on Pacem in Terries from Philosophy, Law, Theology and Political Science*, ed. Heinz-Gerhard Justenhoven and Marry Ellen O'Connell (Baden-Baden: Nomos, 2016), 90 ff.

[8] Schwöbel, *Global Constitutionalism.*

[9] Ibid., 11.

time. They stem from different readings of the same literature to some extent, and in particular to Kantian literature. However, both of these concepts basically tell us something fairly different. Cosmopolitanism particularly, appears as a broader concept along with different traditions, and thus these two concepts are to be discussed under different sections.

3.1.1.1.1.1 Kantian Tradition and Cosmopolitanism

To define in general terms, cosmopolitanism is,

> the view that all human beings share certain essential features that unite or should unite them in a global order that transcends national borders and warrants their designation as "citizens of the world."[10]

Furthermore, there are various approaches to cosmopolitanism. Referring to "*Patriotism and Cosmopolitanism*" of Martha Nussbaum, Berman argues that beyond a utopian universalism, and without rejecting the idea of local, cosmopolitanism is a strand of thought that allows the recognition that people have multiple affiliations from local to global.[11] On the other hand, global constitutionalism has more to do with Kant's works and the Kantian tradition, which represent a universalism, in terms of cosmopolitanism.

Of all others, there is no doubt that Kant and his famous essay "Perpetual Peace" of 1795 are the most remarkable sources of the cosmopolitanist contributions to international law. Despite the fact that Kant is not the only cosmopolitanist of the eighteenth century, among his coevals he is the most inspiring one to contemporary scholars, particularly in terms of the themes of "moral equality of all human beings, the existence of a set of human rights, and the urgency of establishing the political institution of a league of nations."[12] As a moral cosmopolitan, he supposes that all the human beings are citizens of a moral community.[13] Kant's ideas in "Perpetual Peace" are still being discussed in the context of the constitutionalization of international law. In other words, the Kantian project originates one of the cornerstones of this debate.

In a nutshell, according to Kant, the attempts to abolish wars between states concern a worldwide constitutional order.[14] At this point, it is of note that Kant considers international law as the law of the states, and cosmopolitan law as the law that regulates the relationships between states and citizens of foreign states, and that it is not subject to

---

[10] Pauline Kleingeld, "Six Varieties of Cosmopolitanism in Late Eighteenth-Century Germany," *Journal of the History of Ideas* 60, no. 3 (1999): 505.

[11] Paul Schiff Berman, "From International Law to Law and Globalization" (University of Connecticut School of Law Articles and Working Papers, Paper 23, 2005, http://lsr.nellco.org/uconn_wps/23), 540, last visit 11.07.2013.

[12] Kleingeld, "Six Varieties of Cosmopolitanism," 505.

[13] Ibid., 509.

[14] Jürgen Habermas, "Does the Constitutionalisation of International Law Still Have a Chance?," in *Divided West*, ed. and trans. Cionan Cronin (Cambridge: Polity, 2006), 115-193.

the formal procedures of law-making. Cosmopolitan law has to do with international trade and business, travel, migration, and intellectual exchange across borders. The main theme of cosmopolitan law is the "right to hospitality."[15] The state of peace is not the natural situation for states. It must be established by states, and the required conditions can only be provided by regulations through law.[16] The republican constitution is the essential source of peace. Kant defines the republican constitution as follows:

> A Republican Constitution is one that is founded, firstly, according to the principle of the Liberty of the Members of a Society, as Men; secondly, according to the principle of the Dependence of all its members on a single common Legislation, as Subjects; and, thirdly, according to the law of the Equality of its Members as Citizens.[17]

In this respect, the consent of the citizens is central to this constitution, and as such, declaring a war is under the initiative of citizens. Kant prescribes an international federation of peoples under the cosmopolitan condition, but he particularly underlines that it shall not lead to a cosmopolitan state that is made up of nations.[18] All in all, Kant's ideas in "Perpetual Peace" reflect a mechanism on dealing with aggressive nations, and an effective system of collective security.[19]

Given the current level of international law, some scholars advance the claim that the worldwide state practice regarding legal and institutional international restraints on the discretionary use of power on foreign policy has already confirmed Kant's ideas on "Perpetual Peace." Thereby, these ideas have gained a new force in our era.[20] Benhabib opines that the UN Declaration of Human Rights of 1948 marks a turn from international to cosmopolitan norms of justice. Apart from the international norms, she argues that the cosmopolitan norms of justice "accrue to individuals as moral and legal persons in a worldwide civil society."[21]

As one of the authors who follow the legacy of cosmopolitanism, Habermas deals with this as a political matter rather than a moral one.[22] He reconstructs Kantian cosmopolitanism for the contemporary political situations. According to him, the catastrophes of the twentieth century and the social dynamics of globalization led to a new

---

[15] Kleingeld, "Six Varieties of Cosmopolitanism," 513.

[16] Immanuel Kant, *Perpetual Peace: A Philosophical Sketch*, trans. W. Hastie (published by Slought Foundation, Philadelphia and the Syracuse University Humanities Center, 2010, http://perpetualpeaceproject.org/initiatives/publication.php), 12, last visit 08.09.2014.

[17] Ibid., 13.

[18] Ibid., 17,

[19] James A. Yunker, *The Idea of World Government: From Ancient Times to the Twenty First Century* (London: Routledge, 2011), 29.

[20] Ernst-Ulrich Petersmann, "Multilevel Trade Governance in the WTO Requires Multilevel Constitutionalism," in *Constitutionalism, Multilevel Trade, Governance and International Economic Law*, ed. Christian Joerges and Ernst-Ulrich Petersmann (Oxford: Hart Publishing, 2011), 13. Martti Koskenniemi. "Constitutionalism as Mindset: Reflections on Kantian Themes about International Law and Globalization," *Theoretical Inquiries in Law* 9 (2007): 12.

[21] Seyla Benhabib, *Another Cosmopolitanism* (Oxford: Oxford University Press, 2006), 16.

[22] Kleingeld, "Six Varieties of Cosmopolitanism," 505.

opportunity of thinking about Kant's cosmopolitan ideas and cosmopolitan justice in the context of today's global matters.[23] In addition, cosmopolitan solidarity is an integral part of the Enlightenment.[24] Habermas argues that in the aftermath of the two world wars particularly, a constitutionalization process has come about in international law in a parallelism with the cosmopolitan condition, which was described by Kant as a condition for permanent peace. The institutionalization and codification within this process have reflected a new process towards this condition.[25] In this sense, the establishment of the League of Nations in 1920 was also understood in Kantian terms by some notable scholars of that era, since it introduced the need for a cosmopolitan condition, and led to a great turn in international law by prohibiting war among states.[26] From this point of view, a constitutional order for a community of states is required to establish a real law-governed relationship between states and individuals.[27] Such a constitutional order would only be possible through the "republicanism of all states" or through a "world republic."[28] Nevertheless, Kant's opinions gained a new dimension over time, since he realized that such an order has the capacity to degenerate over time and could turn into a universal monarchy. Instead, he mentioned a confederation of nations in "Towards a Perpetual Peace." Furthermore, Habermas states that Kant never renounced the idea of the constitutionalization of international law in the form of a world republic, despite it becoming subject to various speculations.[29]

In Habermas' point of view, a transition from the law of nations to cosmopolitan law can be identified as a constitutionalization process. However, it cannot be considered as a continuation of the "evolution of the constitutional state leading from the national to a global state."[30] He argues that the constitutionalizaton in international law cannot be understood in parallel with the domestic constitutionalization. In this respect, the lack of a supranational mechanism in the international legal order with executive and sanctioning powers is the greatest deficit of international law.[31] By underlining this, Habermas indeed points to the core of the idea of constitutionalization: "It proceeds from the non-hierarchical association of collective actors to the supra- and transnational organizations of a cosmopolitan order."[32] According to Habermas, in the current stage of international law, the legal orders of the United Nations, the World Trade Organization and the European Union promise this progress. He explains the common feature of them as follows:

---

[23] Robert Fine and Will Smith, "Jürgen Habermas's Theory of Cosmopolitanism," *Constellations* 10, no. 4 (2003): 469.

[24] Ibid., 470.

[25] Habermas, "Constitutionalisation of International Law," 115.

[26] Ibid., 156.

[27] Ibid., 122.

[28] Ibid., 123.

[29] Ibid., 124.

[30] Ibid., 132.

[31] Ibid.

[32] Ibid., 133.

> they give the impression of a suit of clothes a couple of sizes too big waiting to be filled out by a stronger body of organizational law – in other words, by stronger transnational and supranational mandates for governance.[33]

He argues that the UN Charter could provide a "global domestic politics without a world government" as it is a conceptual alternative to a world republic in view of its power to impose peace and to implement human rights. That is to say, a world state is not the only means of realizing the cosmopolitan condition. He also highlights that a state is not a precondition for a modern constitution.[34] This idea was additionally shared by others alike, for example by Brun-Otto Bryde, who prescribes a global constitutionalization independent from the nation states:

> Although a constitutional state [Verfassungsstaat] cannot exist at the international level, constitutionalism can; likewise, there cannot be a (global) Rechtsstaat but there can be a (worldwide) rule of law, there cannot be an international welfare state [Sozialstaat] but there can be (global) social justice.[35]

In the contemporary world, Habermas emphasizes the role of "post-national constellations" as well; in other words, law and decision-making centres beyond nation states. The complex relations through these constellations set the stage for a constitutionalization in international law.[36]

However, it is of note that following the end of the bipolar Cold War, the emergence of the American hegemony over international relations has reflected a breakdown in such a development of international law towards the cosmopolitan condition, and under these circumstances, Habermas sees no chance of the realization of a Kantian cosmopolitanism. In other words, he deems the support of USA to the cosmopolitan order as crucial.[37] Under circumstances that are dominated by a hegemonic power, a hegemonic liberalism does not comply with Kantian thinking at all.[38] Further, Habermas was criticized for "subtly downplaying" practical obstacles to the development of the cosmopolitan tradition by referring to such a distinction in liberalism. This is indeed negligence of the fact that cosmopolitanism has always appeared in different forms and has developed into a diverse nature.[39]

---

[33] Ibid., 134.

[34] Ibid., 136-137.

[35] Brun-Otto Bryde, "Konstitutionalisierung des Völkerrechts und Internationalisierung des Verfassungsrechts," *Der Staat Bd.* 42 (2003), H. 1, 61-75 cited by Ibid., 139.

[36] Ibid., 176 ff.

[37] Ibid., 117, 179.

[38] Ibid., 183.

[39] Neil Walker, "Making a World of Difference? Habermas, Cosmopolitanism and the Constitutionalization of International Law" (EUI Working Papers, Law No. 17, 2005, http://cadmus.eui.eu/bitstream/handle/1814/3762/WPLAWNo.200517Walker.pdf?sequence=1), 3, last visit 11.10.2013.

As noted above earlier, the cosmopolitan tradition has relied on various strands of thought from the beginning on. This is also true for the current cosmopolitan views. Habermasian view is also likely to be distinguished from some other cosmopolitan views.[40] First of all, this difference stems from Habermas' scepticism about the conformity of the UN and other supranational structures with democracy. The democratic legitimacy is problematic for the political structures that include everybody and that provide no basis for "collective identity or civic solidarity."[41] Habermas opines that the global society lacks the "ethical-political self-understanding of the citizens of a particular democratic life."[42]

Moreover, the Kantian project could be seen as morally legitimate, on the ground that it basically hinges on the idea that democratized nations shall not wage war with each other. However, how to cope with the conditions that lead to democratized nations' wars with non-democratized nations, rises as a striking question. This is a paradox and it is counted as an essential obstacle to the cosmopolitan condition. On the other hand, cosmopolitanism currently has a broader content than in Kant's era, as Ulrich Beck notes in view of the influence of globalization: "The important fact now is that the human condition has itself become a cosmopolitan."[43]

Grimm argues that whether the juridification on a post-national level can amount to a constitutionalization process is strongly related to the answer to the question of whether or not the concept of constitution can be detached from nation states and can be transferred to the non-state entities that exercise the public power.[44]

Indeed, the term "constitution" has already been used to identify basic texts of international organizations. The "Constitution of the World Health Organization" or the "Constitution of the International Labour Organization" epitomize this fact. The concept of constitution used here can be counted as a synonym of the concept of the "constitutional instrument" that is found in Article 5 of the Vienna Convention on the Law of Treaties.[45]

Andreas L. Paulus argues that the constitutional quality of a system has a lot to do with the coherence of a legal system. That is to say, it is not possible to conclude that a constitutionalization is possible or already ongoing in international law from a point of view that regards international law as an anarchical order.[46] This means that the systemic qualities of international law have priority as decisive aspects in

---

[40] Fine and Smith, "Habermas's Theory of Cosmopolitanism," 474.

[41] Ibid.

[42] Jürgen Habermas, *The Postnational Constellation* (Cambridge: Polity, 2001), 107.

[43] Ulrich Beck, *Cosmopolitan Vision*, trans. Ciaran Cronin (Cambridge: Polity, 2006), 2.

[44] Dieter Grimm, "The Constitution in the Process of Denationalization," *Constellations* 12, no. 4 (2005): 458.

[45] Bardo Fassbender, "The United Nations Charter as Constitution of the International Community," *Columbia Journal of Transnational Law* 36, no. 3 (1998): 538.

[46] Andreas L. Paulus, "International Legal System as a Constitution," in *Ruling the World?: Constitutionalism, International Law, and Global Governance*, ed. Jeffrey L. Dunoff and Joel P. Trachtman (Cambridge: Cambridge University Press, 2009), 73.

a query about global constitutionalism. Accordingly, institutionalization appears as the most important aspect of constructing coherence in the international legal order, and as such, constitutionalization has an intimate relationship with the phenomenon of institutionalization.[47]

This issue was also discussed in terms of some contemporary institutionalization models. For instance, it has been argued that the unique characteristics of the EU make it an unsuitable model for a world-wide constitutionalism.[48] However, according to the same view, the WTO fits better to an international constitutionalization model, notably in view of the legalization of the dispute settlement, and the constitutional principle of non-discrimination through the conventional principle of the most favoured nation and national treatment; as well as the international trade rules introduction, which dispense with the need for domestic protectionist policies and the direct application of GATT rules.[49]

On the other side, to what an extent constitutionalization of institutions such as the WTO can lead to a constitutionalization in the global realm is dubious. Some scholars maintain that in contrast, this would increase the fragmentation of international law.[50] This question will be handled in the details in this chapter later.

3.1.1.1.1.2 The Idea of "World State"

The integrationist ideas can also be discussed in the context of a "World State." As a matter of fact, this idea has a very old history. The long tradition of the idea of a World State in the form of the "Christian World Empire" or Dante's idea of the universal government since the fourteenth century, can be held up as remarkable examples in this context.[51]

Hauke Brunkhorst's "cosmopolitan statehood" can be counted as a sort of bridging account between cosmopolitanism and the World State. The cosmopolitan state, in Brunkhorst's thought, is an empirical datum. That is to say, a kind of World State already exists.[52] However it is an inchoate process.[53] Against this background, the current form of the nation state is merely a specific form of the state evolution, and

---

[47] Ibid., 76.

[48] Anne Peters, "Compensatory Constitutionalism: The Fundamental Function and Potential of Fundamental International Norms and Structures," *Leiden Journal of International Law* 19 (2006): 595.

[49] Ibid. 596.

[50] Jan Klabbers, "Constitutionalism Lite," *International Organizations Law Review* 1 (2004), 32.

[51] Mathias Albert, "World State: Brunkhorst's 'Cosmopolitan State' and Varieties of Differentiation," *Social & Legal Studies* 23, no. 4 (2014): 519.

[52] Hauke Brunkhorst, "The Co-evolution of Cosmopolitan and National Statehood – Preliminary Theoretical Considerations on the Historical Evolution of Constitutionalism," *Cooperation and Conflict* 47, no. 2 (2012), 177.

[53] Albert, "World State," 518.

it draws a borderline between other forms of statehood. The nation state became the dominant form of authority in Europe in the nineteenth century, and in the global sphere only from the second half of the twentieth century on. It also has deep roots in the medieval age. There was always a "co-originality" of a cosmopolitan legal order along with the evolution of modern nation states.[54] On the other hand, the post-war processes of institutionalization, decolonization, individualization and juridicification mark a constitutionalization process. This is a new phase in the evolution of statehood, and this time it is expressed in its own forms.[55]

Brunkhorst's idea of the World State relies on Luhmann's System Theory in some terms. Thus, he proceeds from the idea that the World Society is a normatively integrated society, and the current cosmopolitan legal order consists of three main features:

> (1) the permanently increasing juridification of world society; (2) the emergence of some kind of a hierarchy of norms; and (3) the structural coupling of the systems of world law and world politics.[56]

Brunkhorst argues that a cosmopolitan legal order had developed after the Papal Revolution of the eleventh century in Europe, which is also known as the universal state of the Church. This sacred cosmopolitan state was integrated with the secular states of empires, kingdoms, feudal orders and other public authorities through a legal hierarchy.[57] However, it did not retain the same form. It was reconstructed in the course of the Protestant Revolution, and thereby a new kind of *jus gentium* was born. In this new natural system, divine and treaty law became quite influential in the new European order of states. Afterwards, French and American Revolutions changed the meaning of cosmopolitanism that was now led by universal and individual rights, along with the emergence of the modern republican nation-state:

> The new legal order of the revolutionary nation-state combined the cosmopolitan universal basic law with concrete procedural rules; subjective rights with judicial, legislative and administrative proceedings. From the very outset, such a law is designed as a dynamic order that transcends itself. It not only relies on a new order of international law based on the universal legal principle of individual and popular self-determination, it is also internally cosmopolitan[58]

Finally, Brunkhorst argues that the meaning of cosmopolitanism changed again due to the developments of post-World War II. The contents of French and American constitutions no longer have the same meaning because of various social and political crises, wars and catastrophes; and cosmopolitanism is no longer the same as in Kant's writings. This process also saw a still ongoing juridification and

[54] Brunkhorst, "Cosmopolitan and National Statehood," 177.

[55] Albert, "World State," 524.

[56] Brunkhorst, "Cosmopolitan and National Statehood," 178.

[57] Ibid., 182-183.

[58] Ibid., 186, emphasis belongs to the original text.

constitutionalization.[59] In this respect, the evolutionary constitutionalization of world law has been accompanied by a revolutionary institutionalization.

Matthias Albert mainly agrees with Brunkhorst regarding the idea of the World State. However, he finds his ideas on the "integrative potential of both the globale Rechtsgenossenschaft and the cosmopolitan state" too optimistic. According to him, Brunkhorst makes a mistake by giving too many credits to the segmentation and the primacy of functional differentiation of world politics in a Luhmannian way. Thus, he neglects the fact

> that a variety of forms of differentiation supports a variety of different, partially non-state forms of organizing political authority which potentially support rather than undermine disintegrative effects of functional differentiation.[60]

This means that Brunkhorst overlooks or underestimates the alternative forms of statehood or alternative organizing political authorities; in other words, he is very much into the modern form of nation states.

It is also of note that Brunkhorst deals with cosmopolitan statehood and global constitutionalism in other contexts as well. He also analyses the constitutionalization process within the transnational structures, and points to the democracy deficit and legitimacy problems within these regimes.[61] Brunkhorst discusses the inchoate global legal order in terms of Dewey's distinction to the formation of the public sphere as "strong" and "weak." In this respect, a strong public marks a sphere where "inclusive discussions and binding egalitarian decisions are structurally coupled via legal procedures."[62] A strong public is distinguished from a weak public in terms of the solidity of a democratic organization, and therefore, constitutions are considered as a remarkable component of the public sphere. This is so, because a public can only be weak without constitutional organizational norms.[63] The weak public has no legal impact on political and administrative power, while it has moral influences and a communicative power. In case of a weak public, democratic self-organization and effective access to the legal system are not enabled; therefore, these kinds of societies are hierarchical societies, and not egalitarian in Rawlsian terms.[64] The outcome of these kinds of societies is a hegemonic law of a ruling social group which cannot be legitimated. A true democracy is not possible without the egalitarian procedures of decision making.[65]

Constitutions belong to an advanced stage of strong public spheres. Brunkhorst clarifies this point with these words:

---

[59] Ibid., 187.

[60] Albert, "World State," 525.

[61] Hauke Brunkhorst, *Solidarity: From Civic Friendship to a Global Legal Community*, trans. Jeffrey Flynn (Cambridge: The MIT Press, 2005), 7.

[62] Hauke Brunkhorst, "Globalising Democracy Without a State: Weak Public, Strong Public, Global Constitutionalism," *Millennium - Journal of International Studies* 31 (2002): 676.

[63] Ibid., 675.

[64] Ibid., 679.

[65] Ibid.

> (…) a strong public relies on a public sphere framed by the norms of a constitution. (…) A strong public is a weak public plus the political and administrative power enabled and organized by a constitution.[66]

Thus, given the existence of post-war international organizations, notably the UN, and the binding legal rights and general principles of international law, Brunkhorst advances the claim that the current situation of the global legal order is not tantamount to a strong public, but to a "strong global public in the making."[67]

In this regard, governmental and public networks are components of a strong public at nation states level. On the other hand, the media of global communication and networks of transnational associations constitute the "social preconditions" of this weak global public.[68]

The idea of a World State has also been discussed in a teleological way.[69] Basically, the idea of "World State" differs from cosmopolitanism, on the ground that "World state formation is not only a cosmopolitan process, but a communitarian one as well."[70]

Further, although this debate has a long history, there is a consensus among the current scholars about the impossibility of a world government. As a matter of fact, the UN has been deemed as the highest form of global political authority that is allowed by the current reality of the international community. It has also been found non-desirable, since it can quickly "degenerate into a tyranny, bureaucratic suffocation, cultural homogenization."[71] In addition, it was also considered as a threat against individual liberties and that no form of democracy could meet the needs of a diversity of peoples under a world government.[72] However, there are also some other scholars, such as Alexander Wendt, who argue that a World State would carry out a function in favour of human liberties and more justice.

In this context, the idea of an "empire" appears with a very intimate, conceptual relationship to the world government. This idea stems from an extensive territory and numerous subsidiary political units containing many diverse peoples and cultures in an empire. Therefore, this relationship may lead to a rejection of the idea of a world government by a large majority of the world's population.[73]

As mentioned in the previous section, Kant's "Perpetual Peace" was debated concerning the question of whether or not it reflects an idea of the World State. While examining the idea of the World State, Yunker agrees that Kant's ideas basically

---

[66] Ibid., 677.

[67] Ibid., 676.

[68] Ibid., 680.

[69] Alexander Wendt, "Why a World State is Inevitable," *European Journal of International Relations* 9, no. 4 (2003): 491.

[70] Ibid., 519.

[71] Yunker, *The Idea of World Government*, 5.

[72] Anne-Marie Slaughter, *A New World Order* (Princeton: Princeton University Press, 2004), 8.

[73] Yunker, *The Idea of World Government*, 15.

refer to a confederation, a looser formation, and do not meet a full-scale state. Yet, he argues that this idea has much in common with proponents of an idea of a World State.[74]

The scholars that attempt to construct an idea of the World State refer to the historical fact that there were 600.000 independent political communities on Earth in the past, while there are currently only about 200. In addition to this, contemporary regional sub-systems are further phenomena that support this development.[75] This fact has been employed to prove that unification in the global realm is the final destination of the political evolution, and also to demonstrate the "logic of anarchy."[76]

Wendt constructs the theory of a World State teleologically. For this purpose, he first challeges the modern and post-modern rejections to the teleological methodology that it is thought to "deny human agency" in social relations. In this regard, he argues that these rejections are unfounded.[77] On the other hand, he prescribes a World State that is quite different from modern nation states. According to him, a World State would be shaped in a more decentralized form, even without a government. Following this, he opines that a worldwide EU-like structure would count as a world state.[78] In addition, once a world society is established, a common desire to maintain it, will follow automatically.

Furthermore, Wendt also deals with concerns about the desirability and the possibly negative character of a World State. He examines whether or not Kant would be right in pointing out that a World State would be a despotic state. Wendt argues that this might be true if a World State only meets the "thin" criterion of a Weberian state, namely, a legitimate monopoly of source. However, Wendt presents another model of state. His world state model is not a "stable end-state," but a state where the struggle for recognition would always go on. This struggle occurs at a micro level through the acts of individuals and at the same time, at a macro level through states. However, as he argues, this does not mean that this model is not exempt from the debate on democracy deficit concerning transnational assemblages.[79]

Yunker remarks that Wendt's arguments would be more persuasive for a theoretical philosopher than for an international relations practitioner.[80] On the other hand, Yunker proposes a "Federal Union of Democratic Nations" as a World government model that reflects a limited government instead of an omnipotent state, and also a distinct model compared to the UN. This body has a constitution, the power to levy taxes and its own armed forces along with the legislative, judicial and administrative powers.[81] His proposed constitution consists of five essential sections:

---

[74] Ibid., 29.

[75] Wendt, "World State is Inevitable," 503.

[76] Ibid., 491.

[77] Ibid., 492.

[78] Ibid., 515.

[79] Ibid., 518.

[80] Yunker, *The Idea of World Government*, 93.

[81] Ibid., 106.

> (1) nature and purposes of the Union; (2) the three branches of government (legislative, executive and judicial); (3) powers and responsibilities of the supernational government; (4) rights and responsibilities of nations; (5) rights and responsibilities of citizens.[82]

Consequently, the idea of a World State has been represented by two main opinions. It could be discussed in the form of the idea of the cosmopolitan World State, which is akin to the cosmopolitanist tradition, and also in a teleological way that informs us about the inevitable future-generation of the World State. Without any doubt, these ideas are strongly relevant to the global constitutionalism discourse, although emphasis on the constitutionalization of the latter is fairly weaker. The emergence of a world state and its legal orders bring to the forth the question of its constitutional order. However, these ideas do not tell us much about the idea of their constitutions; therefore, the image of a constitution remains in the dark.

3.1.1.1.2 The UN Charter as a Constitution

The most notable contribution to this category is the theory of German scholar Bardo Fassbender that counts the UN Charter as the constitution of the international community.[83] The UN Charter is originally an international treaty. Nevertheless, according to Fassbender, it must be distinguished from other international treaties as the UN Charter is a "constituent treaty." The idea that the UN Charter has unique qualities was also agreed on by some other scholars. For example, Christian Tomuschat identifies it as a "world order treaty."[84] On the other hand, according to Doyle, the supranational structure of the UN order is the key point of the constitutional features of the UN Charter.[85]

One of the proceeding points of Fassbender is that there is not only one type of constitution that is confronted by domestic constitutions, since local communities and supranational communities can also have a constitution.[86] He predicates his idea on a relatively broad definition of a constitution:

> A constitution is a set of fundamental norms about the organization and performance of governmental functions in a community, and the relationship between the government and those who are governed.[87]

---

[82] Ibid., 107.

[83] Fassbender, "The United Nations Charter," 531.

[84] Christian Tomuschat, "Obligations Arising for States Without or Against Their Will," *Recueil des Cours* 241, no. 4 (1993): 248.

[85] Michael W. Doyle. "The UN Charter – A GlobalConstitution?," in *Ruling the World? Constitutionalism, International Law, and Global Governance*, ed. Jeffrey L. Dunoff and Joel P. Trachtman (Cambridge: Cambridge University Press, 2009), 115.

[86] Fassbender, "The United Nations Charter," 558.

[87] Bardo Fassbender, "Rediscovering a Forgotten Constitution: Notes on the Place of the UN Charter in the International Legal Order," in *Ruling the World? Constitutionalism, International Law, and Global Governance*, ed. Jeffrey L. Dunoff and Joel P. Trachtman (Cambridge: Cambridge University Press, 2009), 139.

Nevertheless, he states that, there is still not a general agreement in identifying a constitution. He refers to two main strands in German constitutional thought to understand the relationship between a constitution and a community. In the first point of view, which is represented by Carl Schmitt, a political entity first emerges and then a constitution arises. This means that it is not possible to set up a constitution through a political entity that does not exist. In contrast, according to the second point of view, a community can only be constructed through a constitutive process. That is to say, the construction of a state hinges on the existence of a constitution. This point of view was also reflected by Rudolf Smend and Hermann Heller.[88] Fassbender supposes that his approach to the constitutional treaties somewhat fits to the latter.

Despite the uncertainty in the definition of a constitution, Fassbender argues that a constitution can still be identified through a number of universal characteristics: "These are sets of fundamental norms about the organization and performance of governmental functions in a community, and the relationship between the government and those being governed."[89] The political community at stake does not need to be a state. For further analysis, he refers to the methodology of Max Weber called the "ideal type" of a phenomenon. The ideal type is a theoretical artefact that does not reflect any reality; instead, it is "determined by intentionally intensifying and combining one or more of its individual features to form a consistent theoretical construct."[90] Fassbender opines that in the international context, the concept of constitution does not need to refer to its origins that are associated with the nation state, but rather a constitution will arise as an autonomous fact beyond the will of states. Proceeding from Weber's ideal type methodology, Fassbender employs the concept of an "ideal constitution" for the UN Charter.[91]

As to the constitutional features of the UN Charter, first of all, Fassbender counts the UN as the main representative of the international community.[92] In his point of view, the UN Charter has constitutional features in various terms. By counting them as constitutional, Fassbender's understanding of global constitutionalism gains a normative perspective. These features are as follows:

> (…) In particular, it includes rules about how the basic functions of governance are performed in the international community, that is to say, how and by whom the law is made and applied, and how and by whom legal claims are adjudicated. The Charter also establishes a hierarchy of norms in international law (Article 103).[93]

Fassbender considers these as the minimum qualities of a constitution. By referring to the Preamble and Chapter 1 of the UN Charter, he states that the will of

[88] Fassbender, "The United Nations Charter," 561.

[89] Ibid., 569.

[90] Ibid., 570.

[91] Ibid., 573.

[92] Ibid., 567.

[93] Bardo Fassbender, "The Meaning of International Constitutional Law," in *Transnational Constitutionalism: International and European Models*, ed. Nicholas Tsagourias (Cambridge: Cambridge University Press), 2007, 322.

the founders is clearly to construct a new legal order through the Charter. Borrowing from Ackermann, he argues that the San Francisco Conference, which ended up with the creation of the UN Charter, is of a characteristic of a "constitutional moment."[94] At this point, Fassbender highlights the words of the US President Harry Truman in the final session of the San Francisco Conference: "The Charter, like own Constitution, will be expanded and improved as time goes on."[95] The UN Charter also aspires to the eternity like any other constitution; it provides for amendment, but not termination.[96]

Fassbender also attributes a special importance to the choice for the word "charter." In this regard, for instance, "covenant" was used for the statute of the League of Nations, and according to him, these choices imply a special meaning. "Charter" was deliberately chosen and in 1945 it was understood as equivalent to a "written constitution."[97] The opening words of the Charter, "We the peoples of the United Nations," prove this opinion since they demonstrate a parallelism with the US Constitution, which opens by the words "We The People of the United States." Contrary to this, the Covenant of the League of Nations opened with the traditional opening words of a treaty: "The High Contracting Parties … "[98]

Accordingly, there is an intimate relationship between general international law and the UN Charter, and there is no international law independent from the Charter. In this respect, the UN Charter is "the supporting frame of all international law" and it ranks in the highest position in the hierarchical order of norms.[99] This means that, other treaties of international law have a position of ordinary law in the presence of the UN Charter. This was also proved by the recognition of the UN Charter as a meta-norm by many international treaties. For example, Article 1(c) of the Statute of the Council of Europe reads as "Participation in the Council of Europe shall not affect the collaboration of its members in the work of the United Nations." A similar statement is also found in Article 7 of the NATO Treaty. In Article 3(5) of the Treaty on European Union, amended by the Treaty of Lisbon, respect for the principles of the United Nations Charter in the context of a contribution to the development of international law is mentioned among the aims of the European Union. The parties of the Vienna Convention on Diplomatic Relations of 1961 and the Convention on the Law of the Sea of 1982, also declare to remain loyal to the principles and purposes of the United Nations Charter.[100] There are numerous other examples. Given these examples, Fassbender argues that states hold the UN Charter in a higher

---

[94] Fassbender, "The United Nations Charter," 573.

[95] Harry S. Truman, Speech at the Final session of the San Francisco Conference (June 26, 1945), in 1 Documents of the United Nations Conference on International Organization 680 (1945), cited by Fassbender, "Rediscovering a Forgotten Constitution," 134.

[96] Fassbender, "The United Nations Charter," 578.

[97] Ibid., 580.

[98] Ibid., 580.

[99] Ibid., 585.

[100] Fassbender, "Rediscovering a Forgotten Constitution," 142-143.

esteem than international law scholars do.[101] On the other hand, Fassbender states that it does not mean that any other international document cannot bear a constitutional rank. For example, "world order treaties" like the Human Rights Covenants and the Genocide Convention, and some by-laws of international law also have additional constitutional features in comparison with the ordinary treaties.[102]

As mentioned above, the UN Charter, as a charter, features a law, distinct from other kinds of international legal instruments, like a covenant.[103] It rather prescribes a vertical integration unlike the League of Nations, as Preuß states that, "The UN Charter set up an international organization—a mechanism for the pursuit of collective goals by means of coordination of action controlled by a central organ."[104]

The constitutional qualities of the UN Charter were discussed by some other authors as well. Habermas argues that the UN Charter has some specific constitutional features. He basically underlines three key features of the Charter:

> the explicit connection of the purpose of securing peace with a politics of human rights; the linkage of the prohibition on the use of violence with a realistic threat of prosecution and sanctions; and the inclusive character of the world organization and the universal validity it claims for the law it enacts.[105]

According to Habermas, due to these features of the UN Charter, states are no longer the subjects of international treaty law. States and their citizens are now "constitutional pillars of a politically constituted world society," and this shift stems from the cultural and economic dynamics of the world society.[106] Furthermore, from a Weberian point of view, it is also noted by some scholars that the UN Charter provides the centralization of the legitimation of the use of force by granting the Security Council the monopoly regarding this matter, except for the cases of self-defence, which proves its constitutional character as well.[107]

The idea that the UN Charter is the constitution of international law has seen many criticisms, but it has also been found inspiring by many. For example, some argue that despite all the developments towards a legal organization in a full sense, a mechanism of separation of powers is hardly to be exemplified within the international legal order, particularly in the UN system, and even between national states and international organizational bodies.[108] Furthermore, the constitutional features of the UN Charter do not suffice at some points, as they are far from controlling the

---

[101] Ibid., 143.

[102] Fassbender, "The United Nations Charter," 588.

[103] Ibid.

[104] Ulrich K. Preuß, "Equality of States – Its Meaning in a Constitutionalised Global Order," *Chicago Journal of International Law* 9, no.1 (2008-2009): 39.

[105] Habermas, "Constitutionalisation of International Law," 160.

[106] Ibid., 161.

[107] Paulus, "International Legal System," 77.

[108] Karl-Heinz Ladeur, "Ein Recht der Netzwerke für die Weltgesellschaft oder Konstitutionalisierung der Völkergemeinschaft," *Archiv des Völkerrechts* 49 (2011): 259.

fundamental issues of a political order, which also constitute the founding block of a political order.[109] In a similar vein, Judge Pinto De Albuquerque from the ECtHR and his colleagues opine that the lack of an effective constitutional control over the Security Council and other bodies of the UN is a major handicap of the UN System that weakens the constitutionalization process.[110] The UN Charter has also seen criticisms that while the UN Charter focuses on the international peace and security, it reduces the importance of other global problems.[111] On the other hand, from more statist perspectives, one may also argue that the UN was not intended to create a World State, and therefore the UN Charter can by no means be counted as a constitution.[112]

It is also evident that the efficiency of the human rights protection through the Human Rights Council of the UN is dubious, since an individual application to this body is not yet possible.[113] Therefore, the protectional function of the Charter for fundamental rights remains in the dark. At this point, Judge Pinto De Albuquerque et al. argue that the UN will not gain a "constitutional nature" until the day a World Human Rights Court is established with compulsory jurisdiction over the bodies and the officials of the UN.[114] Under these circumstances, the constitutional claim of the UN Charter is much weaker than that of the ECtHR in spite of the existence of the *jus cogens* rule of Article 103 of the Charter.[115]

In addition to these, the UN Charter has not been able to establish an efficient fundamental system for international law, and it mainly relies on general international law instead of re-identifying its essential dynamics. Furthermore, despite the monopolization of the use of force through the Charter, the UN cannot employ military force by itself.[116]

---

[109] Preuß, "Equality of States," 41.

[110] Al-Dulimi and Montana Management Inc. v. Switzerland, 5809/08, Concurring Opinion Of Judge Pinto De Albuquerque, Joined By Judges Hajiyev, Pejchal And Dedov (21.06.2016), para. 8, http://hudoc.echr.coe.int/eng?i=001-164515, last visit 12.03.2017.

[111] Preuß, "Equality of States," 41.

[112] Doyle, "UN Charter," 113.

[113] Ladeur, "Ein Recht der Netzwerke," 249.

[114] Al-Dulimi and Montana Management Inc. v. Switzerland, Concurring Opinion, para. 8.

[115] Therefore, UN Law is "subordinated to the primacy of the Convention as a constitutional instrument of European public order." Ibid., para. 59, 71. However, according to Peters, this presumption paves the way for domestic judicial review of the Security Council decisions, and this may give rise to unfair results especially for the people subject to listing decisions of the Security Council. Such a problem demonstrates the urgency of further constitutionalization of the UN, particularly in terms of the sanctions regime. Anne Peters, "The New Arbitrariness and Competing Constitutionalisms: Remarks on ECtHR Grand Chamber Al-Dulimi," *EJIL: Talk*, June 30, 2016, http://www.ejiltalk.org/the-new-arbitrariness-and-competing-constitutionalisms-remarks-on-ecthr-grand-chamber-al-dulimi/?, last visit 03.03.2017.

[116] Paulus, "International Legal System," 78.

3.1.1.1.3 Constitutionalization of the WTO

The academic contributions regarding the constitutionalization of the World Trade Organization mainly proceed from this question: "is the trade regime properly understood as a constitutional entity?"[117] As a matter of fact, constitutionalization of the WTO would be discussed among other sectoral and microconstitutionalization models since the operation of the WTO concerns a sectoral matter, and as such, constitutionalization of a "regime" is questioned under this section. However, as distinct from microconstitutionalization processes within particular transnational regimes, constitutionalization of the WTO should rather be understood as constitutionalization of the world trade, that is to say, in a holistic context. In other words, the WTO is regarded as somewhat a part of a broader international legal system, instead of a self-contained constitutional order.[118] The Appellate Body of the WTO also confirmed this approach in earlier rulings. For example, the Appellate Body states that the WTO agreements "should not be read in clinical isolation from public international law," and "[c]ustomary international law applies generally to the agreements between WTO members," and in so doing it emphasizes the incorporation of the WTO law with general international law.[119]

The World Trade Organization has a special function within the globalization process on the ground that globalization in a sense, denotes the increasing international economic integration.[120] The debate of the constitution of the WTO mainly concerns constitutional attributions to the institutional structure of the WTO, or a set of normative commitments, or the judicial review mechanism.[121] Rather, the contributions to this debate pursue prescriptive methods to explain a constitutionalization process within the WTO Law.

One of the prominent scholars that deal with constitutionalization of the WTO is John Jackson. He basically argues that a rule-oriented approach is necessary to provide security and predictability for decentralised international markets and the WTO could be the best host for a constitution pursuing such aims.[122]

---

[117] Jeffrey L. Dunoff, "The Politics of International Constitutions: The Curious Case of the World Trade Organization," in *Ruling the World? Constitutionalism, International Law and Global Governance*, ed. Jeffrey L. Dunoff and Joel P. Trachtman (Cambridge: Cambridge University Press, 2009), 179.

[118] Joel P. Trachtman, "Constitutional Economics of the World Trade Organization," in *Ruling the World? Constitutionalism, International Law and Global Governance*. ed. Jeffrey L. Dunoff and Joel P. Trachtman (Cambridge: Cambridge University Press, 2009), 217.

[119] Appellate Body Report, United States - Standards of Reformulated and Conventional Gasoline, 16 WT/DS2/AB/R (April 29, 1996); Panel Report, Korea - Measures Affecting Government Procurement, 7.96, WT/DS163/R (May 1, 2000), cited by Koskenniemi, "Constitutionalism as Mindset," 19.

[120] Trachtman, "Constitutional Economics," 206.

[121] Dunoff, "Politics of International Constitutions," 184.

[122] Ibid., 185.

Ernst-Ulrich Petersmann deals with constitutionalization of the WTO in terms of some normative commitments and the protection of some normative values. Human rights are very central to this approach, and economic freedoms are found at the heart of his perception of human rights.[123] According to Petersmann, human rights and economic freedoms depend on the same values, namely,

> individual freedom and responsibility, (…) non-discrimination, rule of law, access to courts and adjudication of disputes; promotion of social welfare through peaceful cooperation among free citizens; parliamentary approval of national and international rules.[124]

On the other hand, the WTO pursues some constitutional functions for all member states. For example, it guarantees freedom and non-discrimination in their domestic legal systems.[125] Petersmann suggests a European model of economic integration for the WTO.[126] His main idea is that a global economic integration on liberal principles confirms the political ideas of Kant and Hume and the economic theories of Ricardo and Smith:

> the mutual gains from voluntary international trade, and from an international division of labour based on liberal rules, offer the most important means to overcome the "Hobbesian war of everybody against everybody else" through peaceful cooperation, even if people and governments act as self-interested utility-maximizers.[127]

In this sense, the turn from anarchic "international law of coexistence" into the "international law of cooperation" in the aftermath of World War II, was the most successful step in international economic law and in the European integration.[128] Accordingly, like the EU Law, "we the citizens" must become the main subjects of the WTO Law.[129]

While dealing with the idea of the WTO constitution, Petersmann proceeds from some common features of constitutions in order to identify the concept of a constitution. According to Petersmann, these are the "higher rank position" and the "abstract and general nature" of constitutions.[130] He views the WTO Agreement and other rules as constitutional documents. In this respect, he argues that the constitutional functions of the WTO law are not only found within the institutional framework of the WTO, but also through its effects on national laws.[131] Furthermore, the WTO rules protect economic freedom and some other relevant rights, and they

---

[123] Ibid., 188.

[124] Ernst-Ulrich Petersmann, "The WTO Constitution and Human Rights," *Journal of International Economic Law* 3 (2000), 19.

[125] Ibid., 20.

[126] Dunoff, "Politics of International Constitutions," 188.

[127] Ernst-Ulrich Petersmann, "Constitutionalism and International Organizations," *Northwestern Journal of International Law & Business* 17 (1996-1997): 399.

[128] Ibid., 400.

[129] Petersmann, "WTO Constitution and Human Rights," 24.

[130] Petersmann, "Multilevel Trade Governance," 15.

[131] Ibid., 31.

prescribe formal techniques for decision-making that are characteristic of constitutionalism. They also have supremacy over conflicting provisions of other multilevel trade agreements annexed to the WTO Agreement and over the relevant trade rules in member states. The WTO law also introduces limits on the power of the trade policy.[132] Further, "embedding the implementation of international trade rules into stronger domestic 'constitutional checks and balances'" may serve the purpose of constitutionalization in the multilevel trade governance.[133] In short, Petersmann prescribes a multilevel constitutionalization process for the WTO, which is entirely different from the national examples.

The Appellate Body and the dispute settlement system are viewed as the main transnational features of the WTO.[134] Deborah Cass puts the Appellate Body of the WTO into the heart of the constitutionalization process. The Appellate Body creates constitutional norms and structures during the dispute resolution process through various methods including interaction with the constitutional values of other systems. In this way, the WTO contributes to the constitutionalization of international trade law.[135]

The WTO, for example, has not yet proceeded with a formal constitution, unlike the European Union. Moreover, the WTO still lacks any mechanism of the separation of powers and of the superiority of any establishing norms on other international norms. Additionally, it is obvious that the WTO has still an underdeveloped legislative capacity. Furthermore, the attitude of the WTO organs and texts regarding a direct effect of the GATT and the WTO legal order has always been adverse. For example, in the dispute panel report of Section 301, it is stated that the GATT and the WTO did not create a legal order producing direct legal effects on individuals.[136] In this regard, this is one of the clearest differences between the WTO legal system and the EU Law. Therefore, from a point of view that applies an analogy between domestic constitutionalism and the WTO Law, one can hardly claim a constitutionalization process within the WTO.[137]

Nonetheless, bearing this deficiency of the WTO in mind, Petersmann points to some recent developments. For example, he points to an increasing agreement on the WTO needing far-reaching institutional and legal reforms in the decision-making, following the reform proposals – including references – to the governance of the EU as a model in the Sutherland Report on "the Future of the WTO" of the Directorate General.[138]

Dunoff notes that although the relatively well-developed dispute resolution mechanism of the WTO is to be regarded as the most notable constitutional aspect, the political pressures from member states and some textual constraints diminish the ability of the dispute panels to produce law. Therefore, he advances the claim

---

[132] Ibid, 32-33.

[133] Ibid., 37.

[134] Trachtmann, "Constitutional Economics," 217.

[135] Dunoff, "Politics of International Constitutions," 190.

[136] Ibid., 189.

[137] Ibid., 180-181.

[138] Petersmann, "Multilevel Trade Governance," 30.

that the dispute settlement mechanism simply reflects a weak ground for a constitutionalization.[139] On the other hand, he argues that whereas the WTO dispute resolution system is fairly deliberative, it is quite weak in terms of participatory or democratic politics.[140]

Under these circumstances, given the adverse facts about a constitutionalization in international trade law, Dunoff questions why so many scholars focus on debating the constitutionalization of the WTO. He concludes that the current queries for the constitutionalization of the WTO also reflect a desire for the stability and legitimacy of a higher law. These inquiries also have to do with "a deep disciplinary anxiety about the nature and value of international law."[141] Petersmann's opinions are in parallel with Dunoff's at this point. Petersmann states that the constitutionalization of the WTO may aim at reforming international law and domestic laws.[142] He also considers the constitutionalization of the WTO as a must, since he believes that international trade cannot be secured otherwise.[143]

3.1.1.2 Micro-Constitutionalization

Not all contributions to the global constitutionalism discourse take a stand in favour of a holistic constitutionalization process. There are also some scholars that highlight the fact that the fragmentation in international law impedes and even renders a global constitutionalization impossible, but still argue that a constitutionalization can occur within the fragmented structures of global law. The most prominent proponents of this view are Gunther Teubner and Andreas Fischer-Lescano, who own distinctive ideas on this matter. The main target of this section is to introduce their academic writings on global constitutionalism. Their theories bear the traces of Luhmann's views on the World Society and the Systems Theory. Before going into details, it would be helpful to first have a look at Luhmann's opinions on the law of the world society and the concept of the constitution, which are also likely to be perceived as alternative readings of globalization.

3.1.1.2.1 World Society and Constitutions as Structural Couplings of Law and Politics

Luhmann's academic works include, *inter alia,* the development of a world society. In Luhmann's theory, one striking point is that the political system does not represent a centre of societal interactions; instead, it is merely a communication system

[139] Dunoff, "Politics of International Constitutions," 183.

[140] Ibid., 195.

[141] Ibid., 204.

[142] Petersmann, "Multilevel Trade Governance," 35.

[143] Ibid., 57.

which is not superior to other communication systems in society.[144] The society consists of a number of systems, such as law, politics, religion etc., and they reproduce themselves only through self-referential communications, which means a synthesis of information, communication, and comprehension.[145] The state has no primary position in this sociological perspective, as it is only a "de-centred nexus of contingent communications amongst a number of others."[146] Luhmann's socio-legal theory envisages that law and society are interactive facts that are empirically researchable variables, and he refuses the sociological premises that prescribe some certain type of norms that can be observed in every society, since natural law was superseded.[147]

As to the globalization debate, Luhmann appears with his own idiosynchratic theory on the "world society." According to Luhmann, the modern society consists of one single coherent social system and it is the "world society" that is based on the worldwide communicative systems.[148] In this system, independent and interdependent states play the main roles and none of them can ignore any political shifts in the world.[149] The global system reflects a serious shift in the evolution of society. That is to say, "all internal boundaries can be contested and all solidarities shift" in the contemporary global system.[150] This system is subject to a functional differentiation through some sub-systems, such as the legal system, the economic system, the religious system and the political system. This sort of functional differentiation is different from the era of Durkheim, in which the division of labour was essential, and it basically developed in the aftermath of World War II along with a new conception of modernization:

> It distinguished between different function systems and proclaimed, under the name of "development," their modernization by way of a market orientation of the economy, a democratization of politics, equal access to school education, the establishment of constitutional legality (rule of law) all over the world, a political control of the military, a free press, self-directed scientific research and so on.[151]

Furthermore, the primary differentiation between nation states is segmentary. That is to say, functional differentiation is secondary and less complex.[152] This system was

---

[144] Ladeur, "Ein Recht der Netzwerke," 321.

[145] Niklas Luhmann, "The Unity of the Legal System," in *Autopoietic Law: A New Approach to Law and Society*, ed. Gunther Teubner (Berlin: Walter de Gruyter, 1988), 17.

[146] Chris Thornhill, "Niklas Luhmann and the Sociology of the Constitution," *Journal of Classical Sociology* 10, no. 4 (2010): 321.

[147] Niklas Luhmann, *A Sociological Theory of Law*, trans. Martin Albrow and Elizabeth King-Utz, ed. Martin Albrow (Florence, KY: Routledge, 2013), 10.

[148] Clemens Mattheis, "The System Theory of Niklas Luhmann and the Constitutionalization of the World Society," *Göttingen Journal of International Law* 4, no. 2 (2012): 637.

[149] Ibid., 641.

[150] Niklas Luhmann, "Globalizaton or World Society: How to Conceive of Modern Society?," *International Review of Sociology: Revue Internationale de Sociologie* 7, no. 1 (1997): 67-79.

[151] Ibid.

[152] Mattheis, "System Theory of Luhmann," 638.

also explained by a metacode of "inclusiveness and exclusiveness" by Luhmann, which was employed in clarifying the differentiation between the centre and the periphery. In this regard, functional differentiation in world society has been only partially achieved, and thus other parts of the world have been excluded from world communication.[153] Moreover, according to Luhmann, we need a new methodology to understand the new "social" in world society by emphasizing the essential differences from the domestic domain:

> At the end of the 20th century we have to learn this lesson. In vain we try to use the leftover vocabularies of a tradition whose ambition it was to define the unity, or even the essence, of the social. Our problem is to define difference and to mark off a space in which we can observe the emergence of order and disorder.[154]

Accordingly, whether or not a world law exists arises as a prominent question. In the Luhmannian perspective, contemporary international law works in this way particularly through international tribunals.[155] Furthermore, Luhmann gives a specific place to the function of the constitution in his academic works.

As a common thread, in post-Luhmannian studies, classical approaches to the constitutions are criticized since they are incapable of explaining factual dispersal of constitutional power beyond nation states, and they still adhere to the insufficient distinctions of public and private law, and to the idea of a foundational normative consensus as the legitimating force of constitutions.[156] These theories deal with constitutional norms as socially formative and structurally embedded elements of society:

> For this theory, in its intention at least, a norm cannot be disarticulated from the factual form of its communication, and a norm's status as norm depends entirely on its enunciation within a set of externally unfounded communications. The constitutional norms of society are thus always also the constitutional facts of the society.[157]

Luhmann's theory is a "fully sociological paradigm" of constitutional studies, which deals with constitutional norms beyond the facts/norms dichotomy, and its aim is to provide a sociology of constitutions that reflects the legitimating function of constitutional norms.[158] His approach to constitutions can be basically analyzed from two points. First, according to Luhmann, constitutions are structural couplings between law and politics. This implies that constitutions have functions of consolidation and simplification of the relationship between legal and political systems, and thereby, they allow the law to explain itself as "politically enforced" and political power to

---

[153] Ibid.

[154] Luhmann, "Globalizaton or World Society."

[155] Mattheis, "System Theory of Luhmann," 640.

[156] Thornhill, "Niklas Luhmann," 320.

[157] Ibid., 323.

[158] Ibid., 325.

explain itself as "legally determined."[159] As a result of this role within this relationship, constitutions acquire the function of providing for the legitimacy of political power.[160] A second contribution of constitutions to the legitimization of political power rises by obscuring the contingency of the foundations of function systems and providing a basis for differentiated and plausible use of political power in a modern society.[161] By virtue of the inclusive facilities of constitutions, they also played a role in the transformation of modern societies from "patrimonial structures and stratified estates" into "fully differentiated aggregate of persons."[162] In addition, constitutions denote a response to the differentiation of society, that is to say, constitutions facilitate political systems in creating their self-differentiation from other social systems, and this results in a contribution to the differentiated structure of modern society.[163]

A second feature of constitutions underlined by Luhmann is that the political system enables social exchanges in order to obtain a legal form.[164] By virtue of constitutions, these social exchanges are filtered out and unnecessary elements of political systems are blocked. This can be regarded as their function for the abstraction of society's political system.[165]

As seen, Luhmann's understanding of constitutions is considerably related to the legitimacy of political power, but beyond a normative context. This approach is rather theoretical oriented and based on external observations.[166] A full differentiation of the political system is a precondition for its legitimacy. In other words, "legitimacy is the adequately differentiated form of political power."[167] His theory is in search of explaining the status of constitutions and the role of constitutional rights in "positivization, differentiation, and de-politicization of society's power" as communicative elements.[168] However, at this point, Luhmann notes that a structural coupling through constitutions is not possible in the world society due to the segmentary differentiation between states.[169]

That political and constitutional norms are both internal products of society's political power is a remarkable contribution of Luhmann's theory to the constitutional inquiries from a sociological point of view.[170] This can open the way for

---

[159] Ibid., 326.

[160] Ibid.

[161] Ibid. 327.

[162] Ibid.

[163] Ibid.

[164] Ibid., 328.

[165] Ibid.

[166] Mattheis, "System Theory of Luhmann," 632.

[167] Thornhill, "Niklas Luhmann," 329.

[168] Ibid., 330.

[169] Mattheis, "System Theory of Luhmann," 642.

[170] Thornhill, "Niklas Luhmann," 332.

various sociological views that depart from "the society's constitution," and unlike some other sociological views of constitutions, Luhmann's theory helps us avoid considering constitutions as external devices imposed on the power.[171] On the other hand, as mentioned above, Luhmann's contributions were studied and beared to another phase by some scholars, who delineated a global constitutionalization in world society by drawing on his findings on the development of world society, as will be mentioned below.

3.1.1.2.2 Teubner and Fischer-Lescano: Constitutional Fragments

The scholarship of Gunther Teubner and Andreas Fischer-Lescano is multifaceted and makes contributions to the global constitutionalism debate in various terms. From this perspective, a constitution cannot be confined to the contours of state law: "not just ubi societas, ibi ius, as Grotius once said, but ubi societas, ibi constitutio."[172] In their very remarkable article titled "Regime Collisions: A Vain Search For Legal Unity in the Fragmentation of Global Law," they proceed from Luhmann's predictions on the emergence of a fragmented global legal order through social sectoral lines, and draw attention to the intersection of these fragments as a new question of this new legal order:

> should the law of a global society become entangled within sectoral interdependences, a wholly new form of conflicts law will emerge; an "intersystemic conflicts law," derived not from collisions between the distinct nations of private international law, but from collisions between distinct global social sectors.[173]

These global social sectors are perceived in a Luhmannian perspective in the writings of Fischer-Lescano and Teubner. In a nutshell, world society is a "society without an apex or a center" and it is not convenient for an organizational or doctrinal unity of law, since there is no authority for coordination of societal fragments.[174] As mentioned above, an autonomous global system emerges in markets, health, tourism, sport, law, politics etc., and each of these sectors operates within their own closure area. To make it more clear:

> Through their own operative closure, global functional systems create a sphere for themselves in which they are free to intensify their own rationality without regard to other social systems or, indeed, regard for their natural or human environment. They do this for as long as they can; that is, for as long as it is tolerated by their environments.[175]

---

[171] Ibid.

[172] Gunther Teubner, *Constitutional Fragments: Societal Constitutionalism and Globalization*, trans. Gareth Norbury (Oxford: Oxford University Press, 2012), 35.

[173] Andreas Fischer-Lescano and Gunther Teubner, "Regime-collisions: The Vain Search for Legal Unity in the Fragmentation of Global Law," *Michigan Journal of International Law* 25, no. 4 (2004): 1000.

[174] Ibid., 1017.

[175] Ibid., 1006.

Furthermore, their findings regarding the fragmentation of global law rely on three fundamental premises. First of all, fragmentation at stake is so radical that it cannot be perceived by any reductionist approaches. Because of the intensive fragmentation, a normative unity is impossible to come about. The legal fragmentation cannot be overcome, but instead, a weak normative compatibility between the fragments can be achieved.[176]

These points deserve some further explanation. According to Teubner, globalization has robust effects on law making processes. As already mentioned, the newly emerging global private regimes are very central to the emergence of the global law. Traditional ways of law making, where the state lies at the core of the process, are no longer in use, and the focus of law making is shifting towards global private regimes: "Increasingly, global private regimes are producing substantive law without the state, without national legislation or international treaties. (…) in short law making is happening 'alongside the state'."[177] Global law is autonomous and it is based on its own sources. "International organizations, multinational enterprises, global law firms, global funds, global associations, global arbitration courts" are its major actors.[178] At this point, it is of note that the concept "regime" used by these authors is completely different from the classical concept of regime; instead, it marks "a kind of loose coupling of patterns of co-ordination, rule-making, standard-setting, etc, for different political arenas."[179] Apart from that, private regimes are also different from customary law although both concepts have some common features. Both of them have a social origin and they are not products of a (national) sovereign. Further, they exclude a central body which would provide validity for them. But, customary law is the product of diffuse communication, whereas private regimes derive from social differentiation.[180] Furthermore, a unitary customary law no longer makes sense. Instead, various social law norms that concern various global sectors and stem from differing internal organization of norm production have to be taken into consideration.[181]

In Teubner's point of view, the newly emerging constitutional conditions of the global order cannot be grasped unless traditional views for a constitution are left aside. The same is true for the logic of the operation of a legal system. Law should also be considered in line with functional differentiation in the global realm instead

[176] Ibid., 1004.

[177] Gunther Teubner, "Global Private Regimes: Neo-Spontaneous Law and Dual Constitution of Autonomous Sectors?," in *Globalization and Public Governance* ed. Karl-Heinz Ladeur (Ashgate: Aldershot, 2004), 73.

[178] Ibid., 74.

[179] Karl-Heinz Ladeur, "Governance, Theory of" Max Planck Encyclopedia of Public International Law, last updated: September 2010, http://opil.ouplaw.com/view/10.1093/law:epil/9780199231690/law-9780199231690-e940?rskey=8nhhTc&result=5&prd=EPIL, last visit, 01.11.2014. Fischer-Lescano and Teubner, "Regime collisions," 1011.

[180] Teubner, "Global Private Regimes," 76.

[181] Ibid., 82.

of national restraints.[182] Today we can talk about a unity of law in the global realm, but this is no longer structure-based like the nation state model. Instead, it is process-based and subject to many internal conflicts as a result of its heterogeneous form.[183] As a result, the traditional hierarchy of norms is no longer valid. A "centre-periphery divide" has replaced the old form. In this new form, the courts lie in the centre, and political, economic, religious and various forms of subjects are found in the periphery.[184] Global private regimes increasingly generate their own law, independently of nation states and traditional structures of international law. In this regard, Teubner and Fischer-Lescano refer to the *lex mercatoria* of international trade and the *lex digitalis* of the Internet as the most prominent private regimes.[185]

From the point of view of Teubner, constitutionalism beyond the nation states relates to

> constitutional problems arising outside the borders of the nation state in transnational political processes, and at the same time outside the institutionalized political sector, in the "private" sectors of global society.[186]

However, the theoretical framework of the current scholarship remains ineligible to perceive these new formations in terms of the constitutional theory:

> The main problem is to overcome the obstinate state-and-politics centricity of these positions. A sociological theory of societal constitutionalism that has so far remained unheard in the constitutional debate will be able to do that.[187]

At this point as a criticism, according to Ladeur, it is of note that Teubner's view on constitutionalization omits the variety of social and legal norms and the diversity of patterns of coordination between them.[188]

These regimes also generate a legal pluralism in the global context, and they exist independently of actions of the nation states by producing their own substantive law. The fragmented subjects of the global domain, – which conduct different issues ranging from human rights to environment or global trade- generate a kind of global law, transcending the traditional understanding of international law. This is "autonomous global law" in Teubner's words, which is

---

182 Fischer-Lescano and Teubner, "Regime-collisions," 1007.

183 Ibid.

184 Ibid., 1012.

185 Ibid., 1010-1011.

186 Teubner, *Constitutional Fragments*, 1.

187 Ibid., 3.

188 Karl-Heinz Ladeur, "The Emergence of Global Administrative Law and Transnational Regulation" (Instiute for International Law and Justice Working Paper, no. 2011/1, Finalized 04.04.2011, http://www.iilj.org/publications/the-emergence-of-global-administrative-law-and-transnational-regulation-2/), 246, last visit 19.12.2013.

> increasingly basing itself on its own resources. International organizations, multinational enterprises, global law firms, global funds, global associations, global arbitration courts, are legal institutions that are pushing forward the global law making process.[189]

From this point of view, constitutionalization occurs in a fragmented plane and through those subjects of fragmentation, namely the self-contained, transnational, regulatory regimes and their highly specialised primary norms. These norms become constitutional insofar as they establish a closer parallel to state constitutions; that is to say, in a Luhmannian view, when they function as "structural coupling of the reflexive mechanisms of law with those of politics."[190] Additionally, these norms demonstrate typical features of constitutional norms: "provisions on the establishment and exercise of decisionmaking (organizational and procedural rules) on the one hand, the definition of individual freedoms and societal autonomies (fundamental rights) on the other."[191]

By virtue of this process, the centre of regulatory power moves from nation states towards international bodies, and non-public actors like transnational corporations and global civil society.[192] These elements stay alive through a self-constitutionalization process. Although they were formed by the international (or intergovernmental) processes at the outset, they set up their own private orders over time, as very frequently exemplified in the WTO case.[193] Such a transformation in the global society is so prevailing. This is one result of the fact that various types of social law with its own norm production centres have superseded the "unique" customs of public international law.[194]

Teubner suggests dealing with the extension of the concept of law and focusing on the non-statal sources of law in order to better understand this development.[195] The independence of these self-contained regimes relies upon the fact that they have their own legal sources. However, these regimes and the global order generated by them do not frame unique societal values, and the concept of justice has always been absent within their nature.[196] Against this background, the viability of global law is strictly related to its effectivity rather than any values embedded into it, since its roots are not traced to natural law.[197]

---

[189] Teubner, "Global Private Regimes," 74.

[190] Fischer-Lescano and Teubner, "Regime-collisions," 1016.

[191] Ibid.

[192] Teubner, *Constitutional Fragments*, 51.

[193] Ibid, 55.

[194] Ibid, 82.

[195] Ibid., 33.

[196] Stefan Oeter, "Theorizing Global Legal Order - An Institutionalist Perspective," in *Theorizing the Global Legal Order*, ed. Andrew Halpin and Volker Roeben (Oxford: Hart Publishing, 2009), 82.

[197] Andreas Fischer-Lescano and Gunther Teubner, "Reply to Andreas L. Paulus, Consensus as Fiction of Global Law," *Michigan Journal of International Law* 25 (2003-2004): 1067. Also Oeter, "Theorizing Global Legal Order," 82.

According to this perspective, the fragmentation of the international legal order is the key point of this debate.[198] It is not plausible to speak of a unification of the international legal order during the globalization era. However, the "collision of regimes"[199] in a polycentric global society reflects the reality of this society better. This means that the fragmented subjects of global law create their own meta-laws; and as a salient problem of global law, these laws may collide at various points, and may lead to a conflict of norms. As a prominent example, the WTO Appellate Body collides with various human rights regimes or environment protection regimes in many cases. The same is also true of the WHO norms colliding with *lex mercatoria* norms.[200]

Under these circumstances of a polycentric global law, the situation of *jus cogens* rules becomes problematic in terms of the private regimes. The private regimes stem from contractual relations and any source giving mandatory effect to these peremptory norms is still missing.[201]

On the other hand, some scholars regard the constitutional qualities of the micro-constitutionalization processes as dubious. For example, according to Paulus, these processes, either those of WTO or those of human rights regimes, lack a very central feature of domestic constitutions which is "namely a mechanism for balancing all the interests of all stakeholders beyond the narrow confines of trade or human rights."[202]

Moreover, Fischer-Lescano reflects the Luhmannian centre-periphery phenomenon in his writings on global constitutionalism, and he draws attention to the role of international tribunals in the constitutionalization process.[203] In the global legal system, various norms and principles emerge, and their validity can only be conferred by the courts, which are located in the centre of the legal system. Further, according to Fischer-Lescano, the global constitution is the structural coupling of global law and global politics, and jurisdictional norms are very central to this character of constitution.[204]

Overall, this view of global constitutionalism highlights the deep fragmentation, plurality and policentricity of global law, and thereby points to the implausibility of the search of a unity in the international legal order:

---

198 Martti Koskenniemmi, *From Apology to Utopia: The Structure of International Legal Argument; With a New Epilogue* (Cambridge: Cambridge University Press, 2005). Martti Koskenniemi, "The Politics of International Law: 20 Years Later," *European Journal of International Law* 20, no.1 (2009): 12.

199 Fischer-Lescano and Teubner, "Regime-Collisions," 999-1046.

200 Ibid., 1013.

201 Ibid., 1032.

202 Paulus, "International Legal System," 82.

203 Andreas Fischer-Lescano, "Die Emergenz der Globalverfassung," *Zeitschrift für ausländisches öffentliches Recht und Völkerrecht* 63, no. 3 (2003): 738.

204 Ibid.

> In the place of an illusory integration of a differentiated global society, law can only, at the very best, offer a kind of damage limitation. Legal instruments cannot overcome contradictions between different social rationalities. The best law can offer-to use a variation upon an apt description of international law-is to act as a "gentle civilizer of social systems."[205]

In this polycentric environment, fragmented bodies produce their own higher laws in a reflexive manner, and as a result, this gives rise to the microconstitutional forms. In a global order where harmony between these regimes does not exist, the collision of norms is inevitable, and thus we need special meta-norms of conflict in order to eliminate this disharmony. Meta-norms of conflict can generate constitutional norms and create a true constitutional agenda in terms of these authors' understanding of constitution in the global realm, instead of a cosmopolitan construction or global unification of law. This is the most distinctive point of this approach compared with the holistic approaches to global constitutionalism.

3.1.1.3 Compensatory Constitutionalism

Apart from these approaches, global constitutionalism has also been discussed in view of the linkage between transnational law and the domestic constitutional legal orders. In this regard, the growing impacts of transnational law on the national constitutional systems are considered as parts of the constitutionalization process.

Christian Tomuschat attributed a supplementary role to international law in operation of national constitutional laws. He qualified some international treaties as "völkerrechtliche Nebenverfassungen."[206] In this perspective, international law has a foundational role in domestic constitutions. However, this role is not only a formal one, and he believes that the classical monist-dualist distinction is illusory. He rather predicates his idea on the international human rights law that developed in the aftermath of World War II. Against this background, the international community has been in a progress towards a value-oriented and an individual-oriented system, where states act as agents of the international legal order; by leaving a sovereignty-oriented order.[207] In his understanding of international law, the constitutional character of international law implies enshrining and securing fundamental legal values.[208]

---

[205] Fischer-Lescano and Teubner, "Regime-Collisions," 1045.

[206] Christian Tomuschat, *Der Verfassungsstaat im Geflecht der internationalen Beziehungen*, Veröffentlichungen der Vereinigung der deutschen Staatsrechtslehrer 36 (Berlin, New York: de Gruyter, 1978), 7, 51–53 cited by Armin von Bogdandy, "Constitutionalism in International Law: Comment on a Proposal from Germany," *Harvard International Law Journal* 47, no.1 (2006): 228.

[207] Ibid., 228.

[208] Ibid., 231.

Furthermore, a very similar idea is central to the compensatory constitutionalism as a component of the global constitutionalist discourse, which is essentially found within the academic works of Anne Peters.

Borrowing from Skinner, Peters and Armingeon have argued that constitution, constitutionalization and constitutionalism are "evaluative-descriptive terms" which "inevitably evaluate whatever they are employed to describe."[209] According to Peters, states and state constitutions underwent a transformation due to the globalization process which resulted in their weakness or uselessness in many fields, and thus state constitutions can no longer be counted as "total constitutions."[210] Due to globalization, nation states have come across some new issues that extend their capabilities. In other words, domestic constitutionalism is no longer in a position to cope with many conventional societal issues. This amounts to a de-constitutionalization process for the nation states, and therefore, a full constitutional protection can only be provided by the global governance which extends constitutional borders of states.[211]

In addition, the intertwinement of international and domestic legal orders occurs in a number of fields due to globalization. These fields mostly relate to the economic, political, military, legal and power relationships.[212] The state activities became extraterritorial, and the effectiveness of nation states has been reduced. As a result, national and international grounds became complementary. Anne Peters calls this a "constitutional network," where constitutional elements of governance from various levels, either national or international, complement and support each other.[213] This sort of network implies the interaction between these norms from various levels, not as a network of institutions. On the other hand, this networking situation is to be perceived as a response to the opponents of the constitutionalist analysis of international law, who mostly stick to arguing the fragmentation of international law. Peters defines it as a "unity in diversity" or a "flexible diversity."[214]

---

[209] Anne Peters and Klaus Armingeon, "Introduction: Global Constitutionalism from an Interdisciplinary Perspective," *Indiana Journal of Global Legal Studies* 16, no. 2 (2009): 387.

[210] Peters, "Compensatory Constitutionalism," 580.

[211] Ibid.

[212] Ibid. 591.

[213] Ibid. 601. However, as she clarifies in her text, what is meant by a constitutional network is quite different from what is implied in various disciplines, notably in recent sociology. Thus, the term of network should not lead to a confusion, in consideration of the term "network" which is largely used in this project, beginning from the first Chapter.

[214] Ibid. 602. At this point, it should be repeated that fragmentation is not only an argument of those who reject the idea of global constitutionalism. As seen in the previous section concerning "Microconstitutionalism," some alternative approaches to global constitutionalism also employ it broadly. In a similar vein, Peters argues that fragmentation should not be viewed as an absolute obstacle against constitutionalization in the global realm. Instead, fragmentation and constitutionalization nourish each other to a great extent, and they can be regarded as "two sides of the same coin." Peters, "Fragmentation and Constitutionalization," 1030.

In Peters' own words, global constitutionalism is

> a strand of thought (an outlook or perspective) and a political agenda which advocate the application of constitutional principles, such as the rule of law, checks and balances, human rights protection, and democracy, in the international legal sphere in order to improve the effectivity and the fairness of the international legal order.[215]

In this respect, constitutional principles stemming from domestic constitutions gain a further function in the international legal order by virtue of global constitutionalism. However, she argues that national and international discourses on constitutionalism are basically unrelated, and the global constitutionalism discourse mostly refers to a "thicker legalization and institutionalization," which could be handled without touching upon the concept of constitution.[216]

Furthermore, her theory refutes other global constitutionalism theories in terms of some further aspects of constitutionalism. For example, borrowing from Ackermann, she focuses on any possibility of constitutional moments in the global realm, and even though she admits that this may be possible when we consider the transformations led in 1945 and 1989, the gradual formation of global law does not comform with the prerequisites of the traditional constitutionalism.[217] Additionally, from a functional approach, it is hard to distinguish constitutional laws from ordinary laws since ordinary regulations of international law are also likely to perform some of the functions of alleged constitutional norms.[218] For these reasons, this theory rejects any possibility of an international constitution in a formal sense.

The theory of compensatory constitutionalism in the first instance suggests linking these two academic discourses, domestic and global ones. The basic function of global constitutionalism is to compensate deficiencies of national constitutions. In this respect, it rather concerns constitutionalizing the global governance.[219]

Some other scholars have analyzed the above-mentioned compensatory relationship between transnational and national domains as well. According to Walter, in parallel with Peters, international law supplements and partially replaces national laws. However, he does not concur with those who assert a constitutionalization in the global realm as a consequence of this process.[220] In conclusion, compensatory constitutionalism relies on the basic idea that contemporary constitutionalism indispensably exceeds the national borders in order to maintain its existence, and for this purpose, it defines constitutionalization in descriptive terms.

---

[215] Peters, "Compensatory Constitutionalism," 583.

[216] Ibid. 597.

[217] Ibid. 599.

[218] Ibid.

[219] Ibid. 610.

[220] Christian Walter, "International Law in a Process of Constitutionalization," in *New Perspectives on the Divide Between National and International Law*, ed. Janne Nijman and Andre Nollkaemper (Oxford: Oxford University Press, 2007), 198.

3.1.2 Global Constitutionalism as a "Noetic" Idea

Apart from these scholars dealing with the assumption of an ongoing constitutionalization in the global realm, some other scholars approach this idea critically on the ground that the idea of a global constitutionalization does not reflect the truth of the international legal order. However, these scholars still presume a future possibility of a global constitution from a different perspective. In this regard, they reconstruct global constitutionalism as an intellectual interest field, and this is why we could name this category as "noetic."[221] This category could be best epitomized by Koskenniemmi's and Schwöbel's ideas on global constitutionalism.

As a prominent scholar, Martti Koskenniemi's opinions on global constitutionalism are quite remarkable. The response of Koskenniemi to the global constitutionalist debate can be regarded as critical. There are a number of grounds for his scepticism in his academic works. According to Koskenniemi, a resemblance between domestic and global constitutionalism can hardly be established. First of all, the international realm lacks a *pouvoir constituant*. In addition, the idea of a global constitution is not desirable, since a constitution in the international realm is likely to belong to an empire; that is to say, it would presumably rise as a constitution of an imperial actor.[222] What is more, the cosmopolitan turn in international law in the aftermath of the end of the Cold War has been overshadowed by a number of subsequent developments. In general, these developments relate to the new regulatory needs, and also to the incapacity of the traditional means to meet these needs. According to Koskenniemi, these developments are the "deformalisation," the "fragmentation" in international law and the "empire," which reflects a single dominant actor in international politics.[223] In this respect, as an "architectural project," constitutionalism is one of the responses developed by the international lawyers against these facts.[224] He underlines the artificial texture of this issue and the constructive efforts of international law scholars in various points: "Constitutionalism and pluralism are abstract responses to the emergence of multiple legal regimes. (…) Constitutionalism and pluralism are generalizing doctrines with an ambivalent political significance."[225]

Given these facts, Koskenniemi rejects one single way for a constitutionalist reading of international law. Instead, he suggests understanding global constitutionalism as "a mindset,- a tradition and a sensibility about how to act in a political world.":[226]

---

[221] Here I basically refer to the ancient Greek meaning of "noetic:" "action of perceiving or thinking" independently of experiments or senses. http://www.merriam-webster.com/dictionary/noetic, last visit 01.03.2015.

[222] Martti Koskenniemmi, "The Fate of Public International Law: Between Technique and Politics," *The Modern Law Review* 70, no.1 (2007): 19.

[223] Koskenniemi, "Constitutionalism as Mindset," 13.

[224] Ibid., 18.

[225] Koskenniemi, "Fate of Public International Law," 24.

[226] Koskenniemi, "Constitutionalism as Mindset," 9.

> (...) constitutionalism is not necessarily tied to any definite institutional project, European or otherwise. Irrespective of the functional needs or interests that laws may seek to advance, a Kantian view would focus on the practice of professional judgment in applying them. Less than an architectural project, constitutionalism would then be a programme of moral and political regeneration. This is what I mean by the description of constitutionalism as a "mindset."[227]

According to Koskenniemi, this would be considered as an alternative reading of the Kantian political philosophy. At this point, he underlines an overlooked feature of the cosmopolitan and republican ideas of Kant. It was fairly important for Kant that regulative universality had become a part of actual politics.[228] In this regard, the use of constitutional vocabulary in his works also reflected a criticism against the actual politics of his age, in particular against the counter-revolutionary attitude of Prussia.[229] The current global constitutionalist discourse has a similar focus, as the constitutional vocabulary targets inequalities in the international realm and universalizes the scope of problems.[230] Accordingly, he argues that the current global constitutionalist contributions are not satisfying, since they rely on the conventional law of diplomatic institutions, instead of the Kantian ideals of freedom and self-determination.[231] In this respect, as demonstrated in the quoted passage above, he suggests understanding global constitutionalism as a mindset for international lawyers in rebuilding their approach to international law by drawing on Kantian principles.

As another noetic idea, the theory of Christine J. Schwöbel argues that the common features of global constitutionalist theories remain incapable of surviving a global project for various reasons, and she underlines the theoretical shortcomings of global constitutionalist ideas. For this purpose, she focuses on some assumptions which are common in all global constitutionalist ideas. One assumption is that the idea of the constitution cannot be confined to nation states constitutions.[232] Proceeding from common features of national constitutions, Schwöbel draws attention to the similar features in some founding documents of international or transnational institutions, and thus she advocates the idea that constitutionalism has a new trajectory in the international and transnational sphere. The second assumption is about the increasing homogeneity of the international domain, which is frequently contested by opinions which focus on the fragmentation of the international legal order and the fact of hegemony in international politics.[233] The third assumption is about the universality of global constitutionalism.[234] Schwöbel at that point emphasizes

[227] Ibid.

[228] Ibid., 35.

[229] Ibid., 34-35.

[230] Ibid., 35.

[231] Ibid., 36.

[232] Schwöbel, *Global Constitutionalism*, 89.

[233] Ibid., 95.

[234] Ibid., 107.

the fact that global constitutionalist ideas are products of the western scholars and the western legal culture, and she examines the assumption of the universality of these ideas in view of this fact.

Nevertheless, she does not leave the issue of the viability of global constitutionalism aside; instead, she suggests dealing with it in a completely different way. Schwöbel questions whether or not the idea of global constitutionalism may be reconstructed in some way. She states that in view of the current structure of the international legal order, global constitutionalism is not entirely unthinkable; rather it would be better to consider it as an ongoing process of international law.[235] Further, she suggests viewing global constitutionalism as a political fact. We should avoid seeking a fixed framework; rather expect, by referring to the notion of Derrida, "democracy to come;" "constitutionalism to come" by considering global constitutionalism as a future project. In other words, the normativity of a constitutional order and a constitution have not become a concrete issue yet, "but are features of the promise of constitutionalism to *come*." She calls such a restructuration "organic global constitutionalism," which arises as a new approach to global constitutionalism, and which is supposed to be purified from the faults and failures of other approaches.[236] While developing this concept, she benefits from Jacques Derrida's idea of the future as a promise without content; that is to say, she means that global constitutionalism is just an open space without a fixed content. What is going to concretize the future promise is the discourse theory of Habermas. In other words, organic global constitutionalism is not a blueprint, a stasis or so. It is a living structure and a forum which has certain functions for debates on the fragmentation, legitimacy and the role of law in the society. At this juncture, she admits that this is not a purely new concept, but a compilation of various approaches. Schwöbel argues that constitutions are frameworks for allocating power, either political or economic, and the ideas of global constitutionalism rely upon the belief that "law has the potency to impact on social reality." In addition, the global constitutionalism debate is held in order to legitimate international law.[237]

3.2 Viability of Global Constitutionalism

As presented above in the preceding section, the discourse of global constitutionalism has seen various contributions regarding the emerging structure of global law under conditions of globalization. Since there is no formally promulgated written constitution in the international legal order, this debate evidently lacks an empirical object. In this regard, the viability of the idea of global constitutionalism basically concerns two main questions: "Is there an ongoing process of constitutionalization," and "can

[235] Ibid., 133.

[236] Ibid., 148.

[237] Ibid.

constitutionalism reflect the truth of current conditions of international law?" In this section, the "factuality" of global constitutionalist ideas will be discussed. To that end, the discourse on global constitutionalism will be held in multiple dimensions. First, the responses to the idea of global constitutionalism from various scholars will be glanced. Following that, the anatomy of the global constitutionalism discourse will be drawn by focusing on the commonalities of the global constitutionalist ideas and the main deficiencies of this discourse that lead to the imperfection thereof.

3.2.1 Responses and Challenges to Global Constitutionalism

The theories of global constitutionalism mentioned above have also seen various responses from the legal scholarship. Some opposing views have arisen; although they agree with some findings of global constitutionalism theories regarding the transformation in international law. In addition, as mentioned above, some of the global constitutionalism ideas have been nourished by such an opposition to the other global constitutionalist theories. The problem mostly arises in the interpretation of legal, political and social developments that are involved in the global constitutionalism discourse. On the other hand, there are some other responses that challenge the fundamental findings of global constitutionalism theories. In this regard, negative responses to the global constitutionalism debate can be classified basically as: (1) those which certainly reject this idea on the ground that it is unrealistic and a result of the false analysis of international law and the international society, (2) those who argue that constitutionalism does not fit with the reality of the global order, although they agree on the need for defining global law in terms of an emerging public order (such as some proponents of global administrative law and legal pluralism), (3) those who focus on fundamental deficits of the constitutionalization process, such as rule of law, democracy etc. as well as desirability thereof (some above-mentioned scholars as participants of the global constitutionalism discourse are also found in this category). Since group (2) was already touched upon in the preceding chapter, the first and third groups will be mentioned below.

3.2.1.1 "Unrealistic" Perspective of Global Constitutionalism

A common objection to global constitutionalism theories rises from those who argue that the idea of a constitution beyond states does not make sense, since the detachment of constitutions from states is not possible. In other words, the proponents of this idea opine that the concept of constitution strictly belongs to states, as it arose and developed through the emergence of modern states. Therefore, it does not fit into a transnational or global scheme. Dieter Grimm explicitly advocates this approach.[238] Furthermore, Grimm states that the legalization of the international legal

[238] Grimm, "Constitution in Process of Denationalization," 447.

order does not amount to a constitutionalization, and does not reach the standards of constitutionalism. The use of constitutionalism in this way results in the exclusion of democratic elements of constitutionalism.[239] In addition, Grimm argues that the UN Charter, in this sense, contributes to the legalization of the international order, however, this legalization process does not amount to a constitutionalization.[240]

As mentioned above, fragmentation is a very central issue of the contemporary international law as well as the global constitutionalist discourse. In view of the fragmentation of international law, some scholars argue that the current international law rather resembles the medieval state orders, where there were many different bearers of public power. Hence, this scattered order is not very compatible with the preconditions for a constitution, like coherence and comprehensiveness.[241] On the other hand, from another perspective on constitutional sociology and history, various codes of modern constitutionalism were embedded in the high-medieval period.[242] Therefore, this analogy is not completely helpful in demonstrating the irrelevance of such a fragmented order to a constitutionalization process. At this point, it is of note that modern national constitutionalization processes were born into very scattered political orders, and that constitutionalization processes inherently trigger the integration of a fragmented order.

Another response to the debate on fragmentation and constitutionalization comes from Anne Peters. Peters opines that the problem of fragmentation have been overstated in this debate, due to the "[e]mpirical findings on the scarcity of conflicts, the prevailing scheme of parallelism and reconciliation of norms from different regimes, and the migration of norms from one regime to another."[243] Irreconcilable norms and case law are rarely found in this context, and international courts act with deliberation in preventing norm and interpretation conflicts. Against this background, Peters advances the claim that international law is in fact less fragmented than propounded in the debate. Further, constitutional perpective is to be viewed as an integral part of the fragmentation debate that "usefully complements" it.[244] A similar argument was also discussed in Al-Dulimi ruling of the ECtHR. Judge Pinto De Albuquerque et al stress that constitutionalization in the international legal order occurs in various fragmented bodies, however such fragmented constitutionalization is an "intra-systemic" matter of the global realm. That is to say, these constitutionalization practices do not mark self-contained, hermetic regimes "as if

[239] Dieter Grimm, "The Achievement of Constitutionalism and its Prospects in a Changed World," in *The Twilight of Constitutionalism?* ed. Petra Dobner and Martin Loughlin (Oxford: Oxford University Press, 2010), 21.

[240] Ibid., 19.

[241] Ibid., 18.

[242] Christopher J. A. Thornhill, *A Sociology of Constitutions: Constitutions and State Legitimacy in Historical-sociological Perspective* (Cambridge: Cambridge University Press, 2011).

[243] Peters, "Fragmentation and Constitutionalization," 1028.

[244] Ibid. 1028-1029.

they were isolated towers." Instead, they highlight that "decentralised plurality may foster cross-fertilisation and synergy between competing legal orders."[245]

3.2.1.2 "Flaws" of Global Constitutionalism

A common challenge to the universalist and cosmopolitan ideas as well as the global constitutionalism theories is the relativism and particularism that basically arise as a critique against western legal tradition.[246] In particular, the negligence of non-western legal traditions and the monolithic and western-centric structure of universal ideas are central to these critiques: "How can one seriously claim to be a universalist, if one is ethnocentrically unaware of the ideas and values of other belief systems and traditions?"[247] From this point of view, the European and Anglo-American character of these studies hinders the establishment of an overarching discourse. According to scholars who point out the hegemonic character of integrationist ideas, the domination of European states and subsequently of the United States over international law, and the facts of imperialism and colonialism hurdle the attempts to view a unified international legal order. From this point of view, international law has always been a western law, and in particular European Law.[248] Under these circumstances, a legitimacy problem is likely to be fixed, and this is true for global constitutionalism theories as well. In this sense, the integrationist approaches to international law and global constitutionalism may serve as instruments to institutionalize the hegemonic domination.[249] However, in view of the historical formation of national constitutional orders, it can hardly be affirmed that unification through a constitutionalization process occurs without the hegemonic domination of any power, or that a constitutionalization always requires an equalization of the components of a social order. Contrariwise, the modern revolutionary constitutions of western countries have reflected the hegemony of the newly emerging social classes over the older

[245] Al-Dulimi and Montana Management Inc. v. Switzerland, Concurring Opinion, para. 71.

[246] Neil Walker, "Universalism and Particularism in Human Rights: Trade-Off or Productive Tension?" (Edinburgh School of Law Research Paper no. 2012/10, 2012, http://ssrn.com/abstract=2021071), last visit 13.04.2015. Also, Boaventura de Sousa Santos, *Toward a New Legal Common Sense: Law, Globalization, and Emancipation* (London: Butterworths, 1995). William Twining, "Implications of 'Globalisation' for Law as a Discipline," in *Theorizing the Global Legal Order*, ed. Andrew Halpin and Volker Roeben, (Oxford: Hart Publishing, 2009). David J. Bederman, *Globalization and International Law* (New York: Palgrave Macmillan, 2008). Jack Donnelly, "Cultural Relativism and Universal Human Rights," *Human Rights Quarterly* 6 (1984): 400-419.

[247] At this point, Twining rejects even more moderate ideas that human rights discourse provides a "framework," "arena" or "meeting ground" for a dialogue, debate of negotiation of values and beliefs between different systems, which were mainly reflected by Habermas and Stuart Hampshire. Twining "Implications of Globalisation," 56.

[248] Schwöbel, *Global Constitutionalism*, 98.

[249] Ibid., 102.

ones. It is indeed a notable characteristic of modern constitutions that constitutions were configured to exclude alternative cultures, and they have never been capable of reflecting the diversity of the modern society.[250] Therefore, this argument is not very convincing. However, questioning possibilities for a constitutional transformation or an existence of an order through some facts, and questioning the legitimacy of that transformation or existence of an order are completely different things. Thus, there is still room to consider these arguments as the challenges to global constitutionalism theories. First of all, the euro- or western-centric character of the global constitutionalist discourse is most likely to lead to the question of "how global" the order envisioned by global constitutionalists is. Further, through what societal dynamics does it operate? Does it have a consent from all the relevant actors, and in whose name has such a constitutionalization process proceeded? It is evident that the idea of universalism is not a spotless idea. Orientalism and interventionism have mostly accompanied this idea.[251] It was employed by the imperialist powers in an illegitimate way, in order to achieve their selfish interests under colonialism. It was even considered a basis for the imperialist expansionism in many interventions to the non-western world. Therefore, as Wallerstein argues, today it needs a restructuration in view of these facts.[252] On the other hand, it has to be noted that some global constitutionalism theories already take this legitimacy problem into consideration, and they do not remain silent to these problems at all. Furthermore, as can be seen in the example of the micro-constitutionalism debate, not all global constitutionalism theories are after a global or universal overarching structure.

Further, the western local political and legal cultures have also been quite influential in the construction of the ideas on global constitutionalism. This fact is also likely to be employed to demonstrate the linkage of global constitutionalism to the European scholarship. As an example, the outnumbering contributions of German scholars to this debate are striking, and it has often been stated that global constitutionalism is a European conception.[253] Armin von Bogdandy argues that this has to do with the German approach to international law in the Post-war era that is inclined to identify the international legal order via common global values and goods: "understanding current international law as a building block of a global legal community has been a constant thread of thought among many German international law scholars."[254] At this point, von Bogdany highlights that the other major European countries, such as France and Britain, pursued completely different approaches to international law during this period.[255]

[250] James Tully, *Strange Multiplicity: Constitutionalism in an Age of Diversity* (Cambridge: Cambridge University Press, 2007), 7.

[251] Immanuel Wallerstein, *European Universalism: The Rhetoric of Power* (New York: New Press, 2006).

[252] Ibid.

[253] Schwöbel, *Global Constitutionalism*, 107.

[254] Von Bogdandy, "Constitutionalism in International Law," 224.

[255] Ibid., 223.

Accordingly, this point was also discussed in terms of the question "how global is global law," which brings the spatial dimension of global law into question.[256] Hans Lindahl opines that the word "global" does not illustrate the spatial dimension of global law at all. According to Lindahl, global law comprises the overlapping legal orders. By referring to Saskia Sassen's idea that "global law is itself a form of local," he argues that the putative spatial divide between local and global is in fact only a fault line of globalization.[257] Against this background, the ideas of global law and global constitutionalism are misleading to some extent since they do not specify the correct spatial basis.

In addition to these, Kirsch argues a striking point that global constitutionalism theories are in search of a continuity with central political concepts and domestic traditions. In so doing, they strive to prevent the normative ruptures in the globalization debate.[258] However, given the intense diversity of global (post-national) realm, such a template of constitutionalism fails to respond to the facts of the global world in a realistic way.[259] The main problem which gives rise to such an incompatibility is, as Tully underlines, the inability of modern constitutionalism to overcome the cultural and social diversity, on the ground that modern constitutionalism hinges on the ideas of impartiality and uniformity.[260] On that account, constitutions arise as the primary, collective political framework of the society; however, they have not been configured to serve for drastically diverse communities. In addition, the core of national or foundational constitutionalism envisages a hierarchical structure in a political order, which cannot easily run in with the heterarchy of the *sui generis* governance on a global level. Hence, the global constitutionalism theories should leave referring to national constitutionalism aside, so as to keep alive the claims on the extension of constitutionalism beyond the state.[261] On the other hand, the global domain is a new and mostly unknown space, although global constitutionalism theories attempt to tame and organize it in a rational way.[262]

Therefore, an analysis of the global domain in strict comparison with the national domains may lead to serious mistakes. Kymlicka points out the same argument, and suggests a new language while dealing with global matters, by cutting off the link between the global discourse and the domestic ones.[263] Consequently, from

[256] Hans Lindahl, "Legal Order and the 'Globality' of Global Law," in *Reflections on Global Law,* ed. Shavana Musa and Eefje de Volder (Leiden: Brill, 2013), 36-44.

[257] Ibid., 37-44.

[258] Nico Krisch, *Beyond Constitutionalism: The Pluralist Structure of Postnational Law* (Oxford: Oxford University Press, 2010), 67.

[259] Ibid., 61. For a similar view on this issue: Ladeur, "Emergence of Global Administrative Law," 243.

[260] Tully, *Strange Multiplicity*.

[261] Krisch, *Beyond Constitutionalism*, 61.

[262] Ibid.

[263] Ibid., 193. Will Kymlicka, *Contemporary Political Philosophy: An Introduction*, 2nd ed. (Oxford: Oxford Books, 2002).

this perspective, to apply the concept of national constitution to the global domain should be seen as a categorical problem and an inadequate argument to frame such an asymmetric domain.[264]

Furthermore, the bitter experience of the European Union regarding the Treaty Establishing a Constitution for Europe has given rise to some further objections as well. From this point of view, the EU has already proven that it does not have the convenient structure for a constitutional order. The lack of a European people and a collective identity has arisen as the prominent issue. These problems have also gone hand in hand with the democracy deficits of the European Union; and the legitimacy level of a constitution has remained too low, compared with the nation states. Against this background, the constitutional treaty does not lead to an internal transformation, that is to say, it does not become a constitution in the real sense. Thus, this reveals the fact that applying national patterns to the European Union is in vain.[265] Another contribution in this context argues that the attempts to build a European constitutionalism within the context of the traditional state constitutionalism reflect a gross fault; since new and hybrid forms of governance, like networks, became widespread and overruled old forms over time.[266] It has accordingly been stated that a new form of administrative action has been emerging, and this is an uncertain form that is open to new experimentations in constitutional law.[267]

In a similar vein, global constitutionalism has seen some further harsh critiques. The critical opinions of Phillip Allot are remarkable. Allot believes that the alleged global constitutional developments, like the UN Charter, are in fact

> the groundwork of international oligarchy of oligarchies –not "We the Peoples of the United Nations," but we, governments speaking in the name of states-with a Security Council that is a collective monarchy.[268]

That is to say, Allott finds more improbable than ever the realization of a republicanization of nations in a Kantian fashion.

Furthermore, the transnational regimes have evolved without any "revolutionary consciousness" unlike the constitutionalization processes of the nation states. Therefore, these regimes have faced a number of specific legitimacy issues. They also pose problems in regard to the democratic principle, as Brunkhorst states, "[t]hey negatively integrate society with a minimum of solidarity, but as for positive integration they lack politically inclusive, democratic solidarity. They are effective, but not democratically so."[269] From this point of view, the rise of the democracy

[264] Walter, "International Law," 192.

[265] Dieter Grimm, "Does Europe Need a Constitution?," *European Law Journal* 1, no. 3 (1995): 297.

[266] Karl-Heinz Ladeur, "'We, the European People…'-Relache?," *European Law Journal* 14, no. 2 (2008): 149.

[267] Ladeur, "Emergence of Global Administrative Law," 244.

[268] Phillip Allott, "The Emerging International Aristocracy" *New York University Journal of International Law and Politics* 35, no. 2 (2002), 336.

[269] Brunkhorst, *Solidarity*, 7.

deficit of these entities is inevitable. The legitimacy problems of these regimes are of other aspects as well. For instance, in terms of the law making processes, the international legal rules are also far from reflecting the justice-oriented legal orders.[270] On the other hand, national democratic regimes are in need of the democratization of the public law of transnational and international organizations.[271]

3.2.2 *Interrogation for Viability of Global Constitutionalism*

The global constitutionalism theories have so far been discussed in terms of two ends of thought. Briefly, one end of the spectrum basically argues that the concepts of constitution and constitutionalism are likely to be applied to transnational law in view of some specific developments, whereas the other end mostly refers to the utopic or morally problematic aspects of this discourse. As stated before, this research project deems global constitutionalism to be an umbrella term. In order to identify this term more specifically, the commonalities of the present contributions should be specified. These commonalities should include what global constitutionalism includes as well as what it lacks. In this regard, unveiling common deficiencies is fairly important in examining the viability of the idea of global constitutionalism.

3.2.2.1 Commonalities of Global Constitutionalism Theories

As touched upon above, the philosophical and ideological backgrounds of global constitutionalism theories vary considerably. This makes it difficult to examine a single idea of global constitutionalism in order to examine its viability.

Nevertheless, according to Schwöbel, global constitutionalism still has a number of common key themes. Global constitutionalism theories basically rely on the limitation of power in international law, the increasing institutionalization, the social idealism that is reflected mostly through the pre-eminence of human rights, the increasing standard-setting capacity of international law and the individual rights protection mechanisms.[272] Even on the assumption that these premises are true, it is still dubious that these themes could be viewed as a foundational basis for a constitutionalization in the global realm. This is a weak point of this discourse since global constitutionalism does not suggest a common framework for the concept of constitution. A constitution has multiple dimensions, such as historical, legal, sociological etc. The true anatomy of the constitution has been largely neglected by overlooking these dimensions, and the concept of constitution has rather been perceived in analytical positivist terms. Above all, constitution was born into the

---

[270] Oeter, "Theorizing Global Legal Order," 81.

[271] Brunkhorst, *Solidarity*, 8.

[272] Schwöbel, *Global Constitutionalism*, 109-132.

newly emerging modern nation states, and it evolved within this framework. Whatever methodology is pursued, every global constitutionalism theory refers to this evolutionary line of the concept of constitution. Therefore, it is evident that national constitutions have constantly been the main reference of this discourse. On the other hand, this proves that the global constitutionalism discourse suffers from the indeterminacy of the concept of constitution. This also rises as a major problem of the constitutional theory, which is dominantly positivist. However, those who follow the Luhmannian conception of a constitution are likely to be counted as an exception. Among the global constitutionalism ideas that were presented in this chapter, the meaning of constitution is clear only in the "microconstitutionalism theory," as the proponents of this approach follow a certain idea of constitution whose contours were clearly drawn. In this regard, as the structural coupling of global law and politics, the global constitution consists of jurisdiction norms, *jus cogens* and norms that determine how norms are validated, such as Article 38 of the ICJ Statute.[273]

Further, some scholars abstain from using a constitutional language although they point to the integrative processes in the global order. For example, Von Bogdandy argues that a democratic federation cannot exist in the global realm. Instead, global institutions that function efficiently can enable national democracies to cooperate successfully in order to build an integrated world.[274]

There are also some other scholars who prefer alternative terms instead of constitutionalization for the developments in the global realm. Given a number of formal and informal developments, Wiener speaks of an "enhanced constitutional quality" of the international order. When this quality of the international relations was raised, the international realm transformed into a ground for pluralist international relations from an anarchic society of states.[275] These developments range from a transformation in the character of treaty law to the newly emerged social practices of the international interaction, the legal cross-referencing, blogging etc.

3.2.2.2 What Does the Global Constitutionalism Discourse Lack?

Above all, the discourse on global constitutionalism lacks an empirical research object, namely a written formal constitution in the global realm. It is beyond doubt that the lack of a written constitution, and of any political movement or attempt at triggering a world constitution is the most significant ground for scepticism for constitutionalization in the global realm.[276] Therefore, the global constitutionalism discourse deals with only the facts that may imply a future establishment of a constitution. However, the question still remains: to what degree does the global constitutionalism discourse involve all the prerequisites of a constitution?

[273] Fischer-Lescano, "Emergenz der Globalverfassung."

[274] Von Bogdandy, "Constitutionalism in International Law," 240.

[275] Wiener, "Global Constitutionalism: Mapping," 11.

[276] Peters, "Fragmentation and Constitutionalization," 1019.

This question is found at the core of the debate of constitutionalism in the global realm.[277] It is also the distinguishing fact of this discourse from other integrationist ideas, say, legal pluralism and global administrative law. In other words, to what degree global constitutionalism reflects the contemporary appearances of the concept of constitution must be the first step of interrogation. The answer to this question is the key to the examination of the viability of the idea of global constitutionalism. That is to say, the viability of the idea of a global constitution relies upon the inclusion of the contemporary constitutionalism by the discursive object of this idea.

In this regard, it is also of note that a missing point of this debate is that the interdisciplinary context of global constitutionalism has not been well established, and the relevant studies mostly express their interest in terms of their own disciplinary approaches.[278] To be more clear, what is pointed here is the inadequacy of conceptual borrowings between different disciplines. More specifically, this problem can be described as the lack of contributions from constitutional theory to international law discourse or *vice versa*.

The constitutional experiences of nation states are very central to the understanding of constitution by the contributors of the global constitutionalism discourse.[279] However, as mentioned before, the main problem is their incapability of providing the continuity of national constitutionalism in the global realm:

> Postnational constitutionalism is an attempt to establish continuity with central political concepts and domestic traditions; it tries to avoid the normative rupture often feared in discussions of globalization and global governance. (…) Most approaches to postnational constitutionalism are too thin to redeem the full promise of the domestic constitutionalist tradition and therefore cannot provide the continuity they seek.[280]

In a similar vein, some argue that the meaning of the concept of constitution undergoes a transformation when it is transferred to the global realm.[281] Accordingly, the idea of constitution in the global constitutionalism debate does not comply with "the reality of constitution" since this debate runs quite far from the contemporary dynamics of the constitutional theory.[282] As a result, the idea of constitution remains in the dark and global constitutionalism deals with a blurred conception of constitution. Kjaer explains this as "[t]he vast majority of the existing works on law and

---

[277] Anne Peters, "Global Constitutionalism Revisited," *International Legal Theory* 11 (2005): 42.

[278] Antje Wiener, "Constitutionalism Unbound: A Practice Approach to Normativity" (Paper presented at 'Practice, Ethics and Normativity' at the Annual Millennium Conference 'Out Of The Ivory Tower - Weaving the Theories and Practice of International Relations, London School of Economics & Political Science, London, 22-23 October 2011, http://ssrn.com/abstract=2103049 or http://dx.doi.org/10.2139/ssrn.2103049), 9, last visit 11.04.2014.

[279] Kjaer, *Constitutionalism in Global Realm*, 7.

[280] Krisch, *Beyond Constitutionalism*, 67.

[281] Walter, "International Law," 194.

[282] Kjaer, *Constitutionalism in Global Realm*, 7.

politics in the global realm assume that the concepts of law and the political remain unchanged."[283]

Seen in this light, one of the most striking quandaries of global constitutionalism theories is that they have so far not found an overarching basis or a common framework to define a constitution. Therefore, these theories reconstruct the concept of constitution as a fairly abstract and broad term, and mostly neglect some contemporary aspects of this concept. However, this leads to a rupture with reality, or to the exclusion of some constitutional experiences. This evidently creates a weak spot for global constitutionalism theories, which discuss constitutionalization through an insufficiently reconstructed image of modern constitutions. In some cases, this issue gains a more ambiguous character, as some scholars make contributions in vague terms, such as the "constitutional quality." As a matter of fact, the nebulous concept of "constitutionalization" reflects this vagueness as well. These contributions often give rise to the negligence of the core issues of the matter. These points require specifying the factual dimension of the concept of constitution.

This issue was also regarded as a "translation" problem among some scholars. According to these scholars, the prominent question that arises in this debate is whether or not the concept of constitution can be translated into the non-state level, and whether or not this is a legitimate attempt.[284] At this juncture, one should also ask whether state constitutions are of a value that is worth transferring and applying to the non-state context.[285]

In this regard, Neil Walker draws attention to a significant point which is mostly ignored among the scholars dealing with global constitutionalism: "(…) what is the added value of the invocation of the term 'constitutional' to endorse the favoured narrative of progress?"[286] This is also related to another question regarding the constitutional quality of international law as argued by some scholars. For instance, whether or not "coherence" and continuous existence of networks of regulation are sufficient enough to generate a constitutional order remains in the dark, since these criteria are very abstract. From this point of view, a constitution includes a set of general standards, and it also functions as a mechanism to implement these standards within a legal order.[287] However, it is not clear how general these standards should be understood.

As agreed by most of the global constitutionalism theories, global constitutionalism is to be considered as a continuum of modern constitutionalism. It has to do with public power, freedoms and institutional settings. It deals with these topics in a progressive manner, and strives to reconstruct their spatial basis. However, this

---

[283] Ibid., 8.

[284] Neil Walker, "Postnational Constitutionalism and the Problem of Translation," in *European Constitutionalism Beyond the State*, ed. J.H.H. Weiler and Marlene Wind (Cambridge: Cambridge University Press, 2003), 27.

[285] Ibid., 32.

[286] Walker, "Making a World of Difference," 10.

[287] Paulus, "International Legal System," 86.

does not affect the fact that it belongs to the discourses of modern constitutionalism and modern society. Therefore, the answer to the question "what is to be translated" is embedded in the identification of the contemporary constitutionalism. In order to examine the viability of global constitutionalism, first of all the "translation subject" needs to be identified clearly through the contemporary constitutionalism. For this purpose, the next chapter shall be dedicated to identifying the contemporary meaning of constitution.

However, this outcome needs a bit further explanation. At this point, a crucial problem of global constitutionalism should be pointed out. As mentioned before, the concept of constitution originates from the experiences of modern nation states; and these experiences are still the only reference points for global constitutionalism, since there is evidently no written, promulgated global constitution. In this regard, global constitutionalism has been identified as an assimilation concept (Assimilationskonzept) since it deals with the idea of a constitution in the global realm independently of any tangible formal development, and it is rather discussed around an idea of an uncompleted process of constitutionalization.[288] The content and claims of global constitutionalism theories have been shaped accordingly, and these theories pursued a method of application of an image of a domestic constitution to the global level. However, the main shortfall of the global constitutionalism discourse is that it neglects the fact that the meaning of a constitution is quite relative, on the ground that different national constitutional experiences spawned various traditions of constitutions. This diversity has also been reflected within many studies on constitutional theory, and it has also been subject to various debates in this field. What is more, Thornhill argues that the global constitutionalist discourse remains silent about various qualitative transformations in the character of modern constitutions, and they lack a paradigmatic framework to explain these changes, while they commonly adhere to the idea that an emerging global constitutional order reflects a breakup from the classical lineage of constitutionalism.[289] Furthermore, Thornhill views this problem as the result of a lack of a sociological perspective to the concept of constitution, despite some global constitutionalist theories having already originated from sociological approaches to transnational law:

> They [global constitutionalist theories] do not examine the inner reflexive meanings of these norms, they do not probe the structural reasons for the distillation of distinct constitutional norms, and they do not directly link changing norms to changing societal structures: the inner meaning of norms for society is not placed in the focus of inquiry.[290]

Consequently, he argues that we need a new paradigm to disclose the relationship between global constitutionalism and the developments in constitutional law in consideration of their deeper sociological causes.[291]

---

[288] Viellechner, "Verfassung als Chiffre," 239.

[289] Chris Thornhill, "Rights and Constituent Power in the Global Constitution," *International Journal of Law in Context* 10 (2014): 371.

[290] Ibid., 372.

[291] Ibid.

Nevertheless, global constitutionalism theories remain silent towards these debates to a large extent. As a result, the global constitutionalism discourse runs without any contributions from the constitutional theory. Therefore, first and foremost, it is crucial to unveil the meaning of the idea of the contemporary constitution in various dimensions, in order to examine the viability of the idea of global constitutionalism. Seen in this light, the "interrogation of viability" gains the meaning of searching the capability of the global constitutionalism discourse to reflect the idea of constitution by preventing any rupture with the modern concept of constitution and by searching common dynamics of modern constitution and global constitutionalism. Thereby, a fundamental aim of this project appears to be the interrogation of to what an extent does the global constitutionalism discourse reflect the idea of the contemporary constitution.

Chapter 4
Meaning of Contemporary Constitution

4.1 Key Concepts

4.1.1 The Main Idea of Contemporary Constitution and Constitutionalism

As discussed in the preceding chapter, the prominent issue in the global constitutionalism discourse is the lack of a clear idea of contemporary constitution. Therefore, this chapter will be devoted to exploring the contemporary idea of constitution. To this end, the meaning of contemporary constitution will be discussed in a broader context since diverse approaches to constitution require this.

The meaning of the concept of constitution is quite problematic in the contemporary world since it has hitherto been subject to numerous controversial definitions. Constitutions are rather broad texts, and they can be drafted by their framers as a political manifest instead of a supreme law. Therefore, they lack precision and need interpretation to fill in the meaning of generalities in many cases.[1] Since a unique reading of a constitution is not possible, ambiguities and some other problems regarding textual interpretation can arise. Constitution can have different meanings depending on various approaches from various disciplines, therefore seeking a single typology of constitutions indeed does not make much sense.[2] This is to be counted as one of the core issues of the global constitutionalism debate on the ground that

[1] Michael J. Horan, "Contemporary Constitutionalism and Legal Relationships Between Individuals," *The International and Comparative Law Quarterly* 25, no. 4 (1976): 859.

[2] Dieter Grimm, "Types of Constitutions," in *The Oxford Handbook of Comparative Constitutional Law*, ed. Michel Rosenfeld and Andras Sajo (Oxford: Oxford University Press, 2012), 98.

A. Atilgan, *Global Constitutionalism*, Beiträge zum ausländischen öffentlichen Recht und Völkerrecht, https://doi.org/10.1007/978-3-662-55647-4_4

global constitutionalism theories rely on different understandings of constitutions. Most of these theories reconstruct the concept of constitution, and they employ different practices of constitutionalism that have appeared since ancient eras. In consequence, constitutions do not have an agreed and coherent framework within this discourse, and thus to what extent they reflect the reality of contemporary constitutions is controversial. This is indeed a problem of the contemporary constitutional theory as well. As Fassbender notes, legal scholars have so far been more interested in the question "how a constitution works" than "what is a constitution."[3] Without doubt, modern constitutions evolved as a subject matter of modern nation states and societies, and national constitutional experiences are still the main reference points for the development of this concept. However, referring to national constitutions is not fruitful in this context since the character of national constitutions is subject to various factors, notably different traditions of constitutionalism that arose in different societies and through interpretive methods, which have largely been under the influence of legal positivism in the evolutionary process of modern law.

Furthermore, the difference between modern constitutionalism and contemporary constitutionalism is important in understanding the current strands of constitutionalism. This is noteworthy, because, as Henkin argues, contributions and roles of modern constitutionalism in contemporary constitutions cannot be determined with confidence.[4] This means that contemporary constitution framers rarely refer to the ideas of Locke, Montesquieu, Kant, Rousseau, and their successors, such as Bentham, Mill, and the socialists regarding modern constitutionalism.[5] Instead, contemporary constitutionalism has its own doctrinal sources. In other words, apart from the enlightenment process, the western democracies created their inherent sources for constitutionalization. The new constitutional experiences led to the new standards for constitutionalization processes. For instance, the US and French Constitutions with universal human rights covenants gave birth to fundamental rights, the Magna Carta of England spawned the idea of limited government, the German constitution helped the promotion of welfare state and so on.[6] A crucial point is that this process is still ongoing and contemporary constitutionalism is creating itself through various phenomena of its era.

Despite various dimensions in defining constitution and constitutionalism, it is still possible to find out some agreed aspects of the concept of constitution. Above all, constitution and constitutionalism have a very basic and ever-standing feature, as McIlwain states:

[3] Bardo Fassbender, "The United Nations Charter as Constitution of the International Community," *Columbia Journal of Transnational Law* 36, no. 3 (1998): 533.

[4] Louis Henkin, "A New Birth of Constitutionalism: Genetic Influences and Genetic Defects," *Cardozo Law Review* 14, no. 3-2 (1992–1993): 533.

[5] Ibid.

[6] Ibid. For further explanations on the revolutionary role of rights over contemporary constitutionalism: Chris Thornhill, "Contemporary Constitutionalism and the Dialectic of Constituent Power," *Global Constitutionalism* 1, no. 3 (2012): 369-404.

> The most ancient, the most persistent, and the most lasting of the essentials of true constitutionalism still remains what it has been almost from the beginning, the limitation of government by law.[7]

Therefore, it can be said that the limitation of government or public power is the *raison d'être* of a constitution. Accordingly, as a very basic part of a constitution, it is stated in Article 16 of the French Declaration of the Rights of Man and the Citizen that: "A society in which the observance of the law is not assured, nor the separation of powers defined, has no constitution at all." This is a very common feature of modern constitutions, as it is explicitly articulated in all constitutional texts or only implicitly implemented, such as in the British constitution.[8] In addition to the separation of powers, other fundamental common pillars of the constitution have appeared as democracy, human rights and rule of law.[9]

Further, Dieter Grimm points to two common aspects of the concept of constitution. In this respect, constitution is a "law with special function and object" and it is of "a regime defining character, which influence the way constitutions try to fulfil their function."[10] In other words, constitutions come about with two basic characters, legal and political.

On the other hand, the concept of "constitutionalization" appears as a more ambiguous term. This ambiguity inherently increases when it comes to a constitutionalization in the global realm.[11] In a simplified manner, constitutionalization is likely to be defined as "connotation of a process;" as Walter states that,

> [i]n using the term "constitutionalization" (instead of constitution), the idea of a static situation is rejected and the term may even imply some degree of imperfection –a situation of transition from one underlying concept to another, the contours of which are not yet entirely clear.[12]

To be more precise, in a common sense a constitutionalization process in all cases refers to an institutional construction in order to provide the "densification of legal

---

[7] Charles Howard McIlwain, *Constitutionalism: Ancient and Modern* (Indianapolis: Liberty Fund, 2007), 24.

[8] Andreas L. Paulus, "International Legal System as a Constitution," in *Ruling the World?: Constitutionalism, International Law, and Global Governance*, ed. Jeffrey L. Dunoff and Joel P. Trachtman (Cambridge: Cambridge University Press, 2009), 92.

[9] Ibid.

[10] Grimm, "Types of Constitutions," 99.

[11] Stefan Oeter, "Global Constitutionalism: Fundamental Norms, Contestation and the Emergence of Constitutional Quality," in *Peace Through Law: Reflections on Pacem in Terries from Philosophy, Law, Theology and Political Science*, ed. Heinz-Gerhard Justenhoven and Marry Ellen O'Connell (Baden-Baden: Nomos, 2016), 86.

[12] Christian Walter, "International Law in a Process of Constitutionalization," in *New Perspectives on the Divide Between National and International Law*, ed. Janne Nijman and Andre Nollkaemper (Oxford: Oxford University Press, 2007), 192.

material."[13] In this sense, constitutionalization pressupposes a legalization process in the public life.[14]

Constitutionalization is a relatively new term in the political literature.[15] Accordingly, its meaning is determined by the terms "constitution" and "constitutionalism," the content of which was indeed formed long before this term. In a general context, in Loughlin's words, constitutionalization is

> the term used for the attempt to subject the exercise of all types of public power, whatever the medium of its exercise, to the discipline of constitutional procedures and norms.[16]

Constitutionalization is rather discussed today regarding developments in the international legal order, despite the fact that it has noteworthy impacts on national orders.[17] In the global realm, constitutionalization rather marks a change towards a more just world order.[18] It is also of note that the idea of domestic constitutionalization has become ripe only recently, by virtue of the political developments at the end of the twentieth century.[19] Further, according to Loughlin, constitutionalization has evolved out of the extension of borders of constitutionalism and the loosened links between constitutionalism and nation states.[20]

Traditionally, constitutionalism has been represented by two different paradigms, namely liberal constitutionalism and republican constitutionalism, which basically stem from the nature of politics.[21] The liberal paradigm has been the dominant perspective since the nineteenth century, and it has reconstructed constitutional states in a legal and rights-based foundation.[22] On the other hand, civic republicans, who prefer acting in accordance with the will of the majority, are still the main opponents of liberal constitutionalists.[23]

---

[13] Karl-Heinz Ladeur, "The State in International Law" (Comparative Research in Law & Political Economy Research Paper no. 27, 2010, http://digitalcommons.osgoode.yorku.ca/cgi/viewcontent.cgi?article=1094&context=clpe), 22, last visit 21.04.2013.

[14] Martin Loughlin, "What is Constitutionalisation," in *The Twilight of Constitutionalism?* ed. by Petra Dobner and Martin Loughlin (Oxford:Oxford Univ. Press, 2010). 47.

[15] Ibid., 61.

[16] Ibid., 47.

[17] Ibid., 62.

[18] Stefan Oeter, "Regime Collisions from a Perspective of Global Constitutionalism," in *Contested Regime Collisions: Norm Fragmentation in World Society*, ed. Kerstin Blome et al. (Cambridge: Cambridge University Press, 2016), 23.

[19] Loughlin, "What is Constitutionalisation," 63.

[20] Ibid., 68.

[21] Dario Castiglione, "The Political Theory of the Constitution," in *Constitutionalism in Transformation: European and Theoretical Perspectives*, ed. Richard Bellamy and Dario Castiglione (Oxford: Blackwell, 1996), 21.

[22] Ibid., 22.

[23] Cornelia Schneider, "The Constitutional Protection of Rights in Dworkin's and Habermas' Theories of Democracy," *UCL Jurisprudence Review* (2000): 103.

As mentioned earlier, constitutions are subject to various interpretive processes in every culture. Likewise, the character of law is generally subject to a disagreement in the society in particular about whether or not the grounds of laws are met in particular cases, and this is likely to be described as an "empirical or theoretical disagreement."[24] Such a disagreement stems from the different empirical observations of law. On the other hand, the definition of a constitution also matters in terms of the interpretive points. For instance, as Dworkin argues, American judges are distinguished as liberal or conservative due to their disagreements on "about what the constitution is a matter of postinterpretive law, about what it standards it deploys for testing official acts," although they agree on which words make a constitution as a matter of "preinterpretive text."[25] However, such a distinction is still not a functional one, as he puts forward, on the ground that it is an elusive and oversimplified distinction depending on the political matches of their decisions. That is to say, there are not very clear boundaries between these views in most cases. Instead, judges in general combine various views that may be defined as either liberal or conservative.[26]

Against this background, constitutionalism can be defined in various ways from different perspectives depending on backgrounds of interpreters. The relationship between a constitution and constitutionalism in terms of an overarching function is crucial. For example, if one accedes that constitutionalism is constructed depending on a concrete constitutional practice, it would be defined as follows:

> Constitutionalism speaks not to what a constitution does, but to a mode of doing it—a particular functional logic—of which the constitution is paradigmatic and which has, as an indispensable secondary effect, the legitimation of exercises of power which accord with that logic. The ideology of constitutionalism, like its legitimating effect, is parasitic upon its particular functional logic: It follows from rather than defines it.[27]

In contrast, some others advance the claim that a constitution is a written expression of constitutionalism in the context of a specific political system; that is to say, constitutionalism is determinative on the character of constitutions.[28] This view may be affirmed when merely the history of constitutional movements is taken into consideration. However, in view of the interpretive processes in enforcement processes of constitutions, the aptness of the former view is obvious. Therefore, in the historical context, both should be taken into consideration in terms of their own referential points. On the other hand, as will be touched upon in the details below, the former

---

[24] Ronald Dworkin, *Law's Empire*, (Cambridge: The Belknap Press of Harvard University Press, 1986).

[25] Ibid., 358.

[26] Ibid., 359.

[27] Paul Scott, "(Political) Constitutions and (Political) Constitutionalism," *German Law Journal* 14, no. 12 (2013): 2162.

[28] Horan, "Contemporary Constitutionalism," 848.

definition of the character of constitutionalism is more likely to be considered in the process of contemporary constitutionalism.

Furthermore, when discussing the meaning of modern constitution, an emphasis should be placed on the fact that modern constitution is, without any doubt, a concept that essentially refers to a state constitution, and therefore it mainly relates to state activities and public power.[29] Therefore, it is a must to elaborate this concept and draw its conceptual anatomy within the borders of state constitutions in order to get the main idea thereof.

As mentioned in the beginning, since contents of constitutions vary and each constitution has different characteristics, a typology of constitution has to be drawn. However, this is not a secured way of reflecting the true character of constitution, as there is always a threat of reductionism. Therefore, this text will not adhere to any unquestionable typology, but will rather discuss some commonalities for this concept. To begin with, the text will choose a ready-made typology that alleges to drawing a framework for contemporary constitutions. Dieter Grimm underlines five fundamental characteristics of the concept of modern constitution, in view of "achieved constitutions" of the past. In this regard, he argues that the achievement of a constitution depends on these five elements:

> (1) The constitution in the modern sense is a set of legal norms, not a philosophical construct. (…)
> (2) The purpose of these norms is to regulate the establishment and the exercise of public power as opposed to a mere modification of a pre-existing public power. (…)
> (3) The regulation is comprehensive in the sense that no pre- or extra constitutional bearers of public power and no pre- or extra constitutional means to exercise this power are recognized.
> (4) Constitutional law is higher law. It enjoys primacy of all other laws and legal acts emanating from government. Acts incompatible with the constitution cannot claim legal validity.
> (5) Constitutional law finds its origin with the people as the only legitimate source of power. The distinction between pouvoir constituant and pouvoir constitué is essential to the constitution.[30]

He argues that these five elements are to be taken as a ground for a typology of contemporary constitutions, as they reflect the commonalities of constitutions that have been able to survive up to the present. Putting this typology into a parenthesis now, in this chapter, the text will explore the contemporary idea of constitution through a conceptual analysis as well as the contemporary discourses on the identity of constitution. For this purpose, a broad range of contributions on the character of contemporary constitution will be drawn on. At the end, a general depiction of the concept of constitution will be sought in terms of various contemporary phenomena

[29] Antje Wiener, *The Invisible Constitution of Politics: Contested Norms and International Encounters* (Cambridge: Cambridge University Press, 2008), 30.

[30] Grimm, "Types of Constitutions," 104.

that shape its current form. This will come to mean a cross-check of Grimm's typology at the same time.

4.1.1.1 Historical Development of Modern Constitution and Constitutionalism

4.1.1.1.1 Pre-modern Developments

In consideration of the facts mentioned in the preceding section, constitutionalism is "a theory of limited government and is concerned mainly with the norms which modern constitutions should contain."[31] In this regard, the fundamental principles of modern constitutionalism are "independence of the judiciary, separation of governmental powers, respect for individual rights, and the promotion of the judiciary's role as guardians of constitutional norms."[32] Hence, it can be said that constitutionalism has to do with the construction of constitutions above all. To put it differently, and in a pure liberal legalist view, constitutionalism is "a system that establishes individual legal rights that the dominant legislature does not have the power to override or compromise."[33] On the other hand, from a political constitutionalist view, constitutionalism is a political doctrine, and an invention of modernity.[34]

The history of the concept of constitutionalism did not run in parallel with constitutions until the last quarter of the eighteenth century. In other words, constitutionalism is a recent innovation in the history of constitutional developments, and the first flag holders of constitutionalism were American and French revolutionists.[35] Afterwards, it became a strong subject of political struggles all around the world. Nevertheless, it did not gain a universal recognition by the end of the twentieth century.[36] To reduce constitutionalism to the submission of politics into law does not reflect the truth, since the concept of constitution existed before the emergence of modern constitutionalization processes.[37] It denotes a fact beyond the legalization of public power. It is rather a special and ambitious form of legalization. However, at this point, it would be helpful to state that a constitution is not the same thing as constitutionalism. To be more precise, borrowing from Weiler and Wind, Italian and

---

[31] Martin Loughlin, "Ten Tenets of Sovereignty," in *Sovereignty in Transition: Essays in European Law*, ed. Neil Walker (Oxford: Hart Publishing, 2006), 55.

[32] Ibid.

[33] Ronald Dworkin, "Constitutionalism and Democracy," in *Constitutionalism and Democracy*, ed. Richard Paul Bellamy (Aldershot: Ashgate, 2006), 3.

[34] Castiglione, "Political Theory of Constitution," 5.

[35] Dieter Grimm, "The Achievement of Constitutionalism and its Prospects in a Changed World," in *The Twilight of Constitutionalism?* ed. Petra Dobner and Martin Loughlin (Oxford: Oxford University Press, 2010), 3.

[36] Ibid.

[37] Ibid. 5.

German constitutions contain very different provisions; however, they share a very similar model of constitutionalism background, by "vindicating certain neo-Kantian humanistic values, combined with the notion of the Rechtsstaat."[38]

In the historical context, constitutionalism can be described as an achievement [*Errungenschaft*] since its prominent functions are to abolish any arbitrary and absolute power over people and to render the use of public power predictable.[39] In other words, constitutionalism marks, as a political movement of the seventeenth and eighteenth centuries in particular, not only seeking a written constitution, but also referring to certain constitutional principles, notably the rule of law, or judicial review.[40]

In another way of expression, constitutionalism is "the political theory that generally accompanies the technique"[41] for establishing modern constitutions. Since a written constitution does not exist in the international legal order, an examination of the global constitutionalism discourse can make sense in the elaboration of the concepts of the constitutionalism and constitutionalization. These two concepts acquire their meanings within the historical and the societal context of constitutions. This is a crucial point on the ground that the concept of the constitutionalization rather refers to transnational processes today, as national constitutionalization processes are rather deemed to be completed.[42]

As will be mentioned below, proto-constitutional orders or pre-modern constitutionalization processes that resulted in modern constitutions came about in the high medieval era. As some scholars who deal with sociology and history of constitutions strictly refer to, the constitutional developments of this era involve significant clues for understanding the evolution of modern constitution.[43]

Despite the fact that constitutions are modern tools, the term of constitution had existed and referred to different forms in the pre-modern times. During the period of ancient (Greek) constitutions, the state as an organic entity possessed the constitution, which was then indeed equivalent to the whole of politics (*politeia*).[44] This means that ancient constitutions did not represent the foundation of a governmental authority.[45] This was so, because there was no clear distinction between the society and the state in Ancient Greece, in particular until Stoics; and law was only one

[38] J.H.H. Weiler and M. Wind, "Introduction" in *European Constitutionalism Beyond the State*, ed. J.H.H. Weiler and Marlene Wind (Cambridge: Cambridge University Press, 2003), 1.

[39] Niklas Luhmann, "Die Verfassung als evolutionäre Errungenschaft," *Rechtshistorisches Journal* 9 (1990): 176, cited by Grimm, "Achievement of Constitutionalism," 10.

[40] Anne Peters, "Compensatory Constitutionalism: The Fundamental Function and Potential of Fundamental International Norms and Structures," *Leiden Journal of International Law* 19 (2006): 583.

[41] Loughlin, "Ten Tenets," 55.

[42] Ibid.

[43] Christopher J. A. Thornhill, *A Sociology of Constitutions: Constitutions and State Legitimacy in Historical-sociological Perspective* (Cambridge: Cambridge University Press, 2011).

[44] Loughlin, "Ten Tenets," 48.

[45] Ibid. 49.

aspect of the polity where no provision was seen subordinated to any other.[46] The only way to remedy unconstitutional acts was through a revolution; that is to say, a complete dissolution of the political life.[47] At this point, one can make the comparison that ancient constitutionalism was rather an instrument for social construction of nomos, whereas modern constitutionalism has been an instrument for polity.[48]

The medieval constitutions were also fairly different from modern constitutions in many terms. The constitutional documents of medieval societies were customary instruments, where consuetudinary laws which were interpreted by the judicial actors were the principal sources.[49] The medieval era was rather significant in terms of the societal transformation that led to the "proto-constitutional orders," which transformed into the modern constitutional systems over time. The presumption of a higher law, or subordination of laws to this sort of law, as the basis for a new and modern constitutionalism in the medieval period was demonstrated as the greatest revolutionary transformation in the history of politics.[50]

Although the word "constitution" acquired its current meaning later, some legal arrangements in various European countries beginning from high medieval period – in other words from the end of the twelfth and thirteenth centuries – can be defined as constitutional documents.[51] Some observers claim that during the fifteenth and sixteenth centuries, various documents in various names functioned as constitutions, particularly in France.[52]

In particular, the features of constitutional developments of transformations from the early feudal system to the high feudalism are striking. During this process, the emergence of a new and progressive differentiation in the economic interactions led to the incidence of various administrative institutions, which performed "at a growing level of social and personal abstraction and consistency," whereas the legal relations were decentralized and they largely hinged on the private, embedded relationships of the former system. This implied indeed an inchoate centralization of European societies' political systems, where a need for a predictable and consistent political and legal system had arisen:[53]

---

[46] McIlwain, *Constitutionalism*, 35.

[47] Ibid., 36.

[48] Antje Wiener, *Invisible Constitution of Politics*, 29.

[49] Thornhill, *A Sociology of Constitutions*, 72.

[50] McIlwain, *Constitutionalism*, 36.

[51] Thornhill, *A Sociology of Constitutions*, 20. However, Grimm does not concur with this opinion. In his point of view, this was not so, because constitutions were not normative tools, but empirical ones, before US and French constitutions arose. The constitutions which arose before these constitutions can just be considered as factual constitutions. After the rise of modern constitutions, these forms of constitutions did not disappear, but turned to a "constitutional reality" that influences law. Dieter Grimm, "The Constitution in the Process of Denationalization," *Constellations* 12, no. 4 (2005): 447-448.

[52] McIlwain, *Constitutionalism*, 88.

[53] However, this did not come to mean a de-feudalization process. Thornhill, *A Sociology of Constitutions*, 21-23.

> That is to say, the gradual extension of monetary transactions and individual property ownership and the disintegration of property-holding groups from feudal tenures created an early urban economic elite, and this class intensified its authority through techniques of governance and legal integration that were not tied to socially embedded customs and feudal arrangements.[54]

At this juncture, the ground for constituting precise and coherent legal forms for the European societies becomes clearer. The transformation process in question was also related to the transformation of power into an "objectively defined" structure, and the emergence of new legal forms was central to it.[55] The salient point is the fact that law had crucial functions in the societal transformation processes. For example, the adoption and consolidation of Roman law had strong impacts on the legal structure of feudalism in the Holy Roman Empire and the de-feudalization process.[56]

The de-feudalization and the early statehood processes in Europe can be characterized as "proto-constitutional orders," borrowing from Chris Thornhill.[57] A relevant fact is that these orders prioritize the modern liberal constitutions of European states. From a sociological point of view, these orders were predecessors of the modern constitutional orders, as a number of constitutional developments took place in these preconstitutional structures. As a matter of fact, scholars in this field argue that each premodern case in Europe has different characteristics. There are a number of reasons for the emergence of these orders in the medieval societies. According to Thornhill, a remarkable one is the increasing density of the governance within the process of transformation of feudal structures as a consequence of the need of the states to perform judicial power.[58] The early states, in this sense, had kinds of "rudimentary constitutions" that determined their representative and consultative functions; and this occurred in parallel with the law-making activities of the early states in written forms, in a way that was borrowed from the church to turn customs into positive laws.[59] One can also state that these constitutions were developed by these states in order to detach the power from private prerogatives and to constitute their power in an abstract, stabilized and autonomous way.[60] This resulted in the construction of an inclusionary power of states by the help of those constitutional structures, and an inclusionary society where all social domains became subject to the newly differentiated power. In short, the political power utilized law for its reproduction through the society and for the inclusion of other politically relevant social actors of the society, regents etc. This also came to mean the abstraction of power from the immuned and privileged individuals or groups, and in a sense the reproduction of power under public law.[61] The formation of statehood

---

[54] Ibid., 24.

[55] Ibid.

[56] Ibid., 40.

[57] Ibid., 68.

[58] Ibid., 73.

[59] Ibid., 74.

[60] Ibid., 75.

[61] Ibid., 76, 109.

went in parallel with an increasement in the "integrity and abstractions of constitutional orders," and the constitutional developments of that period had great impacts over the early modern statehood of Europe.[62] The doctrines of fundamental law and natural law were also quite influential over this result.

This new form of statehood, at the same time, became the initial point of the doctrine of the constituent power.[63] The constitutionality of the statehood emerging in the aftermath of the European revolutions relied on a constituent power, which represented a "single popular will." From this time on, this concept played a very crucial role in stabilizing the political structure of the modern society.[64] It enabled modern states to keep their power alive. On the other hand, states based in a constituent power became much more effective in eliminating the customary forces in order to consolidate the newly emerging legislative institutions.[65] Additionally, modern constitutions eliminated and excluded cultural diversities as constitutive aspect of politics, while setting a uniform political association.[66] This negative aspect of modern constitutionalism remained a major feature thereof.

Furthermore, it is of note that, as a consequence of the fact that the distinction between private law and public law was hardly visible in the medieval societies, the form of the medieval constitutions was different from constitutions of the modern societies.[67] They were also ineligible normative structures, since they were not able to be effective for the whole society.[68] In medieval societies, constitutional developments helped the rise of the rudimentary forms of public law that aimed at abstracting its political resources. However, this function completely changed in the early modern societies, as they led to the consolidation and differentiation of political resources in order to condense the power in unitary institutions.[69] In other words, one could argue that the medieval constitutional developments set the ground for the emergence of public law, and public law found the opportunity to gain a compact form over time. From this point of view, it could be stated that constitutions had a bridging function in the historical development process. This is also quite related to the fact that constitutionalization was the legalization of public power in order to meet needs of the societal transformation. In this respect, the border between private and public law has been a basic tenet of the modern constitutionalism.[70]

---

[62] Ibid., 110.

[63] Chris Thornhill, "Rights and Constituent Power in the Global Constitution," *International Journal of Law in Context* 10 (2014): 359.

[64] Ibid.

[65] Ibid., 361.

[66] James Tully, *Strange Multiplicity: Constitutionalism in an Age of Diversity* (Cambridge: Cambridge University Press, 2007), 63.

[67] Thornhill, *A Sociology of Constitutions*, 11.

[68] Ibid., 11. Ulrich K. Preuß, "Equality of States – Its Meaning in a Constitutionalised Global Order," *Chicago Journal of International Law* 9, no.1 (2008-2009): 17-49.

[69] Thornhill, *A Sociology of Constitutions*, 157.

[70] Grimm, "Constitution Process of Denationalization," 453.

During the emergence of the early statehood in Europe, especially in terms of the example of Italian cities, *ius statuendi* was secured by conferring constitutional character upon the statutes of the cities in the process of gaining autonomy. This is noteworthy for the reason that it exemplifies the fact that concentrating the power around constitutions is vital for the establishment and the political autonomy of statehood.[71] During the emergence of statehood in Europe, general and consistent laws carried out functions for replacing the private justice of former regimes and for restricting individual decisions in order to meet the needs of society for jurisdiction.[72] This new European statehood marked modern constitutionalism, as the concept of modern constitution was identified by a specific set of European institutions.[73]

Beyond giving some historical data on the emergence of modern constitutionalism, this topic is also of a special meaning in terms of our main inquiry. In contemporary global studies, the emergence of modern constitution and nation state through a number of medieval political and legal developments, has been held as a subject of an inquiry on whether constitutional developments in the medieval era could be analogous to the current developments in the fragmented structure of the global order.[74] This question could allow the global constitutionalism discourse to reconstruct the debate on constitutionalization in the global realm through a comparative historical way.

4.1.1.1.2 Rise of Modern Constitutionalism

Modern constitutions are the constitutions that came into force in the aftermath of the American and French Revolutions of the eighteenth century. They were the outputs of a transformation process which impacted the relationships between governments and peoples. During this transformation process, the traditional political orders had undergone a dramatic shift; where status and hierarchy, the main grounds of governments, were replaced by the public consent for the common benefit of the people.[75] These governments were limited, accountable and responsive. In addition, they were based on contract, and on the principles of enumeration of powers, institutionalization of checks over the exercise of powers and the protection of fundamental rights.[76] On the other hand, the rise of modern constitutions in the eighteenth and nineteenth centuries was related to the revolutionary processes, and constitutions

---

[71] Thornhill, *A Sociology of Constitutions*, 50.

[72] Ibid., 58.

[73] This also points to what Kant calls a republican constitution. Tully, *Strange Multiplicity*, 63.

[74] Saskia Sassen, "Neither Global Nor National: Novel Assemblages of Territory, Authority and Rights," in *Laws and Societies in Global Contexts: Contemporary Approaches*, ed. Eve Darian-Smith (Cambridge: Cambridge University Press, 2013), 23-38.

[75] Loughlin, "What is Constitutionalisation," 48.

[76] Ibid.

arose as symbols of national self-awareness, self-determination and independence.[77] Consequently, constitution arose as a concept that reflects a foundational basis for new modern states, and also as an emancipatory term used in political struggles in the modern era.[78]

Although the term of constitution existed before the American and French revolutions, as mentioned above, and its meaning and content underwent a transformation after these revolutions.[79] Grimm argues that the most important contribution of these revolutions to modern constitutionalism was "to turn the ideas from philosophy into law."[80] In other words, as a consequence of the rise of modern constitutions, the concept of constitution no longer remained descriptive, but instead became a prescriptive term.[81] Above all, popular sovereignty became the legitimating principle of the political order, instead of the monarchical sovereignty. Moreover, they achieved this by creating a normative basis and legalization of the societal consensus.[82] This led to the transformation of law into positive law entirely, and to the subordination of ordinary law by constitutional law. In this way, the will of the ruler as the divine law or natural law lost its legal character and turned into a morally binding normative source.[83]

Furthermore, it is noteworthy to mention that, even though both of them have been considered as headstones of modern constitutionalism, American and French constitutions represent different traditions of constitutionalism in some terms. In Article 16 of the French Declaration of the Rights of Man and of the Citizen of 1789, it is stated that "a society in which the observance of the law is not assured, nor the separation of powers defined, has no constitution at all." Whereas the principle of limited government comes to the fore in American constitutionalism, the government appeared rather as an instrument to enable citizens to enjoy their rights in French constitutionalism.[84] This can be explained in Loughlin's words as "the history of the development of the US Constitution is the history of the triumph of liberal-legal [constitutionalism] over republican-political constitutionalism."[85] On

[77] Silke Hensel, "Constitutional Cultures in the Atlantic World During the 'Age of Revolutions'," in *Constitutional Cultures: On the Concept and Representation of Constitutions in the Atlantic World*, ed. Silke Hensel et al. (Newcastle upon Tyne: Cambridge Scholars Publishing, 2012), 5.

[78] Hans Vorländer, "What is 'Constitutional Cultures'?," in *Constitutional Cultures: On the Concept and Representation of Constitutions in the Atlantic World*, ed. Silke Hensel et al. (Newcastle upon Tyne: Cambridge Scholars Publishing), 2012, 23.

[79] Grimm, "Achievement of Constitutionalism," 5.

[80] Grimm, "Types of Constitutions," 102.

[81] Ibid., 103.

[82] Grimm, "Achievement of Constitutionalism," 8.

[83] Grimm, "Constitution in Process of Denationalization," 449.

[84] Ulrich K. Preuss, "Disconnecting Constitutions From Statehood: Is Global Constitutionalism a Viable Concept?," in *The Twilight of Constitutionalism*, ed. Petra Dobner and Martin Loughlin (Oxford: Oxford University Press, 2010), 31.

[85] Loughlin, "What is Constitutionalisation," 58.

the other hand, it should be noted that the American revolution which set the ground for the constitution was not preceded by a state-building process like France, but through some different societal factors still.[86] In addition, the establishment of a government and the transformation of law into reflexive forms were distinguished features of French and American constitutions; compared with the English constitutional developments, which resulted in a partial restriction of the government.[87]

The modern constitutionalism in Europe developed in parallel with the emergence of the modern state, and it was one of the facts restraining the power of states, along with urban autonomy and parliamentarism between the twelfth and sixteenth centuries.[88] Modern constitutions arose as a consequence of a number of societal developments, which can be defined as prerequisites of a modern constitution. First of all, a differentiated system of political rule came about, and the omnipotence of monarchy was defeated. The monopoly of the force of the state was perfected on behalf of the people, the new sovereign.[89] In this respect, for example, the French Revolution did not influence the existence of sovereignty in general terms, but rather it carried out a complementary function for the state building.[90] The modern constitutions arose as an answer to the question of how the state power can be bound by law, even though it produces law itself; and it achieved this by dividing positive laws into two, as the one regarding the state power and the other one which regulates relations of individuals. This was preceded by splitting the public power into two, into a *pouvoir constituant* and *pouvoir constitué*.[91]

According to Dieter Grimm, constitution in the modern sense cannot be considered as a philosophical construct, as it is a set of legal norms that aims at regulating the establishment and the exercise of public power. He indicates functional characteristics of modern constitutions as being comprehensive, enjoying primacy over all other laws and legal acts, and an issue concerning *pouvoir constituant* and *pouvoir constitué*.[92] Substantive characteristics could be enumerated as "democracy, rule of law, separation of powers, fundamental rights."[93] From this perspective, an order that denies the democratic core of public power and the requirement of a limited government cannot be held as a constitutional one.[94]

Modern constitutions became influential over the transformation of the meaning of the term "sovereignty." Although sovereignty was earlier related to "the control over a territory," by virtue of modern constitutions through the democratic revolutions

---

[86] Grimm, "Constitution in Process of Denationalization," 451.

[87] Ibid., 452.

[88] Preuss, "Disconnecting Constitutions," 24.

[89] Dieter Grimm, "Does Europe Need a Constitution?," *European Law Journal* 1, no. 3 (1995): 285.

[90] Grimm, "Constitution in Process of Denationalization," 451.

[91] Grimm, "Does Europe Need Constitution?," 286.

[92] Grimm, "Achievement of Constitutionalism," 9.

[93] Ibid.

[94] Ibid., 10.

of the eighteenth century, it gained a new meaning related to the "collective self-rule or a multitude" or "the constituent power of the people themselves."[95] Since sovereignty is no longer defined relying on territoriality, it has been argued that a contemporary definition of a constitution must include both states and other political entities which are not based on territoriality.[96] At this juncture, Preuss states that,

> whenever a multitude whose members are demarcated against the outside world establish a regime through which they pursue the goals of common defence and/or common welfare and establish rules about the formation of a common will which are able to generate obligations and responsibilities for the individual members this multitude has constituted itself as a distinct entity shaped by the constitution.[97]

This definition highlights a feature of constitutions regarding the social actions that enable individuals to act interdependently. As such, constitutions extend beyond their components and produce a collective will formation:

> In practical terms that means that constitutions establish a political system which provides an institutional space in which the affairs of a multitude as such become the matter of collective deliberation and action and are separated from the spheres of its individual members. They determine the elements of collective will formation, the conditions under which the collective has supremacy over the individuals' spheres and the procedures through which individual obligations are created and their enforcement guaranteed.[98]

Furthermore, the two most striking goals pursued by modern constitutions are to specify the structure of the office of government, and to create a basis for the unity of the nation. That is to say, modern constitutions have a function of nation-building.[99] The concept of equality has a lot to do with constitutional nations, as it points to the equality of citizens and the equality of each nation, and this relationship created the essential ground for the independency of nation states from the Papal and Roman imperialism.[100] On the other hand, beyond these functions, the way of characterizing the public sphere appeared as another issue of constitutional functions in the modern era.[101] However, these features of modern constitutions did not remain stable. One noteworthy example can be given as the fact that constitutions can now exist without presupposing shared values or shared understandings of social practices; and thereby they can exist beyond social and physical demarcations.[102] Given this fact, Preuss concludes that, as a matter of fact, beyond the coercive state power, the new modes

---

[95] Preuss. "Disconnecting Constitutions," 37.

[96] Ibid., 43.

[97] Ibid.

[98] Ibid., 43.

[99] Loughlin, "What is Constitutionalisation," 52. Tully, *Strange Multiplicity*, 68.

[100] Tully, *Strange Multiplicity*, 68.

[101] Loughlin, "What is Constitutionalisation," 53.

[102] Preuss. "Disconnecting Constitutions," 46.

of non-coercive but obligatory cooperation have also been evolving within various social organizations, as newly emerging constitutional problems of the society.[103]

In modern societies, the political power has been broadly exercised through constitutional laws, and the political power is deemed to be legitimate in case it complies with the constitutional framework. Constitutional law is the precondition of self-reproduction of modern societies in terms of its political aspects.[104] In short, modern constitutions reflect outcomes of the legalization of state power in its historical context.[105] In addition, "founding moments" and "democratic politics" have also been heeded as preconditions of modern constitutions.[106] In other words, as a common thread, modern constitutions have arisen as result of some extraordinary historical moments, and they have been marked by the soul of the movements that give rise to these moments.

Last but not least, geographical status is also among the important aspects of modern constitutions. Modern constitutions emerged within territorial borders. However, modern constitutionalism also maintained the idea of universalism.[107] This has given rise to the recognition of the universal validity of constitutions.

4.1.1.2 Identification of Constitution: Discursive Facts

The concept of constitution will not be confined to the formal and written constitutions in this research, as mentioned before. The major claim here is that constitutions are also contextual entities beyond their formal existence. Above all, diverse interpretational traditions prove this claim. As a matter of fact, interpretation is the greatest determinative of identities of constitutions.[108] In other words, constitutional communities are "interpretation communities," and this brings discursive and contestable traits of a normative order into play.[109]

Borrowing from Hayek, Wenzel reminds us of the fact that "'perception is always an interpretation' of the physical world."[110] Furthermore, constitutions are

---

[103] Ibid.

[104] Thornhill, *A Sociology of Constitutions*, 374, 375.

[105] Grimm, "Does Europe Need Constitution?," 288.

[106] Tully, *Strange Multiplicity*, 69.

[107] Grimm, "Constitution in Process of Denationalization," 453.

[108] Michel Rosenfeld, "Constitutional Identity," in *Oxford Handbook of Comparative Constitutional Law*, ed. Michel Rosenfeld and Andras Sajo (Oxford: Oxford University Press, 2012), 756-776.

[109] Hans Vorländer, "Integration durch Verfassung? Die symbolische Bedeutung der Verfassung im politischen Integrationsprozess," in *Integration durch Verfassung*, ed. Hans Vorländer (Wiesbaden: Westdeutscher Verlag, 2002), 22.

[110] Nikolai Wenzel, "From Contract to Mental Model: Constitutional Culture as a Fact of the Social Sciences," *Review of Austrian Economy* 23 (2010): 62.

not unchangeable agreements reached at a foundational moment.[111] As Rosenfeld argues, a common identity of constitutions could be created by referring to the limitation of power, the commitment to adherence to the rule of law and the protection of fundamental rights, as most common features of constitutions. However, the problem is that the existence of these features leads to very different interpretations within the different constitutional frames. The natural consequence of this fact is the "textual sameness and interpretive selfhood" of constitutions.[112] Under these circumstances, speaking of a common identity of constitutions becomes very difficult.

In order to achieve the maintenance of a constitution under changing circumstances, interpretation is required. To put it differently, changes and developments in the evolution of constitutions are results of interpretation.[113] To assign constitutions to a specific category means constraining "the modes of legal analysis appropriate to its interpretation."[114] That is to say, the greatest debates on constitutional law have been regarding the interpretation of constitutions.[115] Therefore, an attempt at understanding the contemporary meaning of constitution requires dealing with interpretation methods.

The reasons for interpretation of constitutions vary. Academic scholars need interpretation in order to construct a typology of constitutions.[116] On the other hand, judges need to interpret constitutions due to their ambiguous, vague, contradictory or insufficiently explicit contents in constitutional disputes.[117] Whether for academic purposes or for judicial needs, the ultimate goal of interpretation is the identification of constitution. In other words, interpretation gives the identity of a constitution.[118] For the purposes of this inquiry to reach an overall depiction of contemporary constitution, this text will not adhere to the definition of modern constitution provided by the traditional constitutional theory. The meaning of contemporary constitution will be sought in a broader context that involves "interpretive selfhood" of constitutions in addition to their "textual sameness." To this end, under this section, diverse interpretive processes will be discussed in order to reach a typology of constitution. At the end, the probability of obtaining an overall idea of contemporary constitution will be examined, in order to employ the reconstruction of the idea of constitution in the global constitutionalism discourse.

---

[111] Tully, *Strange Multiplicity*, 183.

[112] Michel Rosenfeld, "Constitutional Identity," 757.

[113] Grimm, "Types of Constitutions," 100.

[114] James A. Gardner, "Reply: What is a State Constitution?," *Rutgers Law Journal* 24 (1992-1993): 1025.

[115] Dworkin, *Law's Empire*, 360.

[116] Grimm, "Types of Constitutions," 98.

[117] Jeffrey Goldsworthy, "Constitutional Interpretation," in *Oxford Handbook of Comparative Constitutional Law*, ed. Michel Rosenfeld and Andras Sajo (Oxford: Oxford University Press, 2012), 689-717.

[118] Rosenfeld, "Constitutional Identity," 757.

4.1.1.2.1 Traditional Idea of Constitution: Analytical Interpretation of Constitution

Legal definitions of constitutions largely depend on the normativist and positivist interpretations, which rather deal with the "textual sameness" of constitutions. While comparing historical and legal approaches to constitutions, A. V. Dicey states that

> to a lawyer, on the other hand, the primary object of study is the law as it now stands; he is only secondarily occupied with ascertaining how it came into existence.[119]

Oxford Dictionaries give place to a definition of constitutions in the same vein: "the system or body of fundamental principles according to which a nation, state, or body politic is constituted and governed."[120] Likewise, the normativist definitions of constitutions can be found within the remarkable rulings of the constitutional courts. For instance, in the famous Marbury v. Madison case, Chief Justice Marshall of the US Supreme Court defines the concept of constitution as,

> either a superior paramount law, unchangeable by ordinary means, or it is on a level with ordinary legislative acts, and like other acts, is alterable when the legislature shall please to alter it.[121]

As a matter of fact, the constitutional theory is normativist, and thus the societal contingencies do not have impacts on it.[122] The normativist definitions of constitutions in general underline the similar aspects of constitutions, such as outlining the powers of institutions of states, setting out and protecting fundamental rights, constraining the state power and requiring some special procedures to be amended.[123] That is to say, constitutions are legal norms that differ from other norms, as they govern the creation and exercise of political power and are superior to all other norms.[124] They provide standards of behaviour for the public authorities which were formed by them.[125] Additionally, constitutions are legal instruments with special

---

[119] A.V. Dicey, *Introduction to the Study of the Law of the Constitution*, 9th ed. (London: Macmillan and Co., 1948), 15.

[120] Oxford English Dictionary, http://www.oed.com/view/Entry/39848?redirectedFrom=constitution#eid, last visit 01.02.2014.

[121] Marbury v. Madison, US Supreme Court, 5 U.S. 137 (1803), page 5, https://supreme.justia.com/cases/federal/us/5/137/case.html, last visit 21.09.2014.

[122] Joseph Raz, "On the Authority and Interpretation of Constitutions: Some Preliminaries," in *Constitutionalism: Philosophical Foundations*, ed. Larry Alexander (Cambridge: Cambridge University Press, 1998), 156.

[123] Eric Barendt, *An Introduction to Constitutional Law* (Oxford: Oxford University Press, 1998), 1.

[124] Dieter Grimm, "Integration by Constitution," *International Journal of Constitutional Law* 3 (2005): 193. Castiglione, "Political Theory of Constitution," 8.

[125] Grimm, "Integration by Constitution,"194.

methods to fulfil their duties; for example, their supremacy over all the relevant legal order concerns this feature, as they are employed to measure the validity of all other legal acts.[126] In short, in terms of the normative analysis, constitutions are bulks of norms that determine conditions for the use of public power.[127] This was also very central to early modern writings on constitutions. For example, another author who wrote on constitutions earlier, Thomas Paine, having focused on written constitutions of America and France, stated that,

> (…) a government without a constitution is power without right. (…) A constitution is a thing antecedent to a government; and a government is only the creature of a constitution.[128]

Having considered the constitutional experience of England, where a constitutional tradition evolved throughout the centuries, Dicey stated that constitutional law consists of two elements. One is the "constitutional law," as the normative body of constitutions; and the other one is "conventions of the constitution," which consist of practices that do not fall into the scope of law at all.[129] In other words, this view suggests the separation of a legal element from the conventional or extra-legal elements of a constitution, as a requirement for dealing with constitutions in a normative way.[130] In addition to that, in Cardozo's famous definition, the normative body of a constitution should be held as beyond its time, since it denotes a future binding structure:

> A constitution states or ought to state not rules for the passing hour, but principles for an expanding future. In so far as it deviates from that standard, and descends into details and particulars, it loses its flexibility, the scope of interpretation contracts, the meaning hardens.[131]

A normative analysis of constitutions also concerns the whole structure of a legal system. From the normativist perspective, law is simply the system of norms that are acts of will towards the conduct of others.[132] In order to gain a legal character, a norm should be authorized to issue commands. In this regard, in Kelsen's "Pure

---

[126] David Beatty, *Constitutional Law: In Theory and Practice* (Toronto: University of Toronto Press, 1995), 5.

[127] Thornhill, *A Sociology of Constitutions*, 10.

[128] Thomas Paine, "Rights of Man," in *The Complete Works of Thomas Paine* (London), 302-3, 370, cited by McIlwain, *Constitutionalism*, 2.

[129] Dicey, *Introduction to Study of Law*, 24.

[130] At this point it should be noted that Dicey's views rely on the parliamentary sovereignty and reflect a political constitutionalism that basically argues for that a parliament can legislate in any way, either amend or repeal, and other institutions are not capable of disapplying parliamentary decisions. Richard Bellamy, "Political Constitutionalism and the Human Rights Act," *International Journal of Constitutional Law* 9, no. 1 (2011): 94.

[131] Benjamin N. Cardozo, *The Nature of the Judicial Process,* 13th ed. (New Haven: Yale University Press, 1946), 83.

[132] Hans Kelsen, "The Function of a Constitution," in *Essays on Kelsen*, ed. Richard Tur and William Twinning, trans. Iain Stewart (Oxford: Clarendon Press, 1986), 109.

Theory of Law," constitutions have a leading role for the foundation and the validity of the whole legal system, and norms cannot be considered as invalid as long as they comply with constitutions:

> If we ask for the reason of the validity of a positive legal order, we arrive finally at a historically first constitution, which authorizes custom or a legislative organ to create general norms, which, in their turn, authorize judicial and administrative organs to create individual norms. The assumption that these norms are valid presupposes a norm authorizing the Fathers of the Constitution to create the norms instituting legislation or custom as the basis of all the other legal functions. This norm is the reason of the validity of the Constitution and hence the basic norm of the legal order established in conformity with the Constitution. It is a norm presupposed in our juristic thinking; it cannot be a norm created by the act of will of a definite individual (…)[133]

In short, in Kelsenian terms, the function of a constitution is "the grounding of validity."[134] Accordingly, a positive legal system is composed of superordinate and subordinate norms, on top of which the constitution is found; and where the validity of a higher norm grounds the validity of a lower norm, which is subordinated to the higher norm in terms of its creation.[135] On the other hand, from the view of the earlier positivists such as Austin, law, as a positive science, had to deny all kinds of value judgments, and positive constitutional law was not a law at all, but a type of political morality.[136]

Against this background, constitution can also be defined as "a body of metanorms, rules that specify how legal norms are to be produced, applied, and interpreted"[137] when their relations with other norms are taken into consideration. Accordingly, constitutions constitute polities as metanorms, which provide legitimacy for legal rules. At this point, autonomy from the power is a significant criterion for gaining a normative feature for constitutions; and therefore, for example, the absolutist or authoritarian traditions of constitutionalism do not represent a real constitution at all.[138]

"Normative constitutional law" was referred by Louis Favoreu, as a study of sources of the hierarchy of norms in constitutional law.[139] In this respect, this would simply be defined as a method for the application of Kelsenian theory to constitutional law. This theory does not only submit that constitutional norms are subject to

---

[133] Hans Kelsen, "On the Basic Norm," *California Law Review* 47, no:1 (1959): 108.

[134] Kelsen, "Function of a Constitution," 119.

[135] Ibid.

[136] Martin Loughlin, "The Concept of Constituent Power," *European Journal of Political Theory* 13, no. 2 (2013): 4.

[137] Alec Stone-Sweet, "What is a Supranational Constitution? An Essay in International Relations Theory," *The Review of Politics* 56, no. 3 (1994): 444, emphasis belongs to the original text.

[138] Ibid. 446.

[139] Kemal Gözler, *Anayasa Hukukunun Metodolojisi* (Bursa: Ekin Kitabevi Yayinlari, 1999), 193.

a hierarchy of norms, but it also argues that this occurs between different sub-disciplines of law, as constitutional law rises to the top of other sub-disciplines.[140]

Hart deals with functions of constitutions as the founding elements of the whole legal system as well. According to him, constitution is a rule of recognition.[141] The rule of recognition simply provides persons and officials with authoritative criteria for identifying the primary rules of obligation.[142] In a legal system where a variety of sources of law exist, the rule of recognition arises as a criterion for the validity of rules. In his theory, the rule of recognition sets the basis for the whole structure, and constitutions are situated as a basis of the legal order.

As touched upon above, the traditional approaches mostly deal with doctrines of particular constitutions, and they do this by developing philosophical perspectives.[143] When classical accounts of constitutions are viewed from a sociological standpoint, they are criticized for neglecting "the factual dispersal of legal and constitutional power" within the society, since they adhere to the unfruitful distinctions of public law and private law, and for reducing the source of normative and legitimating force of constitutions into a "foundational normative consensus."[144]

From the standpoint of some normativist perspectives, for example constitutions of states in USA, are in fact not real constitutions when compared with the federal constitution; rather they only form a positive law. The reason is that they do not meet the traditional prerequisites of constitutions, e.g. they have no founders, and residents of a state cannot be understood as "people" in a constitutionalist sense since they do not have any ethnic, linguistic or religious concerns.[145]

The borders of the interpretation of a constitution are too narrow within a normative analysis since they neglect a distinction between normative elements and extralegal components of a constitution. This may lead to a breakage in obtaining data regarding the constitutional norms. As Thornhill states very illuminatingly,

> normative inquiry (…) tends to see one set of constitutional norms as categorically distinct from alternative or historically antecedent norms, and it closes its view to the continuous social processes that are reflected through constitutional normativity. For example, it omits to consider ways in which new constitutional norms might refract underlying transformations of societal structure; it does not consider how these norms might reflect changes in the

---

[140] Ibid. 195.

[141] H.L.A. Hart, *The Concept of Law*, 2nd ed. (Oxford: Clarendon Press, 1994), 100. For an opposite view: Raz, "On the Authority," 161. Raz notes that the rule of recognition is always customary and cannot enable a transition to the statutory law. However, this does not comply with the nature of constitutions, which can become statutory in case being changed by legislation.

[142] Ibid.

[143] Denis J. Galligan and Mila Versteeg, "Theoretical Perspectives on the Social and Political Foundations of Constitutions," in *Social and Political Foundations of Constitutions*, ed. Denis J. Galligan and Mila Versteeg (Cambridge: Cambridge University Press, 2013), 3.

[144] Chris Thornhill, "Niklas Luhmann and the Sociology of the Constitution," *Journal of Classical Sociology* 10, no. 4 (2010): 320.

[145] Gardner, "What is State Constitution?," 1029.

> environments to which law needs to be applied and in which it needs to be legitimised; it is curiously inattentive to the nexus between changing norms, changing social functions, and changing demands for law, power and legitimacy.[146]

From Thornhill's perspective, this amounts to missing "inner meanings" and the societal functions of norms achieved through the social practice.

Another striking point is that normativist approaches in the legal discourse can be deemed to be "tautological," on the ground that they advance the claim that all legal systems have a constitution.[147] This indeed results in narrowing borders of analysis in a sense. Furthermore, a constitution that only stands for a textual body may not be identical to a constitution that stands for "the supreme law" in all cases. This difference also makes sense in their interpretation.[148]

In this vein, Dworkin clearly affirms that legal positivism is an inadequate tool for the interpretation of constitutions, as it neglects the essential fact that law is not only what the officials have declared, but also "the principles underlying what they have declared, whether they have recognized those principles or intended to enact them or not. Law is a matter of integrity, not just fiat."[149]

4.1.1.2.2 *Constitutions in Context: The Dichotomy of Political Constitution and Legal Constitution*

In order to demonstrate that the "textual sameness" of analytical interpretations does not work to reflect the truth of constitutional law, the text now proceeds to a contemporary constitutional discourse in which the "interpretive selfhood" of constitutions is the major motive. The debate regarding the legal and political forms of constitution reflects a deep intellectual cleavage in reading the contemporary dimensions of constitution. At this point, the text aims at finding out the dynamics of interpretation that lead to the emergence of these opposite constitutional traditions.

Given the functions of constitutions in the maintenance of democracy, as mentioned in the previous section, contemporary forms of constitutionalism have been perceived in terms of two opposite poles, "political" and "legal" constitutionalism. The central issue of this division is "the role of law in democracy."[150] Basically,

---

146 Thornhill, "Rights and Constituent Power," 357.

147 Raz, "On the Authority," 153.

148 Michael J. Perry, "What is 'the Constitution'? (and Other Fundamental Questions)," in *Constitutionalism: Philosophical Foundations*, ed. Larry Alexander (Cambridge: Cambridge University Press, 1998), 112. It should be noted that in the quoted text, the author focuses rather on the US Constitutions. Therefore, the expression of "the supreme law" should be thought in the context of the US Constitution.

149 Dworkin, "Constitutionalism and Democracy," 6.

150 Panu Minkkinen, "Political Constitutionalism versus Political Constitutional Theory: Law, Power, and Politics," *International Journal of Constitutional Law* 11, no. 3 (2013): 585. Gadamer 174.

this debate reflects the distinction between European and British constitutional traditions.

In a very general sense, constitutionalism would be commonly defined as seeking "to prevent arbitrary government."[151] Beyond this extremely large definition, it is of note that various constitutional traditions can reflect different understandings of constitutionalism, depending on how they understand arbitrary acts and how they commit to prevent these acts.[152] The most striking division between constitutional traditions in these terms relates to the distinction between "political constitutionalism" and "legal constitutionalism." This distinction has become an important part of the contemporary constitutional law discourse, rather by virtue of the debates on British constitutionalism. To be more precise, it was formerly assumed that English law included neither public nor constitutional law until these issues began to be addressed in a case in 1970.[153] Furthermore, the British Constitution, which was formally accorded by the Department of Constitutional Affairs, proved that the UK has its own constitution, whose central pillar consists of the Human Rights Act of 1998 that gives effect to the European Convention on Human Rights in domestic law.[154] That this debate arose in Britain was not surprising since it has no written constitution, despite the rise of various constitutional movements and the constitutional documents of the past. In this respect, a distinction between political constitutionalism and legal constitutionalism through constitutional matters of Britain has recently been subject to the academic works of British scholars in particular, most notably Griffith, Tomkins, Loughlin and Bellamy.[155]

The "arbitrariness" is a keyword for this distinction. According to the classical and neo-republican political constitutionalism, arbitrariness means the domination of the ruled by their rulers, and constitutionalism copes with this situation by constituting a balance of power between the relevant social groups and parties. On the other hand, for the legal constitutionalism tradition, arbitrariness means

[151] Richard Bellamy, "Constitutionalism," in *International Encyclopedia of Political Science*, ed. B. Badie, D. Berg-Scholsser and L. Morlino (IPSA/Sage 2010), http://ssrn.com/abstract=1676321, l, last visit 12.12.2014.

[152] Ibid.

[153] Home Office vs. Dorse Yacht Co. Ltd., A.C. 1004 (1970), cited by Tom R. Hickman, "In Defence of the Legal Constitution," *The University of Toronto Law Journal* 55, no. 4 (2005), 981.

[154] Ibid.

[155] Graham Gee and Grégoire C. N. Webber, "What is a Political Constitution?," *Oxford Journal of Legal Studies* 30, no. 2 (2010): 275. For the most notable academic works of this field: J.A.G. Griffith, "The Political Constitution," *Modern Law Review* 42, no. 1 (1979): 1-21. Richard Bellamy, *Political Constitutionalism: A Republican Defence of the Constitutionality of Democracy* (Cambridge: Cambridge University Press, 2007). Adam Tomkins, *Our Republican Constitution* (Oxford: Hart, 2005). Martin Loughlin, *The Idea of Public Law* (Oxford: Oxford University Press, 2003).

"interference with individual rights, and seeks to establish protections for them via the separation of powers and a judicially protected constitution."[156] The main focus of the classical constitutionalism mentioned above, is on the designation and the function of democratic processes; whereas, the latter rather highlights the judicial protection of a political system and the constitutionally consolidated rights by constitutional courts.[157]

Another key point on the debate of political constitutionalism and legal constitutionalism concerns where the supremacy lies. For political constitutionalists, supremacy (should) lie(s) with the legislature; whereas, it (should) lie(s) with the judiciary according to the legal constitutionalists.[158]

The dichotomy of legal and political constitutions is independent from other conventional distinctions of the constitutional theory. The distinction between legal and political constitutions does not reflect a republican-liberal dichotomy at all. This is proved by the facts that many neo-republican scholars argue for a constitutional form, which involves the same themes as liberal constitutions; and thus a political constitution is not necessarily a reflection of the republican philosophy. Further, the writings of Jeremy Waldron are to be counted as another example, as he is a liberal while he pursues a political constitutionalist theory.[159]

As a matter of fact, the elements of legal and political constitutionalism can be found in most of the constitutions.[160] From the point of advocating liberties, most of the political and legal constitutionalists consider themselves civil libertarians.[161] One of the fundamental differences between a legal and a political constitution has to do with the question of "how best to hold the government to account." In this regard, political constitutionalists privilege political forms and institutions of accountability; whereas, legal constitutionalists think that accountability is best secured through the legal forms and institutions.[162] The political constitutionalists mostly refer to the concepts of "the openness, the possibilities for participation, the effectiveness, and the democracy enhancing features of political constitutionalism," and the legal constitutionalists largely rely on the "reason and reasonableness," as well as the idea that a constitution "protects minorities as well as majorities, and secures for all the enjoyment of basic rights."[163]

---

[156] Bellamy, "Constitutionalism," 1.

[157] Ibid.

[158] Richard Bellamy, "Political Constitutionalism and Human Rights Act," 89.

[159] Marco Goldoni and Christopher McCorkindale, "A Note From the Editors: The State of the Political Constitution," *German Law Journal* 14, no. 12 (2013): 2104.

[160] Richard Bellamy, *Political Constitutionalism: Republican Defence*, 5.

[161] Adam Tomkins, "The Role of the Courts in the Political Constitution," *University of Toronto Law Journal* 60 (2010): 3.

[162] Ibid., 2.

[163] Ibid., 2.

4.1.1.2.2.1 Legal Constitution

4.1.1.2.2.1.1 Theoretical Background

A legal constitution is characterized by the recourse to independent courts that enable the resolution of reasonable disagreements over constitutional issues.[164] The idea of constitutional rights is the main aspect of the legal constitutionalism.[165] In a nutshell, the legal constitutionalists advocate the ideas that a rights-oriented judicial review mechanism impedes the majority tyranny and fecklessness; the rights provide the basic principles in case of coming across multiple interpretations of laws, and furthermore, they construct democratic processes as their basic grounds.[166] On the other hand, the separation of judicial, executive and legislative powers is essential to legal constitutions. The rationale behind this is that a parliament should enact laws that are to be interpreted and applied by courts; and only by this way, freedoms can effectively be protected.[167]

The separation of powers that evolved mainly in the course of the British Civil War of the seventeenth century, was a turning point for the development of legal constitutionalism.[168] The main source of motivation in this process was the idea that "individuals or groups should not be 'judges in their own cause'."[169] The separation of powers also provided the constitutions with more efficiency in terms of the division of labour.[170]

The theory of separation of power and the theory of mixed government have two distinct aims. In short, in Bellamy's words,

> Within the "pure" theory of the separation of powers all three branches were co-equal. As with the theory mixed government, the aim was to prevent any one section of society dominating another by obliging each to collaborate with the others.[171]

The judiciary was not a distinctive function in the theory of mixed government, and it burgeoned in the theory of the separation of powers. Throughout its historical development, the judiciary made its function more clear; and in the era of contemporary constitutionalism, its competences reached the largest of its evolution.[172] In this regard, it could be argued that legal constitution arose as a corrective to the idea of political constitution.[173]

---

[164] Mark Tushnet, "The Relation Between Political Constitutionalism and Weak-Form Judicial Review," *German Law Journal* 14, no. 12 (2013): 2250.

[165] Bellamy, *Political Constitutionalism: Republican Defence*, 15.

[166] Ibid.

[167] Hickman, "In Defence of Legal Constitution," 1004.

[168] Bellamy, "Constitutionalism," 5.

[169] Ibid., 5.

[170] Ibid., 6.

[171] Ibid.

[172] Ibid., 7.

[173] Ibid.

As a common thread, according to legal constitutionalists, once a matter is involved in a constitution, it is a political issue no more.[174] Legal constitutionalism is largely criticized by the political constitutionalists on the ground that they advocate apolitical or depoliticized models of the deliberative democracy.[175]

Legal constitutions are typically marked by a constitutional text and a set of unwritten constitutional principles. In this sense, a constitution stands for a higher law that renders conflicting inferior laws invalid, and the transgressions of constitutional norms can be easily identified. Legal constitutions contain detailed and precise prescriptions on various essential issues of a public order that provide them their basic character, and they limit and bind the political activities.[176]

The academic works of Bruce Ackerman on modern constitutionalism reflects an example for the construction of legal constitutionalism in several terms.[177] First of all, Ackerman argues for a difference between the ordinary politics and the constitutional politics that comes about in the exceptional circumstances where the whole system of governments is at stake, and when these circumstances manage to unite people and lead them to consider a common good instead of their own interests.[178] Thus, constitutional politics are subject to various constitutional moments in consideration of their positions to the constitutional foundation. For instance, in USA, this occurs through "the Founding, Reconstruction and the New Deal" processes. The role of the Supreme Court judges is to uphold not only the founders' intentions, but also the intentions of people that arose at the last relevant moment, and they have to integrate various elements of each constitutional moments.[179] This leads to a greater democratic legitimacy of constitutions, as they are periodically reviewed; and by this way, their adaptation to changing circumstances is secured.

Political constitutionalists challenge this sort of a legal constitutionalism, first of all, by asserting that a distinction between constitutional and ordinary politics is redundant. From this point of view, constitutions are simply products of political processes; and thus they stand at the centre of all societies and there is no need to consider them within an extra-political framework.[180]

John Rawls also accounted on constitutions' roles in a democracy from a liberal perspective. In Rawls' point of view, a constitution should provide the constitutional courts with a competence to the interpretation and the protection of rights and liberties.[181] According to him, political decision-making processes and individual

---

[174] Gee and Webber, "What is Political Constitution?," 284.

[175] Bellamy, *Political Constitutionalism: Republican Defence*, 90.

[176] Gee and Webber, "What is Political Constitution," 286.

[177] Bruce Ackerman, *We the People: Foundations* (Cambridge: Belknap Press of Harvard University Press, 1993).

[178] Bellamy, *Political Constitutionalism: Republican Defence*, 129. Richard Bellamy and Dario Castiglione, "Constitutionalism and Democracy: Political Theory and the American Constitution," *British Journal of Political Science* 27 (1997): 609.

[179] Bellamy, *Political Constitutionalism: Republican Defence*, 131.

[180] Bellamy and Castiglione, "Constitutionalism and Democracy," 615.

[181] Ibid., 603.

considerations must be kept out of rights and liberties through constitutions. The rationale behind this understanding of constitutionalism goes beyond the conventional liberal theory, and it is to be explained by Rawls' conception of justice that basically aims at an "overlapping consensus" on the role and basis of politics, by isolating the core political principles.[182] This is also the key to a peaceful, social co-existence. However, such an insulation of the political sphere has been questioned by political constitutionalists with regard to the desirability and the possibility of such a situation. In this respect, this theory omits reconciling differences through negotiation and debate in a broader sense, and it may result in the de-legitimization of the political sphere.[183] On the other hand, the construction of an overlapping consensus is a political issue, and such a consensus can hardly be constructed without a political deliberation process.[184]

The political constitutionalists challenge legal constitutionalism in some further terms as well. Above all, the reliance of legal constitutionalism on rights comes to the fore. According to the political constitutionalist scholars, most notably Bellamy, constitutional rights are not mediums of reaching justice, even though they carry out some functions for societal well-doing.[185] Additionally, he points to the distinction between "constitutional politics" and "ordinary politics" in writings of some legal constitutionalists, and argues that it is a weak spot of this scholarship that they ignore the constitutional role of democratic politics. While they dismiss the role of democratic politics on constitutional issues, they largely focus on constraining or regulating political power by constitutions.[186]

Another objection to legal constitutionalism concerns the fact that legal constitutionalism reflects an attempt to depoliticize constitutions as a source of domination. Legal constitutionalism seeks to draw boundaries of the political sphere, and it replaces politics with an apolitical politics on some certain matters. However, this leads to a potential source of arbitrary rule and domination.[187]

On the other hand, some legal constitutionalists have developed counter arguments against political constitutionalists; and having referred to Dicey's views, they claimed that the true foundation of a constitution is a legal one.[188] In other words, this has been tantamount to the denial of the existence of a political constitution.

Dworkin's theory, as mentioned above, is likely to be considered as a response to some of the challenges to the idea of legal constitution. Above all, his theory, like that of Habermas, envisages that a true democracy is possible, if a political system provides constitutional protection of rights against the sovereign will.[189] A

[182] Ibid.

[183] Ibid., 604.

[184] Ibid., 608.

[185] Bellamy, *Political Constitutionalism: Republican Defence*, 19.

[186] Ibid., 141.

[187] Ibid., 147.

[188] Hickman, "In Defence of Legal Constitution," 987.

[189] Schneider, "Constitutional Protection," 119.

constitution that prescribes a judicial review mechanism over the executive bodies is mostly criticized as undemocratic, as courts, or better judges take decisions in such processes where a participation of people is not envisaged. On the other hand, it is commonly argued that disabling provisions of constitutions are likely to function as a limiting tool for the power of a majority that wishes its demands to be met. However, Dworkin, borrowing from an example from John Hart Ely, argues that the freedom of speech may prevent any censoring provision that is wished by the majority, but this is an underpinning situation for a democracy rather than a disabling one.[190] In fact, Dworkin affirms that this problem arises from the misunderstanding of democracy by constitutional lawyers who have overfocused on how to interpret constitution, and what constitutions do and say.[191] Instead, he highlights the fact that democracy is somewhat related to the collective actions of people. For this purpose, he makes a distinction between "statistical" and "communal" collective action. The statistical action marks group acts without any consciousness of collectivity; whereas communal action requires assumption of individuals as a collective group that is a separate entity or a phenomenon, and cannot be reduced to a statistical function of individual action.[192] The premise of "Canadian people want a more aggressive and interventionist economic policy" epitomizes the former, and the latter is exemplified by Germans feeling responsible for what their nation did regarding the Nazi crimes, not for what other Germans did.[193] These two forms of collective actions lead to two different readings of democracy. In this respect, the adoption of the former gives rise to a majoritarian outlook; while the communal reading envisages that political decisions in a democracy are taken by a distinct entity, such as people.[194] Accordingly, Dworkin argues that a response to the conflict between constitutionalism and democracy basically depends on which conception of democracy is adopted. In the statistical reading of democracy, structural provisions are limited to those which are expressly structural, that is to say, regarding procedure and organization. On the other hand, in a communal reading, the structural provisions are not limited to them, and a communal collective action is possible if the members of a community share certain ideals. In this understanding of democracy, every citizen is in a position to make a difference, and this difference is not subject to a limitation of power of others that deny any equal respect.[195] Under these circumstances, the maintenance of these ideals through restraints on majority decision is to be seen as a matter of "structuring democracy," but not as an issue of undermining democracy.[196] By this way, Dworkin constructs an account of democracy in the integrated and communal

[190] Ronald Dworkin, "Equality, Democracy and Constitution: We the People in Court," in *Constitutionalism and Democracy*, ed. Richard Bellamy (Ashgate: Dartmouth, 2006), 17.

[191] Ibid., 18.

[192] Ibid.

[193] Ibid.

[194] Ibid., 19.

[195] Ibid., 27.

[196] Ibid., 19.

sense. Integrity is a keyword in Dworkin's thinking about law. It requires judges to interpret law as a part of a self-consistent unity and consistency of principle regarding rights of citizens, in order to create fair and just situations.[197] In this respect, he speaks of an interpretive ideal of integrity that restrains personal beliefs and embraces judges to act with respect to a coherent set of principles about the rights and duties of people.[198] Judges are of a crucial position to determine the rights and duties, since only judges possess the sufficient expertise to employ principles drawn from various parts of law within this process.[199] Integrity requires the fidelity to theories of fairness and justice, in addition to rules and procedures.[200] Moreover, his theory of the law of integrity underpins the legitimacy of the state. That is to say, it establishes citizens' obligation to obey the law and justifies the coercive power. By this way, Dworkin points to a fraternal ideal as the source of the legitimacy.[201] In short, when democracy is considered on this basis, constitutionalism (in legal sense) is not likely to be a threat to democracy, but rather a supporting mechanism.

Furthermore, Dworkin is quite optimistic about the deliberation of people to politics through judicial review. He believes that citizens also have a direct impact on this process:

> [judicial review] provides a forum of politics in which citizens may participate, argumentatively, if they wish, and therefore in a manner more directly connected to their moral lives than voting almost ever is.[202]

This is to be regarded as a response to political constitutionalists, who consider judicial mechanism far from the participation of people.

Apart from that, Dicey's views reflect a sort of legal constitutionalism, as he opines that courts create a foundational basis for constitutions by determining and interpreting the law. Courts are "guardians of legality," by protecting rights and freedoms of citizens from the unlimited power.[203]

As seen, the incompatibility between constitutionalism and democracy is an old matter, and the balance between judicial mechanisms and political power mechanisms still reflects a notable problem. This problem lies at the heart of the challenge of political constitutionalists. In short, the legal constitutionalism has a legitimacy problem on the ground that it is hard to justify various political and executive privileges in this system. Therefore, as Hickman argues, political constitutionalists'

---

[197] T. R. S. Allan, "Dworkin and Dicey: The Rule of Law as Integrity," *Oxford Journal of Legal Studies* 8, no. 2 (1988): 266.

[198] Dworkin, *Law's Empire*, 225.

[199] Allan, "Dworkin and Dicey," 269.

[200] Ibid., 267.

[201] Ibid., 268.

[202] Ronald Dworkin, "What is Equality? Part 4: Political Equality," *University of San Francisco Law Review* 22, no. 1 (1988): 29 cited by Schneider, "Constitutional Protection," 114.

[203] Allan, "Dworkin and Dicey," 269.

objections to legal constitutionalism in fact do not stem from its foundational principles, but rather on the legitimacy problems of liberalism itself.[204]

4.1.1.2.2.1.2 German Basic Law (Grundgesetz) as a Legal Constitution

In view of the strong role of the constitutional court, the current German constitutional system is to be regarded as a genuine example of legal constitutions. The tension between constitutionalism and democracy was true for Germany in the past, as the first liberal constitution was born in a monarchy instead of a democracy in this country; and this had important impacts over the evolution of German constitutionalism.[205] On the other hand, the establishment of the Federal Constitutional Court of Germany and a judicial review mechanism by the Basic Law (Grundgesetz), made profound contributions to the development and perfection of German human rights culture.[206] This also gave a new shape to the constitutional order of Germany. Within this new system, for example, "the principle of Rechtsstaatlichkeit (Rule of Law) involves securing a person's rights by adjudication rather than through participation in the democratic decision making process."[207] This is a striking point, as it proves the role of adjudication over the rights and freedoms of persons. The Court achieves this by enjoying the characteristic powers of a constitutional court. At this juncture, it is of note that unlike the US Supreme Court, the Federal Constitutional Court of Germany is not an integral part of the general judicial system.[208] Furthermore, its decisions are final and binding for all other courts, all federal or state governmental organs and public officials.[209] In this respect, the source and the authority of the Federal Constitutional Court are certain and undisputed. This is to be regarded as a distinguished feature of the constitutional judicial mechanism in Germany. On the other hand, as a contrast example, in the US the main task of the Supreme Court is to find the source and to establish the limits of judicial review, since the Marbury v. Madison ruling of this court.[210] As it is mentioned in the Basic Law, the Federal Constitutional Court of Germany examines governmental actions that violate the constitutionally guaranteed individual rights and freedoms; examines the constitutionality of a rule upon application of a federal, state government, a certain number of Parliament members, or a judge of a lower court; examines controversies

[204] Hickman, "In Defence of Legal Constitution," 1016.

[205] Matthew G. Specter, *Habermas: Entelektüel Bir Biyografi*, (Istanbul: Iletisim Yayinlari, 2012), 36.

[206] Ibid., 37.

[207] Erhard Denninger, "Judicial Review Revisited: The German Experience," *Tulane Law Review* 59 (1984-5): 1014.

[208] Ibid., 1025.

[209] Donald P. Kommers, "German Constitutionalism: A Prolegomenon" (Scholarly Works Paper no. 98, 1991, http://scholarship.law.nd.edu/law_faculty_scholarship/98), 842, last visit 14.04.2014.

[210] Ibid., 842.

between constitutional institutions, e.g. between the executive branch and the Parliament; and examines conflicts between states and the federation.[211] Constitution is regarded as the yardstick of constitutional court judges, who are known as guardians of the constitution (Hüter der Verfassung), and they are able to declare a legislation null, unlike an ordinary judge from lower courts, who can just interpret a legislation in reaching decisions.[212] The Federal Constitutional Court of Germany also took some decisions that identified the scope of the constitutional adjudication through interpretation, and determined the principles and conditions that allowed judges to create new law.[213] Moreover, as the Federal Constitutional Court stated in an earlier ruling,

> No single constitutional provision may be taken out of its context and interpreted by itself .... Every constitutional provision must always be interpreted so as to render it compatible with the fundamental principles of the Constitution and the intention of its authors.[214]

This means that the Court preferred to stick to the will of the founders and in this respect, German constitutionalism differs from the US constitutionalism, which is open to a more dynamic interpretational perception, as will be mentioned below. The German constitutional court shall protect the constitution "as a whole." That is to say, one constitutional value can never be preserved at the expense of one another. Unity and harmonization are key words at this point.[215] In addition, the intention of the Court to fuse positivistic and natural law traditions of legality was manifest in former decisions through an interpretive principle, which is named "the unity of the Constitution as a logical-teleological entity."[216]

The Federal Constitutional Court of Germany also has a priority over the administrative bodies in terms of the doctrine of "indeterminate legal terms" (Unbestimmte Rechtsbegriffe). Due to this doctrine, in case of the existence of an indeterminate term in theory regarding the administrative matters, and its application to a specific case, the correct meaning must be determined only by the court. The Court has the last word in this case and the administration has no power. As Denninger explains it through an example,

> if the "reliability" of an applicant for a license to sell alcoholic beverages is at issue, the administrative tribunal is to scrutinize whether the administrative agency in its decision assessed "reliability" as it has been interpreted by the tribunals.[217]

---

[211] Denninger, "Judicial Review," 1017.

[212] Ibid.

[213] e.g. Soraya case of 1973, cited by Denninger, "Judicial Review," 1019.

[214] Kommers, "German Constitutionalism," 851. The author does not mention the name and any further information of the ruling.

[215] Ibid.

[216] Ibid.

[217] Still there are some exceptions to this principle. Denninger, "Judicial Review," 1021.

Having considered the role of the Basic Law in law and politics, it has been argued that German constitutionalism is characterized by the fact that the political process must adopt hegemony of the constitution.[218] Furthermore, in particular beginning from the 1970s, the Federal Constitutional Court developed a hegemony over German politics through some crucial decisions that impeded progressive activities of the liberal-social democratic majority in the parliament. The Court delineated the polity created by the Basic Law as a "militant democracy," and predicated some rulings on this view. The prohibition of a Neo-Nazi Party in 1952 and of the Communist Party of Germany in 1956 are the most remarkable examples.[219] The court was criticized severely, since intense intervention in politics was considered a breach of the doctrine of separation of powers.[220] This led to some concerns about the future of the democratic culture in Germany:

> The court's present function with respect to judicial review is positive. Nevertheless, some risks remain. The most serious of these is that an autocratic administration of justice might dangerously narrow the concept of pluralism to a monistic view of civic values. Such constricted perception of values, if practiced by the Constitutional Court and other high courts, might suffocate the still delicate flowering of democracy, of freedom of speech, and of active citizenship, which in Germany needs more intense care than in the robust grassroots democracy of the United States.[221]

Some political scholars, like Habermas, pointed to the excessive power of the Court and to a threat for the development of democratization of the German political culture in this sense.[222] This is a very clear-cut indicator of a paradox of legal constitutionalism. On the one hand, a legal constitution, which is subject to the judicial review through courts, comes to the forefront as the guardian of rule of law and human rights. On the other hand, this constitution establishes hegemony over the political realm, which is the natural habitus of democracy. In consequence, compared to other constitutional courts, the German court created a far broader scope of competence. For example, the US Supreme Court rejected all major cases which were heard by the German Constitutional Court, with respect to the procedure of "abstract review of statutes" (abstrakte Normenkontrolle).[223] In this regard, in view

---

[218] Kommers, "German Constitutionalism," 849.

[219] Socialist Reich Party Case, 2 BVerfGE 1 (1952); Communist Party Case, 5 BVerfGE 85 (1956), cited by Ibid., 854.

[220] Apart from the political critics, the court also received judicial protests through some dissenting opinions. The dissenting opinions by Judges von Brüneck and Simon in "University reform case" and "Roe v. Wade" are notable at this point. Denninger, "Judicial Review," 1023.

[221] Ibid., 1031.

[222] Specter, *Habermas*, 40.

[223] The "abstract review" is a remedy that is used when there exist "divergent opinions or doubts about the compatibility of federal or state law with the Basic Law or the compatibility of state law with other federal law," Denninger, "Judicial Review," 1025.

of the political roles and impacts of the Federal Constitutional Court of Germany, some scholars argued that a complete separation of political and judicial power is not possible when it comes to a constitutional order and adjudication; instead they are of complementary functions. Accordingly, the Federal Constitutional Court is supposed to be somewhat a political body instead of a judicial body.[224] Nevertheless, that each justice is elected by the Parliament by a two-thirds vote for a single non-renewable term of 12 years, is likely to be considered as a fact that makes the court's judicial activism "less objectionable."[225]

Last but not least, German constitution "takes rights seriously" in a Dworkinian manner.[226] Human dignity, as mentioned in Article 1, is the very foundation of other rights and the ultimate basis of the constitutional order. The Basic Law gives rights a place in a hierarchical manner. The rights-oriented structure characterizes the whole text. On the other hand, and in connection with this fact, the Federal Constitutional Court was inclined to deal with the Basic Law in terms of the value system that is inherent of it over time, and this led to a task of the Court to create and maintain a nation of shared values.[227] In conclusion, German constitution is to be referred as a "constitution of rights," rather than duties, unlike American constitution.[228]

4.1.1.2.2.2 Political Constitution

4.1.1.2.2.2.1 Theoretical Background

As mentioned above, political constitutionalists basically proceed from the insufficiency of liberal or legal constitutionalism to solve the tension between constitutionalism and democracy, and they view political constitutionalism as an alternative to the legal constitutionalism. To this end, they argue for a republican form of constitutionalism that relies on the political and democratic processes, and that can function without a formal constitution.[229] In this respect, the reasonable disagreements over constitutional issues should be resolved through "open debate and ultimate decision-making by democratically chosen officials."[230] The concept of political constitution, in the context of British constitution, originates from the academic work of J.A.G. Griffith, titled "the Political Constitution," that focuses on the description of the British political system.[231] Griffith's findings were followed by several scholars, and consequently political constitutionalism has become a full-fledged constitutional theory that was raised as an alternative to the liberal legalism

---

224 Ibid., 1024-25.

225 Kommers, "German Constitutionalism," 844.

226 Ibid., 855.

227 Ibid., 861.

228 Ibid., 872.

229 Bellamy and Castiglione, "Constitutionalism and Democracy," 617.

230 Tushnet, "Political Constitutionalism and Weak-Form," 2250.

231 Griffith, "Political Constitution."

or legal constitutionalism.[232] The most remarkable characteristic of this understanding of constitution lies in the belief in "a return to a Benthamite conception of democracy in a bid to reinvigorate parliamentary politics."[233]

The theory of mixed government provides a model of constitutionalism that relies on institutions that determine methods of decision-making, as it was prescribed in Aristotle's Politics and Polybius's Histories.[234] The mixed government did not make any clear distinction between powers; and executive, judicial and legislative powers were shared by different social classes. The theory that relied on this kind of government was challenged by the developments of seventeenth and eighteenth centuries. Through these developments, governmental and loyal oppositions gave rise to a new kind of balance of powers, a new form of political constitutionalism. However, Bellamy argues that, the mixed government did not disappear in this new formation, and it was reproduced in new ways that enabled different kinds of interests to exist within the policy and law-making processes on an equal basis.[235]

On the other hand, approaches of Richard Bellamy and Adam Tomkins, who made their contributions to political constitutionalism later than Griffith, represent "a normative turn" in political constitutionalism, since their idea of political constitutionalism is a normative account thereof.[236] However, this has never amounted to an entirely legalist view. For example, according to Bellamy, there is no non-political world, that is to say, everything –and constitutions as well – is political and there is no chance to deal with them outside of politics.[237]

Political constitutions do not contain any comparable and definitive prescriptions, that is to say, any consistent statement, rights or formalized legal instruments, any entrenching procedures that complicate the amendment of constitutions and fixed constitutional boundaries. In this respect, how they can be prescriptive remains in the dark as it is hard to identify the normative content of constitutions.[238] Hence, normative aspects of political constitutions are weaker than legal constitutions:

> Because a political constitution "lives on changing from day to day" (as Griffith noted), and because, in a very real sense, "the democratic process is the constitution" (as Bellamy noted), a political constitution is, in the final analysis, difficult to identify as a phenomenon distinct from day-to-day political activity. There is no appeal to a reified constitutional text, to a bill of rights or to grand judicial pronouncements. Rather, a political constitution works primarily, and often imperceptibly, inside Parliament and the executive and, where visible, its workings will often appear less dignified and more haphazard than court proceedings, as

[232] Goldoni and McCorkindale, "A Note From the Editors," 2104.

[233] D. Dyzenhaus, "The Left and the Question of Law," *Canadian Journal of Law and Jurisprudence* 17 (2004): 7, cited by Thomas Poole, "Tilting at Windmills? Truth and Illusion in 'The Political Constitution'," *Modern Law* Review 70, no. 2 (2007): 250.

[234] Bellamy, "Constitutionalism," 3.

[235] Ibid., 5.

[236] Gee and Webber, "What is Political Constitution," 282.

[237] Ibid., 285.

[238] Ibid., 286.

> members of Parliament argue amongst each other, harangue the Prime Minister and then, for the most part, rally behind their party whips.[239]

In other words, political constitutionalism does not require a tangible constitution, unlike legal constitutionalism. Political constitutionalism is rather marked by a "living constitution" or a customary constitution. However, this does not mean that a political constitution is not prescriptive, but the nature and content of a constitution are not prescribed in great detail for the reason that it is always subject to change, affected by the ordinary political processes.[240] In Griffith's words, "[e]verything that happens is constitutional, [and] if nothing happened that would be constitutional also," that is to say, a constitution is the expression of daily politics.[241]

A political constitution does not imply that there are no legal restraints on the power of government, although it initially looks like an oxymoron. In addition, it does not mean that existing legal restraints are supervised only by political constitutions instead of courts. Against this background, the questions of "how much law" and "where should the limits of legality be set" arise as significant issues of political constitutionalism.[242]

According to Griffith, societies are by nature authoritarian, and governments are even more so.[243] The key conception of his understanding of political constitutionalism is "conflict," in the sense of either interests or ideology. He believes that the nature of human association is inescapably conflictual, and this is the source of his anti-authoritarian standing.[244] In this respect, politics means "the political management of conflict" and law is just "one means, one process, by which those conflicts are continued or may be temporarily resolved."[245] On the other side, Griffith depicts the judiciary as the "part of the established authority;"[246] and the function of the judicial adjudication under a Bill of Rights is to "pass political decisions out of the hands of politicians and into the hands of judges."[247] That is to say, regardless of who takes a decision, a political decision keeps its political character at any time. Even if it is taken by a judge, a political decision is still of a political character. However, according to Griffith, a political decision should be taken by politicians. This is a more secure way, since they are removable by elections and are also accountable to

---

[239] Ibid.

[240] Ibid.

[241] Ibid.

[242] K. D. Ewing, "The Resilience of the Political Constitution," *German Law Journal* 14, no. 12 (2013): 2117.

[243] Griffith, "Political Constitution," 2.

[244] Graham Gee, "The Political Constitutionalism of JAG Griffith," *Legal Studies* 28, no. 1 (2008): 33.

[245] Ibid., 27-28.

[246] J. A. G. Griffith, *The Politics of the Judiciary* (London: Fontana, 1997), 335.

[247] Gee, "Political Constitutionalism of Griffith," 28.

the Parliament.[248] In his opinion, judges are not neutral actors of these processes, as usually expected:

> because they are placed in positions where they are required to make political choices which are sometimes presented to them, and often presented by them, as determinations of where the public interest lies.[249]

That is to say, the determinations of the public interest reflect the political views of the judiciary. However, according to Griffith, a constitution carries out functions to manage political conflicts at all times, and therefore it must show sufficient flexibility to respond to changing patterns of these political conflicts.[250] He explains the prior role of politics in a democratic constitutional order as follows:

> Constitutions are political structures and should, in democratic societies, be designed so as to incorporate dissent and provide adequate opportunities for the expression of minority views. But laws themselves are used both to suppress and to promote freedom. Only politics will decide which.[251]

As a political constitutionalist, Griffith articulates his concerns on the transformation of the British constitutional order where enlargement of the scope of the judicial review is in process, beginning from the adoption of the Human Rights Act of 1998, in various ways. In this regard, Griffith states that this turn in the constitutional system of Britain will result in an inevitable conflict between the courts and the government.[252] Like many other political constitutionalists, he opines that the idea that judges can keep their impartiality is not true, and the political partiality of judges is a real threat against the British democracy.[253]

According to Poole, Griffith's idea of political constitution aims toward two main points, which are political and philosophical, as the basic constitutional reform and the constitutional theories influenced by natural law.[254] In this regard, Griffith's scholarship is likely to be considered as an opponent of natural law as well as liberal constitutionalism. He castigates Dworkin, as he views the concepts of "moral reading of a constitution" and "community morality" as unreasonable, in view of the reality of law.[255] Further, he argues that natural lawyers also failed in explaining the working principles of constitutions, as they used the nineteenth century language based on the concepts of the eighteenth century.[256] In a kind of

---

[248] Ibid., 29.

[249] Ibid.

[250] Ibid., 33.

[251] JAG Griffith, "The Common Law and the Political Constitution," *Law Quarterly Review* 117 (2001): 59-60, cited by Ibid., 33.

[252] JAG Griffith, "The Brave New World of Sir John Laws," *Modern Law Review* 63 (2000): 159-176.

[253] Ibid.

[254] Poole, "Tilting at Windmills?," 253.

[255] Griffith, "Political Constitution," 11; Poole, "Tilting at Windmills?," 252.

[256] Griffith, "Political Constitution," 6.

"Austinian view," he explicitly denies the moral character of law, and affirms that law only consists of the statements of the power relationships.[257] According to him, the rights are political claims in a "Benthamian sense;" they have no moral connections and they reflect the power relations as well.[258] In that respect, since political issues should be dealt with by politicians, the bill of rights has no function to solve political problems; and politicians only change the direction of conflicts towards the courts instead of the democratic realm.[259] A very fundamental view of Griffith is that legal constitutions usurp the political power without any legitimate basis. Further, a rights centric approach to law is likely to evade responsibilities regarding the truth of real issues and to mythologize these matters.[260]

Given these facts, Griffith describes the British constitution as a living and ubiquitous one, in other words:

> The constitution of the United Kingdom lives on, changing from day to day for the constitution is no more and no less than what happens. Everything that happens is constitutional. And if nothing happened that would be constitutional also.[261]

Griffith's basic opinions reflect the core of political constitutionalism. Further, Mark Tushnet and Jeremy Waldron are other constitutional scholars, whose names are to be mentioned in this debate as they advocate constitutional politics that regard the parliament as the centre thereof.[262]

The prescriptive feature of political constitutions is different from legal constitutions, as it is not as binding as legal constitutions. In this respect, the failure of political constitutions in their basic tasks does not give rise to the invalidity or violence of fundamental law, "but a distancing from the republican ideal and a concomitant source of domination and political inequality."[263] In contrast to legal constitutionalism, which envisages the preexistence of a constitutional text in great details, political constitutionalism prescribes very little in order to let the political actors prescribe the content and the character of a constitution.[264] Indeed, political constitutionalism still concerns the similar issues of legal constitutionalism as individual rights, legality, democracy etc. However, the greatest difference is that political constitutionalism also deals with the "legitimacy of the processes whereby we define and promote or restrict rights through legislation and administrative action."[265] In this regard, a political constitutionalist approach can reveal the illegitimacy of constitutional processes within a different view from legal constitutionalism, as Bellamy notes:

---

[257] Ibid., 19.

[258] Poole, "Tilting at Windmills?," 258.

[259] Griffith, "Political Constitution," 14.

[260] Ibid., 17.

[261] Ibid., 19.

[262] Poole, "Tilting at Windmills?," 264.

[263] Gee and Webber, "What is Political Constitution," 294.

[264] Ibid.

[265] Bellamy, *Political Constitutionalism: Republican Defence*, 145.

> From this perspective, a failure to acknowledge the disagreements that surround constitutional values, and the resulting need for political mechanisms to resolve them, can itself be a source of domination and arbitrary rule that impacts negatively on rights and the rule of law.[266]

When explaining his opinions on political constitutionalism, Bellamy refers to Quentin Skinner and Philip Pettit, as they state that avoidance of domination, or freedom as non-domination marks a neo-Roman reflection of the republican tradition.[267] Political constitutionalism is reflected through the republican principles of non-domination, equality and political mechanisms of public reasoning and balance of power.[268] Against this background, political constitutionalism, in Bellamy's words, advocates democracy against judicial review, on the grounds that democracy upholds and protects constitutional rights, values and rule of law, whereas judicial review weakens constitutional values and attributes of a democratic order.[269]

Bellamy states that he argues for the model of political constitution for the constitutional order of the UK, on the ground that political means provide more secure safeguards for human rights, compared with legal constitutionalism.[270] In this sense, political constitutionalism suggests defining law in a more legitimate basis through associating its source with a democratically elected legislature.[271] According to him, a political understanding of constitutionalism gives rise to deliberation; an adequate realization and protection of constitutional values lead to the operation of real democratic politics instead of ideal democratic politics.[272]

British constitution can still be considered as both a political and a legal constitution from different perspectives.[273] Likewise, most constitutions are likely to have features of both political and legal constitutions.[274] However, in relevant literature, it is largely adopted that British constitution primarily reflects features of a political constitution.[275] Likewise, Switzerland, which adopted the maxim of "democracy

[266] Ibid.

[267] He refers to Quentin Skinner, *Liberty Before Liberalism*, (Cambridge: Cambridge University Press, 1998), and Philip Pettit, *Republicanism: A Theory of Freedom and Government* (Oxford: Oxford University Press, 1997). Ibid., 154.

[268] Ibid., 209.

[269] Ibid., 260.

[270] Bellamy, "Political Constitutionalism and Human Rights Act," 88.

[271] Ibid., 110.

[272] Bellamy, *Political Constitutionalism: Republican Defence*, 210.

[273] Ibid., 295.

[274] Ibid., 5.

[275] Adam Tomkins, "Constitutionalism," in *The Oxford Handbook of British Politics*, ed. Matthew Flinders et al. (Oxford: Oxford University Press, 2009), 242. Tomkins, *Our Republican Constitution*. However, attempts to underline that British constitution is evolving towards a model of legal constitution should not be overlooked. Gee and Webber, "What is Political Constitution," 299.

as the guardian of human rights"[276] (instead of a supreme court), reflects a sort of political constitutionalism.[277]

Richard Bellamy reconstructs political constitutionalism by employing several common features of constitutions. Political constitutionalists agree that a rights-based constitutional law cannot be located above politics. They do not totally deny the requirement of rights for a constitutional system; however, they basically advocate the idea that "any system of rights has to be politically negotiated and will be the product of institutional arrangements that exist to arbitrate these debates," in order to determine the most appropriate system of rights.[278] In this respect, judicial review is also a matter of politics.[279] Political constitutionalists deem the democratic source of a law as an essential feature of its political legitimacy, and thereby they do not reflect parallelism with legal positivism.[280] Another striking point in Bellamy's description is that political constitutionalists deem courts to be less legitimate and less effective mechanisms than legislatures within democratic systems, in view of the deliberative qualities of legislatures and accountability of legislators.[281] Finally, political constitutionalists advance the claim that the rights determined by legislators should be superior to the decisions of courts, in other words a Parliament must be the Supreme Court on constitutional issues and rights.[282]

According to Bellamy, a non-dominating process of politics must meet two criteria:

> First, citizens will need to feel that no difference of status exists between them and the decision-makers. The decision makers cannot be chosen because for some reason they are deemed to be "superior" sorts of people. Second, the reason the views of some citizens may count for less than those of others in the actual decision cannot be because some people hold the "right" view and others the "wrong" one.[283]

These criteria are met in a standard democratic process. The democratic process has a distinctive character of non-domination, when compared with the judicial processes. Legal constitutions can claim legitimacy provided that a constitution is based on terms that cannot be rejected reasonably by anybody, and from this perspective this is not possible.[284]

---

[276] Karl-Heinz Ladeur, "Ein Recht der Netzwerke für die Weltgesellschaft oder Konstitutionalisierung der Völkergemeinschaft," *Archiv des Völkerrechts* 49 (2011): 249.

[277] However, it is of note that Switzerland has an effective Supreme Court and judicial review mechanisms over violation of the constitution, and in this sense, it does not fit into this category perfectly.

[278] Bellamy, "Political Constitutionalism and Human Rights Act," 90.

[279] Ibid.

[280] Ibid., 91.

[281] Ibid.

[282] Ibid., 92.

[283] Bellamy, *Political Constitutionalism: Republican Defence*, 164.

[284] Ibid., 165.

According to political constitutionalists, determining the content of rights is a crucial point in order to understand their political character. In this sense, a consensus on rights is somewhat political, and hence it is not very possible to find out an agreed constitutional framework of rights.[285] This creates a weak spot for legal constitutionalism that claims to offer a common framework of rights. Additionally, these scholars argue that, compared with legislative processes, judicial processes include certain weaknesses in safeguarding these rights. In this regard, judicial review on constitutional matters for example, may render law uncertain in some cases:

> It invites judges to employ their potentially eccentric or debatable moral judgments rather than to be guided by narrower legal considerations that allow citizens to know where they stand with regard to laws by making it more likely they will be interpreted and applied in consistent ways.[286]

A social change can only be enabled by legislation and judicial review may hinder such a process.[287]

In Loughlin's view, public law is part of an autonomous political practice and does not have distinctive characteristics in this sense.[288] Furthermore, political constitutionalists examine how far law is *per se* able to mitigate arbitrariness in governmental matters through the concept of rule of law. The rule of law is a paradoxical concept for them in several terms. For example, Bellamy touches upon the views of Hayek and Dworkin regarding the rule of law and the moral integrity of law. He questions the sufficiency of the criteria of generality, universality and non-discrimination to achieve their goals. In this sense, he goes through examples of racial laws of Nazis and South African Apartheid system, and he concludes that rules that meet these criteria may clearly be prone to consolidate certain biases and injustices.[289] The tyrannical rulers may even have an interest in creating a predictable regime for themselves. The legality may stabilize power, but on the other hand "it also skews the law against the poor and less well-placed."[290] He also argues that, although Hayek believes that rules could even eliminate judicial discretions, this never happens in reality.[291] In addition, he challenges Dworkin, by saying that his theory on the moral dimensions of law is far from being objective, as it is very difficult to sustain objectivity claims because of "the limitations of human reasoning which appear to allow for rival claims to be made."[292] It is also hard to claim that judiciary will reach the morally best view of law. Consequently, this renders law

[285] Ibid., 25.

[286] Ibid., 37.

[287] Ibid., 44.

[288] Hickman, "In Defence of Legal Constitution," 992.

[289] Bellamy, *Political Constitutionalism: Republican Defence*, 70.

[290] Ibid., 81.

[291] Ibid., 71.

[292] Ibid., 78.

indeterminate. Instead, Bellamy advocates a political perspective to the rule of law. From this perspective, the rule of law relies on the conditions where all citizens enjoy an equal status in the making of laws and have no dominion over each other.[293] In this respect, justice is a matter of the balance of power. In addition, this view of rule of law does not rely on a formula that laws must be general, abstract and universal. Instead, "a provision should be justifiable in a mutually acceptable way and bear equally and consistently on all to whom it applies."[294] There is no criterion that determines which rules are to be accepted as law *a priori*, unlike in legal constitutionalism. Such problems are rather to be dealt with in the conformity with polities, and will have different results in different political cultures; thus rule, of law arises as the democratic rule of persons.[295]

In Tomkins' view, legal constitutionalists ignore the role of parliament's rule completely. According to him, courts should not exceed the role which they are designed for in a political constitutional order.[296] They should ensure that parliaments act fairly in terms of decision-making procedures, with the exception of protection of some civil liberties. In short, courts should take a secondary position in constitutional matters, and their roles should be limited to ensuring that the legislative bodies act fairly.

As mentioned in the details, political constitutionalists are somewhat in a defensive position, instead of suggesting a universal model of constitutionalism that is admissible throughout the world. For instance, in case of the political content of rights, they argue that reasonableness and proportionality are functional tools of parliamentary democracies like the UK, when addressing the question of acceptable and unacceptable expression within the framework of Article 10 of the ECHR. Therefore, it can function better than a judicial review mechanism.[297] As seen in this example and in the former ones, political constitutionalists usually think about the British constitution and the British political culture mostly, and about some further potential similar models. It is also of note that, unlike legal constitutionalists, they refrain from advancing universal claims. This is likely to be regarded as a distinguished feature of political constitutionalism.

4.1.1.2.2.2.2 The Human Rights Act and the British Constitution

As mentioned, the concept of political constitution was essentially coined to illustrate the British constitution. However, despite it being based on a political constitution and never having a written constitution, the development of the legal system of the UK induced very important contributions to the development of the legal

---

[293] Ibid., 80.

[294] Ibid., 82.

[295] Ibid., 83.

[296] Adam Tomkins, "What's Left of the Political Constitution?," *German Law Journal* 14, no. 12 (2013): 2280.

[297] Tomkins, "Role of Courts," 5.

constitutions, as it originated the concepts of the separation of powers and the bill of rights.[298] Nevertheless, the weakness of the judicial review mechanisms on public actions throughout the history of this system and the fact that political accountability was seen as the guarantee of a limited government, played a key role in this result. On the other hand, in spite of the overriding power of political traditions on judicial review; in particular, the adoption of the Human Rights Act by the Parliament of the United Kingdom on 9 November 1998, escalated the debates on the character of the British Constitution.

As a matter of fact, the extension of the scope of the judicial review in the UK has been at issue since the 1960s.[299] The Human Rights Act is an act that aims at placing the rights prescribed under the European Convention on Human Rights into the UK Law, and it renders any act of public bodies unlawful if they do not comply with the ECHR. Accordingly, the most striking feature of this act is that it enables individuals to bring human rights cases to domestic courts without a precondition of bringing their case before the European Court of Human Rights.[300] As a corollary, this leads to an overweight of the judicial review of acts of executive bodies instead of the political review, as it was the tradition of the UK constitutional and political system. Although in the Section 3(1) of the Act it is stated that "primary legislation and subordinate legislation must be read and given effect in a way which is compatible with the Convention rights," this is not a judicial restriction of legislative activities, since Section 3(2-b-c) prescribes that an incompatibility with this

> does not affect the validity, continuing operation or enforcement of any incompatible primary legislation; and (…) does not affect the validity, continuing operation or enforcement of any incompatible subordinate legislation if (disregarding any possibility of revocation) primary legislation prevents removal of the incompatibility).[301]

In other words, in terms of constitutional law, the Human Rights Act does not prescribe an exact turn to the judicial review of the primary legislation in a classical sense, as it is done in countries where legal constitutionalism is prevalent. As a matter of fact, the mechanism of the Human Rights Act to review the primary legislation is a unique one. In this regard, courts are empowered to issue a "declaration of incompatibility" in case a primary legislation contradicts rights governed under the ECHR. However, this does not mean that legislation at issue becomes invalid. It remains in force until it is amended by the government or the Parliament. This means that a court itself does not possess the power to overturn a legislative act unlike a classical judicial review mechanism. In case of a declaration of incompatibility, "the court's decision will be likely to trigger the Parliament to amend the relevant law."[302]

---

[298] Bellamy, "Political Constitutionalism and Human Rights Act," 86.

[299] Griffith, "Brave New World," 172.

[300] Section 7 of the Human Rights Act, http://www.legislation.gov.uk/ukpga/1998/42/section/7, last visit 31.03.2015.

[301] Ibid., Section 3(2-b-c).

Under these circumstances, British courts have less power than the courts of other European countries which have been granted the power to annul legislative acts that violate rights governed under the ECHR.[303] However, the Parliament is no longer beyond scrutiny. In addition, Bendor and Segal put forward the idea that the Human Rights Act can indeed be more efficient and functional in the case of proving the compatibility of legislative acts, rather than the incompatibility.[304]

Some British scholars, including J.A.G. Griffith, argued that the adoption of the Human Rights Act will result in the debasement of the legal argument.[305] Griffith's claims basically rely on four arguments. The adoption of convention rights will lead to judges leaving the traditional legal tests in practice of law because of the open-textured and indeterminate nature of rights. Then judges will seek new principles and doctrines that are compatible with this new source of law. Accordingly, the restraints on the power of judges will become weaker, and their individual characters will come forth in judicial processes. Furthermore, the new order of the Human Rights Act brings the "self-reinforcing language of rights" into play, and as such "judicial lawlessness" will come about by virtue of this new order.[306] Griffith was criticized on the ground that he downplays the normative content of a political constitution and his idea of the political constitution was very much stuck to the British constitution.[307]

On the other hand, for example, Ewing explicitly states that the adoption of the Human Rights Act could not be considered a sign of the transformation of the constitution from political to legal.[308] His objection, above all, relies on the opinion that the process of adjudication is itself a political one.[309] As a matter of fact, modern human rights law is not very credible in the eyes of political constitutionalists in terms of its procedural requirements. Despite them agreeing that human rights have a liberty-enhancing dimension, it provides the judiciary with vast power and this is "too high a price to pay."[310] In addition, Griffith draws attention to the conflict creating features of provisions of the ECHR, and he states that Article 10 of the ECHR, which governs the freedom of expression and information, is "the statement of a political conflict pretending to be a resolution of it."[311] Following this, Griffith repeats his doubts about legal constitutionalism:

---

[302] Ariel L. Bendor and Zeev Segal, "Constitutionalism and Trust in Britain: An Ancient Constitutional Culture, A New Judicial Review Model," *American University International Law Review* 17 (2001-2002): 689.

[303] Ibid., 690.

[304] Ibid., 701.

[305] Poole, "Tilting at Windmills?," 250–277, 264.

[306] Ibid., 265.

[307] Gee and Webber, "What is Political Constitution," 280.

[308] Ewing, "Resilience of the Political Constitution," 2112.

[309] Ibid.

[310] Tomkins, "Role of Courts," 4.

[311] Griffith, "Political Constitution," 14.

> If we incorporate the European Convention into our domestic law, questions like those in the thalidomide case will be left for determination by the legal profession as they embark on the happy and fruitful exercise of interpreting woolly principles and even woollier exceptions.[312]

As a common thread, political constitutionalists argue for the true roles of courts: "what they are good at and what they are designed for." Adam Tomkins delineates his view as far as possible from a model of juristocracy, that is to say, the rule by courts.[313] In this respect, he suggests a model regarding the roles of courts in a political constitutional order as follows:

> (i) The courts should ensure that the government acts within the scope of, and not beyond, its legal powers; (ii) The courts should ensure that the government's decision-making is procedurally fair; (iii) The protection of civil liberties should be privileged, so that the courts should ensure that government interference with civil liberties may occur only when justified as being necessary on the basis of evidence; (iv) Some protections of civil liberties are so important that they may be articulated in the form of absolute rights—such as the rule that no-one may be subjected to torture; such rights should be rigorously enforced by the courts; and (v) The courts should have a role in nourishing and supporting the political constitution; when the government acts in a manner that undercuts or circumvents effective parliamentary scrutiny, the court should refer the matter back to Parliament for reconsideration of the matter.[314]

In his point of view, judicial review is not entirely responsive to the constitutional goods, like proportionality and reasonableness, compared with competences of the parliament.[315] Tomkins also highlights the primitive role of the parliament in enacting laws; therefore, parliaments have a larger competence in amending laws for practical purposes.[316] Furthermore, in view of the structure of the judiciary, the interference of judiciary to the rights-based cases should be curtailed, except for the absolute rights (e.g. prohibition of torture) and the process rights (e.g. right to a fair trial).[317]

Paul Craig challenges this approach in various terms. Above all, the major opinion of Craig is that this approach is incoherent and inconsistent. He rejects such a premise against the judicial review, which envisages that judicial review should avoid being involved in cases where "contentious value assumptions" and "difficult balancing exercises" are at stake, since this would destroy the adjudication completely. This can be explained through the example of private law courts dealing with the contestable normative assumptions, while "conceptions of moral responsibility and justifiable excuse" being the themes of the criminal law doctrine.[318] Moreover, in political constitutionalist accounts, it is not clear how to fill in the gap

312 Ibid., 14.

313 Tomkins, "Role of Courts," 3.

314 Tomkins, "What's Left," 2281.

315 Ibid., 2287.

316 Ibid., 2286.

317 Tomkins, "Role of Courts," 6.

318 Paul Craig, "Political Constitutionalism and the Judicial Role: A Response," *International Journal of Constitutional Law* 9, no. 1 (2011): 114.

caused by the absence of the legal remedies.[319] In terms of the British legal order, Craig argues that the outcome of Tomkins' views is to exit the ECHR and to appeal the Human Rights Act. Overall, Craig believes that what Tomkins attempts to do is to undermine his own standpoint, by suggesting an incoherent basis for courts.[320]

On the other hand, some other political constitutionalists suggest various degrees for the efficacy of the judiciary in a constitutional order. A striking one deals with a distinction between the strong and the weak form of the judicial review, as suggested by Mark Tushnet.[321] Political constitutionalism rejects and challenges the strong form of constitutional review. On the opposite side, the weak form of judicial review arises as an innovation in the constitutional design of the late twentieth century.[322] What Tushnet suggests as weak judicial review is that a judicially created meaning may be rejected by the government through a "more-or-less" ordinary legislation, without appealing to a constitutional amendment. Tushnet opines that this kind of judicial review complies with the political constitutionalism, as it is not determinative on the decision-making processes. In this respect, the weak form of judicial review enables executive bodies to exercise the function of rectifying court decisions.[323] Tushnet also advances the claim that the strong form of constitutionalism is not suitable for the judicial enforcement of many social and economic rights, since their implementation is highly information-sensitive, and the strong form of constitutionalism is not flexible enough to gain the necessary information on these matters. Further, Tushnet states that an effective enforcement of these rights requires policy-making processes and bureaucratic regimes of implementation.[324] These sorts of rights have been held as the directive principles that cannot be enforced by judiciary in modern constitutionalism, as done in the Indian Constitution and the Irish Constitution of 1937. This proves to become a paradox for legal constitutionalism. In this sense, the weak form of the judicial review offers a decent institutional design for the enforcement of these rights.[325] In short, Tushnet advocates this form of judicial review, as he supposes that it provides the legitimacy for a political constitution.

Finally, it seems that the debate on political and legal constitutionalism, which runs around the British constitutionalism, has come to the conclusion that the British constitutional order does not feature only a political or a legal constitutionalism, but rather both; that is to say, a "mixed constitution" which requires understanding both political and legal dimensions of this constitution.[326] Against this background, the

---

[319] Ibid., 117.

[320] Ibid., 130.

[321] Tushnet, "Political Constitutionalism and Weak-Form," 2250.

[322] Ibid.

[323] Ibid., 2555.

[324] Ibid., 2258.

[325] Ibid., 2259.

[326] Ibid., 2276. Hickman, "In Defence of Legal Constitution." The use of "mixed constitution" here is different from that of 18th Century.

"mixed" character gains more importance.[327] On the other hand, it is evident that this dichotomy is still of importance, in that it stresses two different understandings of constitutionalism, which basically rely on the role of courts in the making of constitutions and in the maintenance of constitutional orders. As such, the question of whether a constitution is political or legal may still have crucial outcomes in terms of the capacity of a constitution to support the democratic principle.

On the other hand, it is of note that not all contributions view legal and political constitutions as two opposite poles. Instead, in view of the complex structure of modern public law, some suggest to deal with them as partner concepts. In this respect, Hickman suggests to count the British constitution as a legal constitution, but rather in a balanced or mixed formation.[328]

4.1.1.2.2.3 Contextual Identity of Constitution

The debate on political and legal constitutionalism provides significant hints regarding the contemporary character of the concept of constitution. This debate has echoes of various crucial matters of the world constitutionalism. For instance, the relationship between constitutionalism and democracy is on the one hand, whereas the desirability of constitutionalism in view of the tensions between constitutionalism and democracy is on the other. The dichotomy between legal and political constitutionalism reflects one aspect of contextual existence of the contemporary concept of constitution. In this regard, this debate is helpful in demonstrating the fact that constitutions appear in diverse contexts, and this results in the rise of different meanings of constitution in different societies. However, contextual dimensions of constitutions are not confined within this debate. As is the case with international law, constitutional law has been encircled by a number of facts spawned by the globalization process as well as the recent relational rationality of this new era. The implications of globalization have strong impacts on the contemporary identity of the concept of constitution, and these implications will be discussed in the second part of this chapter.

As seen above, the major tension between political and legal constitutionalism relates to the relationship between constitutionalism and democracy. Tension between constitutionalism and democracy also rises as part of the global constitutionalism discourse, in context of the "desirability" of constitutionalism for the global realm.[329] This problem is likely to be discussed in terms of Walker's question

[327] Ibid., 2276.

[328] Hickman, "In Defence of Legal Constitution," 1016.

[329] For caveats on the idea of global constitutionalism regarding the threat of American hegemony and anti-democratic international structures over emerging democratic principles of international law: Jeffrey L. Dunoff and Joel P. Trachtman, "A Functional Approach to Global Constitutionalism" (Harvard Public Law Working Paper no. 08-57, 2008, http://ssrn.com/abstract=1311983), 23 ff., last visit 19.04.2015. Anne Peters, "Global Constitutionalism Revisited," *International Legal Theory*, 11 (2005): 60 ff. On the other hand, for a different approach in the debate of "desirability of global constitutionalism" that views global constitutionalism as "desirable" and also "preferable" to the other alternatives: Michel Rosenfeld, "Is Global Constitutionalism Meaningful or Desirable?," *The European Journal of International Law* 25, no. 1 (2014): 198.

as to whether constitutionalism is worth translating into the global domain.[330] On the other hand, academic contributions to the global constitutionalism debate rather proceed from a presupposition that constitutions provide democratic legitimacy or that they ensure the democratic construction of a regime. A clear idea of the separation of powers is very central to this way of thinking. However, this view neglects the diversity of constitutional types, or in other words, this view reflects a sort of continental Euro-centric approach. On the other hand, as mentioned before, a democratic construction is missing, or the democracy deficiency is manifest in transnational regimes in question. It is evident that constitutions are essential subject matters of a debate on the maintenance of democracy and democratic states. In this respect, the idea of constitutionalism has been challenged by some scholars who are concerned about the maintenance of democracy, since constitutions confine the political majorities with the alleged eternal existence of constitutions. At this point, Dworkin refers to a debate on a potential tension between constitutionalism and democracy, as was also done by some other scholars from the modern political science.[331] The combination of constitutionalism and democracy is likely to reflect a tautology or an oxymoron: "Whereas the first term refers to 'restrained and divided' power the second implies its ultimately 'unified and unconstrained' exercise."[332] Given the features of these concepts, constitutionalism and democracy can be deemed as irreconcilable terms. According to Dworkin, the differentiation of approaches to the relationship between constitutionalism and democracy mainly relies on how democracy is identified. For example, those who principally identify democracy along with the rule of people in a system that is established through the majority voting, suppose that a constitutional order that protects individual rights indeed does not comply with the most fundamental democratic assumption of popular sovereignty. From this point of view, judiciary threatens popular sovereignty as it overrides laws passed by a legislator that reflects the will of the people. Rights and popular sovereignty appear as poles apart. Samuel Huntington's understanding of democracy based on the majority voting is to be held up as an example for this kind of approach.[333]

On the other hand, there is another conception of democracy that is based on the constitutional protection of rights. This conception of democracy implies the "legitimate rule of people," which requires some fixed constitutional restraints on the majority rule.[334] According to Dworkin, a major scholar of this strand of thought, to speak of a tension between liberal constitutionalism and democracy is not realistic, as democracy cannot be defined as merely a majoritarian rule. Instead it must be understood as a legitimate majority rule and a constitutional structure that draws

---

[330] Neil Walker, "Postnational Constitutionalism and the Problem of Translation," in *European Constitutionalism Beyond the State*, ed. J.H.H. Weiler and Marlene Wind (Cambridge: Cambridge University Press, 2003), 27.

[331] Ronald Dworkin, "Constitutionalism and Democracy," 3. Also this debate was very essential in modern German constitutionalism. Specter, *Habermas,* 35-46.

[332] Bellamy and Castiglione, "Constitutionalism and Democracy," 595.

[333] Schneider, "Constitutional Protection," 101-102.

[334] Ibid., 103.

limits for a majority, and therefore is a prerequisite for a real democracy. In this regard, constitution is to be viewed as a must for the legitimation of a democracy.[335] However, it has also been argued that constitutionalism may be supposed to threat democracy in various terms. Above all, as a major problem for a democracy, a constitution prescribes disabling provisions that set limits to the power of a majority.[336] Furthermore, the power of judges through judicial review is a potential threat against political equality, since implementation of constitution is undertaken by a closed-circuit group that does not require the participation of people. According to Dworkin, beyond a positivist view of law-making, who views that judges are not interpreting law but inventing it; the activism of judges is inevitable in the natural evolution of law, and this does not breach political equality and democracy.[337] The mission of judges is not to reproduce the constitutional law, but rather to discover the reality of constitutional law.[338] Further, the judicial interpretation of constitutions is strictly required to control the power of elected officials by individual rights; and the judiciary is the best forum, as it holds the matters in moral terms rather than political ones.[339] In short, Dworkin argues for the opinion that constitutionalism is not hostile to democracy, and it is rather a precondition of democracy as it constitutes "the people;" that is to say, "the democratic community," and thus a communal freedom is not possible without it.[340] According to Dworkin, the true tension is not between constitution and democracy, but between democratic and elitist ways of decision-making over what other values to recognize.[341]

Evidently these points have to do with the dichotomy of legal and political constitutions.

These ideas are also likely to be endorsed by some further philosophical insights. Some scholars argue that the function of a legal constitution is not to make politics inessential, but rather to limit it with some principles.[342] For an originating constitution, the question of moral legitimacy concerns the moral arguments directly. In Raz's view, once legal conditions for legitimacy are met, the moral conditions are also met at the same time.[343] From this perspective, the authority of a constitution does not stem from the authority of their authors. Further, constitutions are "self-validating" structures, as long as they exist within the borders of moral principles.[344] Moral justification is also very central to the interpretation of constitutions.[345]

---

[335] Ibid., 104.

[336] Dworkin, "Equality, Democracy and Constitution," 15.

[337] Dworkin, "Constitutionalism and Democracy," 6.

[338] Ibid., 8.

[339] Ibid., 11.

[340] Ibid., 10.

[341] Dworkin, "Equality, Democracy and Constitution," 16. This could also be read as a response to political constitutionalists.

[342] Grimm, "Constitution in Process of Denationalization," 452.

[343] Raz, "On the Authority," 159.

[344] Ibid., 173.

[345] Ibid., 178.

However, as Raz affirms, there is no general theory of constitutional interpretation that is to be regarded as a general recipe.[346]

Moreover, some other views deal with the validation problem of constitution beyond the matter of democratic principles, and demonstrate exceptions to the moralist approaches in constitutional theory. The coordination theory, which places emphasis on this issue, is to be mentioned here. Apart from Hobbes' theory on draconian force by the state and Locke's contractarian views on obedience to the state, Hume's theory on constitutions is based on a dual convention. This means that the government's power relies on a "specific form of coordination," which is itself a convention and the populace "acquiesces" by its own convention.[347] The existence of these two conventions is a must in order to gain the capacity to exercise power. The acquiescence of the populace is "the compelling fact."[348] The theory of coordination rather points to the causal links between the foundation of a constitution and its success. A constitution may include any content; nevertheless, it may fail to coordinate the people to acquiesce the new government. In such a case, it would be called a "failed constitution" rather than asserting that it is not a constitution. Hardin states that "a successful constitution must have been a successful coordination device" in order to achieve its aims, and since they did not have such a character in their foundation, many constitutions failed soon after their adoption. A coordinating and self-enforcing character makes constitutions work.[349] According to Hardin, the core problem of constitutionalism is how a government is empowered by a constitution.[350] In addition, constitutionalism has a two-fold problem. It coordinates on a constitution and its form of a government in the foundational phase, and then it enables a constitution to maintain order.[351]

These two briefly mentioned philosophical approaches demonstrate that the dichotomy of legal and political constitutionalism may gain multiple dimensions in view of their central themes. The main outcome of this point for this book is that these facts prove the existence of the contextual identity of constitution in terms of the foundational principles of constitutions. Up to this point, this fact has been discussed regarding some scholarly contributions. Nonetheless, the interpretive identification of constitution by judges is also noteworthy. American constitutionalism presents significant examples on this matter. The tension between "originalism" and "living constitutionalism," the two conventional interpretational instruments of the US Supreme Court, epitomizes the role of the judicial interpretation in building the contextual identity of constitution.

The constitution is in general perceived as a "static" conception. This stems from the classical theory whose understanding of liberty envisages the principle of

---

[346] Ibid., 180.

[347] Russel Hardin, "Why a Constitution?," in *Social and Political Foundations of Constitutions*, ed. Denis J. Galligan and Mila Versteeg (Cambridge: Cambridge University Press, 2013), 59.

[348] Ibid., 60.

[349] Ibid., 63.

[350] Ibid.

[351] Ibid., 64.

"non-intervention" on rights.[352] On the other hand, in both common and civil law traditions, the statutory interpretation has a special gravity,[353] and thereby constitutions have been reconstructed through some progressive interpretation methods in the case law of constitutional courts. A contemporary understanding of constitution that originates from the rulings of the US Supreme Court in the twentieth century, reads the constitution as a living organism that is always subject to change. More specifically, the debate around the US Constitution on "the living constitution" stems from the question of the normative constitutional theory. This focuses on whether interpreters of the constitution should be loyal to the mind of the framers or whether they should adapt general constitutional principles to changing circumstances.[354]

The idea of living constitution arose as an opposite term against originalism. It was conventionally acceded as "that the only acceptable method of interpreting the U.S.Constitution is to apply 'the text and original meaning of various specific constitutional provisions'."[355] Originalism has been a very influential theme of constitutional practice in USA and it is still a powerful method for conservative mobilization in the US Supreme Court, particularly in cases regarding the citation of foreign law.[356] It is indeed part of a political culture and practice, as it was recently developed as an instrument of conservatism in particular in the 1980s; and Siegel describes this texture as: "Originalism, in other words, is not merely a jurisprudence. It is a discourse employed in politics to mount an attack on courts."[357] In this respect, originalism was criticized as being an effort for infusing the Constitution with conservative political principles.[358] Originalism left impacts on the structuration of the US Supreme Court in the earlier times. This was indeed necessary by the reason of the relative stability of institutions during the first three quarters of the nineteenth century. However, various developments in the political and legal culture of the country led to discarding originalism as the main interpretive method of reading the constitution. These were increasing efficiency of legal positivism, historicism, pragmatism and anti-formalism.[359]

---

[352] Bertil Emrah Oder, *Avrupa Birligi'nde Anayasa ve Anayasacilik* (Istanbul: Anahtar Kitaplar, 2004), 49.

[353] Charles H. Koch Jr., "Envisioning a Global Legal Culture," *Michigan Journal of International Law* 25 (2003): 40.

[354] Howard Gillman, "The Collapse of Constitutional Originalism and the Rise of the Notion of the 'Living Constitution' in the Course of American State-Building," *Studies in American Political Development* 11 (1997): 191. Arthur Selwyn Miller, "Notes on the Concept of the Living Constitution," *The George Washington Law Review* 31, no. 5 (1963): 881.

[355] Robert C. Post and Reva B. Siegel, "Originalism as a Political Practice: The Right's Living Constitution" (Faculty Scholarship Series no. 171, 2006, http://digitalcommons.law.yale.edu/fss_papers/171), 545, last visit 19.01.2014.

[356] Ibid., 546.

[357] Reva B. Siegel, "Constitutional Culture, Social Movement Conflict and Constitutional Change: The Case of the De Facto ERA" (Faculty Scholarship Series no. 1097, 2006, http://digitalcommons.law.yale.edu/fss_papers/1097), 1347, last visit 19.01.2014.

[358] Post and Siegel, "Originalism as a Political Practice," 561.

[359] Gillman, "Collapse of Constitutional Originalism," 213.

The proponents of the living constitutionalism deal with the constitution beyond its meanings that reflect the will of the framers, and they interpret it rather by updating it in accordance with the actual political and societal conditions. This is the crucial point that distinguishes it from originalism. According to Balkin, a constitution is constructed in two situations: in case constitutions are vague or silent, and in case we need to create laws or build institutions to fulfill constitutional purposes.[360] Contrary tp popular belief, living constitutionalism is in fact produced by the political branches, and what courts do is to respond to these political constructions by rationalizing, supplementing and legitimating them.[361]

In the history of the US Supreme Court, the era of Chief Justice Marshall has been considered as a period in which the constitution was regarded as a dynamic and growing instrument of governance, and this dynamic outlook of the court was also observed in some cornerstone rulings, such as the case of Marbury v. Madison.[362] The Justice Marshall puts forward the idea that the ultimate source of authority resides in the people, that is to say, not in the Congress, the Supreme Court or states. They can only exercise power granted by the people through the constitution.[363]

In addition to these approaches from the Supreme Court, some innovative acts of the US Congress and the local governments in constructing early versions of the regulatory state in the early twentieth century had impacts on the emergence of living constitutionalism.[364] Although these attempts saw a resistance from the courts at the first step, they adopted them over time, and served to legitimize them in a series of landmark decisions.[365] This way of the state-building became quite influential during the New Deal of 1933-38 in USA, as a response to the Great Depression. It is of note that the acts mentioned here were not any kind of amendments; since amendment is just a concept that is completely irrelevant to living constitutionalism. Against this background, Balkin explains the central idea of living constitutionalism as: "state-building by the political branches and judicial constructions are, generally speaking, mutually productive and mutually supportive."[366]

Discarding originalism and the adoption of the living constitution in this era also came to mean a restructuration of the US. This transformation concerned the "expansion of federal legislative authority and the establishment of a modern, regulatory executive establishment" and the fact that "[t]hese features, in particular,

---

[360] Jack M. Balkin, "Framework Originalism and the Living Constitution," *Nortwestern University Law Review* 103, no. 2 (2009): 560.

[361] Ibid., 561.

[362] William H. Rehnquist, "The Notion of a Living Constitution," *Harvard Journal of Law & Public Policy* 29, no. 2 (2006): 404. Miller, "Concept of Living Constitution," 883.

[363] Rehnquist, "Notion of Living Constitution," 404; However, Selwyn Miller notes that, the extent and the meaning of living constitutionalism never became clear in the court rulings. It was rather employed by judges in justifying overruling precedent, or in changing a doctrine or introducing a new interpretation on a constitutional clause. Miller, "Concept of Living Constitution," 884.

[364] Jack M. Balkin, "Framework Originalism," 561.

[365] Ibid.

[366] Balkin, "Framework Originalism," 562.

were difficult to reconcile with prevailing understandings of original intent."[367] By virtue of this jurisprudential transformation, the American reformers who sought to draw on some intellectual currents that were not available at the age of framers, like Darwinism, historicism, pragmatism etc., could construct the state by tackling the obligation to be loyal to the original intentions of the founding fathers.[368]

Overall, these interpretive paradigms of the US Supreme Court have been major instruments of the court in identifying the US Constitution. They had a role in justifying the constitution to a diverse and pluralistic constituency.[369]

Consequently, constitutions have a contextual identity, and in many cases it is hard to uphold analytical approaches in defining the meaning of the concept of constitution. In this part of this book, two notable appearances of the contextual identity of constitution have been discussed. However, contemporary constitutionalism hosts multiple contextual aspects that becloud a clear meaning of the concept of constitution. Some further issues will be discussed below in the context of globalization, which is also a central aspect of the main theme of this book.

4.2 Contemporary Constitutionalism and Globalization

The discursive facts on constitutions do not merely consist of interpretational differences. In addition, the current constitutional law discourse, particularly comparative constitutional law, hosts a number of debates that were also induced by globalization to a great extent. These are basically the migration of constitutional norms and values, changing forms of legitimation from a constituent power to rights, and changing integrative functions of constitutions. The major claim here is that these developments are of key roles in shaping the contemporary concept of constitution. That is to say, a framework of contemporary constitution can hardly be drawn without taking note of these implications that are observed in the contemporary constitutional and transconstitutional facts. As such, they should be counted as essential for reconstructing the idea of contemporary constitution.

4.2.1 Relationship and Communication Between Constitutions

4.2.1.1 Migration of Constitutions and Contemporary Constitution as a Mobile Phenomenon

Mark Tushnet asks whether or not a constitution must be "autochtonous." He proceeds from Hegel's idea of constitution: "A constitution … is the work of centuries;

[367] Gillman, "Collapse of Constitutional Originalism," 193.

[368] Ibid.

[369] Rosenfeld, "Constitutional Identity," 762.

it is the Idea, the consciousness of rationality so far as that consciousness is developed in a particular nation."[370] In this respect, he highlights Hegel's expression of " … a particular nation," and examines the aptness of this expression in the view of the migration of constitutional structures across national boundaries.

As mentioned in the preceding section, the character of constitutions may differ fairly due to various interpretation methods of different political and legal cultures. It is evident that some other constitutional practices could be added to this diverse framework. Some other specific examples, such as socialist, non-liberal, Islamic etc. constitutions would also be discussed in the context of contemporary constitutionalism. At this point, a very quick conclusion could be that constitution is a very relative concept. In the globalization age, in consideration of varieties of constitutions, it is also worth asking to what extent these constitutions communicate and interact with each other? What is the result of these interactions? Is a constitution only a property of a specific nation? A vein of the comparative legal scholarship highlights that modern national constitutions have become "inherently transnational documents," on the ground that they are to a large extent under the influence of transnational processes, and as such they rather reflect international norms and standards promoted by other nations.[371] Indeed this occurs as an aspect of the "migration of constitutional ideas" across legal systems, and it is observed in the use of foreign law in domestic legal matters and particularly in the constitution-making processes.[372] Some from this perspective put forward the idea that this mobility of constitutions leads to "a common liberal democratic model of constitutionalism."[373] According to Goldsworthy, this common model has adopted the form of the US constitution to a great extent, and it includes some certain elements of this model such as democratic elections, recognition of individual rights, an independent judiciary and special requirements for amendment of constitutional provisions which serve for the purpose of the rule of law.[374] On the other hand, it is of note that the migration of codes (or "transplantation" or "reception," as it is called in some academic works) is a very central theme to modern law in terms of other sub-disciplines of law as well.[375]

370 Georg Wilhelm Friedrich Hegel, *The Philosophy of Right*, trans. TM Knox (1967), 286-7, cited by Mark Tushnet, "Constitution," in *The Oxford Handbook of Comparative Constitutional Law*, ed. Michel Rosenfeld and Andras Sajo (Oxford: Oxford University Press, 2012), 218.

371 Galligan and Versteeg, "Theoretical Perspectives," 13.

372 Sujit Choudry, "Migration as a New Metaphor in Comparative Constitutional Law," in *The Migration of Constitutional Ideas*, ed. Sujit Choudry (Cambridge: Cambridge University Press, 2006), 13.

373 Jeffrey Goldsworthy, "Questioning the Migration of Constitutional Ideas: Rights, Constitutionalism and the Limits of Convergence," in *The Migration of Constitutional Ideas*, ed. Sujit Choudry (Cambridge: Cambridge University Press, 2006), 115.

374 Ibid., 116.

375 Lawrence M. Friedman, *The Legal System: A Social Science Perspective* (New York: Russel Sage Foundation, 1975), 195.

The migration of constitutional values has a mandatory effect on the national constitution-making mechanisms or domestic courts, which is to say that it broadens the scope of the effects of traditional non-binding international or transnational law. Therefore, this phenomenon is one of the main aspects of contemporary constitutionalism. The effect of human rights on national laws can be held up as a salient example in this regard.[376]

It has also been argued that this approach refers to the democratic constitutionalist tradition while defining the interaction between national and international law.[377] In other words, the migration of constitutional values and norms is to be considered as an aspect of the development and the evolution of the modern western democratic constitutionalist tradition.

This vein of scholarship in general envisages that a circulation of constitutional values occurs either subtly or clearly among nations. According to the proponents of this idea, constitutions do not only reflect the statements of national identities in a traditional sense, but also have a function as a means of satisfying or influencing various actors, such as foreign investors or some other countries, for economic, political, security or other reasons.[378] As an empirical study of comparative constitutional law – which analyzes 188 constitutions which were enacted between 1946 and 2006 proves, the diffusion of constitutional rights in different countries is interrelated, and this depends on legal origins, religion, a common legal colonizer and a common aid donor.[379] As a matter of fact, this study reveals the fact that constitutions are standardized documents with a limited number of facts lying behind.[380] This depends on various facts, such as "coercion by other nations, competition among nations, learning by one nation from others, and acculturation."[381] As a matter of fact, given all the external effects on constitution-making processes, it is true to say that "constitutions are commonly transported across national borders."[382] This fact results in the standardization and resemblance of the constitutions throughout the world in terms of principles, values and structures; and also casts doubt on a premise that constitutions reflect national identities and values as

[376] Mayo Moran, "Inimical to Constitutional Values: Complex Migrations of Constitutional Rights," in *The Migration of Constitutional Ideas*, ed. Sujit Choudry (Cambridge: Cambridge University Press, 2006), 234.

[377] Mattias Kumm, "Democratic Constitutionalism Encounters International Law: Terms of Engagement," in *The Migration of Constitutional Ideas*, ed. Sujit Choudry (Cambridge: Cambridge University Press, 2006), 260.

[378] David S. Law and Mila Versteeg, "The Evolution and Ideology of Global Constitutionalism," *California Law Review* 99 (2011): 1172.

[379] Ibid.

[380] Ibid.

[381] Benedikt Goderis and Mila Versteeg, "Transnational Constitutionalism: A Conceptual Framework," in *Social and Political Foundations of Constitutions*, ed. Denis J. Galligan and Mila Versteeg (Cambridge: Cambridge University Press, 2013), 104.

[382] Ibid., 103.

unique documents.[383] Furthermore, each national constitution implies a membership in the global constitutional family.[384]

Constitutions that were adopted through coercion from other nations can be exemplified by the dictated constitutions under circumstances of the colonial dependence and military occupation, such as constitutions of the former colonies of Britain in Africa or Caribbean, which were drafted by the Colonial Office in the UK, or the Japanese Constitution of 1946, which was drafted by the US officials in the aftermath of World War II.[385] Among these examples, the Japanese constitution is depicted as the best example of an imposed constitution, since it was drafted under the capitulations and an aggressive occupation in the aftermath of WWII. Pre-war Japanese legal and political traditions were found only as the minor components of this constitution.[386] As to the effects of colonialism over colonial countries, France and Britain, the leading colonialist states, did not wish their colonies to have separate constitutions, since they deemed these colonies to be their departments. Further, in the post-colonial era, the imposition of anything to these countries was not much possible due to the anti-colonialist consciousness, except for several cases. Therefore, colonialism was not very successful in imposing constitutions to the colonial countries.[387]

Migration does not always occur by only imposing the constitutional models of "the imposer;" the imposed model of constitution may well stem from a different system as well.[388] For example, constitutions of the former British colonies in Africa and Caribbean were "a carbon copy" of the European Convention on Human Rights and Fundamental Freedoms.[389] Apart from these, the German Basic Law (*Grundgesetz*) of 1949, and the Iraq Constitution of 2005 or the Afghanistan Constitution, which were drafted "in the shadow of the gun," can also be considered within this category. However, it is of note that even though German Basic Law was drafted under the pressure and approval of the Allied Powers, the framers largely drew on German models and traditions.[390] Therefore, this example should be distinguished

[383] Law and Versteeg, "Evolution and Ideology," 1239.

[384] Ibid., 1240.

[385] Galligan and Versteeg, "Theoretical Perspectives," 13. As to the Japanese case, the adoption of western laws had begun in 19th century, as this was considered as a compulsory method for modernization and economic development. Lawrence M. Friedman. "Borders: On the Emerging Sociology of Transnational Law," *Stanford Journal of International Law* 32 (1996): 73.

[386] Frederick Schauer, "On the Migration of Constitutional Ideas," *Connecticut Law Review* 37 (2004-2005): 908.

[387] Ibid., 909.

[388] Goderis and Versteeg, "Transnational Constitutionalism," 111.

[389] There is also a wide range of constitutions that were made under the influence of other constitutions, such as the Irish Constitution of 1922 or the post-Communist Eastern European constitutions which were inspired by various Western democratic constitutions. Ibid., 103.

[390] Schauer, "Migration of Constitutional Ideas," 908.

from others at some point. This category also comprises constitutions made through material incentives or carrots and sticks policies. The Turkish and Romanian constitutions have been held up as examples of these kinds of constitutions, as these two countries adopted the fundamental rights commitments in their constitutions in order to take part in the western political system, or in transnational organizations like the Council of Europe. The constitutional amendments made by the Mexican parliament before entering NAFTA are also striking.[391] The reason for such a way of foreign interference is found as the need for good institutions for the economic growth, and thus rule of law reforms on the constitutional basis are considered crucial by the transnational organizations as well.[392] Further, "global spillover effects" of democratization in a nation are considered to lead setting the ground for a "democratic peace." This was first argued by Kant, and prescribes that democratic nations do not fight each other, which makes this the key for providing global security.[393]

By "competition among nations" or "learning," it is implied that states can copy and adopt constitutional provisions of other states in case they find them effective, in order to achieve some goals. One goal can be, for example, an attempt to take part in the global markets.[394] In addition to these, the adoption of a constitutional provision by many states also opens the way to make them "standardized norms of world society." In this respect, other states can tend to adopt these norms in order to gain international acceptance and legitimacy. For example, the reason for the enactment of a western style constitution in Taiwan has been explained by the intention of this state to cultivate the goodwill of western countries, during a period that it was isolated from the rest of the world regarding the diplomatic relations.[395] To respect human rights and the security of freedoms also concerns global investments in many terms, and thus it can be stated that "*bad publicity is costly*" for the states that refrain from taking necessary measures in order to be seen as a democratic country.[396] Moreover, the states are also inclined to adopt the constitutional provisions of other states, not only for the material costs and benefits, but also due to the belief that these provisions are beneficial for them. The learning process is prominent in this category, and learning is enabled by social networks that lead to the flow of information as well as social interactions and social relationships.[397] These networks may emerge within international organizations or through "political, cultural, or socio-economic reference groups."[398]

---

[391] Goderis and Versteeg, "Transnational Constitutionalism," 108.

[392] Also the huge supplies for these refoms by the World Bank have to be borne in mind. Ibid., 109.

[393] Ibid., 110.

[394] Galligan and Versteeg, "Theoretical Perspectives," 14.

[395] Ibid.

[396] Goderis and Versteeg, "Transnational Constitutionalism," 114.

[397] Ibid., 114.

[398] Ibid., 116.

"Acculturation" is also a basis for the circulation of constitutional values and rights. In this option, material benefits for the adopters are more ambiguous, but they adopt some constitutional models in order to benefit from "social rewards."[399] The adoption of these models provides legitimacy and makes contributions to enhance the social relationships within the international community by conforming to social norms. The Meiji Restoration of Japan of the nineteenth century, which was functional for creating a western style cabinet, in order to prove that Japan was part of the modern world and an equal to western powers, could be held up as an example of a constitutional acculturation.[400] Furthermore, transnational influence through acculturation may occur as a consequence of the common religion, language or other common cultural facts between some countries, instead of a global foundational basis.[401]

All these facts and the "shared legal standards" yield "constitutional network effects" among countries where a convergence of constitutional values and rights is observed.[402] The relationships within these legal networks also have far-reaching consequences. For example, being involved by a legal network may attract investors from other member countries of these networks, and thus common legal rules may have a considerable influence on the interaction of countries. In this respect, countries in the same constitutional network enjoy closer ties and relationships with their network associates than with non-members.[403] In this networking relationship, not only nation states but also other norm makers, such as church, transnational organizations and NGOs play significant roles.[404] Furthermore, as can be read from Kant as well, democratic countries are less likely to go to war with each other, and this also holds true in terms of constitutional networking. This is also related with enjoying closer trade relations within a given network.[405] On the other hand, in some cases, this is likely to result in the emergence of competing networks.[406]

However, the migration of constitutional values and norms does not mean that constitutions are planted to legal systems directly. The customization is observed and also necessary in each case.[407] Consequently, as empirical studies on comparative constitutional law demonstrate, world constitutions have a tendency to contain "a generic set of rights," that have growingly gained judicial enforcement

[399] Ibid., 119.

[400] Ibid., 121.

[401] Ibid., 122.

[402] Law and Versteeg, "Evolution and Ideology," 1183.

[403] Ibid., 1185.

[404] Schauer, "Migration of Constitutional Ideas," 917.

[405] Law and Versteeg, "Evolution and Iddeology," 1186, As an opposite view, it should be noted that democratic states are still prone to war with non-democratic states, although they do not fight with democratic counterparts. Michael W. Doyle, "Kant, Liberal Legacies, and Foreign Affairs," *Philosophy and Public Affairs* 12 (1983): 205, 225, cited by Ibid., 1187.

[406] Ibid., 1242.

[407] Schauer, "Migration of Constitutional Ideas," 910.

in the aftermath of World War II.[408] Furthermore, the judicial review mechanisms, which were found only in 25 % of the constitutions in 1946, were contained by 82 % of the constitutions by 2006.[409] Last but not least, another striking point is that the ideological identity of constitutions has significantly shifted toward a libertarian one between 1946 and 2006. This leads to a convergence of constitutions, which implies that the average constitution is becoming more libertarian and more comprehensive.[410]

Against this background, one can argue that the comprehensiveness of constitutions can be taken into consideration in order to identify the dimensions of world constitutionalism, along with their ideological aspects as a second instrument for identification.[411] As a result, this fact appears as a main issue of contemporary constitutionalism.

4.2.1.2 Contemporary Constitution and Transconstitutionalism

The fact that contemporary constitution is a mobile and dynamic phenomenon can be understood in two ways. As mentioned in this chapter, various interpretational traditions demonstrate that constitution is not a stable object, but rather a living tool operating through different interpretive processes. It needs to be adapted to changing conditions not only by amendments, but also by various interpretational methods. The "living constitutionalism" practice of the US Supreme Court is a remarkable example of this. However, what is underlined in this section has to do with a different issue. As shown above, constitutions have become "migrant phenomena" in terms of their normative structures and the values that they bear. The most striking consequence regarding these processes is that, the concept of constitution can no longer be confined within national borders. Against this background, such emancipation of constitution from national borders has been defined through the concept of "transconstitutionalism" by Neves.[412]

In the process of the foundation of modern democracies, constitutions have been the basis of foundation and the fundamental order of the newly emerging democratic societies.[413] In the process of dissemination of the western democratic values, as mentioned above, constitutions became the instrument of dissemination. The migration of constitutional rights and values may be successful in some cases, but this is rather dependent on the compliance with the "local spirit of laws."[414] In this

[408] Law and Versteeg, "Evolution and Ideology," 1194.

[409] Ibid.

[410] Ibid., 1234. However, the authors rightly opine that this does not imply that such a result reflects an "across-the-board movement toward libertarianism."

[411] Ibid., 1233.

[412] Marcelo Neves, *Transconstitutionalism*, trans. Kevin Mundy (Oxford and Portland Oregon: Hart Publishing, 2013).

[413] Vorländer, "What is 'Constitutional Cultures'?"

[414] Mark Tushnet, "Constitution," 220.

regard, even universal norms can be identified in different ways in different legal cultures regardless of their universal character.[415]

Contemporary constitutions became mobile objects through the dynamics mentioned above. This constitutes their character to a certain extent. Beyond the transplantation of constitutional norms, the use of foreign legal norms in constitutional interpretation is also a part of this issue.[416] In addition to this, the mobilized nature of constitutions should be taken into consideration in the analysis of the formation of a constitutional culture within and beyond the national constitutional orders.

This trait of contemporary constitutions also has a lot to do with globalization. In view of globalization as a hegemonic instrument, Berman argues that international human rights revolution in the aftermath of World War II led to the spread of rights-based constitutionalism, whose essential model was the US Constitution.[417] This opinion is also likely to be supported by the facts touched upon above, as rights-based legal constitutionalism has been prevailing over the countries where political constitutionalism is central to the constitutional order. Given the dimension of migration of constitutions through historical facts, legal constitutionalism, be it US model or European model, appears as the main destination of this mobilization.

Against this background, transconstitutionalism is marked by the emancipation of constitutional law from the state, and by the involvement of other legal orders in resolving basic constitutional problems.[418] In addition, transconstitutionalism marks neither international, transnational, supranational, nor national and local constitutionalism.[419] It marks an entirely different category:

> Instead, it points to the need to build "bridges of transition," promote both "constitutional conversations" or "dialogue" and "constitutional collisions" as well as strengthen constitutional entanglements among the various legal orders, be they national, international, transnational, supranational or local.[420]

In Luhmannian terms, a constitution serves to the transversal rationality between law and politics. For example, in a supranational system, "the territorially differentiated political and legal systems of the Member States are constructively linked via transversal constitutions."[421] According to Neves, a consequence of

---

[415] Ibid.

[416] Gabor Halmai, "The Use of Foreign Law in Constitutional Interpretation," in *The Oxford Handbook of Comparative Constitutional Law*, ed. Michel Rosenfeld and Andras Sajo (Oxford: Oxford University Press, 2012), 1328-1348.

[417] Paul Schiff Berman, "From International Law to Law and Globalization" (University of Connecticut School of Law Articles and Working Papers, Paper 23, 2005, http://lsr.nellco.org/uconn_wps/23), 553, last visit 11.07.2013.

[418] Marcelo Neves, "Comparing Transconstitutionalism in an Asymmetric World Society: Conceptual Background and Self-Critical Remarks," (Adam Smith Research Foundation Working Papers Series no. 02, 2005, http://www.gla.ac.uk/media/media_401302_en.pdf), 4, last visit 1.3.2015.

[419] Ibid., 5.

[420] Ibid.

[421] Neves, *Transconstitutionalism*, 65.

transconstitutionalism is decoupling constitutional law from classical constitutionalism, which is strictly associated with states, and a need to seek solutions for constitutional problems in the entanglement of various legal systems.[422]

Transconstitutionalism appears in a number of levels. First of all, transconstitutionalism can be seen as a consequence of the relationships between the state and international level, and rather concerns transterritorialization of constitutional law. The entanglement of public international law and domestic constitutional law has various contexts in this regard. As Neves states, "state constitutional norms have international scope, international norms have constitutional scope."[423] Further, according to Neves, transconstitutionalism appears in some further levels: between supranational law and state law, between state legal orders, between state and transnational legal orders, between state legal orders and extra-state local orders, and between supranational law and international law.[424] In the supranational context, and in the example of the EU in particular, unity is to be viewed rather as a matter of legal and judicial space. In this context, Neves states that the European constitutional order reflects the transversality of legal orders "in dealing with common juridico-constitutional problems" instead of an EU Constitution.[425] On the other hand, the migration of constitutional norms and values generates the ground for transconstitutionalism between state legal orders.[426]

A crucial fact is that all these legal systems share the same binary code of legal/illegal in the world society. However, each legal order is of its own structure, operations, and legal procedures, and this leads to a certain differentiation between these orders.[427] Further, Neves argues that the transconstitutional entanglements are deeply influenced by asymmetries of the contemporary world society. As a result, as mentioned when dealing with migration of constitutional norms and values, some legal orders appear as "receivers," while others as "givers" of legal standards.[428] Moreover, what is relevant to the contemporary transformation of constitutional law in the age of globalization is that the means of migration of constitutions have undergone a serious change in this era. Referring to a Canadian Supreme Court judge, Claire L'Heureux-Dube, Neves stresses the fact that the dialogue between legal systems became the dominant form of "legal borrowings" instead of the receptions of the past. A noteworthy example is the South African Constitutional Court that refers to a broad range of foreign constitutional courts and transnational courts by relying on the South African Constitution in some cases, which allows

[422] Ibid., 77.

[423] Ibid., 86.

[424] Ibid., 96-147.

[425] Ibid., 99.

[426] Ibid., 106 ff.

[427] Ibid., 74-80.

[428] Neves, "Comparing Transconstitutionalism," 8.

considering foreign law in cases concerning the Bill of Rights.[429] Evidently, the "dialogue" here reflects the increasing network communications of legal professionals on a large scale.

4.2.2 *Changing Framework of Legitimacy*

4.2.2.1 Transformation of Constituent Power

Michel Rosenfeld argues that constitutions can be categorized in six types in terms of the methods of constitution-making. In addition to the invisible British model, these are the revolutionary-based model (American and French constitutions), the war-based model (German and Japanese constitutions), the pacted transition model (Spanish constitution of 1978), the internationally-grounded model (constitutions of Bosnia and Sudan) and the transnational model (EU constitution).[430] With the exception of the transnational model, which has not yet entered into force in the EU, common features of these models are that each comes after an *ancien regime,* and a constituent power is very essential in the making of constitutions.[431]

As demonstrated in the previous section, contemporary constitutions are subject to a number of restrictions that stem from the interactions between different constitutions. Therefore, we can hardly agree with Hegel in identifying a constitution with an emphasis to its national basis. The changing structure of law through transnationalization had tremendous effects on constitutional law as well. In this regard, the source of legitimacy of a constitution has come into prominence within the new framework of the increasingly transnationalized legal orders. As to the contemporary constitutions, it is argued that the increased transnationalization regarding constitutional matters has had a negative effect on the traditional source of constitutions, namely the constituent power (*pouvoir constituant).* Thornhill notes very illuminatingly that,

> "[t]he extent to which the legitimacy of political institutions can be derived from a single and clearly external source of norms is now widely open to dispute, and the primary constitutional laws of contemporary society show a rapidly decreasing reliance on identifiable acts of constituent power."[432]

---

[429] In addition to the South African Court, the Supreme Courts of India, Zimbabwe, Israel, New Zealand, and Ireland have regularly cited foreign laws and precedents of foreign courts. Neves, *Transconstitutionalism*, 109.

[430] Rosenfeld, "Constitutional Identity," 766 ff.

[431] The British constitution can also be held as an exception in terms of the criterion of following an ancien regime, on the ground that it is an outcome of a long term and a slow evolution, and it is not very easy to determine constitutional moments throughout its historical development.

[432] Thornhill, "Contemporary Constitutionalism," 370; For a contrast view that considers contemporary constitutions in a continuum with modern constitutions and argue that will of the people is still an essential component of contemporary constitutions, Henkin, "A New Birth," 535.

This needs some further explanation.

Thornhill mentions a number of reasons for this observance. First, it would be useful to have a look at how the conventional constitutional theory defines constituent power. From the point of view of the conventional constitutional theory, the legitimacy of a constitution has been understood within the framework of the doctrine of constituent power (*pouvoir constituant*). As Sieyés uttered first in the early revolutionary France, the doctrine of constituent power prescribes the expression of an initial constituent power and the foundation of a stable public authority by a number of protagonists; and afterwards, the silence of constituent power and the expelling of people from further exercise of power.[433] In other words, constituent power reflects the political fact that power is ultimately enjoyed by the people and it regards to "the generative aspect of the political power relationship."[434] This doctrine had a certain role in the subordination of ordinary law to constitutional law so as to emanate law from the political process, and at the same time to bind the political process to law in the new order.[435] In the classical constitutional theory, a modern constitution should be reconstructed through a constituent power that confers its essential characteristic features and enables it to to be maintained by means of the constituted power. In other words, the concept of constituent power reflects a popular will and denotes the source of legitimacy. Constituted power concerns institutionalization and exercise of political power in a normativist sense.[436] Against this background, constituent power and constituted power are two different facts, which function to complement each other in the exercise of public law. However, it is of note that even though it is not that hard to make a distinction between these two concepts theoretically, such a distinction has always been a tough issue in practice, in terms of the functional dimensions of constitutions.[437] Constituent power and constituted power interact in the making of constitutions, as the latter is subordinated by the former.

In spite of the central role of constituent power in the construction of modern constitutions, it is hard to say that constituent power is still exercised within the above-mentioned framework in contemporary constitutions, according to Thornhill: "Instead, constituent force is constrained and predetermined by a body of established transnational norms."[438] These transnational norms are determinative over national constitutional constructions. As a matter of fact, this is the distinctive texture of the contemporary constituent power: "Effective constituent power is freely accorded to judicial institutions applying transnational norms, which are usually underpinned (immediately or more remotely) by guidelines regarding human rights."[439] The erosion

[433] Thornhill, "Contemporary Constitutionalism," 384.

[434] Loughlin, "Concept of Constituent Power," 1, 14. Also see this article for various definitions stemming from different law schools.

[435] Grimm, "Types of Constitutions," 103.

[436] Ibid. 4.

[437] Thornhill, "Rights and Constituent Power," 361.

[438] Thornhill, "Contemporary Constitutionalism," 370.

[439] Ibid., 371.

of constituent power has also been underpinned by multinational polities, such as the European Union.[440] This process is to be viewed as an ongoing multiplication of constitutional powers. The overarching governance structures undermined the accustomed basis of political power that was constituted by traditional sovereign actors, and it eroded the basic premises of governmental legitimacy. At the same time, this led to the loss of the ability of traditional constitutional actors to create primary laws depending on their free wills. This process also gave rise to the significant transformations regarding relationships between law and constitutional designation in legitimate polity.[441] Consequently, law imbibes constituent power, and the roles change completely: "Constituent power, in short, is now intrinsically juridified: it was once the original and external source of law, but it is now stored within the law."[442]

At this juncture, it seems that the identification of constituent power becomes much more complicated in view of the complex relationships in transnational law. However, Thornhill identifies the contemporary substitute of the constituent power very clearly:

> in the contemporary political system constituent power has been supplanted by rights as the dominant source of legitimacy; this shift underlies the changing political form of contemporary society. Transnationally enforced rights norms now increasingly pre-define the constitutional conditions for the legitimate exercise of power, and it is from norms in respect of rights, not from any primary sovereign act of constitution making, that the contemporary political system generally derives its authority and its self-explanation.[443]

In other words, a contemporary political system does not obtain legitimacy from constituent power any more, but rather from its linkage to rights. Rights, so to speak, have captured the traditional position of constituent power. This arises as the most remarkable outcome of the increasing influence of transnational law over constitutional matters. On the other hand, the expansion of the function of rights from the national realm to the transnational also proves the rupture between the transnational and national constitutional systems.[444]

Transnationalization of law has given rise to significant consequences for the fate of law as well as constitutions. Due to the transnationalization process, constitutions lost their historical foundational references, as they have been replaced by rights; in other words, law gained a new role through its reflexive character. The reflexive character of law has been promoted in the course of this process, and it gained an organic relationship with constitutions, as Thornhill argues:

> In contemporary society, thus, transnationally acceded norms (usually shaped by rights) determine the prior form of national laws, and law can no longer be traced to a founding point of regress. The origin of binding law is now in fact commonly law itself, and law

[440] Ibid.

[441] Ibid., 373.

[442] Ibid., 374.

[443] Ibid., 375.

[444] Ibid., 399.

> (even primary, constitutional law) is habitually derived from other laws: law is typically derived from laws established through international charters, conventions, treaties, and, above all, courts with authority to enforce international agreements regarding rights.[445]

This approach gives no credit to the traditional revolutionary processes of constitution-making in contemporary constitutionalism.

This fact is related to the other aspects of contemporary constitutionalism. Evidently, it is more likely to be considered as an underpinning fact for legal constitutionalism. Thornhill has already stated that this shift in constitutional law occurs in parallel with the contemporary democracy which can be characterized by judicial constitutionalism.[446] Very briefly, rights establish and convene constitutional systems, and they carry out fundamental functions to provide legitimacy for a political system. Courts are of the main role as a medium to the functions of rights, but the national domain is no longer the main ground for exercising this function. At this point, rights also appear as a medium for the political inclusion in global society:

> rights promote a condition of virtual political inclusion in global society: that, through reference to rights, social agents are integrated in the political system in often highly fragmented, partial and functionally specific fashion.[447]

This also marks the expansion of legal constitutionalism beyond national borders, and also, the diminishing power and narrowing borders of political constitutionalism to a certain extent.

The transformation of the source of legitimacy of constitutions and the changing character of constituent power also have to do with the migration of constitutional norms and values. The interaction of the transnational level with the national level and in particular the migration of constitutional values makes the supreme position of the transnational level dubious. Hence, an assumption of constitutionalization in transnational level is not entirely independent from national constitutionalism. As a matter of fact, the migration of constitutional and legal values and particularly rights make both levels highly interwoven. On the other hand, a national domain is always necessary for the viability of a transnational domain, as tangible outcomes of legal activities come about on this level. Against this background, the global order can be depicted as a pluriform system, some levels of which are located in the national domain and some of which extend beyond national borders.[448] Therefore, Thornhill's opinion that the global constitutional form is a "rearticulated or intensified expression of the national constitutional form" proves to be right.[449] He comes to this conclusion by relying on the opinion that transnational constitutional forms are strictly linked to

---

[445] Chris Thornhill, "A Sociology of Constituent Power: The Political Code of Transnational Societal Constitutions," *Indiana Journal of Global Legal Studies* 20, no. 2 (2013): 554.

[446] Thornhill, "Contemporary Constitutionalism," 392.

[447] Ibid., 395.

[448] Thornhill, "Rights and Constituent Power," 384.

[449] Thornhill, "A Sociology of Constituent Power," 603.

the national forms, and transnational constitutional structures are concomitants of the extension of constitutional values over the national borders. As discussed in the first chapter, the globalized economic and political relations undermined the centrality of nation states; and new global and hybrid forms of law-producing centres have arisen as a result of this fact. Under these circumstances, as Ladeur argues, it is now evident that the traditional monopolization of legal sources by sovereign states through the separation of norms and implementation was an ideological exaggeration of the legal positivist strand; and what is more, this legal model was historically a "one-off" and no longer has the capacity to guide global and post-national legal formation.[450] Therefore, an analogous view that amounts to a negligence of the continuity of two levels of law production is most likely to be misleading, as it fails in the identification of sources of law, and on the ground that globalization is more than the formation of a unitary economic and legal space, as of nation states.[451] This is blatantly obvious in constitutional law matters, in consideration of the fact that the contemporary constitutional law is marked by a transformation of relations between a national constituent power and a national constituted power. Above all, the efficiency of these concepts for an emerging global law now remains strictly doubtful.

4.2.2.2 Contemporary Constitution as Increasingly a Rights-based Concept

As discussed above, contemporary constitution is rather reflected by a rights-oriented structure, and the gradual transformation of the British constitution from political to legal constitution proves this to a certain extent. Gardbaum argues that rights mark the contemporary constitutionalism in view of the fact that the normative debates on constitutional reviews focus on the rights protection instead of structural issues.[452]

On the other hand, regarding and beyond the British example, the growing rights-based orientation of constitutions is indeed strictly related to the development of transnational law. The rights-based orientation of constitutions implies a transformation on the source of the legitimacy at the same time.

Talcott Parsons said years ago that however precarious its normative control system is, the international order is to be considered as a social system.[453] In view of this fact, the revolution of rights provided the international legal order with a

---

[450] Karl-Heinz Ladeur, "Towards a Legal Theory of Supranationality: The Viability of Network Concept," *European Law Journal* 3, no. 1 (1997): 44.

[451] Ibid.

[452] An exception to this is constitutions of contemporary post-conflict states, such as Iraq, Bosnia, Kosovo, Sri Lanka and Northern Ireland. The structural issues regarding power among ethnic and religious groups are central to these constitutions rather than rights. Stephen Gardbaum, "The Place of Constitutional Law in the Legal System," in *The Oxford Handbook of Comparative Constitutional Law*, ed. Michel Rosenfeld and Andras Sajo (Oxford: Oxford University Press, 2012), 177.

[453] Talcott Parsons, "Order and Community in the International Social System," in *International Politics and Foreign Policy*, ed. J.N. Rosenau (New York: Free Press of Rosenau, 1961) 123.

consistent normative fact by ruling that precariousness out. It also revealed the fact that the national and transnational orders have an organic linkage. While the concept of the constituent power is being replaced by rights, the normative facts of constitutional orders are likely to have a function of elucidating the role of the judicial bodies and legislative organs in the construction of democracy. In view of the democratization problem of the global realm, this remains at the heart of the constitutionalism discourse. International and national courts, as global networking actors, assume the most central role in this process.

4.2.3 *Contemporary Constitutionalism and Integration*

4.2.3.1 Integrative Power of Modern Constitutions

Constitutions are generally deemed to be the instruments for societal integration despite the fact that the aims and mechanisms of this function are not very clear.[454] "We the People," the well-known opening phrase of the Preamble to the United States Constitution marks the integrative power of the modern constitutions. The integrative force of constitutions has also been discussed in terms of contemporary constitutionalism and the transnational political and legal projects. In this regard, the constitutional quality of the integrative projects, such as the European Union, is a notable aspect of this issue. The liberal constitutionalism, throughout its historical development, consolidated the idea of sovereignty of laws through the idea that law and the legal relations generate the core of the process of societal integration. In this regard, the real constitution of the society has to do with neither a constitutional text nor any institutional structure, but the legal system itself.[455] This also complies with the fact that integration through a constitution is a procedural and temporary response to the plurality in a society, rather than the generation of national homogeneity.[456]

On the other hand, the meaning of the integrative power of constitution is not very clear in the constitutional discourse; and to what extent a constitution is able to give rise to a societal integration indeed appears as an open-ended question. Societal integration has various meanings within the sociological discourse, and it was also discussed with respect to the role of constitutions in a society. In Durkheim's view, integration is basically "solidarity," or in other words "spontaneous social cohesion arising from shared beliefs or attitudes or mutual co-operation."[457] In addition, Talcott Parsons is one of the functional analysts of law, who suggests a conception

[454] Vorländer, "Integration durch Verfassung?," 9.

[455] Castiglione, "Political Theory of Constitution," 20-21.

[456] Vorländer. "Integration durch Verfassung?," 11.

[457] Roger Cotterrell, *The Sociology of Law: An Introduction* (London: Butterworths, 1984), 96.

of law as well as constitution, as a mechanism for the integration of society.[458] His academic works are mainly based on the theories of Durkheim, Weber, Pareto, Radcliff-Brown, Malinowski and Freud; and he built on an action theory that amalgamates these theories and that deals with the interaction of cultural system, social system, personality system and organisms. Parsons views society as a system, and specifies the basic function of this system as "integration."[459] The academic works of Parsons are of capital importance for sociology of law, on the ground that they enable us to find out the position of law among the other functional elements of social systems.[460]

According to Parsons, a social system is a result of the interaction of the majority of actors within a society.[461] Modern industrialized societies are comprised of four distinct functional sub-systems. Apart from the "societal community," "polity" and "economy," it is the "integrative sub-system" of the society that concerns citizenship and social solidarity.[462] Integration concerns the maintenance of a society, and this is most likely to be possible through relationships of sub-systems of a society.[463] Law is a distinct component of this differentiation process. The normative structure of the society is highly differentiated and law carries out an integrative function. Law achieves this by enabling socialization of societal values.[464] By reason of the functional specialization of the law, and of its function to foster the organic solidarity in the society, western societies feature an autonomous legal system. Law cannot be associated with values or be put under the order of political administration. Law develops in countries where fundamental societal values do not remain at the forefront.[465] This is also the ground of the independent judiciary in western countries.[466]

In western societies, the economy and political system are intimate functional systems, and law has a role in securing this sub-system differentiation. "The general legal system," in Parsons' own words, is "the most important single hallmark of modern society."[467]

Further, constitutions have a special emphasis in Parsons' theory. According to Parsons, the political aspect of a social system concerns the attainment of collective goals. One of the salient subsystems of the polity is the legitimacy. As Parsons states:

---

[458] Ibid., 73.

[459] Sezgin Kizilcelik, *Sosyoloji Teorileri*, Cilt 1. (Konya: Nüve Kültür Merkezi, 1994), 428.

[460] Cotterrell, *Sociology of Law*, 81.

[461] Kizilcelik, *Sosyoloji Teorileri*, 439.

[462] Cotterrell, *Sociology of Law*, 82.

[463] Kizilcelik, *Sosyoloji Teorileri*, 441.

[464] On the contrary, this view does not comply with Durkheim, who does not distinguish law from morality and societal values. Cotterrell, *Sociology of Law*, 90.

[465] Ibid., 86.

[466] Ibid., 84.

[467] Ibid., 85.

> The legitimation subsystem of a highly differentiated polity, therefore centers around the constitutional system and the judicial agencies that interpret it. This subsystem is a major link between political and legal organization and thereby involves the integrative structures of the society. Any concrete collectivity depends on fulfillment of of these functions, however rudimentary the agencies that implement them may be.[468]

As is seen, Parsons attributes western constitutions a very remarkable function within the societal system. This function is most likely to be delineated as a "contribution" to the societal integration.[469] In other words, constitutions perform a linking function between some societal facts; and in this respect, they are quite reminiscent of the idea of "constitutions as structural couplings" in Luhmann's theory. However, it is noteworthy that the borders of the communicating systems in Parsons' theory are not as clear-cut as the systems in Luhmann's theory.[470]

On the other hand, given the historical and social functions of constitutions, one can specify the preconditions of the integrative power of a constitution beyond its legitimating roles.[471] However, the question of to what extent this integration can come about gives rise to different views. For example, Preuss explains this feature of constitutions as

> constitutions are not restricted to merely forming "a more perfect union," as the preamble of the US constitution declares; rather, they are institutional devices which constitute a union among discrete natural or corporate individuals who live in a society.[472]

In this regard, constitutions play important roles in the construction of the social reality.[473] On the other hand, it has always been a matter of controversy whether (or to what extent) the expression of "We the people" reflects the real founders of the constitution or not, although it appears in this form in the Preamble of the US Constitution.[474] The US Constitution was made in the name of the people of the US, but the African-American slaves were excluded from the imagination of the American people by the constitution. In addition, the current American population largely consists of the descendants of immigrants that came to the US in the last two centuries; and accordingly, Rosenfeld aptly asks "how can today's 'We the People' identify with its 1787 counterpart and accept the latter's constitution as its own?"[475]

---

[468] Talcott Parsons, *Politics and Social Structure* (New York: Free Press, 1969), 339.

[469] Thornhill, *A Sociology of Constitutions*, 4.

[470] Cotterrell, *Sociology of Law*.

[471] Grimm, "Integration by Constitution," 198.

[472] Preuss, "Disconnecting Constitutions," 40.

[473] Ibid.

[474] Perry, "What is 'the Constitution?'," 104.

[475] Rosenfeld, "Constitutional Identity," 761.

4.2.3.2 Changing Face of Integrative Function

The Constitution of the United States is generally held up as an example of integrative constitution, since it played a significant role in the creation of the national myth. On the other hand, the history of constitutions also saw some bad examples of constitutions that failed in the integration of the society, such as the Weimar constitution.[476] Nevertheless, the effects of constitutions in the integration processes can be only limited, and they are not capable of determining all aspects of these processes.[477] Indeed a constitution cannot be regarded as the only integrative factor in a polity; other factors like history, culture, religion, and nationhood may have more important impacts on integration processes. The European Union can be viewed as an example with poor non-legal integrative factors in this regard.[478] Nevertheless, it is evident that the European Union has been broadly proclaimed as a constitutional polity by an enormous academic circle.[479] Habermas points out that a European constitution can enhance the capability of the EU to act jointly without being affected from the daily policies.[480] However, following that, he argues that the European-wide public sphere should not be considered as the reflection of the national designs in an upper (the European) level. That is to say, this would not (and ought not) occur as a stratified public communication, but rather as "an interpenetration of mutually translated national communications."[481]

Grimm draws attention to the fact that the integrative function of constitution concerns the extralegal effects of a constitution.[482] However, their legal effects are crucial for social integration mainly.[483] The act of constitution-making is indeed an act of "collective self-attribution" of a multitude and a way of constituting a political community.[484] That is to say, from this point of view, the main function of the constitution is "to establish a regime of collective self-rule by constituting 'We the

[476] Karl-Heinz Ladeur, "'We, the European People… '-Relache?," *European Law Journal* 14, no. 2 (2008): 153. Grimm, "Integration by Constitution," 195.

[477] Grimm, "Integration by Constitution," 195. In a similar vein, according to Luhmann, the unity of law is independent from the unity of society. Niklas Luhmann, "The Unity of the Legal System," in *Autopoietic Law: A New Approach to Law and Society*, ed. Gunther Teubner (Berlin: Walter de Gruyter, 1988), 13-18.

[478] Grimm, "Integration by Constitution," 196.

[479] Stone-Sweet, "Supranational Constitution," 442.

[480] Jürgen Habermas, "Why Europe Needs a Constitution," in *Developing a Constitution for Europe*, ed. Erik Oddvar Eriksen, John Erik Fossum and Agustín Menéndez (London: Routledge, 2004), 22.

[481] Ibid., 27.

[482] Dieter Grimm, "Integration by Constitution," 193.

[483] Grimm, "Does Europe Need Constitution?," 287.

[484] Preuss, "Disconnecting Constitutions," 41.

people.'[485] The "We" here has a reflexive character, that is to say, the self-empowerment of a collective actor.[486]

The self-reflexivity of a constitution is reflected by people's expectations. The constitution also has the role of an indicator of the social consensus that shapes the identity of a society:

> (…), a constitution is subject to expectations that extend far beyond its normative regulatory function. People expect the constitution to unify their society as a polity, thereby transcending the differences of opinion and conflicting interests that exist in all societies. The constitution is regarded as a guarantee of the fundamental consensus that is necessary for social cohesion. If a constitution is successful in this respect, it can even help shape a society's identity. The constitution then serves as a document in which society finds its basic convictions and aspirations expressed. This aspect of a constitution can be termed its integrative function.[487]

Following that, Dieter Grimm goes further and argues that constitutions must possess some specific qualities, in order to be defined as integrative forces:

> In general, one might say that a constitution will only have an integrative force if, within its area of application, it stands for more than what it is in juridical terms, that is, more than a mere legal text. The quality that allows a constitution to exceed its legal efficacy is its symbolic power. A constitution will have an integrative effect only if it embodies a society's fundamental value system and aspirations, and if the society perceives that its constitution reflects precisely those values with which it identifies and which are the sources of its specific character.[488]

Consequently, he highlights that an integrative function can come into question beyond legal qualities of a constitution, and that this completely depends on some sort of societal development. However, in Grimm's writings, how the perception of constitution by society gives rise to integration is not clear, as he focuses on normative texts rather than sociological ones. For example, borrowing from Vorländer, he argues that the society must perceive the constitutional system "good," in order to adopt it.[489] According to him, this "goodness" hinges on a "high degree of inclusivity."[490] That is to say, if the constitutions include more interests of the people, they will provide more social integration. This poses a problem, since integrative functions of constitutions in the relevant academic studies of this field lack any support from empirical data.[491]

---

[485] Ibid., 42.

[486] Ibid.

[487] Grimm, "Integration by Constitution," 194.

[488] Ibid., 199. For a similar opinion referring to the symbolic forms in which political imaginations are represented, as the central factor for achievement of a constitution: Vorländer, "Integration durch Verfassung," 18.

[489] Grimm, "Integration by Constitution," 199.

[490] Ibid., 200.

[491] Ibid., 198.

With regard to the matter of integration, the examination of the societal conditions that give rise to the creation of a constitution is vital. Grimm states that this is a relative matter:

> "In order for integration by constitution to occur, (...) the circumstances under which a society is founded play a crucial role."[492] At this point, Ackerman's contributions are striking. He highlights the relationship with the constitutional moments and integrative force of a constitution. A constitution, in this sense is a "symbolic marker of a great transition in the political life of a nation."[493]

In contrast to Ackerman, Grimm argues that constitutional moments are not such absolute prerequisites for the integrative constitutions.[494] To prove this idea, he gives examples from the Swiss Constitution, as it mainly updated the old one, or some other constitutions which did not provide any integration, like some of the former French constitutions. Be it in terms of the Maastricht Treaty of 1992, or from the point of the so-called European Constitution of 2003, the European Union constitutionalism is also not based on a radical breakthrough, but rather on a gradual process. On the other hand, in the case of US constitution, it had very important impacts on social integration, as it had a strong capacity of founding a nation.[495] In this respect, the German and the US constitutionalism are noteworthy examples, since both countries were not able to rely on the traditional means for social integration, but their constitutions provided an opportunity to fill this gap.[496]

On the other hand, when it comes to the transnational context, the integration of constitution becomes a harder issue. In view of the European constitutionalism and the failed attempt at enacting a European constitution, Ladeur puts some objections, and states that in contrast to the usual facts of the constitutional discourse, the demos in question consists of only arguments instead of the people in this process. The core of his argument is the fact that such constitutionalist ideas neglect the fragmentation of social systems, that is to say, "post-modern conditions of the functionality of legal systems" that have recently arisen.[497] At this account, an analogy between the language of American constitutionalism and European constitutionalism is also unfruitful, in particular adopting the wording "We the people ... ," on the ground that this has a completely different meaning in American political history, considering that it has a character of declaration of independence from the former political ties and also of the foundation of a society.[498] A constitutional

---

[492] Ibid., 200.

[493] Bruce Ackerman, "The Rise of World Constitutionalism" (Occassional Papers, Paper 4, 1996, http://digitalcommons.law.yale.edu/cgi/viewcontent.cgi?article=1005&context=ylsop_papers), last visit 11.10.2013.

[494] Grimm, "Integration by Constitution," 201.

[495] Ibid., 201.

[496] Ibid., 204.

[497] Ladeur, "'We, the European People," 149.

[498] Ibid., 150.

treaty does not reflect the character of a constitution at all, and in this respect, this creates another oversight of the European constitutionalism debates. From this point of view, deliberative constitutionalism, or the Habermasian understanding of this issue reflects a fundamental misunderstanding of the facts.[499] In addition, Ladeur puts forward the idea that, integration would only become possible through practical functions of European institutions, but not through a normative foundational act. Since a European identity is still defined through national European identities (Italian, Irish, German etc.), a societal integration in this way is not very likely to occur.[500] At this juncture, European constitutionalism should be dealt along with some other factors, e.g. the new governance structures affecting the attributions of supranationalism. Networks and network-like hybrid organizations, being in the first place, alter the traditional forms of governmentalism, and this also has some results on the societal relationships and potential or possible ways of integration. The conventional borders between private and public, market and organization do not exist anymore. Transformation in governance inevitably has deep impacts on the institutional structure of the EU. However, what is meant by a constitution for the EU is clearly the liberal-modern constitution model of French and American constitutions, that arose at the end of the eighteenth century.[501] Under these circumstances, a state-centred perspective that ascribes a character of a "super state" to the European Union in a traditional manner creates a paradox.[502]

Furthermore, it would be very difficult to clarify the general manner for constitution-making as to whether it functions for a societal integration or a political foundation. Having considered the historical development of British constitutionalism McIlwain stated that:

> Constitutional history is usually the record of a series of oscillations. At one time private right is the chief concern of the citizens; at another the prevention of disorder that threatens to become anarchy.[503]

In any case, it would be apt to state that constitutions have a historical function to impede former political conditions from coming back, and to safeguard the existing political order.[504] However, beyond the symbolic meanings of political facts, a societal integration can be desired, but this does not imply that every constitutionalization process shall result in integration. Historical examples are clear enough in this sense. However, another fact is that successful constitutions are those which could achieve societal integrations, as mentioned above, in addition to a political foundation. Nonetheless, integrative function was a claim of modern constitutionalism, and since demands for recognition of diverse cultures in

---

[499] Ibid., 152.

[500] Ibid., 154.

[501] Grimm, "Does Europe Need Constitution?," 284.

[502] Ladeur, "We, the European People," 159.

[503] McIlwain, *Constitutionalism*, 128.

[504] Grimm, "Does Europe Need Constitution?," 288.

contemporary societies arose in particular in the post-colonial period, it no longer remained a keyword in modern society. In this respect, modern constitutions can no longer meet the needs of contemporary diverse societies, as they were configured to create an overarching unified structure that rejects these diversities. In this new phase, constitutions proved not to be a keyword for the construction of nations in particular.[505]

Briefly, the modern constitutionalism theories assumed a certain role of constitutions in the integration of a society in building a nation. As mentioned above, constitutions were assumed as the instruments that give rise to the notion of "We the People." However, for a number of reasons, constitutions can no longer bear this function in contemporary societies.

The failed constitution of the EU is the most remarkable example of the result of seeking a constitutionalization within an entity that had difficulties with creating a common identity. In addition, democratic principles and individual rights are now in the centre of contemporary constitution, and rights have become the foundational components of a contemporary constitution in this regard. This is important, because it proves that contemporary constitutionalism now takes individuals as the central addressees of rights. In other words, a contemporary constitution has to exist for individuals, not for any other entities, beliefs, ideologies, nations that are supposed to consist of a single ethnic entity, etc. The contemporary society is diverse, and a constitution that aims at working for it cannot function as an integration driven modern constitution.[506]

As emphasized before, the integrative function of a constitution concerns its extralegal effects. Above all, as Talcot Parsons argues, this has to do with societal aspects of an integration process and construction of a collective identity. Modern constitutions feature integrative functions particularly in creating a nation, national identities, citizenship etc. This complies with the political ambitions of their framers. As to the contemporary constitutions, this feature is a bit more complex. Contemporary constitutions are basically the bearers of rights, that is to say, identities created by them mainly rely on the rights they underpin. In this regard, the rights-based integrative function of constitutions has to do with law and legal relationships. Consequently, it is not plausible to seek a common foundational base for contemporary constitutions, which is the same as that of modern constitutions. In other words, "We, the people" is more likely to be formulated as "We, the bearers of rights" for contemporary constitutionalism. This can be the solution to the paradox of attempts to apply modern constitutionalism to the contemporary constitutional practices.[507] However, it is evident that as a combination of the rights holder diverse units, "We" here gains an entirely different ontological background.

---

[505] Tully, *Strange Multiplicity*, 187.

[506] Ibid., 187.

[507] Ladeur, "We, the European People," 159.

4.2.4 *Meaning of Contemporary Constitution*

4.2.4.1 A Deviation or a Continuance of Modern Constitution?

As is the case with international law, constitutional law has not been exempt from a transformation imposed by globalization and other transformative dynamics of the twentieth century, as mentioned above. The challenges against modern constitutions regarding social complexity were also associated with the organizational questions of limitation and control of power.[508] At this point, the question arises to what extent modern constitutions, which were led by American and French constitutions, can meet the needs of contemporary society. Some scholars answer this negatively, and draw a certain borderline between modern and contemporary constitutionalism.[509] In other words, they argue that contemporary constitutionalism is by no means equivalent to modern constitutionalism. From this point of view, contemporary constitutionalism is structured and maintained by new dynamics different from the revolutionary American and French constitutions. In addition to a normative basis, contemporary constitutionalism is also subject to the constructive ideas from the contemporary legal scholarship. For example, Tully suggests discovering a post-imperial intercultural dialogue that refrains from a comprehensive language in order to break with the conventional understanding of modern constitutionalism. Without achieving this, contemporary constitutionalism has to grapple with an impasse caused by cultural diversities.[510] As a matter of fact, this was already uttered by legal pluralists of the 1980s, such as Sally Falk Moore, Clifford Geertz and others who claimed that the comprehensive language of modern constitutionalism cannot represent the post-colonial societies, which consist of a wide variety of legal and customary systems of authority.[511] According to Tully, this means that contemporary constitutionalism was marked by struggles of diverse cultures for recognition, and accordingly the "hidden constitutions of contemporary societies." Tully depicts this situation as "[t]hey [hidden constitutions] are hidden by the rule of modern constitutionalism and the narrow range of uses of its central terms."[512] These hidden constitutions carried out a function to struggle with diversities that modern constitutions were not able to cope with.

To make it more clear, James Tully put forward the idea that modern constitutionalism remained insufficient for responding to cultural diversities of society for over 300 years. The cultural diversity is "analogous to ecological diversity" in Tully's mind; however at the same time it challenges "a powerful norm of uniformity in modern constitutionalism" and gives rise to a serious objection to the

---

[508] Neves, "Comparing Transconstitutionalism," 4.

[509] Tully, *Strange Multiplicity*, 30 ff., and 183.

[510] Ibid., 57.

[511] Ibid.,101.

[512] Ibid., 99.

politics of cultural recognition.[513] That is to say, modern constitution has not been democratized since it did not overcome the challenge of societal diversities yet. Further, according to Tully, modern constitutionalism reflected a very Euro-centric strand of thought and the language of its own age, as it was found in the writings of Kant, Hobbes, Paine, Rousseau etc. The residue of this age currently creates a flaw of modern constitutionalism. Moreover, the traditional constitutionalism also saw serious challenges of post-modernism, cultural feminism and inter-culturalism that pushed modern constitutionalism towards a number of transformations.[514] In this respect, for example, the main concepts in constitutionalism, such as culture, citizen, community, association, nation, people were discussed and attempted to be reconstructed under the common title of identity by postmodernists.[515] Moreover, indigenous peoples, suppressed and divided nationalities and minorities sought constitutional recognition as intercultural citizens.[516] Seen in this light, contemporary constitutionalism stands for a different phenomenon, although it still reflects a continuance of the constitutional movements of the past.

Overall, beyond the various discursive facts that mark contemporary constitutionalism, it is necessary to take note of a very serious impasse of contemporary constitutionalism that is inherited from modern constitutionalism, that is to say, the cultural diversities.[517] As touched upon above, contemporary constitutionalism has been challenged by the demands of diverse indigenous and other cultures for a constitutional recognition, but contemporary constitutionalism still lacks the sufficient instruments for responding to them, since contemporary constitutionalism still reflects modern constitutionalism in many respects. Furthermore, the constitutional movements continue in different forms, as post-modern and feminist demands put contemporary constitutionalism under pressure in order to widen the recognized themes of constitutional law. According to Tully, a crucial theme in this sense is the dysfunctional comprehensive language of modern constitutionalism and the need for a new intercultural language. Seen in this light, contemporary constitutionalism reflects a multifaceted problematic field, which lays out both a continuance of and a disengagement from modern constitutional tradition of the eighteenth and nineteenth centuries.

4.2.4.2 Typology Problem

As Grimm states very clearly, "[t]ypologies presuppose clarity about their object."[518] Further, he also affirms that the typifying of constitution is a very relativistic issue,

---

[513] Ibid., 26.

[514] Ibid., 43.

[515] Ibid., 45.

[516] Ibid., 53.

[517] Ibid., 57.

[518] Grimm, "Types of Constitutions," 100.

and relevant criteria vary from author to author, and further innumerable criteria can also appear.[519] Therefore, as an attempt to limit them, a typology always faces a risk of missing various aspects of an issue.

As demonstrated in this chapter, contemporary constitutionalism differs from the traditional perception of modern constitutionalism to a great extent, as it was reflected by the French and American revolutionary constitutions. The objection points to the characterization of modern constitutions by Grimm, which were mentioned in the very beginning of this chapter, seem clearer at this juncture. First of all, constitutions still retain their philosophical features. However, Grimm states that "[t]he norms emanate from a political decision rather than having their source in a pre-established truth." He evidently refers to the medieval constitutional orders here. However, in contemporary constitutionalism, by virtue of its expanding "legal" character, "rights" have already been established as the new pre-established truth of constitutions. This also has to do with the fifth remark of Grimm. Grimm considers *pouvoir constituant* and *pouvoir constitué* essential to the concept of constitution. Nevertheless, "rights" as the contemporary pre-established truth of constitutions make this distinction insignificant. Rights have already replaced the *pouvoir constituent,* and they became the cardinal source of legitimacy for constitutions. In his second remark, Grimm underlines the function of constitution to regulate public power. The enduring and eternal function of constitution was mentioned before. The problem is that Grimm views this function as a stable one. He stresses the changing conditions for modern constitutions in contrast to the pre-modern proto-constitutional orders. However, as it was discussed in the first chapter, one of the major implications of globalization in the transformed structure of law concerns a transformation in the identification of public order and public law. Due to a growing number of contractual relations, public law becomes permeable with private law, and thus the borderline between the two becomes more blurred. Therefore, this remark does not meet reality at this point. This means that public order in the traditional sense faces a challenge and undergoes a transformation; and as a result, constitutions need to adapt to this new process. Constitutional law arises as an instrument of this transformation. This fact also has to do with the ground to reject the fourth remark. By the reason of this new process where private law penetrates into public law, it is no longer possible to speak of a unique form of public power that acts as unrivalled. In short, the far-reaching effects of globalization on public law make this characteristic of constitution unconvincing. The fourth remark mentions supremacy of constitutions over other legal norms. It is beyond doubt that a constitution must have a "meta" position towards other laws. In terms of the hierarchy of norms in domestic laws, this is an essential characteristic of constitutions. As mentioned before, this feature of constitutions arose so as to institutionalize legal orders and to emancipate law from political influences in the newly emerging modern states. However, to what extent is it an absolute characteristic of contemporary constitutions? The question is the "absolute" quality of higher law, therefore this text does not have a claim

[519] Ibid., 98.

for denying it entirely. This remark is also the most relevant one to the question of global constitutionalism. Under current circumstances, it is basically problematic in two terms. In consideration of the power of interpretive traditions over constitutions, it is necessary to ask what grants this interpretive power. What is implied here is not the authority granted by constitution or other laws to amend constitutions. The interpretive power appears as an extralegal fact. The "living constitution" tradition of the US Supreme Court arises as a striking point for further arguments. To make it clear, in light of the relevant section regarding "living constitution" above, the question arises on how come a legal norm incompatible with the constitution can launch the amendment of a constitution process? How can a constitution become compatible with a lower norm instead of the opposite way? In this respect, how can it be affirmed that "higher law" is the commonality of contemporary constitutions? The second aspect of this matter is the position of transnational law toward domestic constitutions. Evidently, the "higher law" character of constitutions would be seen absolute in the world of *Lotus* doctrine. In a world where nation states were the only decision makers for their own fates and where they were bound by international law only in cases they accepted to be bound, constitutions could be defined as meta-laws of absolute sovereign nation states. However, as mentioned in the first two chapters, when considering the complementary functions of transnational legal institutions and tribunals on domestic constitutions, the label of "higher law" becomes dubious and somewhat relatively apt, rather than an absolute feature. To put it differently, the depiction of "higher law" makes sense in terms of a narrower approach to formal law. On the other hand, if it is dysfunctional to lower laws, the meaning of "higher law" needs to be questioned seriously. Seen in this light, it would be argued that "higher law" is deliberately used, instead of "the highest law." All in all, the characterization of modern constitution by Grimm seems insufficient in reflecting the truth and commonalities of contemporary constitution, and thus in applying to the global constitutionalism discourse.

Against this background, a new way of reading contemporary constitutionalism is required. A new overarching framework is necessary for explaining the meaning of this multifaceted, immigrant, rights-based project. All things considered, any identification of constitutions in descriptive terms would be insufficient to depict commonalities of contemporary constitutions, since they tend to define constitution without a contextual basis. As such they miss the points of the permeability and the mobility of constitutional structures as well as the relativity of their meanings for each society. They miss cultural backgrounds, historical developments of constitutions in each society. Therefore, such a reductionist and descriptive identification of constitution does not give good results for an inquiry to develop a common understanding of constitution, in order to apply it to the discourse of global constitutionalism. However, is it not possible to take up a common idea of constitution? This book could surely opt for an existing one and go through it by explaining the reasons for choosing it. However, for the purposes of this study on global constitutionalism, the relativity of the idea of contemporary constitution cannot be ignored. In order to understand both commonalities and relativity, dynamics of the variations in question need to be understood. Contemporary constitution needs a holistic category to search its identity in order to reflect the diverse and relative character thereof, and to understand its truth. In consideration of these, constitutionalism appears as a social process of interpretation:

> Constitutionalism, in this sense, is a system of interpretive canons, practices, and expectations, in which governmental command may appropriately be evaluated and justified in terms of higher or deeper principles that themselves are not sanctioned by courts.[520]

At this point, Goldsworthy emphasizes several facts that affect different interpretations of constitutions, such as the age and the precedents of a constitution, legal and political culture in which a constitution was born, and "the felt necessities of the time."[521] When considering the relevant academic literature, for a mediate platform between law and politics, "constitutional culture" arises as a fitting category to explain these facts aggregately.[522]

4.2.4.3 A New Paradigm to Explain Diversity and Relativity of Constitutions

In view of the contemporary appearance of constitution as discussed in this chapter, it is most likely to conclude that a single meaning of constitution can hardly be unveiled. Given the diverse forms and functions of constitutions, Heringa and Kiiver make a division between the "narrow or formal" meaning and the "broad or substantive" meaning of a constitution. In a narrow or formal meaning, a constitution is simply a constitutional written document regarding the basic rules that apply to the states. For instance, the constitutional texts of the US Constitution or the Basic Law of Germany etc. In a broad or substantive meaning, constitution refers to

> the entire body of fundamental rules that govern that socio-political entity: be they contained in a central document or in many documents, be they written down or be they customary rules.[523]

Evidently, the British Constitution reflects the second meaning very explicitly; there is no written document called a British Constitution. However, numerous rules and

---

[520] John Ferejohn, Jack N. Rakove and Jonathan Riley, "Editor's Introduction," in *Constitutional Culture and Democratic Rule*, ed. John Ferejohn, Jack N. Rakove and Jonathan Riley (Cambridge: Cambridge University Press, 2001), 8, 14.

[521] Goldsworthy, "Constitutional Interpretation," 706 ff.

[522] Ferejohn et al., "Editor's Introduction," 14.

[523] Aalt Willem Heringa and Philipp Author Kiiver, *Constitutions Compared: An Introduction to Comparative Constitutional Law*, 3rd ed. (Cambridge: Cambridge University Press, 2012), 2-3. A variant form of this categorization is the "big-C" and "small-c" constitutions. Gardbaum, "Place of Constitutional Law," 170-171. However, in this categorization, "small-c constitution" is rather used to imply the customary British Constitution. This book aims at highlighting common broader contexts for all constitutions. Therefore, such categorization may not answer the purpose.

principles embody a constitution, as some of them are judge-made case law, or some of them are the Parliament decisions or statute norms, while others appear in the form of customs, conventions, or gentlemen's agreements.[524] In the same vein, constitutions of Israel, New Zealand and the Swedish Constitution can be put into the same category, as their constitutions are not represented by a central written document. However, the broad meaning of constitution does not only stand for unwritten or customary constitutions. Many constitutions that are embodied by written documents also reflect the broad meaning of constitutions. This means that written constitutions can also have unwritten rules that create their broader constitutions.[525] For example, the US Constitution does not empower judges to declare a legislation unconstitutional, but judges have acquired this power by virtue of case law.[526] Some customary rules can also form a part of the constitution. For example, the relations between the parliament and the ministers are governed by customary rules in Netherlands.[527] The constitutional rule in Turkey that the president appoints the leader of the major party as the prime minister is not found in the constitutional text, but it is entirely a customary rule. Furthermore, some other constitutional rules, for example regarding election systems, the statute of a constitutional court, the rule of procedure of a parliament etc. may be found in ordinary laws. International treaties or international court decisions can also have domestic constitutional effects.[528]

Another important fact about constitutions that cannot be captured by written constitutions is the "working constitution," which means "entirety of rules and perceptions regarding this subject in society."[529] Various examples can be employed to explain this fact. For example, many constitutions refer to the rule of law as a fundamental principle of their constitutional systems. However, in reality, some of them may reflect only words on paper, as we observe many practices against an independent judiciary, or regarding autocratic methods in government and fundamental rights that reflect a tendency toward an arbitrary power. It is a very common issue in countries that come forth with human rights abuses. For instance, the provision of the Soviet Constitution that guarantees the right to freely leave the Soviet Union to every constituent republic can be considered in this context, on the ground that this right had no value in reality except for propagandist purposes.[530] Another striking point relates to the interpretation of the constitution by courts. As mentioned above within the framework of the US constitutionalism, a supreme court may be dominated by interpretive trends relying on ideological and cultural backgrounds of the court members.

---

[524] Heringa and Kiiver, *Constitutions Compared*, 3.

[525] Ibid., 3.

[526] Ibid.

[527] Ibid., 4.

[528] Ibid.

[529] Ibid. Heringa and Kiiver prefer naming this fact as "working constitution." It would also be called as "Constitution in Action" with a reference to the idea of "Law in Action" of Roscoe Pound.

[530] Ibid., 5.

The same provisions and principles may gain entirely different meanings in different eras and in the hand of judges with different ideological and political backgrounds. Further, in a comparative context we come across a similar situation. The same or very similar constitutional provisions in constitutions of very similar national political cultures can be interpreted very differently. A very common example is the abortion rulings of the US Supreme Court and the German Federal Court regarding abortion in the 1970s. It is quite striking that these courts concluded in opposite ways on the same subject matter, which relied on very similar constitutional provisions.[531]

Furthermore, Heringa and Kiiver point to the circumstances of two presidents who have the exact same legal powers and whose effective powers are different because of different social conditions under which they operate, or different levels of political support.[532] All in all, a constitution can appear in different forms when it is considered in its broader meaning. The content of a broader constitution may also deviate from the written form of constitution.[533]

By employing this meaning of constitution, it is evident that one can find out commonalities of political and legal constitutions, or constitutions whose identities have been subject to flexibilization through interpretive activities of courts, like the US Constitution.

The broader definition of constitution better serves for the purposes of this research for two reasons. First, when considering the general overview of contemporary constitutionalism, this definition can display commonalities of constitutions, which arise as very diverse facts, given the different constitutions all around the world. Second, as there is no formally promulgated constitution in the international legal order, the global constitutionalism discourse deals with some assumptions regarding an ongoing constitutionalization. Simply, the global constitutionalism discourse embraces a number of facts and normative bodies in international law, and regards them as indicators of a constitutionalization process. Further, the contributors of this debate rely on some secondary facts in consolidating their presumptions. While doing this, they do not rely on a constitution in the narrow meaning, but rather in the broader meaning. Therefore, it is more likely to express it in such a way that the constitution of global constitutionalism is a broad constitution.[534] On the other hand, in the second chapter, it was noted that the global constitutionalism discourse already lacks a certain idea of contemporary constitution; and instead, the idea of constitution reflected by global constitutionalism is blurred and amorphous. At this point, this expression complies with this finding of the second chapter to a great deal. In other words, the global constitutionalism discourse needs to clarify how it

[531] Roe v. Wade, 410 US 113 (1973) and Schwangerschaftsabbruch II, BVerfGE 88, 203, cited by Vorländer, "What is 'Constitutional Cultures'," 22.

[532] Heringa and Kiiver, *Constitutions Compared*, 4.

[533] Gardbaum, "Place of Constitutional Law," 171.

[534] For example, Fassbender's definition for constitution: Bardo Fassbender, "Rediscovering a Forgotten Constitution: Notes on the Place of the UN Charter in the International Legal Order," in *Ruling the World? Constitutionalism, International Law, and Global Governance*, ed. Jeffrey L. Dunoff and Joel P. Trachtman (Cambridge: Cambridge University Press, 2009), 139.

approaches contemporary constitutionalism. Nevertheless, to this end, global constitutionalism needs to reveal how to contour the broader meaning of constitution.

In this regard, the mainstream constitutional law discourse does not offer a variety of alternatives. To look into comparative constitutional law does not change this fact. At this point, comparative law is crucial, since the contemporary concept of constitution is still considerably associated with state constitutions, and borders of state constitutions are interwoven due to the increasing communication between constitutions.[535] Comparative constitutional law studies make an analogy, distinction and contrast across legal systems. However, as a matter of fact, comparative constitutional law offers an underdeveloped subdisciplinary structure in some terms. As Hirschl argues, comparative constitutional law studies have "(…) fallen short of advancing knowledge through tracing causal links among pertinent variables, let alone contributing to theory building through substantiation or refutation of testable hypotheses."[536] As to the matter of constitutional migration, comparative constitutional law literature has not yet provided a systemic methodology.[537] Another great gap in comparative constitutional law is that it only compares written constitutions, and therefore cannot reflect the broader context of constitution.[538] Yet, a methodological approach is required to explain the diverse constitutive elements of legal and political cultures, in order to understand the contemporary diverse typologies of constitutions.[539]

To put a parenthesis, it is of note that to deal with the wider meanings of law and legal facts is not a recent problem in legal theory. Particularly in the earlier twentieth century, a number of scholars from the sociological jurisprudence defined law in a broader context, that is to say, within its social environment. They refused to define law in positivist ways and depending only on black letter law. Eugene Ehrlich, Leon Petrazyski, Georges Gurvitch, and Roscoe Pound were the most notable ones. As a commonality, these scholars drew attention to the various forms of law in the society other than black letter law, and they defined law in consideration with the broader contexts in societal application. However these theories did not overreach a polemic platform, and they lacked empirical supports to a great extent.[540]

On the other hand, in the recent comparative law theory, some scholars challenged the functionalist approaches that focus on the unity or similarity of facts,

---

[535] Peer Zumbansen, "Carving Out Typologies and Accounting for Differences Across Systems: Towards a Methodology of Transnational Constitutionalism," in *The Oxford Handbook of Comparative Constitutional Law*, ed. Michel Rosenfeld and Andras Sajo (Oxford: Oxford University Press, 2012), 82.

[536] Ran Hirschl, "On the Blurred Methodological Matrix of Comparative Constitutional Law," in *The Migration of Constitutional Ideas*, ed. Sujit Choudry (Cambridge: Cambridge University Press, 2006), 40.

[537] Choudry, "Migration as a New Metaphor," 14.

[538] Herringa and Kiiver, *Constitutions Compared*, 4. William Twining, *Globalisation and Legal Scholarship*, Tilburg Law Lectures Series, Montesquieu Seminars 4 (Nijmegen: Wolf Legal Publishers, 2009), 48.

[539] Zumbansen, "Carving Out Typologies," 77.

[540] Cotterrell, *Sociology of Law*.

and explored the usefulness of the cultural paradigm to explain the diverse forms of law.[541] From this perspective, culture can be an effective instrument in understanding the diverse meanings and the practices of law in different societies. For Pierre Legrand, culture in essence excludes universality, on the ground that, "[c]ulture refers to features that are not universal but that transcend the individual."[542] With respect to the legal borrowings and transplantations, Legrand suggests approaching law as "an incorporative cultural form (...) buttressed by important historical and ideological formations" instead of by only propositional statements.[543] To put it differently, culture has to do with the intangible elements of a legal community and it "organises (not always seamlessly) the identity of such legal community *as legal community*."[544] Law is a social subsystem and is inextricably linked to "the non-legal reality" of the society.[545] From this point of view, we can speak of an exact legal transplantation, only if the rule and its context can be transferred between legal systems.[546] The cultural paradigm enables a comparative approach to avoid considering differences as "irreducible." According to Legrand, the universal grammar of law is "fatally and damagingly, reductionist."[547] Moreover, it is not clear whether the proponents of sameness in legal literature consider the connection of law with the society. In this regard, Legrand puts forward the idea that the aim of cultural paradigm is to "resist 'the imperialism of the Same'."[548] To put it differently, he demonstrates a radical stance against the functionalist views of the comparative law theory in the identification of other laws: "comparatists must resist the powerful drive towards the construction of abstract commonalities."[549] Although not as

[541] Choudry, "Migration as a New Metaphor," 17. Michael King, "Comparing Legal Cultures in the Quest for Law's Identity," in *Comparing Legal Cultures*, ed. David Nelken (Aldershot: Dartmouth, 1997), 119.

[542] Pierre Legrand, "European Legal Systems are not Converging," *International and Comparative Law Quarterly* 45 (1996): 56.

[543] Pierre Legrand, "What 'Legal Transplants'?," in *Adapting Legal Cultures*, ed. David Nelken and Johannes Feest (Oxford: Hart Publishing, 2001), 59, cited by Choudry, "Migration as a New Metaphor," 17.

[544] Pierre Legrand, "Comparative Legal Studies and The Matter of Authenticity," *Journal of Comparative Law* 1 (2006): 374. Emphasis belongs to the original text.

[545] Legrand, "European Legal Systems," 58.

[546] And therefore it is impossible, says Legrand, cited by Choudry, "Migration as a New Metaphor," 17. Also Legrand, "European Legal Systems."

[547] Legrand, "Comparative Legal Studies," 367.

[548] Geoffrey Samuel, *An Introduction to Comparative Law Theory and Method* (Oxford: Hart Publishing, 2014), 164.

[549] Legrand, "Comparative Legal Studies," 368. At this point, in contrast to Legrand, it could be argued that functionalist views about world systems do not reject cultural differentiation at all times. For example, King demonstrates that cultural views are not incompatible with the autopoetic theory of Luhmann; instead, each subsystem of communication attributes different meanings to the concept of culture, from its own standpoint. In this sense, legal culture means "law and its environment." King, "Comparing Legal Cultures," 119-134.

radical as Legrand, the cultural paradigm has also been represented by legal cultural studies in particular beginning from the earlier contributions of Lawrence M. Friedman within the framework of socio-legal studies.[550] These studies basically deal with law in its cultural context. On the other hand, it is of note that the constitutional law discourse is not completely blind to this debate. A newly emerging idea, that strives to explain the diverse meanings of the concept of constitution, is that constitutions are to be dealt with in terms of their distinctive cultures. In this regard, some scholars argue that any particular form of constitutionalism reflects a certain constitutional culture as well as a constitutional political system and a constitutional theory.[551] However, the concept of constitutional culture is used in different meanings. While some scholars refer to the political culture of a society, others consider it along with the concept of legal culture, which is a better established discourse in socio-legal studies. In this respect, constitutional culture reflects an intermediate position between the legal and political culture of a society.[552] Tully reflects the cultural feature of contemporary constitution as follows:

> A constitution should be seen as a form of activity, an inter-cultural dialogue in which the culturally diverse sovereign citizens of contemporary societies negotiate agreements on their forms of association over time in accordance with the three conventions of mutual recognition, consent and cultural continuity.[553]

At this point, various questions come to the fore with regard to the mediating function of constitutions between law and politics.[554] The secret of success for a constitution has been considered as related to its success in communication with the society, and between rulers and the ruled by some scholars. Thus, cultural aspects of constitutions are the key points of this communication.[555] The concept of culture rises as a response to the variety of interpretive meanings of constitutions. Wenzel advances the claim that constitutional culture is determinative over the interpretation of a constitution.[556] That is to say, it is aimed to explain, through the use of the concept of culture, why the British focus on the need for a political constitution for maintenance of democracy, while Americans or Germans do the opposite in favour of a strong judicial review mechanism.[557] Franklin argues this very clearly in the context of the character of American constitutionalism:

---

[550] Lawrence M. Friedman, *Law and Society: An Introduction* (New Jersey: Prentice Hall Inc., 1977). For a summary of historical development and different approaches to legal culture: Sally Engle Merry, "What is Legal Culture? An Anthropological Perspective," *Journal of Comparative Law* 5 (2010): 40-58. Menachem Mautner, "Three Approaches to Law and Culture," *Cornell Law Review* 96 (2011): 839-867.

[551] Ferejohn et al., "Editor's Introduction," 10.

[552] Siegel, "Constitutional Culture," 1327.

[553] Tully, *Strange Multiplicity*, 30.

[554] Siegel, "Constitutional Culture," 1327.

[555] Hensel, "Constitutional Cultures," 5.

[556] Wenzel, "From Contract to Mental," 70.

[557] Ibid., 67.

> American constitutionalism depends to a great degree on cultural values. In other words, the rule of law exists in the US as much because there is an extraordinary level of social consensus as because of the structure of the legal and political system.[558]

More questions can be produced in this context. Why are some constitutions duty-based, while some others are rights-based? Another point is how, why and to what extent they interact or whether they keep their independent structures while constitutional norms and values migrate. For example, to what extent does the conception of rights-based constitution penetrate into the British constitutional culture through the Human Rights Act, and to what extent could it be effective within this constitutional culture? Another relevant issue is legal impacts of constitutions in the reality. As Karl Loewenstein argues in an attempt for creating a typology of constitutions, some constitutions are effective, since they are internalized by governors and the governed. On the other hand, there are also some constitutions which are ineffective, since socio-economic and political conditions prevent them from being applied faithfully. Further, some others, such as those of dictatorial or totalitarian regimes, comply with the political reality, but cannot impose binding rules on it.[559] This means that some constitutions may only have a symbolic meaning as they are not effective over the legal orders, despite meeting formal preconditions of a constitution. At this juncture, Michel Rosenfeld argues that a constitutional identity emerges in three meanings: The first one is the *fact* of having a constitution. The second one is the *content* of a constitution. Finally, the third one is the *context* in which a constitution operates: "different cultures envision fundamental rights in contrasting and even sometimes contradictory ways."[560] In other words, the identity of a constitution transcends mere constitutionalism and the content of a constitution, and it emerges in a dynamic tension with other identities in a society.[561] According to scholars like Post and Ferejohn et al., constitutional culture is the key to understanding these dynamics in the constructional process of the identity of a constitution.[562]

According to Griffith, constitutions reflect all cultural deposition of societies. As a response to liberal legalist constitutional accounts, he argues that,

> [b]ehind all constitutions lie the political, social and economic histories which have shaped the present day nation states; also the histories of their religions and their arts; the games people play; their drinking and eating habits; the way they treat their children and their old people; and so to everything that makes the totality of the national culture.[563]

---

558 Daniel P. Franklin, "American Political Culture and Constitutionalism," in *Political Culture and Constitutionalism: A Comparative Approach*, ed. Daniel Franklin and Michael Baun (Armonk: M.E. Sharpe, 1995), 43.

559 Karl Loewenstein, *Political Power and the Governmental Process* (1957), 147 ff., cited by Grimm, "Types of Constitutions," 107.

560 Rosenfeld, "Constitutional Identity," 757.

561 Ibid., 758.

562 Ferejohn et al., "Editors's Introduction," 11. Post.

563 Griffith "Brave New World," 175.

These cultural aspects of constitution, which consist of histories and habits, stem from the deep and inescapable conflicts of modern society, and political conflicts lie at the heart of these aspects.[564] This interconnectedness also relates to the actual problems of restriction of democratic choice and freedom through global financial problems.[565] In a similar vein, Weimar-era legal scholar Hermann Heller argues that a constitution does not merely consist of constitutional text, but of "customs, ethics, religion, tact, fashion, and so on" and the "whole natural and cultural milieu, the anthropological, geographic, national, economic and social normalities."[566] In this regard, for Heller, content of a constitution reflects the culture of citizens as well as the characteristics of legislators.[567]

Given the contemporary debates in identifying and interpreting constitutions, a number of conclusions have arisen regarding the cultural character of a constitution. First of all, these debates prove that constitutions and constitutional law are not independent from the beliefs and values of non-judicial actors. That is to say, even from the perspective of legal constitutionalism or originalism, various political and societal factors affect the development of constitutions, and this makes them facts that extend beyond the borders of a legal order.[568] At this point, the crucial question is how to determine the scope of these beliefs and values. Is a constitution merely a political or an ideological instrument, if it is considered beyond the legal domain? According to Robert C. Post, culture is the right term for depicting "beliefs" and "values" of non-judicial actors, and it has a dialectical relationship with the constitutional law.[569] A constitutional culture comes in various forms. Not only official, but also ordinary individuals' convictions about their constitution give rise to a constitutional culture. In this sense, Post explains the integrated structure of the Supreme Court as follows:

> It is virtually unimaginable that the Court's articulation of these principles should find their ground exclusively in the professional opinions of judges, without some dialectical connection to the actual political self-conception of the nation.[570]

The decisions of the Supreme Court reflect a communication between the court and the people. Not only individual reactions of constitutional court justices, but even

[564] Gee, "Political Constitutionalism of Griffith," 43

[565] Goldoni and McCorkindale, "A Note From the Editors," 2108.

[566] Hermann Heller, "The Nature and Structure of the State," trans. David Dyzenhaus, *Cardozo Law Review* 18 (1996): 1139, 1185–1186, cited by David Schneiderman, "Property Rights and Regulatory Innovation: Comparing Constitutional Cultures," *International Journal of Constitutional Law* 4, no. 2 (2006): 375.

[567] Ibid.

[568] As an originalist, Chief Justice Rehnquist supposes the opposite about the character of the constitution and constitutional law. In his view, a constitution should be regarded within the scope of the positive law. Robert C. Post, "Foreword: Fashioning the Legal Constitution: Culture, Courts, and Law," *Harvard Law Review* 117 (2003): 30

[569] Ibid., 8.

[570] Ibid., 37.

rights themselves reflect a constitutional culture, where they gain their roots from.[571] He employs three cases heard before the Supreme Court, namely Hibbs, Grutter and Lawrence, in order to support his idea.[572] In this respect, referring to the Hibbs case, Post argues that, the capacity of the Supreme Court to establish effective constitutional law depends on the constitutional culture. In this case, the Supreme Court applies a sex discrimination jurisprudence, which was produced as a constitutional cultural issue reflected in the constitutional interpretations of the Congress.[573]

From Post's point of view, an ideological conviction of autonomy or claiming that the constitutional law must remain completely autonomous from the constitutional culture is an obstacle to constructing a bridge between constitutional law and constitutional culture. Constitutional culture renders a constitutional interpretation possible, since it enables courts to make a dialogue with the societal beliefs and values.[574] Referring to the anthropological accounts, Post regards constitutional culture as an active process that evolves over time and he does not deem it to be a diachronically and synchronically singular fact. Instead, a constitutional culture, as a living phenomenon, is subject to deep divisions in a society.[575] The decisions of the Supreme Court, from time to time, reflect those divisions and tensions, as the Court can opt for constitutional values of one region to another region of the country.[576]

On the other hand, constitutional law and constitutional culture are dialectically interconnected phenomena. However, this does not mean that constitutional law is a sufficient tool to reflect a constitutional culture. Rather it intervenes in constitutional culture to shape it.[577] Post explains that as follows:

> There can be no constitutional law without constitutional culture, but neither can constitutional law be reduced to constitutional culture. (…) For both judges and historians, constitutional culture is the medium within which constitutional law is fashioned.[578]

The dialectical relationship between constitutional culture and constitutional law is to be structured in various ways. Against this background, the US Supreme Court acts in some cases in order to meet the demands of constitutional culture, and shapes the substance of the constitutional law in this direction.[579] Furthermore, constitutional culture is the source of constitutional legitimacy; and thus any intervention in the constitutional law by a constitutional court must rely on constitutional culture, that is to say, fundamental convictions and beliefs of the society.[580]

---

[571] Ibid., 10.

[572] Ibid.

[573] Ibid., 24-34.

[574] Ibid., 40-41.

[575] Ibid., 54.

[576] Ibid., 55.

[577] Ibid., 54.

[578] Ibid., 76-77.

[579] Ibid., 105.

[580] Ibid., 107.

In conclusion, constitution is a matter of culture. The debates on the character of various constitutional traditions and their interpretations, notably in the case of British, American or continental Europe prove that character of constitution.[581] In other words, whether a constitution is political or legal, or other interpretive outlooks towards a constitution are mainly related to the cultural character of a constitution. A constitution is merely neither a legal matter nor a political one, but rather a sum of them, along with other categories, like religion or ethics that give rise to "beliefs" and "values." When it comes to the interpretation of constitutions by courts, as a usual behaviour of the judiciary, courts largely interact with the cultural codes of the society that they serve. This is indeed the only possibility in creating a judgment.[582]

However, it does not mean that constitutional law is just a cultural phenomenon. Post states that when the textual meaning of a constitution is not clear and other legal sources do not suffice, the courts must make constitutional law by looking at cultural practices. In this respect, he argues that even the strictest originalists need to deal with the constitutional evolution. The changing cultural norms and practices constitute new conditions that justify the pliability of constitutions; or in other words, they change the dimension of interpretation of constitutions, and constitutional law properly evolves as culture evolves.[583]

---

[581] Vorländer, "What is 'Constitutional Cultures'," 31.

[582] Post, "Foreword," 77.

[583] Ibid., 82.

Chapter 5
Contemporary Constitution and the Cultural Paradigm

5.1 Constitution as a Cultural Phenomenon

5.1.1 Cultural Paradigm and the Concept of Constitutional Culture

As commonly underlined by the contributions to this field, the meaning of culture is highly blurred. While the traditional meaning of culture includes "everything humanly produced," contemporary studies rather point to its features as a system of symbols, meanings and "their associated social practices."[1] Further, Geertz points to the contextual relevance of culture:

> culture is not a power, something to which social events, behaviors, institutions, or processes can be causally attributed; it is a context something within which can be intelligibly –that is, thickly- described.[2]

In the legal context, culture is rather utilized to explain the foundational basis of a legal order and social forces impacting on its foundation and implementation. Against this background, legal culture is determinative over the identity of legal systems.[3] Eisenstadt argues that "[n]o social order or pattern of social interaction

---

[1] Susan S. Silbey, "Legal Culture and Cultures of Legality," in *Handbook of Cultural Sociology*, ed. John R. Hall, Laura Grindstaff and Ming- Cheng Lo (London: Routledge, 2010), 471.

[2] Clifford Geertz, *The Interpretation of Cultures* (New York: Basic, 1973), 14, cited by Ibid., 471.

[3] Michael King, "Comparing Legal Cultures in the Quest for Law's Identity," in *Comparing Legal Cultures* ed. David Nelken (Aldershot: Dartmouth, 1997).

A. Atilgan, *Global Constitutionalism*, Beiträge zum ausländischen öffentlichen Recht und Völkerrecht, https://doi.org/10.1007/978-3-662-55647-4_5

can be constituted without the symbolic dimension of human activity, especially of basic cultural and ontological visions."[4] In this sense, culture appears as a foundational element of the social order. Culture, in general, has a special place in the construction of social order by virtue of its "order-maintaining" and "order-transforming" functions.[5] Studying the relationship between constitutional orders and cultures, or culture as an element of these orders, is a recent fact in the constitutional theory. As a matter of fact, the domination of positivist school over legal reasoning from the end of the nineteenth century on, was a tremendous obstacle for thinking law along with its cultural environment. Thus, the idea of constitutional culture did not find an academic interest until recently.[6]

The cultural paradigm can be described as "one in which the phenomenon being considered is regarded as being the product uniquely of its cultural context."[7] The cultural paradigm began to gain influence in the social sciences during the 1980s.[8] It arose as a significant methodology in socio-legal studies and comparative law in particular.[9] The constitutional paradigm has a well-established background in legal cultural studies, and it had serious impacts on the socio-legal scholarship. According to Lawrence M. Friedman, who is often celebrated as the founder of this concept, legal culture provides legal research with a special dynamism:

> (…) cultural factors are an essential ingredient in turning a static structure and a static collection of norms into a body of living law. Adding the legal culture to the picture is like winding up a clock or plugging in a machine. It sets everything in motion.[10]

According to Silbey, it abandoned "the law-first" paradigm of research and introduced the dynamics of daily life to the socio-legal research. Further, it abandoned the focus on measurable behaviour in comparing national laws:

> "From this perspective, law is not merely an instrument or tool working on social relations, but also a set of conceptual categories and schema that help construct, compose and interpret social relations." In addition and most importantly, by virtue of the cultural paradigm, the subject of legal research shifted from native categories of actors, such as rules,

[4] S.N. Eisenstadt, "The Order-maintaining and Order-transforming Dimensions of Culture," in *Theory of Culture*, ed. Richard Münch and Neil J. Smelser (Berkeley: University of California Press, 1992), 83.

[5] Ibid. 67.

[6] Hans Vorländer, "What is 'Constitutional Cultures'?," in *Constitutional Cultures: On the Concept and Representation of Constitutions in the Atlantic World*, ed. Silke Hensel et al. (Newcastle upon Tyne: Cambridge Scholars Publishing, 2012), 22.

[7] Geoffrey Samuel, "Comparative Law and Its Methodology," in *Research Methods in Law*, ed. Dawn Watkins and Mandy Burton (London: Routledge, 2013), 102.

[8] Silbey, "Legal Culture and Cultures of Legality," 473.

[9] Susan Silbey, "Legal Culture and Legal Consciousness," in *International Encyclopedia of Social and Behavioral Science*, ed. Neil J. Smelser and Paul B. Baltes (Amsterdam: Elsevier, 2001), 8625.

[10] Lawrence M. Friedman, *Law and Society: An Introduction* (New Jersey: Prentice Hall Inc., 1977), 76.

> institutions etc. to "*an analytically conceptualized unit of analysis, the researcher's definition of the subject: legal culture.*"[11]

Silbey argues that legal researchers were dealing with insufficiently theorized concepts before exploring the cultural paradigm, and through this way, they acquired new research methods in order to understand how law works. The appropriation of the European Social Theory tradition through new research methods was also another profit of this process.[12]

As mentioned in the previous chapter, in Post's opinion, constitutional culture reflects traces of the civic culture in constitutional law, and as such, communication with the society. In other words, Post accentuates the cultural environment of a constitution. However, how to determine this environment remains in the dark in Post's article. Likewise, some other studies remain silent about an exact and precise meaning of constitutional culture as well, and they rather employ this concept in order to demonstrate the extralegal facts that create and nourish differences between different constitutional traditions.[13] On the other hand, the current discourse of constitutional culture achieves this in various ways. Thinking of constitutional culture in parallel with the idea of legal culture and in a dialectical relationship with political and societal discourses reflects two different approaches to this problem.[14] Rather than a coincidence, this evidently stems from the mediating position of the constitutions between law and politics. Zumbansen opines that the mediating function of constitution between law and politics is more noteworthy in contemporary society due to the impacts of heterarchical societal structure:

> The fluidity of institutional structures in the emerging "network society" suggests that constitutional law, based either on a text or emerging from historical common law practice, is best seen as a forum through which an endless number of linkages are constantly created, processed, changed, rejected, and affirmed, between law and politics. (…) constitutions – written or unwritten- and constitutional law must facilitate the intersection of law and politics in a radically heterarchic, modern society.[15]

---

[11] Silbey, "Legal Culture and Cultures of Legality," 474. Emphasis belongs to original text.

[12] Ibid., 474.

[13] For example: Jeffrey Goldsworthy, "Constitutional Cultures, Democracy, and Unwritten, Principles," *University of Illinois Law Review* 2012, no. 3 (2012): 683-710. Reva B. Siegel, "Constitutional Culture, Social Movement Conflict and Constitutional Change: The Case of the De Facto ERA" (Faculty Scholarship Series no. 1097, 2006, http://digitalcommons.law.yale.edu/fss_papers/1097), 1347, last visit 19.01.2014. David Schneiderman, "Property Rights and Regulatory Innovation: Comparing Constitutional Cultures," *International Journal of Constitutional Law* 4, no. 2 (2006): 371–391

[14] David Schneiderman, "Banging Constitutional Bibles: Observing Constitutional Culture in Transition," *University of Toronto Law Journal* 55, no. 3 (2005): 836.

[15] Peer Zumbansen, "Carving Out Typologies and Accounting for Differences Across Systems: Towards a Methodology of Transnational Constitutionalism," in *The Oxford Handbook of Comparative Constitutional Law*, ed. Michel Rosenfeld and Andras Sajo (Oxford: Oxford University Press, 2012), 96.

Contributions on this field also underline the relevance of constitutions to both political and civic cultures in a society. Yet, constitutional culture is to be distinguished in terms of its specific substance at this point, as Wenzel states: "Constitutional culture contains only the elements pertaining to meta-rules, the general organization of law and society, and willingness to be constrained."[16] In consideration of these two main perspectives, constitutional culture will be analysed under two categories that deem political culture and legal culture central to constitutional culture respectively.

5.1.2 Constitutional Culture as a Reflection of Political and Civic Culture

5.1.2.1 Constitutional Culture as a Political Culture

How to link a "constitution" and a "culture" is problematic in several terms. First of all, culture is a very broad concept that can involve everything. In the context of constitutions, Tully defines culture as "an irreducible and constitutive aspect of politics."[17] In the same vein, Vorländer prefers to bridge constitution and culture through the concept of "political culture."[18] According to those who think of constitutional culture as linked with political culture, a constitutional culture has the same essential qualities, attitudes, opinions, values, emotion, information, and skills as a political culture. In this context, constitutionalism rises as a component of constitutional culture.[19] Evidently, constitution also reflects expressions of political ideas as well as positive law.[20] In this respect, political culture is "the combination of solidified opinions and values and those forms of thought, imaginations and patterns of political behaviour."[21] It is highly related to the general culture of a society, but it is not identical with it; instead it is a differentiated part of the general culture.[22] Elazar draws attention to the fact that political culture intrinsically "makes its demands

---

[16] Nikolai Wenzel, "From Contract to Mental Model: Constitutional Culture as a Fact of the Social Sciences," *Review of Austrian Economy* 23 (2010): 61.

[17] James Tully, *Strange Multiplicity: Constitutionalism in an Age of Diversity* (Cambridge: Cambridge University Press, 2007), 5.

[18] Vorländer, "What is 'Constitutional Cultures'," 25.

[19] Rett R. Ludwikowski, "Constitutional Culture of the New East-Central European Democracies," *Georgia Journal of International and Comparative Law* 29 (2000): 4.

[20] Dieter Grimm, "Types of Constitutions," in *The Oxford Handbook of Comparative Constitutional Law*, ed. Michel Rosenfeld and Andras Sajo (Oxford: Oxford University Press, 2012), 115.

[21] Vorländer, "What is 'Constitutional Cultures'," 26.

[22] Daniel J. Elazar, "Globalization Meets the World's Political Cultures," Jerusalem Center for Public Affairs, http://www.jcpa.org/dje/articles3/polcult.htm, last visit 06.10.2015.

on the political system" as a political phenomenon. In this sense, what is "fair" in the political realm is completely different in family or business relationships.[23] Political culture expands the scope of political studies; it makes it involve normative ideas on the social foundation of a political order.[24] Against this background, intersubjective meanings that are created through various symbolic forms of meaning, say, speech, symbols and shared understandings are the basis of a community, and political culture of interpretation is created within these instruments of meaning.[25] On the other hand, political culture is a temporal phenomenon. In this sense, it is a component of the *zeitgeist*, which deals with the public policy of its era.[26]

As a matter of fact, by this way, the concept of constitutional culture is employed to articulate a condensed form of the broader concept of political culture:

> The concept of constitutional culture includes all those aspects of political life and its symbolic representation directly connected to the fundamental structure of the political order which is expressed in the legal text of the constitution.[27]

According to Hensel, these aspects can be fundamental political ideas of a nation or sovereignty as well as further discourses and practices regarding constitutional institutions. Accordingly, constitutional culture is a mirror of the political order. From this point of view, constitution is an identifying and unifying symbol for a political order.[28] In parallel with this, Vorländer states that the role of constitutions and constitutional jurisprudence over structuring political orders increasingly made constitutions "a forum in which discourses about political identity take place." Further, because of this, Vorländer highlights the fact that many social theories, such as Rawls' or Habermas' are concerned with constitutional questions.[29]

A cultural perspective concerns the relativity of the meaning of a constitution, that is to say, a text may have different meanings depending on different cultural backgrounds.[30] Cultural differences can be used to explain differences in interpretation of constitutional principles and norms. A noteworthy example on this matter is that, as touched upon earlier, the US Supreme Court and German Federal Court concluded differently on the practice of abortion in the 1970s, despite the fact that

---

[23] Ibid.

[24] Vorländer, "What is 'Constitutional Cultures'," 26.

[25] Ibid. 27.

[26] Daniel P. Franklin and Michael J. Baun, "Introduction," in *Political Culture and Constitutionalism: A Comparative Approach*, ed. Daniel Franklin and Michael Baun (Armonk: M.E. Sharpe, 1995), 4.

[27] Silke Hensel, "Constitutional Cultures in the Atlantic World During the 'Age of Revolutions'," in *Constitutional Cultures: On the Concept and Representation of Constitutions in the Atlantic World*, ed. Silke Hensel et al. (Newcastle upon Tyne: Cambridge Scholars Publishing, 2012), 6.

[28] Ibid.

[29] Vorländer, "What is 'Constitutional Cultures'," 23.

[30] Ibid., 21.

the constitutional provisions referred to were very similar in these cases.[31] It has been argued that the societal values of these countries were determinative. That is to say, the autonomy and freedom of individuals were quite influential over the Supreme Court's decision, while the human dignity and protection of unborn life marked German Federal Court's decision. On the other hand, German and US constitutional traditions differ in various terms. A striking point is "the ethical mission of the state." Against this background, most German intellectuals believe in such a mission of the state, which historically led to *Sozialstaat* and the state's obligation to enhance human welfare.[32] However, US constitutionalism developed in an opposite dimension. For example, in a case delivered in 1989, where the state was sued due to not rescuing a little child from his father's torture and depriving him of the liberty protected by the fourteenth amendment, the US Supreme Court rejected the application, by stating that,

> The Clause is phrased as a limitation on the State's power to act, not as a guarantee of certain minimal levels of safety and security .... [Its] language cannot fairly be extended to impose an affirmative obligation on the State to ensure that those interests do not come to harm through other means.[33]

These two constitutions reflect "different visions of personhood and social reality."[34] Another striking example is the "supremacy clause" that is found in both American and German constitutions. Although the two provisions are ostensibly very similar, there exists, in fact, a great difference between them. As Denninger underlines, the German version concerns the abstract ranking of rules, while the American one is about the state competence.[35] All in all, in view of these examples, what Vorländer says succinctly gains a deeper meaning: "the culture says what the constitution is."[36]

From this point of view, constitutional cultures differ depending on a number of reasons. First, they strictly concern their principles of a political order and the interpretation of these principles, which are under the strong influence of culture and history. In addition, this difference may rely on whether constitutions are written documents, or on their codifications, interpretation, customs or oral representation; and on their symbolic status for the integration of a political community.[37] In this sense, some democracies can identify themselves as constitutional, or they can

[31] Roe v. Wade, 410 US 113 (1973) and Schwangerschaftsabbruch II, BVerfGE 88, 203, cited by Ibid. 22.

[32] Donald P. Kommers, "German Constitutionalism: A Prolegomenon" (Scholarly Works Paper no. 98, 1991, http://scholarship.law.nd.edu/law_faculty_scholarship/98), 867, last visit 14.04.2014.

[33] Deshaney v. Winnebago County, 489 US 189 (1989), cited by Ibid., 868.

[34] Ibid., 872.

[35] Erhard Denninger, "Judicial Review Revisited: The German Experience," *Tulane Law Review* 59 (1984-5): 1016.

[36] Vorländer, "What is 'Constitutional Cultures'," 22.

[37] Ibid., 31.

adopt national, ethnic, and cultural ideas to determine their identity. For instance, the American constitution has been considered an integrating instrument for the American nation, and it has also been viewed as a distinctive feature of this constitution.[38] At this point, to what extent can American constitution be considered a model of contemporary constitutionalism? This question was discussed in various terms. For example, as Goldsworthy points out by referring to Jack Balkin, the American constitution is defined as a "basic law" and a "higher law" that stands for a supreme law and a repository of values and principles respectively, whereas British and New Zealand constitutions do not have this character. At this point, it is of note that, having referred to Hanna Arendt, Vorländer highlights that the foundational period of the US constitution served to the sacralization of the constitution, since it was perceived as the self-constitution of the people. The Supreme Court even kept this tradition alive and always acted in favour of the construction of the symbolic integration of people. The constitution became a forum for the resolution of political conflicts, and its foundational role was consolidated over time. Therefore, an identity creating and integrating effects of a constitution are manifest in American experience.[39] On the other hand, Goldsworthy argues that the Australian constitution has a basic character, but not a higher position and it cannot be identified as a "peoples' law" (or "our law"), unlike the others.[40] For instance, the American constitution is marked by "a constitutive narrative through which [they] imagine themselves as a people, with shared memories, goals, aspirations, values, duties, and ambition," whereas Australians consider themselves as a "historically continuing people" for whom constitution does not play a basic role in the foundation process. Goldsworthy puts forward the idea that in this sense it is not a problem for them to leave outside the constitution the common values and commitments that identify Australians as a people.[41]

On the other hand, Vorländer argues that a political culture can accommodate a constitution as a system of rules embedded into itself. In this case, referring to the unwritten and customary constitution of England, which has functioned as a "symbol of consensus on fundamental questions of political order," he states that no explicit written constitution is necessary to meet preconditions of a constitution. According to him, this is to be seen as the secret of English constitution for success. Thus, the symbolic meaning of a constitution in a political culture rises as a commonality of constitutions.[42]

Having considered these variations of constitutional cultures, Vorländer has argued that although constitutionalism is a relatively more recent phenomenon in the Anglo-American world, constitutions and constitutional practices of this area provide a more convenient environment for the analysis of constitutional culture.[43]

---

[38] Ibid.

[39] Ibid., 33-35.

[40] Goldsworthy, "Constitutional Cultures," 685.

[41] Ibid., 686.

[42] Vorländer, "What is 'Constitutional Cultures?'," 36.

[43] Ibid. 24.

Beyond the relationship between the political and constitutional culture of a society, constitutional transplantations also have a significant impact on constitutional culture. Goldsworthy notes that in Canada, Australia and India, national constitutions were created through the pragmatic reforms of the imperial British government; and the British constitutional tradition of parliamentary sovereignty was quite influential on the judges of the constitutional courts of these countries.[44] In this respect, constitution carried out the function of a mediator regarding the issues of the migration of a political culture. On the other hand, in some cases, the opposite situation can come into question. For example, as Henkin argues, the US constitutional system was a result of seeking an alternative to the Westminster parliamentary system.[45] In that case, constitution was an instrument for excluding a specific political culture.

5.1.2.2 Constitutional Cultures Between Political Decisions and Social Discourses: Theory of Richard Münch

The German sociologist Richard Münch views constitution as a component of the cultural discourse. In Münch's writings, the concept of constitution is found basically in two different, but dependent ways. Firstly, he deals with constitutions as a political cultural issue and in the context of constitutional cultures. In addition, he is in search of a new methodology to elucidate new constitutionalization processes sociologically, and for this purpose, he examines transnational (in particular European) constitutionalization through the lens of the Durkheimian theory.[46]

Münch also focuses on the concept of constitution within the framework of political culture. In this context, constitution is the core of the crystalization in a society.[47] According to Münch, the main function of the political system is the specification of social spaces through collective decisions and objectives.[48] Constitution in this framework generates the latent code of political acts. It builds the connection between political decisions and socio-cultural discourses. The Constitution fulfills this function through some subsystems, such as constitutional culture,

---

[44] Jeffrey Goldsworthy, "Constitutional Interpretation," in *Oxford Handbook of Comparative Constitutional Law*, ed. Michel Rosenfeld and Andras Sajo (Oxford: Oxford University Press, 2012), 712.

[45] Louis Henkin, "A New Birth of Constitutionalism: Genetic Influences and Genetic Defects," *Cardozo Law Review* 14, no. 3-2 (1992 – 1993): 536.

[46] Richard Münch, "Constructing a European Society by Jurisdiction," *European Law Journal* 14 (2008): 519-541.

[47] Richard Münch, *Die Struktur der Moderne: Grundmuster und differentielle Gestaltung des institutionellen Aufbaus der modernen Gesellschaften* (Frankfurt am Main: Suhrkamp, 1984), 336.

[48] Ibid., 303.

constitutional decision-making structure and communication between experts and society.[49]

Having proceeded from Weber's theory, Münch has argued that a constitution is built by a normative order which distinguishes legitimate political actions and legitimate force from illegitimate force and actions. The institutionalization of this sort of a political order is a characteristic of modern states.[50] Constitution is engaged with the cultural discourse due to the necessity for reasoning (Vernunftverpflichtung). According to Münch, this is the primary element of modern constitutions. The reasoning concerns four intellectual capabilities, such as understanding (hermeneutic reasoning), knowledge of the reality (theoretical reasoning), moral knowledge (practical reasoning), and aesthetical and technical judgement (judicial power).[51] This occurs in the context of constitutional interpretations. Thereby, cultural discourse excludes the irrational argumentations.[52] Further, Münch argues that to what an extent a cultural discourse affects a constitution independent from stake-holders is a matter of character of the experts, who deal with the interpretation of constitution and are under different obligations to the community of constitution. In this regard, he draws attention to the differences between interpretational traditions of Europe and the US.[53] The steering core of the constitutional culture consists of the constitutional principles whose interpretation is a matter of cultural discourse through scientific rationalism and relevant professionals.[54] Münch concludes that constitutions vary depending on four points. These are obligations for reasoning, contraining state force, democracy and performing governance. Accordingly, there are four different constitutions; reasoning-oriented, liberal, democracy-oriented and state-oriented. These types can interact with each other in various circumstances.[55]

Münch advances the claim that Protestantism's conception of a human being had a huge impact on the construction of western modern societies, and thus on western modern constitutions. In addition to that, the major shifts in freedoms, rights and democratization; the impacts of labour movement of the nineteenth and twentieth centuries, and the rise of social rights were other leading dynamics in shaping the fundamental structure of modern constitutions.[56] However, western cultural patterns fairly vary, and they created serious contrasts in the constitutional realm, such as conservative-progressive or liberal-socialist etc. Münch also refers to the fundamental differences between Anglo-Saxon constitutionalism and Continental European constitutionalism. He argues that Anglo-Saxon constitutions have more integrative power than the latter in virtue of their community formation role, while the

[49] Ibid., 311.

[50] Ibid., 315.

[51] Ibid., 338.

[52] Ibid., 334.

[53] Ibid., 335.

[54] Ibid., 336.

[55] Ibid., 354.

[56] Ibid., 336.

Continental European constitutions are not able to enjoy this power since they are open to diverse interpretations of less integrative political sub-cultures.[57]

5.1.3 Constitutional Culture as a Variation of Legal Culture

5.1.3.1 The Idea of Legal Culture

Constitutional culture is a recently unveiled concept, and scholars dealing with this underdeveloped issue refer to "legal culture" as a grounding concept in some cases, as it has become a better-established concept since Friedmann's first introduction in the 1970s. As mentioned before, culture is a concept without a clear and common definition and in general, it is considered in very broad terms in academic works. The concept of culture can refer to many things and facts, such as "collective identity, nation, race, corporate policy, civilization, arts and letters, lifestyle, mass-produced popular artifacts, ritual"[58] etc. The same unclarity also applies to legal culture and the cultural meaning of law to some extent. On the other hand, the contemporary socio-legal scholarship responded to this unclarity in various ways. According to scholars that deal with law from a cultural perspective, law is a dynamic cultural artifact that permanently responds to cultural, social and political changes of society, despite its disillusioning appearance as objective, apolitical and fixed set of rules.[59] According to legal culture scholars, law can be understood in different ways in different societies. For example, as Nelken argues, law is somewhat seen as an ideal aspiration in civil law regimes, due to a number of reasons such as deference to state, philosophical idealism or influence of religion; while in Anglo-American law it is rather understood as a "blueprint for guiding behaviour."[60]

Friedman puts forward the idea that one can speak of a legal culture of a country or of a group, if it has distinguished patterns from the culture of other countries or groups.[61] Every country and also many societies have or had a legal system, as anthropological research demonstrates.[62] In this respect, legal cultural studies concern the cultural specificity of legal systems. "No two cultures are the same,"

[57] Ibid., 354.

[58] Naomi Mezey, "Law as Culture," in *Law and Societies in Global Contexts: Contemporary Approaches*, ed. Eve Darian-Smith (Cambridge: Cambridge University Press, 2013), 57.

[59] Eve Darian-Smith, *Laws and Societies in Global Contexts: Contemporary Approaches* (Cambridge: Cambridge University Press, 2013), 41.

[60] David Nelken, "Using the Concept of Legal Culture" (UC Berkeley, Papers Presented in the Center for the Study of Law and Society Bag Lunch Speaker Series, 2004, http://escholarship.org/uc/item/7dk1j7hm) last visit 09.05.2013.

[61] Lawrence M. Friedman, *The Legal System: A Social Science Perspective* (New York: Russel Sage Foundation, 1975), 194.

[62] Friedman, *Law and Society*, 75.

says Friedman, yet cultural aspects of legal systems create affinities as well as distances. In other words, one can expect Honduras and Nicaragua to have similar legal systems and cultures that are different from Afghanistan or France.[63] Every country or society has a unique substantive law and each requires a special study and correspondingly, legal cultures are

> bodies of custom organically related to the culture as a whole, not neutral artifacts that a society can pick or buy and which do not bear the genetic mark of any particular society.[64]

In addition to this, it is of note that according to Merry, legal culture can also refer to broader dispositions of law, such as human rights culture or rule of law culture.[65] Further, "legal families" can also differ in cultural terms. From a comparative law perspective developed by Zweigert and Kötz, six different legal families come to the fore: "Romanistic, Germanic, Anglo-American, Nordic, Far East, and Religious."[66] Nevertheless, generally, two main streams are employed in identifying western law, civil law and common law. In this regard, for example, civil law systems are generally dominated by scholars and academic lawyers, while common law systems are rather under the domination of practitioners and judges.[67] Clear distinctions can be made between the legal interpretation traditions of these legal families, and these are also determinative in identifying differences between legal cultures. For example, civil law judges rather pursue a "grammatical" interpretation in which finding out the meaning of words is essential; whereas in the US tradition, the realist tradition of interpretation enables judges to legislate to a certain extent, in addition to interpreting texts.[68]

According to Friedman, a legal culture in particular is to be observed in values, ideologies and principles of legal professionals. He makes a distinction here, and states that legal culture refers to two sorts of attitudes and values. One is that of the general public, namely "lay or external legal culture," and the other one is that of lawyers, judges and other professionals, namely "internal legal culture."[69] External legal culture may appear in various forms. According to Friedman, each cultural group in a society represents a different legal culture.[70] In general, values are the residue of social structure. This means that,

---

[63] Ibid., 72.

[64] Friedman, *The Legal System*, 194.

[65] Sally Engle Merry, "What is Legal Culture? An Anthropological Perspective," *Journal of Comparative Law* 5 (2010): 40.

[66] Konrad Zweigert and Hein Kötz, *An Introduction to Comparative Law*, Tony Wier trans., 3rd ed. (1998), 67-68 cited by Charles H. Koch Jr., "Envisioning a Global Legal Culture," *Michigan Journal of International Law* 25 (2003): 50.

[67] Ibid., 41.

[68] Ibid.,, 44.

[69] Friedman, *Law and Society*, 76.

[70] Ibid., 76.

> the complex behaviour of the insiders, is by no means an autonomous growth and by no means an exception to the general proposition about the primacy of society over law.[71]

In other words, social values are always embedded in legal implementation, and the actions of legal professionals can by no means be a basis for an autonomous structure. That can be counted as a response to the opinions that transnational law is of a non-democratic character as it mainly reflects actions of legal or administrative professionals, as mentioned before. However, the question then arises on whether a reflection of social values by legal acts is enough to constitute a democratic order. As political constitutionalists underlined, a tyranny that relies on a legal constitutionalism may formally claim a democratic legitimacy as well. Nevertheless, the true character of that regime would only be found out through the content of social values reflected within that constitutional system.

On the other hand, the concept of legal culture has been defined by various other scholars in various ways as well.[72] According to Nelken,

> legal culture (…) points to differences in the way features of law are themselves embedded in larger frameworks of social structure and culture which constitute and reveal the place of law in society.[73]

Further, Nelken argues that the legal cultural studies strive to understand complex features of role and rule of law in different societies:

> Why do the UK and Denmark complain most about the imposition of EU law but then turn out to be the countries which have the best records of obedience? Conversely, why does Italy, whose public opinion is most in favour of Europe, have such a high rate of non compliance? Why does Holland, otherwise so similar, have such a low litigation rate compared to neighbouring Germany? (…)[74]

From this point of view, legal culture does not aim at establishing a concept of law by establishing universal truths of law, but instead it concerns the mapping of different concepts of law by depicting various ways of practising and living law.[75] However, at this point Merry argues against this kind of understanding of legal culture, as it does not explain how to deal with the mobility between different legal cultures.[76] In other words, it is not clear from this perspective how legal transplantations or transfers can be explained, as mentioned before. However, Nelken also argues that subject of legal cultural inquiries must not be reduced to nation states, on

---

[71] Friedman, *The Legal System*, 194.

[72] For different understandings of the concept: Silbey, "Legal Culture and Cultures of Legality."

[73] David Nelken, "Towards a Sociology of Legal Adaptation" in *Adapting Legal Cultures,* ed. David Nelken and Johannes Feest (Portland: Hart Publishing, 2001), 25.

[74] Nelken, "Concept of Legal Culture."

[75] Ibid.

[76] Merry, "What is Legal Culture," 41.

the ground that many national laws have been shaped by the imposition or transfer of different legal cultures; and furthermore, national legal cultures are currently encompassed by globalization, and thus these two facts cannot be ignored in the formation of legal cultures. In addition, he states that reifying national stereotypes is a threat for legal culture studies, since this would mean overlooking the changeable character of culture.[77] On the other hand, Silbey distinguishes "culture of legality" from legal culture by observing legal objects in a broader framework that extends borderlines of the legal system. In this regard, legal culture is "the schematic structure of legality" that produces a general and historical truth. Instead, the cultural approach can enable us to assess law within its broader meanings, extending beyond a legal order.[78] In that vein, Mezey argues that a cultural understanding of law counts law as discursive and productive as well as coercive; that is to say,

> [l]aw participates in the production of meanings within the shared semiotic system of a culture, but it is also a product of that culture and the practices that reproduce it.[79]

From Mezey's point of view, the relationship between culture and law can be unveiled in three ways. It can first be done by observing the hidden power of law in the field of culture, or the power of culture over legal institutions. Furthermore, beyond a relationship, law and culture can be synthesized, and they can be dealt with as one, the same notion that refers to an endless recycling between formal legal meaning-making and cultural practices.[80]

How to determine what a legal culture rises, is a major problem of the legal culture scholarship. Merry argues that there exist four distinct social phenomena that are mostly referred as legal culture by various approaches. These phenomena are "practices and ideologies within a legal system," "public's attitude towards law," "legal mobilization" (mobilization in a different meaning here), and "legal consciousness."[81] Legal facts can be dealt with in different dimensions in accordance with these approaches and their distinct methodologies.

Cultural aspects of law also have a certain relationship with international and global realms. Against this background, law is "assemblages of legal systems" and a notion that is "constituted through interaction with other legal systems that are similarly culturally constituted."[82] This means that, law's constitution is strictly related to culturally akin legal orders. International and global settings of law have a certain function in the formation of linkages between different legal orders. In this sense, the legal pluralism of the twentieth century is strictly connected with cultural pluralism.[83]

---

[77] Nelken, "Concept of Legal Culture."

[78] Silbey, "Legal Culture and Cultures of Legality," 475-476.

[79] Mezey, "Law as Culture," 60.

[80] Ibid., 62, 69.

[81] The first two are named as "Internal legal culture" and "external legal culture" by Friedman. Merry, "What is Legal Culture," 43-44.

[82] Darian-Smith, *Laws and Societies*, 39.

[83] Ibid., 42.

In terms of international law, the matter of legal culture is of importance in various terms. Having referred to Edward Said's concept "Orientalism," Darian-Smith argues that "legal orientalism," which is a western legal acknowledgment that puts the Euro-American legal systems into the centre and that marginalizes the law of the other world, is a salient cultural aspect that continues to undermine international law and prevents a sincere global dialogue.[84] In addition, Sally Engle Merry highlights that how to deal with the extensive migration of legal ideas and forms should be considered as a challenging problem for those who deal with the concept of legal culture.[85] Today many legal orders and cultures resemble each other in many terms. According to Friedmann, the cultural convergence is of a certain impact over the migration of legal codes or values, and as a matter of course, similar legal cultures adopt laws of similar cultures. That is to say, capitalist economies need capitalist law and modernizing economies need modernizing law. However, borrowing is an official action, which is to say, the answer to the question of how far a borrowing has social roots still remains in the dark.[86]

On the other hand, the aptness of the idea of "legal culture" was questioned by some scholars. Notably, Cotterrell denied the idea of Friedmann, and instead recommended the use of "legal ideology" since it relates to the doctrine and does not lead to a holistic view like culture.[87] Cotterrell opines that legal culture is a vague term. According to Cotterrell, "[l]egal doctrine in contemporary conditions is typically fragmented, intricate and transient; it is in continuous process of reformulation, supplementation and amendment (…)."[88] Therefore, culture does not suffice to reflect its truth, and instead, legal ideology can be helpful in understanding structures of beliefs, attitudes and values and in translating them into regulatory practices. In his reply to Cotterrell, Friedman indeed concedes that legal culture is not the only concept to be utilized in order to understand variations between different orders, but he does argue that legal ideology stands for something different and it is not apt to replace legal culture. Moreover, he puts forward the idea that legal culture is an umbrella term that refers to a range of measurable phenomena.[89] Further, what makes legal culture a special term is that "legal culture is an essential intervening variable in the process of producing legal stasis or change."[90] To make this clear, he mentions that many external events and situations, such as war, earthquakes, birth control pills, computers etc. lead to changes in law. For example, somebody invents the motor car and this leads to modifications in tort law and some other regulations. This means that "[w]hat sets these processes in motion, or determines their shape

[84] Ibid., 51.

[85] Merry, "What is Legal Culture?," 41.

[86] Friedman, *The Legal System*, 195.

[87] Roger Cotterrell, "The Concept of Legal Culture," in *Comparing Legal Cultures*, ed. David Nelken, (Aldershot: Dartmouth, 1997), 21. Merry, "What is Legal Culture," 41.

[88] Cotterrell, "Concept of Legal Culture," 22.

[89] Here Friedman particularly notes that he does not refer to the "measured." Ibid., 34.

[90] Ibid., 34.

or their outcome, are the pressures that are the direct result of changes in legal culture."[91] Friedman argues that an equation which considers social change X to cause legal result Y, is not satisfying. Instead, he suggests another form of equation:

> social change X leads to a change in legal culture Y, which results in this or that kind of pressure on legal institutions, and what comes out is legal result Z. In other words, "legal culture" is a generic term for states of mind and ideas, held by some public; these states of mind are affected by events, situations and the like in society as a whole, and they lead in turn to actions that have an impact on the legal system itself.[92]

Further, Friedman points to the uselessness of conventional concepts of legal families in distinguishing between "living laws" of different countries. He questions how these concepts, such as common law and civil law, can be functional to understand if living legal systems of England, France or Haiti related. Against this background, without legal culture, it seems hard to put any criterion in understanding what draws borderlines between these legal systems. Legal culture, in Friedman's point of view, relates to living law, not law in books.[93]

These features of legal culture are of importance in terms of understanding contemporary constitutionalism. Evidently, constitutions have a foundational relationship to legal orders as they provide the source of legitimacy.[94] Therefore, as some scholars do, proceeding from the concept of legal culture to understand constitutional culture is to be considered as a right move. The concept of legal culture enables us to rightly understand legal families and what differentiates them. Thereby, it provides an overarching concept that is necessary to understand the convergence of constitutional systems in an era in which laws and constitutional norms and values migrate to different legal orders. In short, contemporary constitutionalism proves to be a matter of culture, apart from the legal and political doctrine.

5.1.3.2 Constitutional Culture as Legal Culture

According to some scholars, constitutional culture is a facet of legal culture; however, it is a narrower concept.[95] In this respect, according to Snyder, a constitutional culture refers to "actual provisions" and "unwritten principles" of a constitution.[96] According to Wenzel, constitutional culture, perception of constitutionalism, institutions and informal constraints to power, such as "willingness to be bound"

---

[91] Ibid., 34.

[92] Ibid., 35.

[93] Ibid., 36.

[94] Grimm, "Types of Constitutions," 108.

[95] Francis Snyder, "The Unfinished Constitution of the European Union: Principles, Process and Culture," in *European Constitutionalism Beyond the State*, ed. J.H.H. Weiler and Marlene Wind (Cambridge: Cambridge University Press, 2003), 60-69.

[96] Ibid., 69.

or "public understanding," are of more importance than formal aspects of a constitution to apprehend the power of constitution. In his point of view, the concept of constitutional culture is key to understand the social forces that grant the power to constitution.[97] Against this background, constitutional culture is "a complex emergent phenomenon" and it basically emerges from "theories and worldviews of individuals through the interactions among individuals and groups of individuals and those groups' interactions with other groups and the rest of the world."[98] In addition, Wenzel points to the relativity of constitutional culture, that is to say, the fact that different groups in society can have different constitutional cultures, and there can be a predominant constitutional culture among them.[99]

Further, some other scholars refer to the legal culture discourse in order to explain the making of a constitutional culture. In this respect, in parallel with Friedman's definition of legal culture, a constitutional culture is defined as

> disposition of regular citizens to recognize and accept that they are governed by a written document, one that creates institutions of government and sets limits on what the government may do; the accepted belief that the governing charter is created by the citizenry; the knowledge that the charter is not timeless, but rather that the citizens may change it or revoke it under certain circumstances; and the understanding that until the charter is changed we are bound by it and required to go along with its ultimate results even though we are free to disagree with them.[100]

However, this definition is likely to be found too narrow, since it does not reflect political constitutionalism in every sense, as it deems constitutions as written documents and neglects the role of external factors and constitutional traditions. It reduces constitutional culture to a somewhat consciousness of the ruled on a constitution. In other words, "internal culture," in Friedman's terminology, is ignored in that definition. A definition which clearly identifies political and moral aspects of a constitution seems more appropriate:

> A constitutional culture is a web of interpretative norms, canons, and practices which most members of a particular community accept and employ (at least implicitly) to identify and maintain a two-level system of the appropriate sort.[101]

A constitutional order is a distinctive type of political and legal system. As Ferejohn et al. argue, not all systems have the two level structure of rules and norms that are essential to constitutionalism.[102] In this two level structure, not only are

---

[97] Wenzel, "From Contract to Mental," 57.

[98] Ibid., 59.

[99] Ibid., 61.

[100] Jason Mazzone, "The Creation of a Constitutional Culture," *Tulsa Law Review* 40 (2005): 672.

[101] John Ferejohn, Jack N. Rakove and Jonathan Riley, "Editor's Introduction," in *Constitutional Culture and Democratic Rule* ed. John Ferejohn, Jack N. Rakove and Jonathan Riley (Cambridge: Cambridge University Press, 2001), 10.

[102] Ibid., 11.

constitutional norms and rules superior to ordinary norms, but also constitutional culture is a framework that enables constitution to subordinate other laws. As they argue further, this structure is different from HLA Hart's idea of "rule of recognition":

> In our view, a political and legal system is a constitutional one if and only if it distinguishes between constitutional and ordinary political rules such that the former constrain what can count as valid examples of the latter and also place binding limits – legal or moral, as the case may be – on the share of authority that any group of government officials has either to create valid ordinary rules or to settle the meaning of constitutional rules. The constitutional rules – legal or moral- cannot properly be ignored or dismissed by government officials in a constitutional culture. (…) Granted, officials may have some room for maneuver. After all, they do have a share of authority, and constitutional rules must be interpreted on a continuing basis. But the interpretive norms and practices composing the culture also have bite to some extent, and no group of officials has all the authority to resolve conflicts.[103]

Against this background, the most significant difference in Hart's theory is that the Hartian rule of recognition does not prescribe any binding moral or legal limits over authorities to pass valid laws or determine the meaning of constitution in the case of conflicts. That is to say, neither an absolutist rule nor an unlimited rule of elected representatives is constitutional government. A limited power is essential for a constitutional culture, and this must be enforced somehow even though it is not possible through any constitutional mechanisms, such as the separated powers, independent judicial review, any barriers to amendment of constitution etc.[104] In a nutshell, unlike the Hartian perspective, a norm inconsistent with a constitution may not be illegal in all cases: "Whether illegality follows from unconstitutionality depends on other features of a governmental system."[105] Therefore, invalidity comes into question when a norm violates constitutional culture, not only the text of a constitution. This outlook is helpful for understanding various cases in contemporary constitutionalism. Evidently, it is very illuminating to explain the enforcement and amendment dynamics of the political form of constitutionalism. For instance, this outlook sheds light to the fact that acts of Parliament retain their legal force in case of the violation of constitutional norms in the UK, and it amounts to the amendment of constitution.[106] A similar case is the interpretive method of "living constitution" of the US Supreme Court. One could state that the above-mentioned perspective was also influential in the development of the living constitution method to interpret constitutional conflicts. As mentioned in the third chapter, the US Supreme Court developed this interpretational method so as to highlight the existence of a wider environment of the constitution, which determines its character. Ferejohn et al. also refers to some constitutional rules regarding the US constitutionalism that had and did not have legal force throughout the history of this constitution. The legal force

---

[103] Ibid.

[104] Ibid., 12.

[105] Ibid.

[106] Ibid.

of "'guarantee clause' (assuring the states of a republican form of government)" and "the Ninth and Tenth Amendments (reserving enumerated rights and powers to the people and states)" of the US Constitution was relatively weaker.[107]

The "two-level system," in the words of Ferejohn et al., draws attention to the norms and rules of interpretation and the institutional and governmental practices. This definition includes both "internal" and "external" legal cultures in the Friedmanian sense. In other words, a constitutional culture involves the normative and institutional traditions as well as the interests of ordinary people. Seen in this light, various interpretive approaches to contemporary constitution, as discussed above, rise as an issue of internal constitutional culture. Yet, constitutional culture also relates to "external culture" in the Friedmannian manner.

Mazzone highlights the local civic associations that emerged in the early years of the US, as they took crucial roles in creating the constitution as the bearers of the external constitutional culture. These associations appeared in the form of charity organizations, agriculture societies, women organizations, missionary organizations, Masonic lodges, reformist organizations etc. in various towns throughout the country. Civic associations had become a distinctive feature of the American society as of the early eighteenth century, and at the same time they were quite influential in instilling "the values and habits of constitutional government" in the people.[108] These civic associations created their own constitutions and own mechanisms for their enforcement and amendments that resulted in a sort of self-government; so that they contributed to the development of constitutional cultures in local bases.[109] They helped constitutional values and principles to be understood and adopted among the people, so that had a role in the construction of the American citizenship. Hence, civic associations of this era were significant components of the constitutional culture. Likewise, the knowledge of the people about their constitutional government, the role of public opinion or the people's position in the constitutional foundation or amendment processes concern the (external) constitutional culture. This outcome of constitutional culture is also akin to another one that points to the guardianship function of constitutional culture to constitutions. This function plays a key role in the maintenance of a constitutional culture, and this role has been manifest in the history of the British constitution.[110] According to Wenzel, the constitutional culture in Britain acted as an informal guardian of the constitution, and thus it enabled the constitution to survive for such a long time. He states that, in the US too, we can observe a constitutional culture that underpinned the success of the constitution. This was related to the positive response of the constitution to the historical and contextual demands from the people. However, this was not the case in Argentina, despite the fact that the Argentinian constitution was almost a verbatim of the American constitution, and the same political system of the US was intended

---

[107] Ibid.

[108] Mazzone, "Creation of a Constitutional Culture," 673.

[109] Ibid., 676.

[110] Wenzel, "From Contract to Mental," 71.

to be constituted in this country. The Constitution of Argentina was first drafted in 1853, amended a few times, and the current version is a result of the amendments done in 1994.[111] Wenzel argues that due to the incompliance of the imported constitution with the constitutional culture, the Argentinian constitution failed to achieve economic growth and political stability as expected, whereas it succeeded in the US. Instead, the Argentinian constitution opened the path to military dictatorship and civilian plundering.[112] Such a decisive and supreme position of constitutional culture to constitution was articulated in these words:

> A constitutional regime is secure when its ways have become ingrained in the habits and instinctive reactions ... of the political nation: it safeguards civilized life, but it presupposes agreement and stability as much as it secures them; and it can hardly be expected to build up, recast, or dissect the body in which it resides.[113]

Legal culture is also fairly influential on the character of a constitutional order. Goldsworthy in particular, points to the effects of internal legal culture in the construction of a constitutional culture. Goldsworthy gives the example of British principles of the statutory interpretation being prevalent among judges of the Privy Council and the Canadian Supreme Court, the Australian High Court and the Indian Supreme Court initially, since they were trained in the British legal tradition. Sociological jurisprudence, legal realism and scepticism about the legal determinacy did not have an effect in this legal tradition, unlike in the US tradition.[114] In the case of Germany, Goldsworthy argues that the legalist thinking of the Federal Constitutional Court stems from the civilian-positivistic tradition in Germany, in which legal codes imply "unified bodies of law covering all possible contingencies arising out of human interaction."[115] In this respect, the content of legal education and the perception of notion of law by lawyers are conveyed to constitutional law.

At this point, it is of note that Silbey argues that Friedman was influenced by some European scholars, such as Savigny, while exploring the concept of legal culture. Savigny is indeed viewed as the hidden founder of legal cultural studies by some scholars. Savigny defined law as an expression of "the spirit of people" (Volksgeist) that means "a continuous thread in an evolving culture" and inspired Friedman's approach to law and culture in that sense.[116] In that vein, constitutional culture was also depicted in the same metaphysical dimension by some other scholars. Howard

---

[111] National Constitution of the Argentine Republic, http://pdba.georgetown.edu/Constitutions/Argentina/argen94_e.html, last visit 10.04.2015

[112] Wenzel, "From Contract to Mental," 71.

[113] L Namier, *1848: The revolution of the intellectuals* (London: Oxford University Press, 1944), 31 cited by Ibid.

[114] Goldsworthy, "Constitutional Interpretation," 709.

[115] Donald P. Kommers, "Germany: Balancing Rights and Duties," in *Interpreting Constitutions*, ed. Jeffrey Goldsworthy (Oxford: Oxford University Press, 2007), 207-8, cited by Ibid., 710.

[116] Silbey, "Legal Culture and Legal Consciousness," 8625.

Caygill and Alan Scott described a constitutional culture as Rousseau's "social spirit" of the constitution.[117] This refers to the idea that a constitution requires a "social spirit" as well as a constitutional text. In Rousseau's own words,

> the social spirit, which should be created by these institutions, would have to preside over their foundation; and men should be before law what they should become by means of the law.[118]

Therefore, according to Rousseau, a "social spirit" or a "constitutional culture" is also necessary, besides a written constitutional document, for a constitution to emerge.[119] This spiritualism has been discussed more concretely by some American constitutional law scholars, by pointing to the "unwritten principles" of constitutions, which is a core issue of the debate on the constitutional interpretation in US constitutionalism, as mentioned above.[120]

5.2 Reflections on Constitutional Culture

As explained above, constitutional culture concerns both the political and legal culture of a society. As a matter of fact, this complies with the fact that a constitution possesses both political and legal status. As was explained in the preceding chapter, some constitutions may have only political status, as seen from the British case. On the other hand, the legal status of some other constitutions can be stronger, as known particularly from the current German constitutionalism. This means that the dominant dimension of each constitution should be analyzed independently.

5.2.1 Constitutional Cultures in Territorial Basis

The differences in identities of constitutions can be explained in the light of the cultural discourse. In this regard, culture can be employed to understand constitutions with different characters that were touched upon in the preceding chapter. In this section, the focus will be on how constitutional cultures differ in different national societies. For this purpose, British, German and US cultures will be elucidated. Evidently, some other constitutional cultures could be discussed at this point as well.

---

[117] Howard Caygill and Alan Scott, "The Basic Law versus the Basic Norm? The Case of the Bavarian Crucifix Order," in *Constitutionalism in Transformation: European and Theoretical Perspectives*, ed. Richard Bellamy and Dario Castiglione (Oxford: Blackwell, 1996), 99.

[118] Jean-Jacques Rousseau, *Social Contract and Discourses*, trans. GDH Cole (Dent, 1973), II vii: "The Legislator," cited by Christine E.J. Schwöbel, *Global Constitutionalism in International Legal Perspective* (Leiden: Nijhoff, 2011), 106.

[119] Ibid., 106.

[120] Goldsworthy, "Constitutional Cultures," 683.

However, these constitutional cultures have been deliberately chosen, since they reflect the prototypes of the western constitutions, and also the dichotomy of legal and political constitutionalism. Following this dichotomy is also supposed to be helpful for preserving the coherence of this research since a constitutional culture arises mainly in two dimensions, namely legal and political.

5.2.1.1 The British Constitutional Culture

The political culture of Great Britain is one of the major components of the stable and effective democracy of this country. "Pragmatism, and moderation of the political elites, the widespread consensus about the political procedures, and the deference to rulers" have been the noteworthy aspects of this culture.[121] Against this background, Britain has been viewed as a model of civic culture, in which traditional and modern, subject and participatory values were blended in state and nation building; in contrast to other national formations in France, Germany and Italy, where nation building came about by drawing certain borderlines between the traditional and modern forces.[122]

In terms of constitutional culture, Britain is a special case, as it is the home to an unwritten and customary constitution. This constitution has been maintained by a long standing political tradition. The more striking point is that the British constitution reflects a "political constitution," that is to say, has no legal status at all, as was explained in the third chapter; and customary rules that generate the constitutional norms can be changed by an act of the Parliament. That is to say, the British constitution as well as the constitutions of New Zealand and Israel, do not enjoy superiority over the norms made by legislature.[123] This superiority is articulated by a British maxim of "Parliament can do no wrong." As Bendor and Segal draw attention, this can be perceived in two ways. The first meaning arises due to British people believing that all acts of Parliament are legal at all times, since law is embodied by law. The second is that the British people believe that the Parliament never tends to violate common moral norms.[124] It is supposed that this form of Parliamentary sovereignty is a consequence of cultural beliefs, rather than a legal technicality.[125] Further, the British political culture does not accommodate a strong

---

[121] Dennis Kavanagh, "Political Culture in Great Britain: The Decline of the Civic Culture," in *The Civic Culture Revisited*, ed. Gabriela A. Almond and Sidney Verba (London: Sage Publications, 1989), 124.

[122] Ibid., 125.

[123] William B. Gwyn, "Political Culture and Constitutionalism in Britain," in *Political Culture and Constitutionalism: A Comparative Approach*, ed. Daniel P. Franklin and Michael Baun (Armonk: M.E. Sharpe, 1995), 20.

[124] Ariel L. Bendor and Zeev Segal, "Constitutionalism and Trust in Britain: An Ancient Constitutional Culture, A New Judicial Review Model," *American University International Law Review* 17 (2001-2002): 701.

[125] Ibid., 701.

distrust in Parliament or Government, while in other countries such as USA, distrust in governmental authorities leads to the existence of the judicial review of constitutional norms. The three separated powers including judiciary are co-equal in USA, whereas the British judiciary is subordinated to the will of the legislature, although it has an independent structure.[126] As a result of its political features, the British constitutional norms that consist of constitutional conventions are found in the political culture of the country.[127]

One of the most remarkable features of this legal system is the inability of courts to review the primary legislation. Unlike legal constitutional orders, courts do not enjoy any competence over constitutional matters. In this sense, British courts are described as "crippled law makers" that only function as "law-declarers," and it is claimed that this has also become a main component of Britain's social culture.[128]

The political and constitutional development processes in Britain did not see radical changes recently, but rather a slow evolution that came about over centuries. As a result of this,

> (…) many people have been unaware of its taking place, and concern about it has therefore been minimal. It has also meant that some of the most important innovations in the British constitution cannot be dated with precision.[129]

Accordingly, the political and constitutional processes became very intertwined in Britain. this is also true of the legal system. That is to say, the British constitution is also very immanent in the legal order.[130] It has been argued that the people of Britain do not have an inherent suspicion in the political authorities; and therefore, this set the ground for the exclusion of a judicial review mechanism for the constitutional system.[131]

However, the political constitutionalism of Britain has recently seen the challenge of the adoption of the Human Rights Act. The Human Rights Act basically changed the role of the judiciary by providing for an extension of judicial powers. The Human Rights Act introduced a novelty that basically derived from the legal constitutionalist tradition of continental Europe and constituted a challenge to the old British concept that "Parliament can do no wrong."[132] As discussed earlier, this has been considered as a power shift from the Parliament to the judiciary among constitutional law scholars. However, this is to a certain extent different from the judicial powers in legal constitutionalism. Above all, the government retains its

---

[126] Ibid., 699.

[127] Gwyn, "Political Culture," 21.

[128] Bendor and Segal, "Constitutionalism and Trust," 684.

[129] Gwyn, "Political Culture," 13.

[130] Michel Rosenfeld, "Constitutional Identity," in *Oxford Handbook of Comparative Constitutional Law*, ed. Michel Rosenfeld and Andras Sajo (Oxford: Oxford University Press, 2012), 764.

[131] Bendor and Segal, "Constitutionalism and Trust," 686.

[132] Ibid., 685.

central position; as a legislation which has been declared incompatible, remains in force until it is amended by a government minister or the Parliament. Therefore, it would be better to consider this model as a unique model.[133] Beyond all these, according to Vorländer, the most significant lesson from the British constitutionalism is that constitutional symbolism proves that constitutions "manage to describe a symbolic space within which a debate about the fundamental ideas of political order can take place and have an integrative effect."[134]

5.2.1.2 The German Constitutional Culture

The German constitution (*Grundgesetz*, i.e. the Basic Law) is a special model, as it is an outcome of the aftermath process of World War II. The process towards the constitution was launched by the victors of the war; yet, the most striking point was the success of this constitution in spite of the foreign initiative in the drafting period.[135] In Germany, the outcomes of the disastrous experience with the Nazi government structured the post-war constitutional order. As mentioned above, the most important aspect of the new constitutional order was the operation of a strong constitutional court accompanying a rights-based constitution. The distrust of politicians that stemmed from the Nazi experience "made the soil particularly fertile for expansive rule by untainted constitutional judges,"[136] and thus the constitutional court could become so influential in the enforcement and interpretation of the constitution in Germany. Another ground concerns the character of this constitution. The German Basic Law is termed as "the total constitution" by some scholars, on the ground that

> it essentially resolves-or strongly influences- virtually *all* moral, legal, and political conflicts in a society. Through an expansive interpretation of constitutional rights so that almost any governmental action triggers one or more, a broad conceptualization of the impact of constitutional law on private law, and a robust set of protective duties on the state, there are a few issues on which the Basic Law is silent and so relatively little that is left to the free, unmediated play of political forces.[137]

As to the success of the current German constitution, it is also of note that this was not the case in German constitutionalism at all times. The main reference for this fact is the failure of the constitution of the Weimar Republic of 1919. Despite

---

[133] Ibid., 689.

[134] Vorländer, "What is 'Constitutional Cultures'," 37.

[135] Rosenfeld, "Constitutional Identity," 768.

[136] Michel Rosenfeld, "Constitutional Adjudication in Europe and the United States: Paradoxes and Contrasts," *International Journal of Constitutional Law* 2 (2004): 641, cited by Goldsworthy, "Constitutional Interpretation," 712.

[137] Stephen Gardbaum, "The Place of Constitutional Law in the Legal System," in *The Oxford Handbook of Comparative Constitutional Law*, ed. Michel Rosenfeld and Andras Sajo (Oxford: Oxford University Press, 2012), 174. Emphasis belongs to the original text.

the Weimar constitution being drafted as a liberal and democratic constitution, the regime collapsed within 14 years, and Nazis took power. Along with a number of reasons, the main reason was explained as "the prevalence of anti-liberal and authoritarian values in German society."[138] These values became the main concern regarding the new constitution of the new regime, which was established in 1949. A number of studies in the 1950s about the attitude of the German people towards democratic processes explicitly proved these concerns. The lack of political participation and a low interest and pride in political institutions were common. Rahl Dahrendorf described this situation as follows: "political system that is authoritarian in effect if not in intention."[139]

However, this time, contrary to the expectations, the new Republic proved to be a stable democratic regime over decades. As a matter of fact, this outcome overturns the belief that culture is highly influential in institutions, since it demonstrates that a political culture lacking a robust democratic tradition can be transformed in accordance with the democratic principles.[140]

Internal factors – such as a new beginning in the political arena to overcome the consequences of Nazi experience – combined with the economic growth and the distrust in polity among people, contributed to the success of the new constitution of Germany. Another contribution came through external factors as well, in particular those for staying in a stable and secure international realm through an integration into the Western economic and political institutions.[141] In addition, German politics saw new political movements and an increase in popular participation during the 1970s and 1980s. After all, studies on the political character of the German society began to underline that (West) Germany could be viewed as a normal and stable democratic country that does not differ from other advanced democracies; although some such as Habermas, advanced the claim that this was an incomplete process.[142]

Furthermore, Rosenfeld argues that one of the most striking and distinguishing features of the German constitution is the *ethnos* that arises in contrast to the *demos*, which is found in the French constitution. This means that the German constitution was constructed on the self-governance of a single and homogenous ethnic group. In this model, the constitution and the state are at the disposal of a ready-built nation, which rises on a common language, ethnicity, culture etc., instead of

---

[138] Michael J. Baun, "The Federal Republic of Germany," in *Political Culture and Constitutionalism: A Comparative Approach*, ed. Daniel P. Franklin and Michael Baun (Armonk: M.E. Sharpe, 1995), 79.

[139] Rahl Dahrendorf, *Society and Democracy in Germany* (New York: Doubleday, 1967), 424, cited by Ibid., 85.

[140] Indeed some scholars like Peter H. Merkl advance the claim that lack of democratic values and the supervision of westerns powers in drafting the Basic Law were exaggerated, and the Basic Law largely relies upon German constitutional traditions. Ibid., 80-81.

[141] Ibid., 83.

[142] Ibid., 86.

being an agent of a nation-building process.[143] This feature has also been reflected by the citizenship notion of the German constitutionalism, and some scholars hold it critically. Baun argues that the citizenship understanding of the German constitution that gives priority to ethnicity, threatens the liberal and democratic identity of the constitution.[144]

5.2.1.3 The American Constitutional Culture

Franklin argues that American constitutionalism depends on cultural values to a great extent, and this has to do with the societal demands on rule of law, the expansion of political participation and nationalization of Bill of Rights.[145] Further, he emphasizes that the US Constitution echoes a unique American culture, as it reflects the exceptionalism of American political culture, political philosopy of the eighteenth century, and the great emphasis on property rights over political rights.[146]

A very noteworthy example of the relationship between political culture and constitutional interpretation and culture is the case of the US Supreme Court. As mentioned in the previous chapter, different paradigms have dominated the interpretive methodologies of the Supreme Court. These interpretive methodologies, namely "living constitutionalism" and "originalism," were at the same time a reflection of certain political movements that became influential in their own eras.[147] They basically played a role in the identification of the US Constitution by justifying the constitution to diverse subjects of the constitutional order.[148] Moreover, the transformation of the constitutional theory in the meantime and the development of new outlooks have also been dependent on the jurisprudential development. For example, the development of living constitutionalism in the US owes much to the lessons taken from the sociological jurisprudence, which demonstrates that law inevitably imbibes societal change and development, and legal principles and categories need to be reconceptualised periodically.[149]

Constitutional interpretation is still a very important element of the identity of the US Constitution. The tension regarding interpretation of the constitution is still among very crucial issues of the US Supreme Court, and it leads to a

---

143 Rosenfeld, "Constitutional Identity," 763.

144 Baun, "Federal Republic of Germany," 93.

145 Daniel P. Franklin, "American Political Culture and Constitutionalism," in *Political Culture and Constitutionalism: A Comparative Approach*, ed. Daniel Franklin and Michael Baun (Armonk: M.E. Sharpe, 1995), 43.

146 Ibid., 45.

147 Goldsworthy, "Constitutional Interpretation," 714.

148 Rosenfeld, "Constitutional Identity," 762.

149 Howard Gillman, "The Collapse of Constitutional Originalism and the Rise of the Notion of the 'Living Constitution' in the Course of American State-Building," *Studies in American Political Development* 11 (1997): 193.

polarization among adjudicators. For example, referring to foreign law in interpretation is a noteworthy issue that splits justices of the Court very sharply. For instance, this was the case in a debate between Justice Antonin Scalia and Justice Stephen Breyer. There exist two opposite camps of thinking separately on the matter of using foreign law. One is the exclusivist view, which reflects the ideas of political conservatives, and the other one is the universalist view, which is held by progressives.[150] The first group puts forward the idea that USA is a country with exemplary values and ideals, and as such, a model for the rest of the world; whereas the latter highlights that USA consists of a diverse cosmopolitan nation that is influenced by the values from abroad. Therefore, the exclusivists advance the claim that the US Constitution must remain purely American and free from any foreign influence. The universalists respond to this by alleging that the convergence of constitutional norms and values could be useful through cross-fertilization.[151] This example demonstrates that the US constitutionalism is identified by sharp ideological and cultural polarizations that derive from the political cleavages in the society.

On the other hand, the American constitution is deemed to be a very crucial instrument in nation-building. It is a future-oriented constitution, in this sense a symbol of the national unity and a cohesion of the society. Transforming a multi-ethnic and multi-cultural population into a nation has been demonstrated as the major feature of the American constitution.[152] Huntington explains this as follows: "[i]n other c.ountries, one can abrogate the constitution without abrogating the nation. The United States does not have that choice."[153] The US Constitution was achieved by virtues of its success in the mirroring of the political culture to a great extent; in other words, compliance with the liberal ideology, common immigrant background of the American people, meritocracy, and Protestantism of the original European settlers.[154]

All in all, there is a direct connection between constitutionalism and the cultural facts of a society. As viewed in national cases above, distrust or trust in authorities and political power in a society can be determinative on the structure of a constitution. Societies that distrust governmental and legislative authorities can opt for a stronger judicial review mechanism, as in post-war Germany or USA; while long standing, stable authority structures do not require it, as seen in the case of Britain.

As seen in cases of three major western constitutional systems, national identities determine constitutional identities; and culture is of the leading role in defining these identities.

---

[150] Rosenfeld, "Constitutional Identity," 772.

[151] Ibid.

[152] Ibid., 764.

[153] Samuel Phillips Huntington, *American Politics: The Promise of Disharmony* (Cambridge: Belkap Press, 1981), 11, cited by Vorländer, "What is 'Constitutional Cultures'," 32.

[154] Franklin, "American Political Culture," 47.

5.2.2 Constitutional Culture in Context: Case of Human Rights

From the point of the cultural paradigm, meanings of societal facts are understood in a relative way. As Legrand underscores, the cultural context may be viewed as a barrier to the sameness of facts in different societies.[155] In constitutional law, in particular in the interpretation of constitutions while identifying them, cultural relativism comes to the fore in some specific contexts by challenging universalism particularly. One of the most relevant issues in this context is evidently human rights.

As it has to do with the cultural and historical variabilities, cultural relativism is a "doctrine that holds that (at least some) such variations are exempt from legitimate criticism by outsiders; a doctrine that is strongly supported by notions of communal autonomy and self-determination."[156] Cultural relativism is based on two facts. The first one is the infinity of cultural diversities, and the second is that all principles for assessment and judgement of behavior are relative to culture.[157] In the context of international law, cultural relativism is viewed as the major obstacle for the western law to constitute a universal law. In this regard, it is impossible either to transform or even understand a different culture:

> In order to fully understand a culture, one must be a product of that culture. A culture produces its own unique mode of thought that acts as a schematic guide for conceptual thinking.[158]

Cultural relativism also involves relativities in ethical, epistemological, historical and linguistic fields in the context of international law.[159]

The interpretation of fundamental rights is a very striking matter in this sense. The idea of human rights has a special position in cross-cultural communication. Proceeding from this, Santos argues that, as a matter of course, human rights politics is cultural politics.[160] Given its overarching meaning concerning all human beings, human rights are universal by definition. Against this background, universal human rights and cultural relativism appear as rival conceptions. In particular, this rivalry is clearer in terms of the "radical cultural relativism" and the "radical universalism," in Donnelly's words. The radical cultural relativism regards the culture as

---

[155] Pierre Legrand, "Comparative Legal Studies and The Matter of Authenticity," *Journal of Comparative Law* 1 (2006): 368.

[156] Jack Donnelly. "Cultural Relativism and Universal Human Rights," *Human Rights Quarterly* 6 (1984): 400.

[157] Christopher C. Joyner and John C. Dettling, "Bridging the Cultural Chasm: Cultural Relativism and The Future of International Law," *California Western International Law Journal* 20 (1989-1990): 277.

[158] Ibid., 279.

[159] Ibid., 280 ff.

[160] Boaventura de Sousa Santos, "Towards a Multicultural Conception of Human Rights," in *Global Culture: Nationalism, Globalization and Modernity, A Theory, Culture & Society*, ed. Mike Featherstone (London: Sage Publications, 1990), 215.

the fundamental source of the validity of a moral right or rule; whereas the radical universalism asserts that culture does not have to do with moral rights and rules, since they are universally valid.[161] On the other hand, cultural relativism does not appear only in the radical form. One can also speak of a "weak relativism" that gives credit to universality to a little extent.[162]

The western understanding of human rights underlines the inherent moral qualities of individuals and emphasizes a moral autonomy.[163] However, the problem is that many non-western cultures view the individual as strictly attached to his social role; thereby, they never perceive it by detaching it from his social role. For example, East Asian societies, either Chinese, Korean or Japanese, are depicted as group-oriented, which means that emancipation comes about through the group life. In Africa, where in particular kinship relationships have a special role in the identification of individual, the situation is not very different.[164] This means that different cultures identify the individual at a different basis, and this also affects the character of normative orders. For example, in Islamic tradition of social and political organization, duty has a priority over rights, depending on the primacy of the community.[165]

In consideration of this distinction between western and non-western cultures, some critical views point to the Euro-centric nature of human rights that reflects a continuance of the Euro-centric colonial project.[166] These critical views mostly focus on the tension between European culture and cultures of precolonial African villages, the Islamic society and the South American tribes.[167] From this point of view, the universality of human rights is a disillusion; it is somewhat based on marginalising non-European cultures. It considers actors of human rights issues as in superior and subordinate positions, and glorifies some certain values that are central to western legal systems and cultures. According to the proponents of this idea, human rights discourse mainly aims at imposing them to non-European cultures and legal systems. The human rights corpus relies upon an "arrogant and biased" rhetoric. This strategical drive of the official human rights discourse does not allow a real communication between cultures and a cross-cultural legitimacy. Accordingly, the result is mostly "dumb copies of original;" and as an alien ideology to non-western societies, the human rights movement is doomed to fail.[168] In parallel with these ideas, Santos argues that the universal claim for human rights in fact conceals a

[161] Donnelly, "Cultural Relativism," 400.

[162] Ibid., 401.

[163] Joyner and Dettling, "Bridging the Cultural Chasm," 286.

[164] Ibid., 287.

[165] Ibid., 288.

[166] Makau W. Mutua, "Savages, Victims and Saviors: The Metaphor of Human Rights," in *Laws and Societies in Global Contexts: Contemporary Approaches*, ed. Eve Darian-Smith (Cambridge: Cambridge University Press, 2013), 88.

[167] Donnelly, "Cultural Relativism," 410.

[168] Mutua, "Savages, Victims and Saviors," 89, 92.

"globalised localism," or in other words, a form of "globalization from above" that reflects the globalization of a specific local culture dominantly in a hegemonic form.[169] That is to say, this form of human rights only serves to the struggle of the western world against the rest of the world. In this regard, the content of human rights gives too much credit to the ideas of human nature and absolute dignity and autonomy of individual, and the priority of political and civil rights over economic and social rights mark the liberal western character of the idea of human rights.[170] Accordingly, Santos means that universal human rights are not cosmopolitan. The antidote to this situation is the multicultural reconstruction of human rights that can underpin the relationship between "global competence" and "local legitimacy."[171]

In addition to this, it has also been argued by some western universalist scholars that human rights are western artefacts, and most of the non-western societies lack both the concept and practice of human rights. That is to say, there is a great chasm between these cultures, and a reconciliation is hard to achieve. For instance, some severe sanctions, such as preventive detention, the death penalty, and also a judiciary subordinate to the sovereign ruler, and the lack of a juridical mechanism for appeals are allowed in the Islamic legal doctrine.[172] Evidently, according to the proponents of this view, these facts can by no means comply with the western human rights doctrine. Therefore, they deny a probability for cross-cultural communication.

This problem in human rights rhetoric is also true of the whole Euro-American legal knowledge. This is a result of a downplaying of "existence of epistemological plurality" in the global realm by western nations and of imposing their own legal knowledge on other nations.[173] Darian-Smith argues that the lack of recognition of different epistemological systems always requires asking three questions in order to adopt global socio-legal perspective:

> (1) whose legal knowledge is in play; (2) what cultural biases does such knowledge embody and convey; (3) and what alternative or additional forms of legal knowledge and consciousness may be present that up to now, given the historical dominance of a Euro-American formal understanding of law, have been silenced, ignored, or deemed to be irrelevant.[174]

---

[169] Santos, "Towards a Multicultural Conception," 219.

[170] Ibid., 220.

[171] Ibid., 219. On the other side, Donnelly reflects a different approach on the meaning of universal and cosmopolitan character of human rights. He argues that universality is in fact "relative" in the context of human rights. It applies across all of a particular domain, e.g. universal health care, universal suffrage etc., and due to this relativity, universality does not apply to everyone in the globe. Therefore, he draws attention to that universal claims in human rights matters do not neglect relativity of the matter at all. Thus, he affirms that the tendency to see universalism and relativism as opposite concepts has become obsolete over time. Jack Donnelly, *Universal Human Rights: In Theory and Practice*, 3rd ed. (Ithaca and London: Cornell University Press, 2013), 93-103.

[172] Joyner and Dettling, "Bridging the Cultural Chasm," 295.

[173] Darian-Smith, *Laws and Societies*, 97-98.

[174] Ibid., 98.

Furthermore, these critical views do not reject the idea of universal human rights at all times. Instead, they suggest reconstructing them by finding out their true global and democratic roots. Immanuel Wallerstein's ideas can be held up as an example. According to Wallerstein, the human rights discourse should be reconstructed by challenging the official roots of human rights.[175] To this end, the historical continuance of European colonialism must be broken, and thereby the idea of human rights must be reconstructed in a morally legitimate way.[176] In a parallel way, Santos argues that struggling to give a real cosmopolitan character to human rights is the main task of contemporary emancipatory politics.[177] Furthermore, it has been argued that a few cross-culturally valid moral values can still be found to reconstruct human rights in a legitimate way. A very notable one is the concept of human dignity. Some scholars argue that human dignity is to be regarded as a common moral value in this sense, despite it being largely determined by culture in every society.[178]

Furthermore, some scholars also highlight the flaws and threats of cultural relativism. For instance, Donnelly draws attention to possible misleading aspects of the communitarian rhetoric, and to "cynical manipulations of a dying, lost, or even mythical cultural past," in addition to the legitimate claims of self-determination and cultural relativism. In many cases, these may be performed by corrupt and westernized elites who have weak connections to the indigeneous cultures and have no sincerity.[179] According to Donnelly, cultural relativism is mostly open to misuse for self-interests and arbitrary rules. For example, he refers to the following statement of All Africa Council of Churches on this matter:

> some leaders have even resorted to picking out certain elements of traditional African culture to anesthetize the masses. Despite what is said, this frequently has little to do with a return to the positive, authentic dimensions of African tradition.[180]

The utilization of traditional courts to repress political oppponents by political leaders in order to deal with them outside of the legal system in Malawi, Zaire and Zambia are striking examples. In that vein, Santos argues that both universalism and cultural relativism are detrimental to the conception of human rights:

> Against universalism, we must propose cross-cultural dialogues on isomorphic concerns. Against relativism, we must develop cross-cultural procedural criteria to distinguish

[175] Immanuel Wallerstein, *European Universalism: The Rhetoric of Power* (New York: New Press, 2006).

[176] Mutua, "Savages, Victims and Saviors," 94.

[177] Santos, "Towards a Multicultural Conception," 220.

[178] Donnelly, "Cultural Relativism," 405. Also, Santos, "Towards a Multicultural Conception," 221.

[179] Donnelly, "Cultural Relativism," 411.

[180] All Africa Council of Churches/World Council of Churches Human Rights Consultation, Khartoum Sudan, 16-22 February 1975, cited by Donnelly, "Cultural Relativism," 412.

> progressive politics from regressive politics, empowerment from disempowerment, emancipation from regulation.[181]

Santos affirms that all cultures are relative, but the solution has to do with something beyond the dichotomy of relativism and universalism. For this purpose, he offers a midway, so to speak, by providing a communication between cultures, but at the same time by considering concerns for creating the common criteria. He points to the conception of human dignity as a common value for every society for this communication. In this regard, Santos proceeds from the incompleteness of the conception of human dignity in every society, and from the difficulties to understand a culture from the point of another culture. He proposes *diatopical hermeneutics,* as a method to establish the cross-cultural dialogue. This method does not aim at achieving completeness, but

> to raise the consciousness of reciprocal incompleteness to its possible maximum by engaging in the dialogue, as it were, with one foot in one culture and the other in another. Herein lies its *dia-topical* character. (…) [The diatopical hermeneutic approach] requires a production of knowledge that must be collective, interactive, intersubjective and networked.[182]

In Santos' point of view, the great non-western civilizations, such as Indian and Islamic ones, already have a potential to realize this communication with other cultures.

Further, it has been argued that the widespread adoption of the universal human rights treaties by almost all countries demonstrates a consensus on the universal character of human rights, although this remains unfulfilled in practice in many countries. Donnelly argues that this can be taken as a *prima facie case* for weak relativism. He puts forward the idea that a minimum of common moral values can still be found out for every society. This proves the existence of a certain core of a common human nature that can be considered as a basis for the universal human rights.[183] At this point, the question is to find out these commonalities. Despite the fact that many non-western cultures identify the individual and his/her rights and duties in different ways, this is not to say that these cultures entirely lack any protecting conceptions for individuals. Instead, as some highlight, these cultures possess concepts of "respect for the dignity of the individual, absence of arbitrariness, [and] availability of remedies against despotic rule."[184] This leads to the further question of whether or not western and non-western traditions of individual protection can converge. At this juncture, Joyner and Dettling maintain that western welfare states have already created a model that partially reflects social and economic considerations in human rights understanding of non-western societies.[185]

---

[181] Santos, "Towards a Multicultural Conception," 221.

[182] Ibid., 221-226.

[183] Donnelly, "Cultural Relativism," 414.

[184] Raul S. Manglapus, "Human Rights are not a Western Discovery," *Worldview* 21, no. 10 (1978): 5, cited by Joyner and Dettling, "Bridging the Cultural Chasm," 295.

[185] Ibid., 302.

Under the circumstances of globalization, it is evident that there is no culture that can be isolated from others entirely, as none of them can remain unknown and closed to effects from other cultures.[186] Against this background, neither cultural relativism nor universalism can explain the diversities of human experience itself.[187]

As it is seen, contemporary constitutionalism acquires new dimensions through a cultural approach. The issues revealed in the debate between universalism and relativism arise as a gross problem of contemporary constitutionalism as well. As mentioned before, referring to Tully, one of the most significant assignments of the contemporary constitutionalism is to respond to the needs of diverse societies so as to enhance legitimacy. This has not been achieved by modern constitutionalism so far. In order to overcome this, contemporary constitutionalism needs to find answers stemming from the tension between universalism and cultural relativism in both domestic and international levels. However, as touched upon above, although these two lines are now found unfruitful by some scholars, the issues that are introduced by them are still significant, actual problems of contemporary constitutionalism.

5.2.3 Cultural Identity of Constitution

Constitutional culture is an overarching concept that is employed to understand differences between different constitutions and constitutional orders, and to understand contemporary constitutionalism. In other words, constitution is not immune to the results of cultural differentiations between various societies. What is more, constitution is to be perceived as a phenomenon that is structured by culture itself. Therefore, these cultural aspects come into prominence while examining the viability of the idea of global constitutionalism. Above all, the fact that constitution is a cultural concept demonstrates that a single and an overarching meaning of constitution can hardly be revealed. However, constitutional culture is still an underdeveloped concept, and it also lacks sufficient empirical support. Nonetheless, when dealing with this point along with other aspects of contemporary constitutionalism, some further questions arise. Culture is a mobilized fact in the globalized world; accordingly, what is the consequence of this mobilization in terms of the diversity of constitutions? To what extent do constitutional cultures resemble each other, apart from the textual resemblance? Evidently, these questions are vital for the global constitutionalism discourse where a unification of fragmented elements is sought. At this point, Schneiderman argues that the major benefit of dealing with constitution in cultural terms is "understanding the changes occurring in national constitutional systems resulting from the constitution-like disciplines associated with economic globalization."[188]

---

[186] Ibid., 299.

[187] Ibid., 300.

[188] Schneiderman, "Property Rights," 371.

As Goldworthy stresses, not all constitutions have the same character of "basic law," "higher law" and "the people's law," since they were constructed in different forms and ways.[189] Therefore, a unique form of contemporary constitutionalism is not likely to be manifested. Furthermore, a prototype of modern constitution does not suit to contemporary constitutions. This is a result of the cultural diversity of constitutions. Goldsworthy thinks of this problem in particular in the context of the difference of American and Australian constitutions. On the other hand, as touched upon in the last chapter, differences between political and legal constitutional traditions also prove these cultural borderlines. All in all, constitutional culture appears as an overarching concept for contemporary constitutionalism and it provides a single ground in understanding contemporary constitutions. In conclusion, "constitutional culture" appears as the key issue to understand the diverse meanings of contemporary constitutionalism.

Finally, having considered all cultural relativities and Dicey's perspective, Ferejohn et al. has reached a functional definition of constitution that is supposed to reflect commonalities for comparative purposes.[190] However, they concede that a functional definition misses requirements of a moral reading of constitution as suggested by Dworkin. In this respect, a functional definition to constitution cannot be taken as the single understanding of commonalities. Contemporary constitution requires a more complex reading:

> Constitutional definition depends, unavoidably we think, on constitutional theory – on some particular conception of constitutional culture and of what is that a constitutional government (or, perhaps *this* constitutional government) is aimed at achieving.[191]

Therefore, they highlight a distance between the textualist constitutional theories and theirs. This distance stems from the fact that textualist theories "lack the resources to distinguish procedural from substantive constitutional elements," and this leads to only reading constitutions literally.[192] In this regard, an originalist reading of a constitutionalism underdetermines a constitutional culture as it adheres to only one dimension of constitutional evolution.[193]

Towards the end of the examination of the meaning of contemporary constitution, a conclusion would be that the identity of a constitution is embedded in the cultural codes of a society. In other words, formal institutions cannot guarantee achievement of a constitution without an underpinning culture thereof. Baun explains this relationship as follows:

> (...) unless a constitution reflects the predominant values of a society, its prospects for stable and successful operation –and prospects for constitutionalism- are poor. Accordingly, a democratic constitutional order presupposes and requires a democratic political culture.[194]

[189] Goldsworthy, "Constitutional Cultures."

[190] Ferejohn et al., "Editor's Introduction," 17.

[191] Ibid., 18, emphasis belongs to the original text.

[192] Ibid., 18-19.

[193] Ibid., 22.

[194] Baun, "Federal Republic of Germany," 79.

However, this is not to say that the political and legal culture behind a constitution are the only factors in the achievement of a constitution. As viewed in well-achieved constitutions, a legitimate and workable institutional design must also exist besides cultural underpinnings of a constitution.[195] Moreover, in some cases, democratic constitutionalism cannot succeed, although the traditional political culture is not viewed as a barrier. In this sense, Nigeria is to be held up as an example, since democratic constitutionalism was hindered by "statist values of modernising elites and regimes."[196] On the other hand, as evident from German constitutional history (in particular regarding the history of *Grundgesetz*), a constitution which does not find its roots in the cultural infrastructure of a society, may still succeed by transforming the political culture.[197]

Overall, a constitutional culture is not an unchangeable phenomenon, and constitutional norms and institutions may undertake a role to change it. Consequently, as demonstrated in this chapter, the most significant advantage of dealing with a constitutional culture is to understand shifts in constitutional values and norms beyond the formal structure of a constitution.[198] The cultural paradigm paves the way for dealing with contemporary constitution in terms of legal culture and political culture that gives rise to the constitution in question. By this way, different empirical variations of constitutional practices and interpretive meanings of them can be understood in the age of globalization. Thus, the cultural paradigm appears as a convenient instrument in depicting contemporary constitutionalism. In the next chapter, this paradigm will be used as an instrument to examine the viability of the discourse of global constitutionalism in terms of contemporary constitutionalism.

[195] Daniel Franklin and Michael Baun, *Political Culture and Constitutionalism: A Comparative Approach* (Armonk: M.E. Sharpe, 1995), 222.

[196] Ibid., 226.

[197] Ibid., 226.

[198] Schneiderman, "Banging Constitutional Bibles," 838.

Chapter 6
Contemporary Constitutionalism to Understand Global Constitutionalism

Finally in this chapter, viability of the global constitutionalism discourse will be examined with regard to its capability to reflect contemporary constitutionalism. As discussed in the previous chapter, contemporary constitution has narrower and broader meanings, which are required to reflect its complexity. We employed Grimm's criterion of "Achieved Constitutions" to explain its narrower meaning, and cultural paradigm for the broader meaning. The former is fairly normativist, while the latter has at all times problems in drawing the contours of the research problem. Nevertheless, they arise as the best instruments of contemporary constitutional law theory in order to depict dichotomous, narrower and broader construction of meaning when considering purposes of this research. Therefore, in examining global constitutionalism discourse in terms of the idea of contemporary constitution, these two theoretical instruments shall be our main guides.

6.1 Global Constitutionalism and the Narrower Meaning of Constitution

6.1.1 Global Constitutionalism from the Point of 'Achieved Constitutions of the Past'

This book has not constrained itself to the idea that the concept of constitution particularly belongs to states. As a matter of fact, such a presumption would create a deadlock for this research. Nonetheless, this research has been sensitive to the phenomenon of "modern constitution," which is the main focus of the global constitutionalism discourse, and which was born into and maintained within the framework of modern

A. Atilgan, *Global Constitutionalism*, Beiträge zum ausländischen öffentlichen Recht und Völkerrecht, https://doi.org/10.1007/978-3-662-55647-4_6

states. On the other hand, as demonstrated in the previous chapter particularly, it is not apt to argue that modern constitutionalism, which was basically a product of the seventeenth and eighteenth centuries, remains no longer the same as its original form. Modern constitutionalism is still a component of contemporary constitutionalism to a certain degree. However, some specific features of modern constitutionalism have undergone change and they no longer reflect the contemporary formation.

As mentioned earlier, the discourse of global constitutionalism relies on the conventional idea of modern constitution. This means that many crucial discourses within contemporary constitutional law have been neglected and have not been considered as an inherent part of the global constitutionalism debate. Instead, the global constitutionalism debate was structured on discussions about the existence of a "modern constitution" beyond nation states. In other words, the transfer of a specific form to another level was envisaged, and diverse meanings of this form in contemporary societies were overlooked. This evidently results in the employment of a static form of constitution in the global constitutionalism debate. In this section, these remarks on global constitutionalism and contemporary constitutionalism will be touched upon in details. To this end, this section will begin with the common assumptions about the character of a modern constitution. As discussed in the third chapter in details, these are basically unifying functions of constitution: a constituent power in the establishment process of a constitution, the function of limitation of power and separation of powers, and a hierarchical position of constitution.

In the third chapter, Grimm's typology for the modern constitutions was introduced. Grimm proceeded from the "achieved constitutions"; and at the end, he emphasized five common features of modern constitutions. At the expense of a repetition, these common features are as follows:

> (1) The constitution in the modern sense is a set of legal norms, not a philosophical construct. (…)
> (2) The purpose of these norms is to regulate the establishment and the exercise of public power as opposed to a mere modification of a pre-existing public power. (…)
> (3) The regulation is comprehensive in the sense that no pre- or extra constitutional bearers of public power and no pre- or extra constitutional means to exercise this power are recognized.
> (4) Constitutional law is higher law. It enjoys primacy of all other laws and legal acts emanating from government. Acts incompatible with the constitution cannot claim legal validity.
> (5) Constitutional law finds its origin with the people as the only legitimate source of power. The distinction between pouvoir constituant and pouvoir constitué is essential to the constitution.[1]

At the end of the inquiry regarding the truth of contemporary constitutions, the objections against this typology were expressed above under the Sect. 3.2.4.2.

[1] Dieter Grimm, "Types of Constitutions," in *The Oxford Handbook of Comparative Constitutional Law*, ed. Michel Rosenfeld and Andras Sajo (Oxford: Oxford University Press, 2012), 104.

Nevertheless, it would be helpful to examine to what extent the idea of global constitutionalism meets these prerequisites. At this point, it is of note that only normative ideas can be taken into consideration for this examination since Grimm approaches modern constitutions in a normativist sense. This means that, for example, the idea of microconstitutionalization of Teubner and Fischer-Lescano should be exempt from this examination, on the ground that their understanding of constitution reflects a discursive one. Likewise, Koskenniemmi's "global constitutionalism as a mindset" also lies in a different category. On the other hand, normative ideas on global constitutionalism represent the core of this debate, and they have been the ones provoking further contributions to the discourse. Therefore, it makes much sense to focus on the normativist contributions to global constitutionalism from this point of view. On the other hand, this proves that a normativist understanding of constitution remains insufficient in understanding global constitutionalism, as it is a multidimensional discourse.

When Grimm's typology is employed in examining the idea of the UN Charter as a constitution, the most probable conclusions are as follows:

(1) As a normative construction that consists of legal rules, the UN Charter can meet this precondition very well. The UN Charter evidently originates from political decisions.

(2) The efficacy of the public power established by the UN is quite controversial for several reasons. Nevertheless, it is true that the UN Charter was supposed to establish a public power. The UN Charter brings norms for limitation of this power. In terms of formal purposes, it could be said that the UN Charter meets this criterion as well. However, it is of note that a very formalistic idea is approved in this case. What is more, even though the UN Charter would be viewed as a constitution for a moment in this sense, it is to be considered as a "failed" or a "crippled" constitution, on the ground that it has not created a collective identity, nor a systemic unification in terms of modern constitutionalism. As mentioned before in Chapter 3, the theory of coordination puts forward the idea that a constitution may fail to coordinate the people to acquiesce the new government and in this case, it becomes a failed constitution.

(3) It is evident that the UN Charter would be dismissed in consideration of this criterion particularly. The modern constitutions presuppose a single power for the public. The fact of fragmentation in international law is the greatest obstacle in viewing the subject of the UN Charter as a holder of a single power. Likewise, it is more likely to think of the UN Charter as a failed constitution, as in the second criterion, since it has not been able to create and retain comprehensiveness in international law.

(4) The UN Charter has been able to partially achieve this through Article 103 that governs the *jus cogens* rule. This is indeed one of the strongest facts that are relied upon by the proponents of the idea of the UN Charter as constitution of the international community.

(5) The reflection of the will of people through the UN Charter is a quite controversial issue. International law is in general performed by various experts in processes that are not open to the public. To imagine a constitutionalist revolutionary

movement in its making process is not realistic. Both drafting and ratification processes of the UN Charter did not include any public access and did not become a part of any public movement. To what degree drafting and ratifying national bodies can be regarded as the representatives of the will of their people is quite doubtful.

Seen in this light, from the point of Grimm's typology for modern constitutions, the UN Charter can hardly be viewed as a constitution. The same may apply to debates over the WTO constitution, for example. Of all these criteria, the will of people or existence of a legitimate constitutent power would be problematic in this context. Accordingly, whether or not the WTO Constitution could establish a single power remains in the dark from this perspective.

However, as discussed in the third chapter, these criteria are not preferable for the purposes of this research. Contemporary constitution is a multifaceted and multidimensional phenomenon, and an analysis thereof in terms of normative aspects would not give the most realistic results. On the other hand, before employing the cultural paradigm, there are some further points of the conventional idea of constitution that have to do with the idea of global constitutionalism.

6.1.2 Some Further Aspects of Modern Constitutionalism: Integration, Unity, Separation of Powers

As discussed in the third chapter, modern constitution has been supposed to have a function in contributing to societal integration. Some mentioned this function as a prerequisite for an "achieved constitution," thinking in the context of the failure of the Weimar constitution and some other well-established constitutions. As mentioned above, Parson's functional sociology endows a special function to constitution within the legitimation subsystem of a highly differentiated polity. In this regard, constitution and constitutional institutions are very central to the legitimation subsystem. Further, a constitution is fairly crucial in a society since it is a major link between political and legal organizations, and thus a major instrument in the emergence of a concrete collective identity.[2] A constitution gives rise to expectations for a society to transform itself into a polity.[3] At the cost of repetition, Grimm specifies preconditions of an integrative power as follows:

> A constitution will have an integrative effect only if it embodies a society's fundamental value system and aspirations, and if the society perceives that its constitution reflects precisely those values with which it identifies and which are the sources of its specific character.[4]

---

[2] Talcott Parsons, *Politics and Social Structure* (New York: Free Press, 1969), 339.

[3] Dieter Grimm, "Integration by Constitution," *International Journal of Constitutional Law* 3 (2005): 194.

[4] Ibid., 199.

Grimm states that the harmony between societal values and a constitution is necessary. However, as mentioned before, constitutional theory remains silent on how to determine this harmony, and any empirical work is also missing to prove the existence and degree of such a harmony.[5]

This function of modern constitutions is also prescribed for a global constitutionalization process within the global constitutionalism discourse. For example, holistic views on global constitutionalism seek a unity of the international community, the world society or a specific sector. The World State approach seeks the unification of the world society and its legal system through international law, while cosmopolitan approaches seek a purposive unification of law. The UN Charter appeared as a unifying instrument for a world law, whereas the WTO marked unification of trade sector by the proponents of the idea of constitutionalization in the WTO. The idea of microconstitutionalization envisaged the functional unification of fragmented global sectors. In a general sense, it could be said that the global constitutionalism discourse presupposes a unity or homogeneity in progress in the international society and its law as a consequence of the constitutionalization process. In this regard, the unity of a legal order is generally understood as homogeneity.[6]

Further, many critiques on the global constitutionalist ideas trigger the issue of unity in the international legal order. Most notably, the fragmented structure of international law has been discussed in demonstrating that it is not apt to think of a constitutionalization process in the international legal order.[7] In a similar vein, the idea of the UN Charter as the constitution of the international community has been criticized on the ground that the international legal order is of a fragmented structure, and the UN Charter does not provide the unity of a legal order as expected from any constitution.[8] This problem needs to be dealt with in view of the question of the unity of what is to be expected by virtue of a constitution.

It is beyond doubt that modern constitutions played a key role in the unification of public power, by eliminating the plurality of premodern power centres. Constitutions currently retain this role to a certain extent. However, as demonstrated in the previous chapter, the idea of contemporary constitution does not include such a strong emphasis on integration as traditional constitutions did, and the idea of contemporary constitution needs to follow a trend to embrace various diversities in a society. The demands and struggles for the recognition of cultural diversities were quite influential in the rise of this situation. Further, this new situation opened the path for the dialogue of diverse subjects that were formerly excluded or neglected

---

[5] Ibid., 200.

[6] Christine E.J. Schwöbel, *Global Constitutionalism in International Legal Perspective* (Leiden: Nijhoff, 2011), 95.

[7] Andreas Fischer-Lescano and Gunther Teubner, "Regime-collisions: The Vain Search for Legal Unity in the Fragmentation of Global Law," *Michigan Journal of International Law* 25, no. 4 (2004): 999-1046.

[8] Schwöbel, *Global Constitutionalism*, 107.

by modern constitutions. Therefore, modern constitutions cannot be counted as integrationist and unifying projects in real terms.

On the other hand, it is of note that, as James Tully underlines, modern constitutionalism suffers from the lack of a new language that could work out to shift its unifying function towards an embracing one. This problem also stands in front of the global constitutionalism discourse. The prominent question in this regard becomes to what extent international law enables communication and recognition of diverse groups and cultures. In other words, the idea of a global constitution as a unification project does not respond to the main question of contemporary constitutionalism. Such a constitution would not be desirable for the international community for reasons concerning the representation of diverse cultures and societies. This is also related to the fact that in societies where intense cultural and ethnic conflicts take place, the character of constitutions lies at the heart of the problem.[9]

Therefore, as a liberal democratic discourse, global constitutionalism is to be reconstructed; in view of the problems led by modern constitutions, for diverse communities particularly. In the global constitutionalism literature, it is from time to time noted by some scholars that a global constitution would not be desirable under the current circumstances, on the ground that it would consolidate the hegemony of a superpower or empire.[10] Accordingly, democracy concerns come to the fore in this debate. However, these concerns should not only be viewed related to the hegemonic power of USA over international relations, but also to the core of modern constitutionalism that is still incapable of responding to the needs of diverse societies, as Tully underlines.

Nevertheless, it can be argued that "unity" may still make sense in terms of unity of a legal order, as a constitution plays the role of a "hub," or it determines the hierarchical structure of a legal system. As a matter of fact, many facts dealt with in this text already proved that contemporary constitutions can hardly achieve this. As mentioned in the second chapter, Anne Peters argues that contemporary constitutions remain incapable of meeting the needs of new circumstances that concern the transboundary issues, and that transnational entities play a key role in remedying

---

[9] A prominent example is the Turkish Constitution of 1982, in which Turkish ethnonationalism is strictly preserved by "irrevocable provisions." The amendment of this constitution by recognizing different languages spoken and ethnic cultures living in this country is viewed as the keypoint in resolving the Kurdish issue. Dogu Ergil, "The Kurdish Question in Turkey," *Journal of Democracy* 11, no. 3 (2000): 122-135. In a similar vein, the current German constitution leads to some difficulties in terms of citizenship and other rights for the foreigner labour force of the country by reason of the ethnonationalist emphasis in the citizenship law. Michael J. Baun, "The Federal Republic of Germany," in *Political Culture and Constitutionalism: A Comparative Approach*, ed. Daniel P. Franklin and Michael Baun (Armonk: M.E. Sharpe, 1995), 93.

[10] Martti Koskenniemmi, "The Fate of Public International Law: Between Technique and Politics," *The Modern Law Review* 70, no.1 (2007): 19.

the deficiencies of national constitutions.[11] They have complementary and in some cases, determining functions for national constitutions. Under these circumstances, it does not make much sense to adhere to the unity function and integrative power of modern constitutions to understand their contemporary identity.

As discussed in the third chapter, the integrative force of a constitution has somewhat to do with its extralegal effects. Therefore, it is vain to seek integration by virtue of a constitutional text. If it is true that the UN Charter is the constitution of the international community, then it is to be considered as a "failed" or "crippled" constitution; on the ground that it has not created a collective identity, nor has it created a systemic unification in terms of modern constitutionalism. A striking example is the non-hierarchical operation of international courts, for example the incapacity of the ICJ to bind human rights tribunals in particular.[12] In addition, the same incapacity is true of the WTO Appellate Court, decisions of which are not considered as binding by other transnational trade courts.[13] However, as mentioned in the third chapter, the monolithic body of modern constitution cannot meet demands that stem from the societal diversity in the postcolonial era, and it is no longer an effective political instrument in realizing integrative ambitions.

In conclusion, seeking societal integration as a prerequisite for a constitution does not make sense. Therefore, modern constitutions would not be good instruments to identify the developments in the global realm in terms of this criterion. It would lead to a great mistake and an anachronism to inquire a constitutionalization in the global realm through a modern constitution that served for the construction of the modern state under circumstances of a restricted period.

A normativist understanding of constitution does not remain incapable to fit to the global constitutionalism discourse only in terms of integrative force, but also of limitation of power through separation of powers. It was originally Montesquieu's idea that separating three branches of power (judicial, legislative and executive) and preventing them to unite in a single power could be the only solution to impede despotism. Since then, the separation of powers has been counted as essential for democratic constitutionalism.[14] However, it is of note that the development and evolution of a global public order has not been the same as modern domestic public orders. As mentioned earlier in the first chapter, the global public order is currently quiet permeable with the private sphere, and it can hardly be claimed that there is a global public order that can be subject to an analogy with domestic public order.[15]

---

[11] Anne Peters, "Compensatory Constitutionalism: The Fundamental Function and Potential of Fundamental International Norms and Structures," *Leiden Journal of International Law* 19 (2006): 579-610.

[12] Charles H. Koch Jr., "Envisioning a Global Legal Culture," *Michigan Journal of International Law* 25 (2003): 60.

[13] Ibid. 60.

[14] Schwöbel, *Global Constitutionalism*, 110.

[15] See above, Chapter 2, Section 2.1.2.5. This was also the ground of a major critique of Nico Krisch towards the idea of global constitutionalism. Nico Krisch, *Beyond Constitutionalism: The Pluralist Structure of Postnational Law* (Oxford: Oxford University Press, 2010), 67.

This mixed and hybrid public order features quite differently from the conventional understanding of a public order. Above all, private actors rise as significant actors in the making of law, and transnationalization consolidates this process. *Lex mercatoria*, as recognized in the UN Convention on the International Sale of Goods (CISG), is a noteworthy example. On the other hand, the changing nature of public contracts is to be noted, as they lose their public character to a great extent, since the gravity of private parties increases consistently. This leads to a heterarchical order instead of a hierarchical order, which is traditionally known from the domestic public orders. Finally, as mentioned in this section, the intervention from the Appellate Body of the WTO to public domestic orders is a good example for the permeable public-private relations. Consequently, the current structure of public power is quite complex in the global realm. As such, limitation of power cannot be achieved in the global realms through classical separation of powers, as the roles of these powers are ambiguous in some cases and particularly in cases where private parties take significant roles in maintaining power. Therefore an analogy with national public orders does not make sense in terms of the limitation of power.

6.1.3 Fragmented Global Order: A Proto-Constitutional Order?

Last but not least, the relationship of the fragmented global order and modern constitution could also be elucidated from another point. As touched on above, the emergence of modern constitution by unifying public power was strictly related to some proto-constitutional orders of the late medieval period.[16] In order to find out whether or not a global constitutionalization process is a result of a similar structure, it is necessary to find out whether the current fragmented global legal order can be viewed as equivalent to the fragmented high-medieval period, in which political and legal developments gave rise to the emergence of modern constitution. To put it differently, does the current fragmented and deterritorialized global legal order reflect a proto-constitutional order? This question has already entered into the research agenda of the global studies scholars. For instance, Saskia Sassen questions the aptness of such an analogy between two orders. Her answer is simply negative.[17] In fact, Sassen finds out a similar logic of transition in the contemporary denationalization process.[18] However, she proceeds from very fundamental differences between the medieval and global orders in the foundational features thereof. According to Sassen, in the medieval European era, normative units were strongly emcompassing,

[16] Christopher J. A. Thornhill, *A Sociology of Constitutions: Constitutions and State Legitimacy in Historical-sociological Perspective* (Cambridge: Cambridge University Press, 2011).

[17] Saskia Sassen, "Neither Global Nor National: Novel Assemblages of Territory, Authority and Rights," in *Laws and Societies in Global Contexts: Contemporary Approaches*, ed. Eve Darian-Smith (Cambridge: Cambridge University Press, 2013), 31-32.

[18] Saskia Sassen, *Territory, Authority, Rights: From Medieval to Global Assemblages*, Updated Edition (Princeton: Princeton University Press, 2008), 32.

and these units contained a fairly complete structure involving very complex elements of the social life, such as different classes, norms, judicial systems etc. During feudalism, there was also a kind of central authority led by the church and the empire, which was not based on territoriality.[19] On the other hand, current fragmented units of the global order are "highly specialized, partial, and without much internal differentiation."[20] As mentioned earlier above, in this complex structure of the high medieval order, there was a fatal struggle for power by the reason of the overlapping powers. Constitutionalization meant the abolition of the undesired rivals for power by generating a single power. This intersection is missing in the fragmented global order, as Sassen points out, since these fragments are specialized and partial ones. In addition, internal differentiation is relatively simple and significant conflict zones cannot be observed for power struggles, such as class struggles, etc. Thus, a common ground in the foundational basis of these two historical facts can hardly be found out. In short, such an analogy does not serve the purpose of examining whether or not a current fragmented global order may reflect a proto-constitutional order.

6.2 Global Constitutionalism from the Point of the Cultural Paradigm

The issue of culture has a special weight in global studies. As a widespread implication of globalism, the ongoing movement of people between different countries leads to the dysfunction of the settled meanings of territories and identities. Diasporas as transnational settings threaten nation states implicitly, and they are to be viewed as one of the driving forces of this dysfunction. They have a key role in blending cultures and identities: "[p]rocesses of migration, displacement and deterritorialization are increasingly sundering the fixed association between identity, culture, and place."[21] As such, demographic circulation and cultural imminence undermine our imagination of national borders: life is lived beyond borders and we are always under the influence of implicit cultural codes. This means a disillusionment with the imagination of a modern nation state:

> if communities are based not on fixed attributes like geographical proximity, shared history, or face-to-face interaction, but instead on symbolic identification and social psychology, *then there is no intrinsic reason to privilege nation-state communities over other possible community identifications that people might share.*[22]

---

[19] Ibid., 33.

[20] Sassen, "Neither Global Nor National," 31-32.

[21] Akhil Gupta and James Ferguson, ed., *Culture, Power, Place: Ethnography at the End of an Era, in Culture, Power, Place: Explorations in Critical Anthropology* (Durham, Duke University Pres, 1997), 179, 196, cited by Paul Schiff Berman, "From International Law to Law and Globalization" (University of Connecticut School of Law Articles and Working Papers, Paper 23, 2005, http://lsr.nellco.org/uconn_wps/23), 516, last visit 11.07.2013.

[22] Ibid., 518. Emphasis belongs to original text.

As a corollary, culture has also been dealt with in terms of the impacts of globalization over it. The emergence of a global culture was discussed by numerous scholars in various aspects.[23] By virtue of the cultural paradigm, the idea of a global constitutional culture can now be discussed in the context of global constitutionalism.

6.2.1 Prospects for a Global Constitutional Culture

The concept of constitution has been depicted in a broader context in this book, as it involves not only written basic law texts, but also some further unwritten facts, which generate a constitutional culture. As a matter of fact, in so doing this text has broadened the "achievement criteria" to be considered in the definition of constitution, borrowing from Grimm. This means that, unlike Grimm, it has been pointed out that "achieved constitutions" were indeed results of not only some formal achievements, but also the achievement of some further cultural facts. In other words, these formal criteria were in fact achieved in a cultural environment, and without this environment the contemporary meaning of constitution could not have been grasped.

Constitutional culture has an overarching function in a constitutional order, and it is essential to determine the existence of a constitutional regime, as Ferejohn et al. states:

> In effect, the question of whether a political system can be understood as a constitutional regime depends on the existence of a constitutional culture that contains shared normative expectations about appropriate governmental conduct.[24]

This means that a constitution is a broader issue than a written text or normative principles. From this point of view, a constitutional culture is to be identified in a process in which internal and external cultural factors play a role.

At this juncture, how could this information be used within the context of the global constitutionalism? As a consequence of the inquiry of the above section, it would be a mistake to stick to the question of whether the global order has a constitution or not. There is not only one way of constitution-making and only one

[23] Anthony D. Smith, "Towards A Global Culture?," in *Global Culture: Nationalism, Globalization and Modernity, A Theory, Culture & Society*, ed. Mike Featherstone (London: Sage Publications, 1990), 171-192. Roy Boyne, "Culture and the World-System," in *Global Culture: Nationalism, Globalization and Modernity, A Theory, Culture & Society*, ed. Mike Featherstone (London: Sage Publications, 1990), 57-62. Immanuel Wallerstein, "Culture as the Ideological Battleground of the Modern World-System," in *Global Culture: Nationalism, Globalization and Modernity, A Theory, Culture & Society*, ed. Mike Featherstone (London: Sage Publications, 1990), 63-66.

[24] John Ferejohn, Jack N. Rakove and Jonathan Riley, "Editor's Introduction," in *Constitutional Culture and Democratic Rule* ed. John Ferejohn, Jack N. Rakove and Jonathan Riley (Cambridge: Cambridge University Press, 2001), 13.

meaning of constitution, as is known from contemporary constitutionalism. A constitution can appear in a single written charter, in a sum of various legal texts, or even in the form of customs. On the other hand, the only common form of these distinct constitutions is a constitutional regime that is determined by a constitutional culture. Further, even if it is in some way proved that there is not a written constitution in the global realm; the emergence of constitutional values, such as rule of law, fundamental rights, judicialization at the global level cannot be explained. This would remain a useless truth, so to speak. As a matter of fact, this could be viewed as another deadlock of the global constitutionalism discourse. Therefore, by drawing on the results of this inquiry, the global constitutionalism discourse can be reshaped in a different way by reconstructing constitution in a cultural, discursive form. This can be achieved by focusing on the development of a constitutional culture in the global realm. In other words, the global realm appears suitable only for a "broader" meaning of constitution. At the cost of a repetition, "constitution of global constitutionalism is a broad constitution," in the sense dealt with above in the third chapter.

Whether or not a global constitutional culture exists or evolves, is to be questioned in terms of two perspectives of constitutional cultural studies: constitutional culture as a legal culture and constitutional culture as a political culture. As touched upon in the previous chapter, a constitutional culture can be perceived as a condensed form of a political culture or a variation of a legal culture. Therefore, this question should be handled in view of these two forms of constitutional culture.

6.2.1.1 Global Constitutional Culture as a Global Legal Culture

As pointed out in the previous chapter, constitutional culture as legal culture concerns the extralegal features of a constitutional text, such as "willingness to be bound" or "public understanding" by people. From this perspective, what distinguishes constitutional culture from legal culture is the major theme of the legal culture in question. Constitutional culture has somewhat to do with a legal culture behind a constitution. More specifically, it concerns the "web of interpretative norms, canons, and practices which most members of a particular community accept and employ."[25] Against this background, Friedman's insights on legal culture, through a distinction between internal legal culture and external legal culture, can also work in constitutional culture. In other words, constitutional culture can be dealt with in the context of the practice of lawyers and other relevant professionals, and the public understanding of constitutional law.

In the global realm, where a manifested formal constitution does not exist, it seems harder to deal with the notion of a constitutional culture. However, proceeding from the global constitutionalist ideas, which attempt to identify the character of some international law documents such as the UN Charter as a constitution or WTO

[25] Ferejohn et al., "Editor's Introduction," 10.

Law; searching the character of legal culture behind these documents can be illuminating. That is to say, a focus on global legal culture while questioning a global constitutional culture is fairly required. To make it clear, it is necessary to ask whether or not practices of global legal professionals reflect constitutional practices, and also, whether or not these documents reflect a constitution from the point of public understanding. As mentioned above, Sally Engle Merry highlights four common phenomena that are mostly referred as legal culture by scholars. These phenomena are "practices and ideologies within a legal system," "public's attitude towards law," "legal mobilization," and "legal consciousness."[26] She explains which specific methods of research are required by four fundamental dimensions of legal culture:

> The first [legal practices] requires organisational analysis and ethnographic study of legal institutions, the second [public's attitude towards law] a survey of public attitudes and perspectives, the third [legal mobilization] the analysis of recourse to legal remedies, and the fourth [legal consciousness] a study of how people conceive of problems and the relevance of the law to these conceptions.[27]

The first two of these methods can work for our purposes here, as they reflect the understanding of legal culture by Friedman.

As a matter of fact, any empricial work, such as a survey, will not be referred to underpin the theoretical background under this section. Instead, a number of phenomena of global law mentioned in previous chapters will be handled, and their relevance to the cultural paradigm will be demonstrated here. In other words, the major purpose under this chapter is to propose a cultural view to global issues, and to demonstrate that the cultural paradigm can work in global law matters as well.

A distinction between internal and external legal cultures in international law is not that easy, on the ground that international law is, in a generic way, performed through the work of experts and legal professionals. That is to say, public or ordinary people are generally affected by the consequences of international legal activities in an indirect way. Nonetheless, this book will remain loyal to the distinction of Friedman to a great extent, and reconstruct the distinction between international legal professional's culture and public attitudes including states' policies towards international law.

6.2.1.1.1 Global Internal Legal Culture

In terms of global internal legal culture, first of all, cultural practices of legal professionals in international tribunals come to the fore. As a matter of fact, internal legal culture is of a great importance in shaping the legal culture of the international community, on the ground that international law is in general described as the law

[26] Sally Engle Merry, "What is Legal Culture? An Anthropological Perspective," *Journal of Comparative Law* 5 (2010): 43-44.

[27] Ibid., 44.

of experts that run decision-making processes behind the closed doors. Internal legal culture "refers to the way practitioners within the law see the rules, the legal system and the kinds of people who use it."[28] In this respect, many variables, such as the educational background of people, their connection to political processes, the individual views that they bring into their institutions, their implicit judgments on gender, class, race etc. affect culture of legal institutions.[29] Therefore, revealing the attitude of legal experts to the character of law, the making of which they undertake is crucial for the examination of viability of constitutionalization in the global realm. For example, the judicial globalization between judges through networks, which was noted by Anne-Marie Slaughter, is deemed to be an example of a spreading legal culture by some scholars.[30]

Slaughter refers to the increasing communication between judges all over the world as a result of globalization, and the role of this communication in constructing a global legal system. According to her, the increasing interaction between judges leads to a cross-fertilization between legal cultures.[31] This communication has several aspects: "exchanging opinions, meeting face to face in seminars and judicial organizations, and even negotiating with one another over the outcome of specific cases."[32] They occur between national and transnational courts; and also between national courts in various countries, in formal and informal ways through networking. One result of this communication is that courts refer to the rulings of other countries' courts or transnational courts in their rulings regarding a broad range of issues, most notably human rights. Slaughter draws attention to the success of the ECHR, as "a source of authoritative pronouncements on human rights law for national courts" since it is currently the most cited transnational court in the world, although it has no formal authority on countries outside of the CoE. By this way, courts become active components of legal borrowings across borders.[33] Further, the interaction between courts can be very constructive. Slaughter gives the example of the EU legal order, the construction of which was made possible by relationships between the ECJ and national courts of Member States, although this was not anticipated while drafting the Treaty of Rome.[34]

However, this fact does not mean that the increasing communication between national courts and/or transnational courts does not meet any objection from national judiciaries. Some scholars refer to the idea that domestic constitutional exceptionalism burgeoned in the US Supreme Court against the postwar constitutional law paradigms, which was marked by a strong resistance to referring to

[28] Ibid., 43.

[29] Ibid., 48.

[30] Koch, "Global Legal Culture," 17.

[31] Anne-Marie Slaughter, *A New World Order* (Princeton: Princeton University Press, 2004), 102.

[32] Ibid., 65.

[33] Ibid., 66.

[34] Ibid., 67.

non-US constitutional law.[35] In this regard, numerous judges of the Supreme Court already exchanged their views through dissenting opinions, and showed a strong resistance against citing or drawing on foreign court decisions in the US Supreme Court.[36] This resistance from the US Supreme Court has been stronger than from many other constitutional courts.[37]

Furthermore, "internal legal culture" also fits better as an instrument to examine constitutionalization of the WTO from the point of the cultural paradigm, since WTO Law is somewhat an expert based process, in which contributions from the public are excluded to a large degree. However, it is of note that there is not a strong borderline between internal and external legal cultures. That is to say, this is a result of the fact that legal experts are eventually former non-professionals, who join the legal system after a training process.[38]

There are several different approaches about the emerging character of international legal culture in international organizations and judiciary in particular. These approaches place an emphasis on the originating role of national legal cultures by creating an amalgamation at the international level. Some advance the claim that the international legal culture develops through a "clash" of different cultures. This clash creates a legal culture different from its origins.[39] Furthermore, some others advocate the idea that some particular national cultures remain dominant in the international institutions where they interact, such as the leading position of the American common law culture at the ICTY, or of the French civil law tradition at the ICC.[40] Another major claim is that international legal culture emerges independently, and it has a discrete reality and values that grant it this independence. In this regard, for instance, international criminal law appears as a new *sui generis* legal culture.[41] Apart from that, Campbell puts forward the idea that international criminal law evidences a particular "legal mentalité." This means that international criminal law reflects a distinctive legal culture that cannot be reduced to a clash between different national legal traditions. She gives the example of newly developed norms with respect to sexual violence at wars, in particular through prosecutions of ICTY and ICTR in the 1990s, as this matter was not subject to international regulations to this day.[42] In this vein, one can multiply examples from international criminal law. For

[35] Mark Tushnet, "The Inevitable Globalization of Constitutional Law," *Virginia Journal of International Law* 49 (2008-2009): 986.

[36] Slaughter, *A New World Order*, 76.

[37] Sujit Choudry, "Globalization in Search of Justification: Toward a Theory of Comparative Constitutional37 Interpretation," *Indiana Law Journal* 74 (1999): 820. Also the Australian legal system can be mentioned in this context. Tushnet, "Inevitable Globalization," 986.

[38] Merry, "What is Legal Culture?," 48.

[39] Kirsten Campbell, "The Making of Global Legal Culture and International Criminal Law," *Leiden Journal of International Law* 26 (2013): 158.

[40] Ibid., 158.

[41] Ibid., 160.

[42] Ibid., 161.

instance, from the same perspective, lifting the traditional principle of exemption to impunity for state leaders is a remarkable example. In this regard, the prosecution of Kaiser Wilhelm II pursuant to the Versailles Treaty of 1919, and the abolition of head of state immunity in the 1945 International Military Tribunal Charter and in the International Military Tribunal for the Far East Charter, were the first exceptions to this principle in the twentieth century.[43] As a consequence of these exceptions, the international community developed a new customary rule that "international immunities do not apply to international criminal prosecutions for certain international crimes."[44] This exception became a rule through pertinent provisions of statutes of international criminal tribunals. In Article 27 of the Rome Statute for the International Criminal Court, this rule is articulated as follows:

> (…) In particular, official capacity as a Head of State or Government, a member of a Government or parliament, an elected representative or a government official shall in no case exempt a person from criminal responsibility under this Statute, nor shall it, in and of itself, constitute a ground for reduction of sentence. (…) Immunities or special procedural rules which may attach to the official capacity of a person, whether under national or international law, shall not bar the Court from exercising its jurisdiction over such a person.[45]

Furthermore in Article 7(2) of the Statute of the ICTY, it is stated that,

> [t]he official position of any accused person, whether as Head of State or Government or as a responsible Government official, shall not relieve such person of criminal responsibility nor mitigate punishment.[46]

Slobodan Milosevic, the former Serbian president; Charles Taylor, the former Liberian president; and Jean Kambanda, former Rwandan president were indicted or tried by international tribunals within this new era. To conclude, internal legal cultures of these tribunals, or to put it differently, values and principles convened by legal professionals involved in the international criminal judiciary, were quite influential in overturning the principle of head of state immunity.[47] Accordingly, it has been proved that international criminal tribunals rely upon a particular legal mentalité. This is marked by the "constant process of becoming international," which is

---

[43] Jake Hirsh-Allen, "Bashir's Immunity: Arguments in Support of the Prosecution of an Incumbent Head of a Non-State Party by The International Criminal Court," 2008, http://jake.contemporaryfuture.com/docs/transystemicLaw/BashirsImmunity.pdf), last visit 12.09.2011.

[44] M. Cherif Bassiouni, *Introduction to International Criminal Law* (New York: Transnational Publishers, 2003), cited by Ibid.

[45] Rome Statute of the International Criminal Court, https://www.icc-cpi.int/nr/rdonlyres/ea9aeff7-5752-4f84-be94 0a655eb30e16/0/rome_statute_english.pdf., last visit 11.09.2011..

[46] Statute of the International Tribunal for the Prosecution of Persons Responsible for Serious Violations of International Humanitarian Law Committed in the Territory of the Former Yugoslavia since 1991, http://www.icty.org/x/file/Legal%20Library/Statute/statute_sept09_en.pdf, last visit 11.09.2011.

[47] Hirsh-Allen, "Bashir's Immunity."

to say, it is shaped by its own distinct values and practices.[48] Furthermore, international criminal law is not a way of internationalization, "but a way of universalizing liberal legal form by constructing persons as global legal subjects, which exist in legal relations to all humanity."[49]

On the other hand, when it comes to the constitutional character of this legal culture, as mentioned in the first chapter above, the earlier rulings of international tribunals give clues about what sort of a legal culture was prevailing among legal professionals. The prevailing paradigms of international law mentioned in the first chapter, mark at the same time the prevailing legal cultures of international courts. Of these rulings, the Lotus ruling of the PCIJ denotes that the legal culture of the early twentieth century viewed that international law was subordinate to the will of sovereign states.[50] However, the need for an increased cooperation in the aftermath of the catastrophic wars of the twentieth century; and the changing structures and agents of international relations, became quite influential in the transformation of this culture. In the course of transformation, internal legal culture of the international community gained "constitutional" qualities to some extent through some remarkable rulings of international tribunals.

As mentioned in the first chapter, a number of rulings are of a great importance in international law literature to demonstrate that a new paradigm was emerging in international law. In this period, the International Court of Justice took some significant decisions demonstrating a communitarian approach, by referring to *jus cogens* and *erga omnes* rules in international law. The Barcelona Traction and Lockerbie cases are noteworthy in this sense.[51] International tribunals operating in particular in the human rights field, made significant contributions to shape a global internal legal culture with the constitutional characteristics by taking the increasing integration of the international realm into account. For instance, some of these rulings placed an emphasis on the constitutional character of the UN Charter or the ECHR. The European Court of Human Rights identified the European Convention on Human Rights as "a constitutional instrument of European public order" in

---

[48] Campbell, "Making of Global Legal Culture," 165.

[49] Ibid., 168.

[50] The Case of the S.S. Lotus, (France v. Turkey), PCIJ, Series A, No. 10 (1927), para. 18, cited by Bardo Fassbender, "Sovereignty and Constitutionalism in International Law," in *Sovereignty in Transition: Essays in European Law*, ed. Neil Walker (Oxford: Hart Publishing, 2006), 117.

[51] Barcelona Traction, Light and Power Company, Limited, (Belgium v. Spain), ICJ 3, 32 (05.02.1970), http://www.icj-cij.org/docket/index.php?p1=3&p2=3&case=50&p3=4, last visit, 25.09.2013. Questions of Interpretation and Application of the 1971 Montreal Convention Arising from the Aerial Incident at Lockerbie" (Libyan Arab Jamahiriya v. United States of America), Provisional Measures, Order of 14 April 1992. (14.03.1992), http://www.icj-cij.org/docket/index.php?sum=460&code=lus&p1=3&p2=3&case=89&k=82&p3=5, last visit 19.09.2013.

several decisions.[52] Furthermore, in Al-Dulimi case, Judge Pinto de Albuquerque and his two colleagues highlight the gradual disconnection of constitutionality from the statehood, and also the fragmented nature of constitutionalization in the global realm.[53] They also draw attention to "intra-systemic" conflicts between these fragmented bodies, and to the weaker position of the constitutionalization of the UN. According to these judges, this fragmented structure gives rise to a cacophony at the same time, and only a "World Human Rights Court" may overcome this issue.[54] In the same vein, *ad hoc* courts of the 1990s also proned to describe international legal order as a constitutional order. The Tadic case of the ICTY is one of these noteworthy examples. As mentioned before, in this case, the ICTY underscored the constitutional character of the UN Charter and explicitly identified the UN Security Council as a body operating within a constitutional framework.[55] Therefore, a tendency for a constitutional character is likely to be observed in the global legal culture in these rulings, although they appear rarely and it is hard to speak of a canon that deals with the constitutional traits of international legal order in a coherent manner.

Consequently, the global internal legal culture basically forms in two ways. Globalization gives rise to more interaction between judicial bodies both in transnational and national levels. This evidently contributes to increasing commonalities and the convergence of legal cultures. On the other hand, international tribunals can demonstrate a communitarian approach to international law, which can be interpreted in favour of a global constitutional culture to some extent. However, the external legal culture in the global realm needs to be analyzed as well, in order to reach more robust information about the content of the global legal culture.

6.2.1.1.2 Global External Legal Culture

"Public's attitude towards law," or "external law" in Friedman's words, is also related to global constitutionalism. This sort of legal culture also concerns why people obey law and public perceptions of the fairness of the legal system. In some cultures, law can be either viewed as a source of order or as corrupt and erratic by the public.[56] At this point, as a pertinent example, constitutionalization of the EU

---

[52] Loizidou v. Turkey, Judgment (Preliminary Objection), 15318/89 (23.03.1995), para. 75, http://hudoc.echr.coe.int/sites/eng/pages/search.aspx?i=001-57920, last visit 01.11.2013. Bosphorus Hava Yolları Turizm ve Ticaret Anonim Şirketi v. Ireland, Judgment (Merits), Grand Chamber, 45036/98 (30.06.2005), http://hudoc.echr.coe.int/sites/eng/pages/search.aspx?i=001-69564, last visit 29.10.2013.

[53] Al-Dulimi and Montana Management Inc. v. Switzerland, 5809/08, Concurring Opinion Of Judge Pinto De Albuquerque, Joined By Judges Hajiyev, Pejchal and Dedov (21.06.2016), para. 8, http://hudoc.echr.coe.int/eng?i=001-164515, last visit 12.03.2017.

[54] Ibid., para. 71.

[55] Prosecutor v. Dusko Tadic a/k/a "Dule," ICTY IT-94-1-AR7, 22.10.1995, para. 28, http://www.icty.org/x/cases/tadic/acdec/en/51002.htm, last visit, 20.03.2012.

[56] Merry, "What is Legal Culture?," 44.

could be discussed, and it could be concluded that "the people of the EU" did not ascribe a "constitutional" character to the EU, due to the rejection of the Treaty establishing a Constitution for Europe by Dutch and French voters in 2005.

In addition to Friedman's categories of internal legal culture and external legal culture, legal mobilization refers to "instances when individuals in various social groups and situations turn to the law for help" and also, "[s]ocial movements that rely on legal discourse and legal strategies."[57] This phenomenon is likely to be helpful in observing to what extent global law and its specific rules are adopted and utilized by the people. Moreover, it can provide important data to understand to what extent different cultures respond to legal issues in the same way. That is to say, in some legal cultures, people tend to go to courts facing a legal matter, as they may be labelled as "overly litigious;" whereas in some other cultures, they prefer utilizing social or religious norms instead of legal instruments. For example, a study concluded that individuals in Thailand increasingly deal with injury cases through religion, instead of relying on law as a response to globalization. As another example, people may see local police helpful, corrupt or indifferent, and this affects their willingness to apply to the police.[58] These are crucial examples to note that law is not understood in the same way in every culture; or to put it differently, cultural differentiation appears as an obstacle for a common legal perception throughout the world.

As mentioned before, different traditions in the interpretation of law are also a crucial point of legal cultures. In this regard, Koch points out that how to create a balancing interpretation approach in global level is quite problematic. In terms of current international law, the Vienna Convention on the Law of Treaties prescribes a strong commitment to text and history, and also "subsequent practice" in Article 31(3)(b).[59] In general, civil law and common law systems share some basic principles, but this is not enough to avoid any tension between legal cultures, as it is difficult to find common grounds with other cultures, such as Islamic, Hindu or indigenous cultures in many cases. Koch also underlines the religious sources of the western law, for instance, role of canon law in the emergence of the civil law system, although they have been secularized to a great extent.[60] The legal system of Thailand has also never been compatible with the Westphalian assumptions that law is a positivist and communitarian construct, on the ground that it has always been based on Buddhist law, except for some specific fields, such as criminal procedure and administrative law.[61] When it comes to Chinese law, it becomes more puzzling. The Chinese business practices, namely *guanxi*, are striking examples regarding the interaction of China with global law. In the Chinese culture, *guanxi*

---

[57] Ibid., 44.

[58] Ibid., 50-51.

[59] Koch, "Global Legal Culture," 47.

[60] Ibid., 48.

[61] Russel Menyhart, "Changing Identities and Changing Law: Possibilities for a Global Legal Culture," *Indiana Journal of Global Legal Studies* 10 (2003): 188.

stands for a "local subculture of connections aimed at facilitating the exchange of favours."[62] *Guanxi* is a special personal relationship between people, a value system of the Chinese society; and it "emphasises the value of interpersonal relatedness, long-term mutual benefit, harmony and obligations, rather than individualism, competition and the maximization of self-interest."[63] In other words, it is a sort of business networking that help businessmen deal with risks and uncertainties in business relationships. Banakar points to its expanding structure that gained a transnational dimension in growing relationships of the Chinese business community with other countries. On the other hand, one salient point about *guanxi* is that it leads to a nepotism in Chinese business life in that it creates a close network that consists of family and personal relations.[64] *Guanxi* is not a formalistic system that is governed by legal instruments as those of western legal cultures; and Banakar argues that this leads to the critiques of westerners, in particular, regarding cronyism, corruption and unreliable banking practices.[65] At this point, some western observers seek western standards or legal practices in Chinese business relationships, advancing the claim that a globalized market requires superiority of the rule of law. Banakar criticizes them on the ground that they neglect the fact "that Chinese business culture is embedded in social organisation and tied up with pre-existing social (family/kin) relations and obligations."[66] In contrast to westerners' expectations, *Guanxi* is a very important part of the southeastern legal culture; and how to adjust it to western centric legal principles that claim universality, remains in the dark. The historical tendency to depict China as a "lawless" society in western norms is a striking point. As a current example of the orientalist views in international law, Ruskola points to the arguments that China's entrance into the WTO will eventually give rise to the rule of law in this country.[67] This is desired by western global actors in particular, as China is an increasing global actor whose relations with western countries are growing, and its compliance with western norms of trading are particularly sought in this context.

Given these facts, which values or rights will be given priority, the relative meanings of values and rights or the dismissive nature of universalism can be a source of tension in the interpretation of global legal issues. As mentioned above, there is no common approach to the tension between universalism and cultural relativism,

---

[62] Reza Banakar, "Who Needs the Classics? - On the Relevance of Classical Legal Sociology for the Study of Current Social and Legal Problems," 2012, http://ssrn.com/abstract=2140775, 26, last visit 03.04.2014.

[63] Ibid., 26.

[64] Ibid.

[65] Ibid., 27.

[66] Ibid., 28. Some scholars argue that *guanxi* is now viewed as secondary to the market imperatives of price and quality by many market actors, yet this does not mean that *guanxi* lost its significance in Chinese business culture. Douglas Guthrie, "The Declining Significance of Guanxi in China's Economic Transition," *The China Quarterly* 154 (1998): 254-282.

[67] Teemu Ruskola, "Legal Orientalism," in *Laws and Societies in Global Contexts: Contemporary Approaches*, ed. Eve Darian-Smith (Cambridge: Cambridge University Press, 2013), 75.

and rights-based approaches need to find solutions for challenges from relativism in many cases, despite them spreading faster during the age of globalization.

Snyder draws attention to the fact that European legal culture can be identified as a relatively single legal culture, in comparison to the diversity of Asian legal cultures. On the other hand, this does not evidently mean that Europe is not home to a great deal of diversity.[68] As to the legal order of the European Union, he opines that the supranational legal order is of a different legal culture than a national legal order. The legal culture of the European Union, in this sense is threefold, consisting of a modern or postmodern legal culture, western legal culture and a specific legal culture for the European integration.[69] The first layer, in a Friedmannian sense, consists of the culture of change, with a special emphasis on rights, entitlements and individualism, and of globalization. The second layer is identified by "personalism, legalism and intellectualism." The third layer refers to the specific governance mechanisms of the EU.[70] Snyder's observation can be affirmed in consideration of the success of legal orders brought about in particular by the EU and the CoE. On the other hand, the European law has seen various legal cultural clashes and tensions between national legal orders and orders of these bodies. Various examples of cases can be mentioned regarding the conflicts between internal and external legal cultures. "The doctrine of the margin of appreciation" of the ECtHR is a good example for the discretion of local agents on local situations that is recognized by the Court. This doctrine basically "entails the ECHR accepting determinations made by national authorities regarding, for instance local situations, and will allow national authorities quite a bit of leeway in determining how to behave."[71] The Handyside ruling of the ECtHR is a noteworthy example on this matter. Very briefly, this case was related to a claim of a publisher in the UK that his right to freedom of expression, which is governed under Article 10 of the European Convention of Human Rights, was violated through the seizure of a schoolbook due to its sexual content. This schoolbook was freely published in many European countries, such as Belgium, Finland, France, the Federal Republic of Germany, Greece, Iceland, Italy, the Netherlands, Norway, Sweden and Switzerland as well as several non-European countries.[72] The Court created a discretion space for local authorities by limiting its scrutiny over the matter instead of asserting that the book in question should not offend the British, if it did not offend other Europeans, such as Danes, the Dutch or Germans.[73] As to the European Union, the ECJ saw many tensions

[68] Francis Snyder, "The Unfinished Constitution of the European Union: Principles, Process and Culture," in *European Constitutionalism Beyond the State*, ed. J.H.H. Weiler and Marlene Wind (Cambridge: Cambridge University Press, 2003), 67.

[69] Ibid., 69.

[70] Ibid., 69-70.

[71] Jan Klabbers, *International Law* (Cambridge: Cambridge University Press, 2013), 114.

[72] Handyside v. United Kingdom, 5493/72, Judgment, 07.12.1976, para. 11, 20-23, http://hudoc.echr.coe.int/eng?i=001-57499#{"itemid":["001-57499"]}.

[73] Klabbers, *International Law*, 115.

with the Member States' courts regarding the scope of its competence. The Solange decisions taken by the European Court of Justice and the German Federal Constitutional Court are noteworthy.[74] These decisions basically reflected a tension between the German Federal Court and the European Court of Justice on the superiority of national constitutional laws in the face of the EU Law. In the first Solange case, the German Federal Court concluded that the EU Law cannot take precedence over fundamental rights protected by the German Basic Law.[75] Despite the fact that the German Federal Court softened its approach in the last case, it has been argued that the Solange cases proved that the European Communities still keep their intergovernmental character that provide Member States to hold the ultimate control over the ECJ.[76]

In addition to these, a very significant tension arises between the character of constitutional law and international law. International law was accused of assimilating multicultural values of society, unlike domestic law. In this regard, international law has always been severely criticized by cultural relativists, on the ground that it lacks a common corpus of law, as it is basically grounded in western values and ideological parochialism.[77] On the other hand, some other scholars, such as Joyner and Dettling are sceptical about this conclusion, since they believe that the failure of international law does not depend on mutually conflictive cultures, but rather it concerns only the will of states based on their interests, which impedes cultural interactions beyond nation states to a certain extent.[78] However, this approach is most likely to be viewed as being too much state-centrist by reducing international law to the will of states. Further, it could be partially accepted, on the ground that an international law that reflects the values beyond the will of states may provide a basis for a culturally engaged, or at least culture-oriented international system.

Nonetheless, one cannot advance the claim that contemporary international law is completely blind to the diversity of legal cultures. As a striking example, in Article 9 of the Statute of the International Court of Justice, it is stated that the UN shall

---

[74] Solange I: Judgment of the Court of 17.12.1970, Internationale Handelsgesellschaft mbH v. Einfuhr- und Vorratsstelle für Getreide und Futtermittel. - Reference for a preliminary ruling: Verwaltungsgericht Frankfurt am Main - Germany. - Case 11-70, http://eur-lex.europa.eu/legal-content/EN/TXT/?uri=CELEX%3A61970CJ0011; Solange II: Judgment of the Court (First Chamber) of 12 April 1984. - Wünsche Handelsgesellschaft GmbH & Co. v Federal Republic of Germany Case 345/82. http://eur-lex.europa.eu/legal-content/EN/TXT/?qid=1451330857112&uri=CELEX:61982CJ0345. Solange III (or Maastricht case): Decision from 12.12.1993, 2 BvR L 134/92 and 2159/92, WW(1993) 3047, cited by Joachim Wieland, "Germany in the European Union - The Maastricht Decision of the Bundesverfassungsgericht," *European Journal of International Law* 5 (1994): 259.

[75] Solange I case.

[76] Koch, "Global Legal Culture," 15.

[77] Christopher C. Joyner and John C. Dettling, "Bridging the Cultural Chasm: Cultural Relativism and The Future of International Law," *California Western International Law Journal* 20 (1989-1990): 303.

[78] Ibid., 307.

adopt a principle taking different legal cultures of the world into account in selecting members of the ICJ. Article 9 reads as follows:

> At every election, the electors shall bear in mind not only that the persons to be elected should individually possess the qualifications required, but also that in the body as a whole the representation of the main forms of civilization and of the principal legal systems of the world should be assured.[79]

In addition, the newly emerging international criminal law has also been deemed as a hybrid mixture of common law and civil law cultures. In this context, the International Criminal Tribunal for the Former Yugoslavia stated that:

> [T]he legal system that applies before this Tribunal is not common law nor civil law. It is a hybrid, and it is a system that applies and develops on its own premises and its own terms.[80]

Also the International Criminal Court states that: "[T]he drafters of the Statute (…) deliberately adopted a hybrid procedure which borrows from different legal cultures and systems."[81] At this point, these articulations give rise to the question of what this cultural hybridity means. First of all, as the ICC points out, it has somewhat to do with the procedures pursued by the court. These procedures concern "technical rules governing the conduct of proceedings and evidence, to the structure of proceedings (such as the role of the parties and judges), to the determination of guilt and appeals" and they are supposed to be the main conflict areas of legal cultures. However, international criminal law also reflects a hybrid culture in terms of substantive law.[82] For example, as seen from the cases regarding sexual offences particularly, elements of crimes concern various national laws as well as different bodies of law, such as human rights law and international humanitarian law.[83] In this respect, international criminal law reflects the Post-Westphalian values and principles, which are deemed to have universal validity and to exist for the collective interests of humanity.[84]

A crucial point in terms of the global legal culture relates to the question of why some states accept jurisdiction of international courts and why some others do not.[85] Powell and Mitchell argue that this has to do with the character of national legal

---

[79] Statute of the International Court of Justice, http://www.icj-cij.org/documents/?p1=4&p2=2, last visit 21.09.2014.

[80] The Prosecutor v. Stanisic and Zupljanin, IT-08-91-T1, 15.10.2009, 1508 (ICTY), cited by Campbell, "Making of Global Legal Culture," 155.

[81] The Prosecutor v. Katanga and Ngudjolo Chui, ICC-01/04-01/072, Reasons for the Oral Decision on the Motion Challenging the Admissibility of the Case, 16 June 2009, 18–19, (ICC), cited by Ibid.

[82] Ibid., 156.

[83] Ibid., 157.

[84] Ibid., 166.

[85] Emilia Justyna Powell and Sara McLaughlin Mitchell, "The International Court of Justice and the World's Three Legal Systems," *The Journal of Politics* 69, no. 2 (2007): 397.

cultures. They also reveal a fact that the ICJ has not become a legitimate and effective conflict manager yet. For example, they focus on the grounds of the fact that civil law countries are most likely to accept the jurisdiction of the ICJ. However, in return, Islamic and common law states have demonstrated more durable commitments than civil law states, "which stem from strong norms of contractual obligation and more precise obligations."[86] They opine that these three different legal systems reflect significant variances between the cultural and historical experiences of states, and they underscore three fundamental features of these systems in order to portray these variances:

> the use of precedents (*stare decisis*) [common law], good faith in contracting (*bona fides*) [civil law], and conditions under which contracts must be fulfilled (*pacta sunt servanda*) [Islamic law].[87]

In this regard, "[f]reedom of contracting and lack of religious principles" make common law and civil law countries relatively free to sign contracts and increase their international commitments compared to the Islamic states.[88] Moreover, the lack of good faith and the compliance principles in common law systems have been viewed as reasons for common law states to be more cautious of international obligations. Contracts are not very much detailed in civil law systems, but overly detailed in common law systems; and it is argued that this can have effects over commitments of legal cultures to international court decisions. On the other hand, with regard to the Islamic legal cultures, Powell and Mitchell argue that once an Islamic state adopts an international commitment, it is expected to be firmly committed to those rules due to the effects of *pacta sund servanda* principle in this legal culture.[89] Powell and Mitchell apply an empirical analysis to these hypotheses regarding the relationship between the acceptance of the jurisdiction of the PCIJ and ICJ and legal systems. The empirical research supports their predictions to a great deal. In this respect, 64.6 % of civil law states accept the compulsory judgement of the PCIJ and ICJ, whereas these rates are 20.9 % for common law states, 6.2 % for Islamic states and 8.3 % for the mixed systems. This research also demonstrates that civil law states are by far leading to other states of other systems in accepting the Court's jurisdiction without reservation. However, this research also indicates that civil law countries are more likely to renege on their commitments regarding rulings, and that common law states are more prone to place reservations to the declaration of the acceptance of the Court in comparison to the other legal cultures.[90]

On the other hand, it is of note that under the current conditions of globalization and migration of laws, legal culture arises as a hybrid phenomenon.[91] This means

---

[86] Ibid., 398.

[87] Ibid., 399 ff.

[88] Ibid., 404.

[89] Ibid., 405.

[90] ibid., 408.

[91] Merry, "What is Legal Culture?," 52.

that it is hard to prove the existence of a purely local legal culture. Various elements of legal systems are imported into other legal systems, and they are reconstituted in a new assemblage, so that they give rise to a hybridity. At this point, Merry gives the example of a local women's court, called *nari adalat,* established in rural India in the 1990s as a result of the long term activities of the Indian women's movement in order to resolve cases about the violence against women and other family conflicts. These courts demonstrated a highly hybrid character: "They operated according to sociocultural principles drawn from the women's movement and human rights as well as local and national law."[92] Members of these courts were not legal professionals, but local women from the rural areas of India. Therefore, they did not have a deep knowledge of international conventions and human rights texts regarding women's rights. Nevertheless, they took and utilized the idea of human rights in their arguments and at the end, "[t]hey translated the language of human rights produced in New York, Geneva, Vienna and Beijing into a set of ideas that made sense locally,"[93] and thereby they achieved to set up a hybrid regime for women's rights to constitute an alternative to defend their rights. This can be considered as a proof of the universal thinking on rights and human dignity as well as "vernacularization" of global legal norms and practices, in Merry's words.

Given its relevance to the global legal culture, the attitude of states towards the international judiciary is also noteworthy. It seems that there has been a stable increase in using international adjudication beginning from the 1950s.[94] On the other hand, the empirical evidence suggests that powerful states mostly refrain from initiating proceedings in international tribunals, and rather less powerful states prefer going to court in case of violation of international law. Zangl places an emphasis on the fact that this occurs due to the restricted access for non-state actors to international courts, and states do not use this way mostly for diplomatic reasons.[95]

In conclusion, Schwöbel argues that in an age of diversity on the international sphere, it is quite unrealistic to seek a common global constitutional culture. In this respect, particularity and diversity preside over unity or commonality in the international legal order.[96] Despite the overwhelming diversity of legal cultures in the global realm, some scholars are quite optimistic in the evolution of a global legal culture through merging of various local legal cultures. In this regard, Koch states that civil and common western legal systems provide a merged order relying on some statistical data:

---

[92] Ibid., 53.

[93] Ibid., 56.

[94] Bernhard Zangl, "Is There an Emerging International Rule of Law?," in *Transformations of the State*, ed. Stephan Leibfried and Michael Zürn (New York: Cambridge University Press, 2005), 78.

[95] Ibid., 79.

[96] Schwöbel, *Global Constitutionalism*, 106.

> At present, 33.8% of the world's jurisdictions, encompassing 55.6% of the world's population, are based upon the civil law model, or civil law systems mixed with others (indigenous or religious legal ideologies, for example). The common law model, along with systems mixed with it, include 28.24% of the jurisdictions, and 14.68% of the world's population. Hence, combined, civil and common law-based legal cultures cover over 70% of the world's population in over 62% of the jurisdictions.[97]

Further, Koch highlights the legal culture constituted by the ICJ and the ICC. These courts have already begun to create a universal legal culture based on rights as well as the global trade.[98] At the same time, they are governed by similar constitutional systems.[99] On the other hand, the rest of the world is still regulated by other legal models, such as Sharia or indigenous legal cultures.

To conclude, under circumstances of fragmentation in international law, the diversity of legal cultures and the disagreement on fundamental rights and values; some scholars explicitly express their pessimism about the birth and maintenance of a global legal culture.[100] In contrast, Friedman clearly argues that there exists an emerging common legal culture of our age. This is somewhat true of the legal systems of developed countries. Globalization leads to a convergence between legal systems, and the most notable commonality of these legal systems is its individualistic structure and the enshrining fundamental human rights.[101] Against this background, it would be misleading to suppose that cultural diversity impedes a global legal culture.[102] A legal culture may exist independently from formal legal regulations, as touched on above, and in some cases a legal culture may exist in a subordinate form. The communitarian approaches to international law from internal culture, and a convergence between legal cultures already mark the existence of a global legal culture, even though it does not constitute the only culture in the transnational context. The matter in question here is whether or not this culture has a constitutional character. To conclude on this, it is also necessary to analyze the global constitutional culture in the form of political culture.

[97] Koch, "Global Legal Culture," 2-3.

[98] Ibid. 9.

[99] Ibid., 19.

[100] Menyhart, "Changing Identities," 180.

[101] Lawrence M. Friedman, "Is There a Modern Legal Culture," *Ratio Juris* 7 (1994): 117-31.

[102] Also Friedman opines that different cultural traditions of the eastern societies do not create obstacles to absorb values of the western societies. According to him, modern legal culture is Western because the West modernized before the rest of the World: "Indeed, most so-called "Western" concepts are not really Western at all, at least not in the sense that they are part of ancient traditions. They are, rather, distinctively modern. After all, the West, too, had its traditional period. There are pre-modern fragments and vestiges of customs, habits, and ways of life that linger on in small, remote corners of Europe, and in rituals and ceremonies." Lawrence M. Friedman, "Borders: On the Emerging Sociology of Transnational Law," *Stanford Journal of International Law* 32 (1996): 84-85.

6.2.1.2 Global Constitutional Culture as a Global Political Culture

Global constitutionalism also appears as an agenda of world politics from time to time. In particular, a demand for a financial global constitution that would have a capacity to preclude further global financial crises and to provide a stable global economic order has been expressed by major politicians as an alternative to current governance instruments in economic globalization.[103] In order to understand to what extent global political culture reflects a constitutional culture, it is necessary to have a look at those who define constitutional culture from a political perspective.

To remind us of Vorländer's definition, constitutional culture fuctions as "a forum in which discourses about political identity take place."[104] In this regard, global constitutionalism can be viewed as an element of global political culture that is a candidate for an emerging distinctive political identity. Münch considers constitution as the latent code of political acts that builds a connection between political decisions and socio-cultural discourses.[105] From this perspective, global constitutionalism can be supposed to be a bridge between the global polity and global socio-cultural discourses. In comparison with the theories that define constitutional culture as a legal culture, these definitions remain more blurred. On the other hand, as they connect constitution with the whole cultural discourse, these theories provide a greater area to place the idea of constitution into.

As mentioned in the first chapter, it is broadly agreed that contemporary international law has been marked by the Post-Westphalian transformation. Globalization is found in the centre of this process as a cultural determinant.[106] The Post-Westphalian era is marked by a number of values ascending in the international legal order, such as universal claims to the rule of law and human rights. These Post-Westphalian values stand at the junction point of constitutional and political themes of the global realm. These values also create a proceeding point for the discourse of global constitutionalism. From the perspective of the cultural paradigm, the issues of legitimacy and constituent power, a consensus for a constitution and a global rule of law in respect to Post-Westphalian values can be discussed.

---

[103] For example, the former British Prime Minister Gordon Brown explicitly articulated this need from his own perspective once in a meeting at Harvard University. Harvard Gazette, September 24, 2010, http://news.harvard.edu/gazette/story/2010/09/gordon-brown%E2%80%99s-prescription/, last visit 12.09.2015.

[104] Vorländer, "What is 'Constitutional Cultures'?," 23.

[105] Richard Münch, *Die Struktur der Moderne: Grundmuster und differentielle Gestaltung des institutionellen Aufbaus der modernen Gesellschaften* (Frankfurt am Main: Suhrkamp, 1984), 311.

[106] Roland Robertson, "Mapping the Global Condition: Globalization as the Central Concept," in *Global Culture: Nationalism, Globalization and Modernity, A Theory, Culture & Society*, ed. Mike Featherstone, (London: Sage Publications, 1990), 15-30.

6.2.1.2.1 Post-Westphalian Values and Consensus

Is there a global political culture to discuss within the framework of a global constitutional culture? If the determinant values of current international law are Post-Westhalian values, are they suitable for generating a global constitutional culture? To put it differently, could they be read as constitutional values for the global realm, as indicators of a global consensus? On the other hand, to what degree is consensus the right word for an agreement on the constitutional issues?

In the context of the idea of a global constitution, to begin with Cass Sunstein's question would be helpful: "[h]ow is constitutionalism possible, when people disagree on so many questions about what is good and what is right?"[107] This question indeed becomes more pressing when it comes to the global realm, a domain reflecting vast diversities regarding cultures.

The beginning of the modern era saw a number of developments, strictly connected to the rise of nation states. Very briefly, these developments were the establishment of a Westphalian order of states, the elimination of religion as a major ground of political conflicts as of the end of the Thirty Years' War, the rise of capitalism, the rise of modern science, and political liberties through great revolutions.[108] This new structure and its relational rationality engraved its own political culture, which was contoured by borders of nation states. This structure underwent serious transformations, beginning from the aftermath of the catastrophic wars of the twentieth century, and through increased globalization of the twentieth century and the end of the Cold War. As mentioned earlier, during the globalization process, the dominant position of nation states in determining framework of cultures disappeared, and a new world of network communications has arisen. Under circumstances of this postnational, postindustrial and postmodern era, culture is supposed to be only continental or global; in other words, it is not tied to any place or period.[109] In this framework, international law is more likely to be viewed as a bearer of global culture, as the culture of international organizations appear as "a social agency, a driving force of political change and continuity," rather than a macrostructure that overlays other social agencies.[110] However, the idea that culture exists only globally has been contested in terms of political cultures in local meanings. In other words, globalization has not received the same response from every country and every state, but instead, varied responses from country to country. This issue has been discussed in various terms by academic scholars.

---

[107] Cass Sunstein, "Incompletely Theorized Agreements in Constitutional Law" (Public Law and Legal Theory Working Paper no. 147, 2007, http://chicagounbound.uchicago.edu/cgi/viewcontent.cgi?article=1149&context=public_law_and_legal_theory), 1, last visit 11.07.2015.

[108] Daniel J. Elazar, "Globalization Meets the World's Political Cultures," Jerusalem Center for Public Affairs, http://www.jcpa.org/dje/articles3/polcult.htm), last visit 06.10.2015.

[109] Smith, "Towards A Global Culture?," 175.

[110] Antonia Zervaki, *Resetting the Political Cultural Agenda: From Polis to International Organization* (Cham: Springer, 2014), 23.

One striking point is the diverse contents of political cultures in national and regional basis.[111] Elazar analyzes political cultures of the world in terms of five sets of orientation. These are the orientation to political organization, polity, civil society, political action and political economy. For example, Elazar identifies five basic political cultural orientations to structure the civil society: civic (republican, e.g. Canada and New Zealand), corporatist (e.g. Austria and Sweden), statist (e.g. France), subject (e.g. Saudi Arabia and Gulf states), and tribal (premodern).[112] On the other hand, regional differences in the orientation to polity are also striking. For example, Elazar argues that North American political culture is marked by the "participatory and populist" orientation to polity, while Northern and Southern Europe and Southern Asia are marked by "participatory and elitist," Eastern Europe, Middle East and North Africa are marked by "leader oriented and populist," East Asia and Africa are marked by "elitist," and Latin America is marked by "Elitist, Traditional and Populist" orientations to polity. The orientation to political economy also demonstrates a broad range of diversity. Elazar depicts common European, Latin American and South Asian orientation to political economy as "state involved and common market," while he depicts North American as "commonwealth, market," Middle East, North Africa and East Asia as "state controlled, corporatist," and Africa as "state involved."[113]

Apart from diverse orientations in political cultures, different values conveyed by different cultures form a greater part of this debate. As mentioned above, the debate on universal claims of human rights come to the fore in this context. The earlier imperial liberals assumed that modern European cultures were the "superior cultural bases" for individual rights and freedoms. This superiority was a result of modernism, and it provided the liberal governments with the authority to destruct the diversity of primitive cultures.[114] The relativist and universalist views still debate on the existence of an objective ground to justify rights. At this point, Santos argues that the universal claim for human rights implies a "globalized localism," which means the globalization of western local cultures in a hegemonic way.[115] He instead suggests "human dignity" as a common category, which would be welcomed by every culture.[116] In this regard, Santos advocates the idea that there is no room for justifying objective and universal rights that can be adopted by all cultures. According to him, human rights are a sort of "Esperanto" which can hardly become the daily language of human dignity across the globe.[117] Santos demonstrates sources of the

---

[111] Elazar, "Globalization."

[112] Ibid.

[113] Ibid.

[114] James Tully, *Strange Multiplicity: Constitutionalism in an Age of Diversity* (Cambridge: Cambridge University Press, 2007), 189.

[115] Boaventura de Sousa Santos, "Towards a Multicultural Conception of Human Rights," in *Global Culture: Nationalism, Globalization and Modernity, A Theory, Culture & Society*, ed. Mike Featherstone (London: Sage Publications, 1990), 219.

[116] Ibid., 212.

[117] Ibid., 227.

concept of human dignity in various cultures including oriental cultures, yet whether an absolute commonality would be found out between all cultures remains doubtful. In addition, it is not clear that replacing dignity with rights could appease this debate. The meaning of dignity in western cultures could be taken in a Kantian manner as "man's 'ability to act as a general legislator' in moral *and* legal matters alike."[118] The "other" is of a special meaning in this sort of understanding of dignity, and this is also determinative on social and cultural inclusiveness through the public autonomies and a public democracy.[119] From this perspective, dignity still remains a relative political concept, and it seems a consensus can also hardly be achieved on its meaning.

According to Tully, a common point for the values of a contemporary constitutional culture could be found, if a constitution nourishes the self-respect of components of a constitutional order. This can be ensured through the protection of cultural diversity in a society. He argues this very explicitly as:

> If a liberal constitution is to provide the basis for its most important values of freedom and autonomy, it thus must protect the cultures of its members and engender the public attitute of mutual respect for cultural diversity that individual self respect requires. To put this differently, the primary good of self respect requires that popular sovereignty is conceived as an intercultural dialogue. Various cultures of the society need to be recognised in public institutiuons histories and symbols in order to nourish mutual cultural awareness and respect.[120]

Further, he advances the claim that if a contemporary constitution is to be culturally neutral, it should not privilege one culture and exclude the others, but should mutually recognize all of them. In addition, according to Tully, a culture-blind constitutionalism, or as he names it, the "Esperanto Constitutionalism," which is usually advocated by liberal theories, is disillusionary, as these theories hide the fact of imperialism embedded in liberal constitutionalism.[121] He gives the example of the Canadian Charter of Rights and Freedoms of 1981. According to him, this document ignores the cultural diversity of the society, and rather it works for disunity of the society. Instead, a just form of constitution must meet the need for the mutual recognition of different cultures of its citizens.[122]

These debates also have to do with the issue of consensus for a constitutional polity in diverse societies. As a matter of fact, for many scholars who deal with the diversity problem in a constitutional order, "consensus" is mostly considered as a secondary term to a great extent. Evidently, the existence of consensus in a political system can hardly be determined. Instead of this ambiguous term, Franklin

---

[118] Hauke Brunkhorst, "The Co-evolution of Cosmopolitan and National Statehood – Preliminary Theoretical Considerations on the Historical Evolution of Constitutionalism," *Cooperation and Conflict* 47, no. 2 (2012): 192.

[119] Ibid., 192.

[120] Tully, *Strange Multiplicity*, 190.

[121] Ibid., 7.

[122] Ibid., 7-8.

and Baun argue that tolerance and trust are to be regarded as central concepts of a collective political culture:

> A societal consensus must embrace an "agreement to disagree" based on the assumptions that other citizens have a right to different views and that the political process is a legitimate forum for disputes resulting therefrom. For any procedural structure to endure, it is important that when decisions are made through the appropriate process, citizens, even losers in the political game, abide by the outcome.[123]

Furthermore, they argue that building an institutional structure is not sufficient to generate a self-sustaining democracy, which should normally be the target of a constitutional system. Above all, institutional bodies and political culture must be compatible with each other in order to achieve this.[124] In a similar vein, referring to Russel Hardin, Wenzel argues that constitutionalism requires "relatively wide agreement on core issues," as it is a coordination mechanism.[125]

As mentioned before, the modern constitutional theories consider the agreement reached in dialogue foundational and universal.[126] However, this is not true of contemporary constitutionalism, and indeed it reflects a disillusion. In culturally divided societies, constitutional communication between diverse groups does not need to trigger common universal conclusions. While analyzing constitutional issues between Aboriginal groups and common law systems, James Tully argues this as follows:

> Also, the aim of negotiations over cultural recognition is not to reach agreement on universal principles and institutions, but to bring negotiators to recognise their differences and similarities, so that they can reach agreement on a form of association that accommodates their differences in appropriate institutions and their similarities in shared institutions.[127]

Tully believes that in a "multiverse" of constitutionalism, universality is a misleading concept. As a result, the concept of "reaching agreement" is fairly different from modern constitutionalism.

On the other hand, this idea can be analyzed in a different way by considering the opinions of Cass Sunstein on the role of the incompletely theorized agreements amidst sharp disagreements in the emergence of constitutionalism. Incompletely theorized agreements are the "agreements on abstracts formulations (freedom of speech, equality under the law)" and the "agreements on particular doctrines and practices." Sunstein deems these agreements to be crucial for making constitutions

---

[123] Daniel P. Franklin and Michael J. Baun, "Introduction," in *Political Culture and Constitutionalism: A Comparative Approach*, ed. Daniel Franklin and Michael Baun (Armonk: M.E. Sharpe, 1995), 6-7.

[124] Ibid., 9.

[125] Nikolai Wenzel, "From Contract to Mental Model: Constitutional Culture as a Fact of the Social Sciences," *Review of Austrian Economy* 23 (2010): 58.

[126] Tully, *Strange Multiplicity*, 135.

[127] Ibid., 131.

possible in societies where diverse cultures clash and cannot concur on many fundamental issues.[128] These incompletely theorized agreements make law-making possible. Further, they promote stability and reduce the costs of disagreement in a society. In this regard, people may be attracted by various factors when agreeing on a rule or principle, but Sunstein states that "what ultimately accounts for the outcome, in terms of a full-scale theory of the right or the good, is left unexplained."[129] The common behaviour of agreements of ordinary people about constitutional rules is in reality different from what consensus theories prescribe. People and groups only rarely accept a general theory and its far-reaching consequences:

> Thus we often have an incompletely theorized agreement on a general principle—incompletely theorized in the sense that people who accept the principle need not agree on what it entails in particular cases.[130]

Sunstein does not reject the weight of consensus in achievement of a constitution, but he draws attention to the fact that a just constitution is more important than an unjust constitution that is agreed on by everyone.[131] At this point, incompletely theorized agreements are acceptable, provided that they do not conceal injustice. In this respect, as long as a constitution leads to fair outputs, it could also comply with Tully's arguments for a legitimate constitution. However, the main dimensions of the ideas of Tully and Sunstein should be distinguished in some way. Sunstein does not give attention to under what societal conditions a constitution is fair or not. He only mentions a just constitution that reflects equilibrium between agreements. For Tully this seems impossible. He rather pursues a moral driven approach, and argues that there is not much chance to depict modern constitution as fair due to the structural and historical grounds, as mentioned above.

Overall, a consensus on the Post-Westphalian values cannot be sought in a moral way, as Santos argues, on the ground that they rely merely on western values that spill over towards the rest of the world. However, as contemporary works on consensus in the constitutional orders of diverse societies demonstrate, this cannot be viewed as a core issue of a consensus for a constitution. A consensus does not always rely on moral-based convictions. The abstraction level of constitutional

[128] Sunstein, "Incompletely Theorized Agreements," 1.

[129] Ibid., 3. In a similar vein, Hanna Lerner argues that in cases of deep political and cultural disagrements, constitutions can potentially undermine political stability and democratisation. The incrementalist strategies adopted in the constitution making processes of the deeply divided societies, such as Ireland, Israel and India, drafters of constitutions left the resolution of contentious foundational problems to the political domain by refraining from any clear solution and a clear language for these problems in the constitutions. However, it is also noteworthy that, according to Lerner the success of such an incrementalist approach in these countries hinge on the strong democratic organisations and judicial mechanisms. Hanna Lerner, "Constitution-writing in Deeply Divided Societies: The Incrementalist Approach," *Nations and Nationalism* 16, no. 1 (2010): 68, 84.

[130] Ibid., 10.

[131] Ibid., 20.

values may be the fundamental point for a constitution to survive. In other words, a constitution may be achieved through "incompletely theorized agreements," in a society. Such agreements could also be viewed as the ground for the maintainability of international law. Further, as touched upon above, a consensus does not provide a constitution with legitimacy at all times.

6.2.1.2.2 Global Constitutional Culture and Legitimacy

With regard to transformations in the global political culture, it is also necessary to be reminded of contemporary transformations in the political components of constitution. This concerns mainly a change in the legitimacy mechanism of constitutions on account of the transformation in global political culture through transnational political and legal mechanisms. As mentioned in the third chapter, the classical constitutional theory relies on the idea that the constitutional foundations are fundamentally based on the will of the people, or more specifically the constituent power. However, in consideration of globalization and transnationalization in the contemporary society, this idea can no longer be advocated. The contemporary society has seen a shift in constitutional foundations as a consequence of various developments that were partially mentioned above, and this shift mainly occurred through the transformation of constituent power into "rights."[132] First of all, in parallel with the idea that the formation of national laws only occurred once in the historical context, constituent power was a concept produced by modern societies so as to stabilize the distinctive modern political formation, and it was an outcome of the process of functional differentiation in the modern society.[133] This foundational ground also provided the states with an effective power to consolidate their legislative institutions against the former traditional forces or powers.[134] Further, modern political systems were able to abstract and differentiate their power from local and private power milieux, the former, fragmented holders of the power.[135] This illuminates the historical background of the concept of constituent power. However, increasing functional differentiation and internalism of functional realms of the global society led to the rise of rights that have gradually supplanted constituent power. Once rights, which were formerly depositories of constituted power, have replaced the constituent power; that is to say, once they became the essential reference for legitimacy in constitutional matters, constituent power and constituted power became fused concepts.[136] Additionally, by virtue of this fact, the concept of constituent power now itself does not have the sufficient capacity to produce legitimacy for

[132] Chris Thornhill, "Rights and Constituent Power in the Global Constitution," *International Journal of Law in Context* 10 (2014): 357-396.

[133] Ibid., 359.

[134] Ibid., 361.

[135] Ibid., 386.

[136] Ibid., 363.

political institutions. This shift also concerns the actors of constitutionalization and legitimization processes. The most prominent actor of this process has become the judiciary, which implement primary laws either in global or national levels, and they are now in the position of a legitimizing power that replaced the conventional actors.[137] As is seen from the decisions below, courts play the most crucial role in interpreting and guarding rights.[138] As Friedman argues, the increasing power of courts, in particular through transnational law, was not actually expected by the classical socio-legal scholarship.[139] Therefore, the increasing impacts of litigation law are to be seen as relatively new for socio-legal studies. On the other hand, judicial bodies – particularly at transnational level- which rely on a pluralist legal order rather than a public authority, carry out the function as founders and legitimizers of a constitutional order, where they constitute the centre of a centre-periphery system.[140] According to Thornhill, this resembles the early modernity's juridical conditions which were demolished by the rise of the constituent power as an external factor for legitimization; and now similarly, contemporary judicial bodies "apply internally authorized norms as ground rules for legal validity."[141] Moreover, from an analogical view, having replaced the constituent power, rights became the source of legitimacy, and thereby enabled the contemporary political system to abstract the power in a post-national way.[142]

As mentioned in the first chapter, rights and individuals stand at the core of the Post-Westphalian change. As such, rights arise as common values of both Post-Westphalian order and contemporary constitutionalism. As to the global constitutionalism discourse, having replaced historical functions of constitutent powers, rights could be portrayed as constituent powers of a global constitutionalization. As mentioned under Sect. 3.2.2.1 above, emerging transnational law as bearer of rights, which are now deemed to be new constituent powers, provides a basis for this. Rights appear as the intersection zone of domestic and global constitutional cultures. However, to what extent rights dominate global law has to do with the question of whether or not a global rule of law is emerging.

6.2.1.2.3 A Global Rule of Law?

Beyond any doubt, the concept of rule of law currently appears as a worldwide concept and has a universal claim as such in the case of human rights. In this regard, at the United Nations World Summit of 2005, Member States articulated the need for

---

[137] Ibid., 365.

[138] Friedman, "Borders," 82.

[139] Ibid., 81.

[140] Andreas Fischer-Lescano, "Die Emergenz der Globalverfassung," *Zeitschrift für ausländisches öffentliches Recht und Völkerrecht* 63, no. 3 (2003): 717-760

[141] Thornhill, "Rights and Constituent Power," 369.

[142] Ibid., 386.

"universal adherence to and implementation of the rule of law at both the national and international levels," and they declared their commitment to "an international order based on the rule of law and international law."[143] Further, the rule of law is found in many other international conventions or charters, in particular regarding human rights. For example, in the Preamble of the Universal Declaration of Human Rights, it is stated that,

> [w]hereas it is essential, if man is not to be compelled to have recourse, as a last resort, to rebellion against tyranny and oppression, that human rights should be protected by the rule of law (…).[144]

In addition, the Preamble of the European Convention of Human Rights states that the Member States agreed on this convention,

> [b]eing resolved, as the governments of European countries which are likeminded and have a common heritage of political traditions, ideals, freedom and the rule of law, to take the first steps for the collective enforcement of certain of the rights stated in the Universal Declaration (…).[145]

Beyond its discursive form, rule of law has also been fairly influential in the construction of transnational political cultures through a liberal democratic perspective; as Helfer and Slaughter states: "The European experience of supranational adjudication is the experience of two supranational tribunals operating within a community of liberal democracies with strong domestic commitments to the rule of law."[146] Evidently the rise of the principle of rule of law in a global context has been a very serious factor in the development of the idea of global constitutionalism.

While the rule of law looks a very robust universal principle, as seen from these international documents; Chesterman draws attention to a dissensus on its meaning:

> on the right, Friedrich Hayek placed it at the heart of development policy; on the left, the Marxist historian E.P. Thompson called it an "unqualified human good." It is a term endorsed by both the World Social Forum and the World Bank.[147]

That is to say, rule of law is still a contested term, despite its wide use in legal texts.

---

[143] Simon Chesterman, "An International Rule of Law?," *The American Journal of Comparative Law* 56, no. 2 (2008): 332.

[144] The Universal Declaration of Human Rights, 1948, http://www.un.org/en/universal-declaration-human-rights/, last visit 02.09.2015.

[145] The European Convention for the Protection of Human Rights and Fundamental Freedoms, Rome, 1950, http://www.echr.coe.int/Documents/Convention_ENG.pdf, last visit 02.09.2015.

[146] Laurence R. Helfer and Anne-Marie Slaughter, "Toward a Theory of Effective Supranational Adjudication," *Yale Law Journal* 107 (1997): 331.

[147] Chesterman, "An International Rule of Law?," 332.

It is also of note that rule of law gained slightly different meanings in different national constitutional cultures. The concepts "Rule of Law," "Rechtstaat," "Etat de droit" and "Stato di diritto" point to different practices regarding the superiority of law.[148] In England, which is viewed as "the bastion of the rule of law," Dicey defined the rule of law in the nineteenth century as "the absolute supremacy or predominance of regular law as opposed to the influence of arbitrary power, and [it] excludes be punished for nothing else."[149] Further, according to Dicey, rule of law also has to do with the principle of equality before law and parliamentary sovereignty.[150] On the other hand, the German concept of "Rechtstaat" rather emphasizes on the nature of the state than the judicial process, as it is chiefly based on three elements: self-limitation of state, the theory of subjective rights and the theory of primacy of law.[151] Long after the rise of German "Rechtstaat," French constitutional doctrine developed the "Etat de droit," which means,

> the State equipped with the legal means to ensure that the individuals would be in a position to oppose the will of the parliamentary legislator acting in breach of fundamental rights.[152]

That is to say, the rule of law evolved into different contents in these countries that were shaped by three constitutional cultures. Furthermore, it has also been observed that these understandings of the rule of law can change over time, since constitutional cultures are changeable phenomena. As a striking example, Lord Tom Bingham's recent definition of rule of law can be taken into consideration, when compared with Dicey's classical definition. Lord Bingham defines the rule of law as,

> that all persons and authorities within the state, whether public or private, should be bound by and entitled to the benefit of law publicly made, taking effect (generally) in the future and publicly administered in the courts.[153]

As seen, the recent transformations in the political constitutionalism of Britain through the Human Rights Act can be traced in this definition, while Dicey's definition of the rule of law reflects a pure form of political constitutionalism. Overall, different constitutional practices spawned different meanings of rule of law, and as

---

[148] David Nelken, "Using the Concept of Legal Culture" (UC Berkeley, Papers Presented in the Center for the Study of Law and Society Bag Lunch Speaker Series, 2004, http://escholarship.org/uc/item/7dk1j7hm) last visit 09.05.2013. Ricardo Gosalbo-Bono, "The Significance of the Rule of Law and Its Implications for the European Union and the United States," *University of Pittsburgh Law Review* 72 (2010): 240 ff. Chesterman, "An International Rule of Law?," 336.

[149] Gosalbo-Bono, "Significance of the Rule of Law," 253.

[150] Ibid., 254.

[151] Ibid., 241-242.

[152] Ibid., 249.

[153] Lord Bingham, "The Rule of Law," *Cambridge Law Journal* 66 (2007): 67, cited by Ibid., 259.

such it remained a contested concept in the meantime.[154] Nevertheless, Chesterman argues that a core definition of rule of law would be possible by underlining three elements of the concept. Firstly, the state cannot be exercised arbitrarily; secondly, the law must also apply to the sovereign and the state; and finally the law must apply to everybody equally.[155]

As to the global realm, a number of developments can be deemed to be complying with this core definition of the rule of law. As a result of the developments in international criminal law, the abolition of the Head of State immunity in terms of some specific crimes, and the consolidation of effective remedies in transnational courts epitomize this.[156] The concept of rule of law has also been used in various contexts at the global level. One of these is "good governance" in the development discourse, where rule of law has in general been referred along with the principles of participation, accountability and transparency.[157]

The relevance of rule of law in terms of international relations has so far been unclear, on the ground that there is no sovereign power in the international order, unlike in domestic orders.[158] In this regard, according to Chesterman, there exist three possibilities for thinking of rule of law in the global context. The first one is the application of the rule of law to relations between states and the international institutions. Secondly, it can refer to the primacy of international law over national law, particularly in terms of human rights. As a third possibility, it means the emergence of a normative regime that is capable of protecting individuals without the mediation of any domestic legal arrangements.[159]

Some scholars point to an emerging rule of law in some specific fields of international law, such as the international trade, security, labour and environmental law.[160] From this perspective, this also leads to a paradigm shift and the reconception of rule of law. In this sense, the new paradigm shifts away from states and associates international law with individuals and peoples.[161] For example, from this point of view, the establishment of international regimes with independent enforcement instruments reflects the reconceptualization of the rule of law in international law. This mounted to the expansion of legalism, which was observed in the field of international criminal justice and human rights most strikingly.[162] According to those who consider rule of law as a new paradigm in the international realm, rule

[154] Chesterman, "An International Rule of Law?," 340.

[155] Ibid., 342.

[156] Ibid., 345.

[157] Ibid., 347. Winston P. Nagan and Garry Jacobs, "New Paradigm for Global Rule of Law," *Cadmus* 1, no.4 (2012): 142.

[158] Chesterman, "An International Rule of Law?," 350.

[159] Ibid., 355.

[160] Zangl, "Emerging International Rule of Law?," 73-91.

[161] Rutti G. Teitel, "Humanity's Law: Rule of Law for the New Global Politics," *Cornell International Law Journal* 35, no. 2 (2002): 362.

[162] Ibid., 364-368.

of law reflects an output of the interaction between law and globalization. On the other hand, on normative basis there are also some indications that a rule of law is emerging, in view of the international norms regarding freedom, non-discrimination and *"obligations erga omnes."*[163] According to Petersmann, the WTO epitomizes an international organization in which rule of law has been ensured to a great deal, as this organization provides significant guarantees for transnational freedom and non-discrimination as well as a quasi-judicial, mandatory dispute settlement system.[164] In this regard, he enumerates the important aspects of judicialization in the WTO, as a major contribution to the rule of law in international law:

> compulsory jurisdiction of the WTO Dispute Settlement Body, court-like procedures and stringent time limits for the conclusion of the panel procedures within 6 to 9 months, explicit recognition of the "right to a panel" (Article 6) and of subsequent access to the standing Appellate Body composed of independent judges, automatic and speedy adoption of panel and Appellate Body reports by the Dispute Settlement Body, "expeditious arbitration within the WTO as an alternative means of dispute settlement," multilateral surveillance procedures to ensure prompt compliance with dispute settlement rulings and recommendations, procedures for agreed compensation or authorized retaliation as temporary measures pending the withdrawal of illegal measures and the implementation of dispute settlement findings, obligations to have recourse to, and abide by, the DSU when Members seek redress of a violation or impairment of WTO law, and to refrain from international law remedies inconsistent with the DSU, a large number of requirements to make available judicial, arbitral or administrative tribunals and independent review procedures at the *domestic* level.[165]

However, the compulsory third-party adjudication and appellate review are still exceptional in many regional and worldwide international organizations, other than the EU and the WTO.[166] In addition to this, with regard to other international organizations, which are in particular subject to the debates of global constitutionalization -for example the UN-, whether or not they are bound by human rights treaties is doubtful. This issue was discussed in a number of cases. For example, in the famous Yusuf case, the European Court of First Instance declared that UN Security Council decisions can be restrained only by *jus cogens* norms, by referring to Article 103 of the UN Charter.[167] In addition, the lack of a constitutional court for the UN may cause confusion over the interpretation of the power of organs of the UN, as this

---

[163] Ernst-Ulrich Petersmann, "How to Promote the International Rule of Law? Contributions by the World Trade Organization Appellate Review System," *Journal of International Economic Law* 1 (1998): 31.

[164] Ibid., 31.

[165] Ibid., 35. Emphasis belongs to the original text.

[166] Ibid., 33.

[167] Ahmed Ali Yusuf and Al Barakaat International Foundation v. Council of the European Union and Commission of the European Communities, Court of First Instance of the European Communities, T-306/01, para. 277, 21.09.2005, cited by Chesterman, "An International Rule of Law?," 352.

is generally done by these organs themselves.[168] Further, as equality before law is a part of the core concept of rule of law, even though the UN Charter Article 2(1) states that the UN is based on the sovereign equality of members, current structure and powers of the Security Council are to be considered great obstacles against exercising this equality.[169] Apart from the veto power of the permanent members and the fact that powerful states do not hesitate to use it; the major problem of the Security Council is that it cannot be activated without invoking powerful states, most notably USA.[170] In addition, the independence of the Security Council is still contested as its decisions are mostly shaped by political motivations.[171] Similar problems are also found in the operation of the ICJ. Compared with the WTO Dispute Settlement System, the ICJ is a less developed judicial mechanism. This is because it requires a special agreement among the parties of a dispute, instead of providing a compulsory jurisdiction; its rulings are not subject to an appeal review; and it also is more state-centred as it does not allow complaints of non-state actors.[172] Given these features, to what extent the UN system is based on rule of law remains in the dark. On the other hand, rule of law has been referred in some further international documents too. In Article 9 of the Millennium Declaration, it is stated that Member States resolve,

> [t]o strengthen respect for the rule of law in international as in national affairs and, in particular, to ensure compliance by Member States with the decisions of the International Court of Justice, in compliance with the Charter of the United Nations, in cases to which they are parties.[173]

It has been argued that these kinds of "cautious endorsements" reflect that international law is of a primitive nature as a legal system, although they intend to conceal this truth.[174] On the other hand, judicialization in the international legal order through the construction of a judicial dispute settlement system under the WTO, and the establishment of the International Criminal Court and the International Tribunal for the Law of the Sea were viewed as positive developments towards an international rule of law, although traditional realist views consistently deny this by referring to the power imbalance in favour of big states.[175] The key point of this development in terms of rule of law was that courts became increasingly politically independent and more accessible, and they relied increasingly on the compulsory

---

[168] Ibid., 353.

[169] Chesterman, "An International Rule of Law?," 354.

[170] Zangl, "Emerging International Rule of Law?," 83.

[171] Ibid., 77.

[172] Petersmann, "How to Promote," 35.

[173] Millennium Declaration, Resolution adopted by the General Assembly173 55/2, U.N. Doc. A/RES/55/2, 2000, http://www.un.org/millennium/declaration/ares552e.htm, last visit 12.10.2015.

[174] Chesterman, "An International Rule of Law?," 357.

[175] Zangl, "Emerging International Rule of Law?," 73-74.

jurisdiction.[176] However, as there is no state like body in the international legal order to impose sanctions, the ignorance of court rulings is also another notable problem regarding rule of law. For example, the ignorance of the UN Security Council resolutions, especially regarding severe wars, such as Bosnia, Somalia and Kosovo, led to serious doubts about the efficiency of this body.[177] On the other hand, Zangl highlights the increasing rates of compliance with international rulings over time, particularly by powerful states.[178]

It seems that the international legal order has not yet developed a rule of law in real terms, unlike in the domestic level. According to Petersmann, although national legal systems are currently less separated than the international realm due to the developments in global law, they still focus very much into the "national rule of law" and neglect any contributions for improving the international rule of law.In this regard, the major problem is that nation states neglect providing sufficient constitutional, legislative and judicial restraints on foreign policy powers.[179] Against this background, he points to the importance of more effective mandatory dispute settlement mechanisms in the international realm. He holds up the WTO Dispute Settlement system as a good example for other international judicial mechanisms.[180]

Nevertheless, it is of note that rule of law can be found as an emerging component value of global, legal and political culture. As to the global constitutionalism debate, it has not established itself very well yet in terms of the structural features of international organizations, and also in terms of the relations between other elements of global law and these organizations. In this respect, it could be set forth that rule of law still exists as a rival concept to the arbitrary actions of states stemming from sovereignty in the global political culture; and therefore it has not been put into practice precisely.[181]

6.2.2 Global Constitutionalism and Constitutional Culture

As mentioned in this text at some points, referring to the ideas of James Tully; modern constitutions fell short of responding to the needs of diverse societies, and instead they enhanced the inequalities and dismissive traits of modern polities.[182] From this perspective, modern constitution suffers from a very serious legitimation

[176] For example, compulsory jurisdictions of the WTO Dispute Settlement Body and the UN Security Council. However a contradictory point is the veto power of five permanent powers of the Security Council. Ibid., 76.

[177] Ibid., 87.

[178] Ibid., 86.

[179] Petersmann, "How to Promote," 28-30.

[180] Ibid., 47.

[181] Zangl, "Emerging International Rule of Law?"

[182] Tully, *Strange Multiplicity*.

problem. Therefore, it cannot be viewed as a desirable object for international law. If constitutionalism should be reconstructed in terms of the needs of the global realm, this point needs to be taken into consideration in the first place. However, the global constitutionalism discourse runs mostly without questioning the desirability of the concept of modern constitution for such a diverse realm.

In consideration of all these facts touched upon in this chapter, it could be argued that globalization has not achieved a globalized polity and a globalized legal system yet. However, when it comes to the concept of culture, speaking of the achievement of constitutions does not make much sense. That is to say, whether or not a phenomenon like constitution has been achieved, does not affect the existence of cultures. Culture does not exist only in supreme and dominant forms, as it can exist in the form of subcultures, culture of opponent movements, or culture of minorities. In this regard, the absence of a constitution cannot be an evidence of the absence of a constitutional culture. As seen above, a constitutional culture was in progress in the high medieval era in spite of the lack of any formal constitutional developments. It could also be stated that constitutional culture exists in the global realm, and it is in progress. Given the examples above, constitutional culture can be considered a component of diverse cultural factors of the global political and legal orders. This is evident when considering the international design of human rights, the emerging international rule of law and the emerging transnational legal cultures with constitutional themes. Basically the new legal and political culture embedded in these institutional practices reflects the Post-Westphalian values. This fact also gives rise to an intersection of constitutional values and the Post-Westphalian values. Such a perspective also clarifies what Oeter states: "we are facing a constitutional question in the global realm today, without having clear-cut answers."[183]

The major consequence of this inquiry appears to be that the global realm is of a constitutional culture; although it is still underdeveloped, and lacks a formal basis. To sum up, as elucidated in this chapter, a constitutional legal culture can be identified through a number of rulings of international tribunals. A convergence of legal cultures to a certain extent within certain legal traditions, particularly western, can be observed; although there is still a strong resistance from some other legal cultures. In terms of the political aspects of a constitutional culture, some specific categories regarding constitutional law have already been transferred to the international legal order. The international guarantees of fundamental rights, and the international will towards a global rule of law epitomize this. In addition, as one of the major components of constitutional law, constituent power has already been transformed into rights, which basically carry out functions through transnational law in the contemporary world. These constitutional facts can now be observed within the framework of global law.

---

[183] Stefan Oeter, "Regime Collisions from a Perspective of Global Constitutionalism," in *Contested Regime Collisions: Norm Fragmentation in World Society*, ed. Kerstin Blome et al. (Cambridge: Cambridge University Press, 2016), 22.

This gives rise to an interesting situation. All these facts imply that the global legal order has a constitutional culture, although there is no formal constitution in this realm. How could this situation be explained?

As Ferejohn et al. argues, when referring to contemporary constitutionalism, a constitutional culture does not imply a coherence of ideas and values. Different interpretive ideologies and perspectives are indeed viewed as prerequisites of well-being of a constitutional culture. In this regard, constitutional culture rather appears to indicate diverse meanings and uncertainties of a constitution.[184] Therefore, when examining a constitutional culture, the target is not to find out a set of coherent ideas or values. Further, global or transnational constitutional issues can emerge in different contexts, and therefore their values and other cultural norms can also be different from national constitutions. For example, when it comes to the EU constitutionalism, in particular to the failed constitution of the EU; several specific observations come to the fore in this context. First of all, EU constitutionalism has some particular features that are not observed in national constitutional orders. The EU lacks a sufficient common *ethnos* and *demos* since the institutional structure hinders their emergence.[185] Therefore, as commonly argued, the EU constitutional culture lacks cultural elements regarding *demos* and *ethnos*, such as a consensus or an agreement on a constitutional polity.

The contemporary global legal and political culture is based on the Post-Westphalian values. The Post-Westphalian values envisage the universality of some specific phenomena, such as human rights, rule of law and free trade. This means that, the Post-Westphalian values comply with the values produced by contemporary liberal democratic constitutionalism. However, this culture does not take the form of an overarching culture over global legal and political culture. To make this clear, some formidable points regarding global constitutionalism need to be stressed. First of all, the Post-Westphalian values of global law cannot be applied to every legal culture of the world. There exist some legal cultures, where law is identified differently from the western understanding of law. That is to say, an alleged global constitutional culture can hardly prove to be "global." On the other hand, the question of "how global global constitutionalism is" is not very fruitful in this context. Instead, it should be underlined that the focus here is on the international community that adopts values of the Post-Westphalian world. In other words, the discourse of global constitutionalism interrogates a conceivable constitution for the sector of the international community that adopts western and liberal democratic values. This interrogation would be found apt and accurate in view of the recent transformation of the international legal order; nevertheless, it fails in terms of its methodology. It is true that a "meta legal mentalité" is being constructed in global law; but it is not apt to say that this occurs within the framework of international law, in other words in a vertical dimension. International law represents an ambitious realm for the

[184] Ferejohn et al., "Editor's Introduction," 14.

[185] Michel Rosenfeld, "Constitutional Identity," in *Oxford Handbook of Comparative Constitutional Law*, ed. Michel Rosenfeld and Andras Sajo (Oxford: Oxford University Press, 2012), 765.

international community of the Post-Westphalian values. However, the most striking deficiency of international law is that it reflects a culturally fragmented realm as well as a functionally fragmented one. What is meant here can be made clear by examples from the challenge of USA to the ICC (but not to the whole international criminal law), or distinct legal cultures of some UN Security Council members, such as Russia and China, which view the concept of law entirely different from their western counterparts, and resist against the mentalité of globalism in some cases as mentioned above. The Hindu and Islamic legal cultures can be also added in. In this regard, international law does not reflect a meta legal culture or a legal culture determined by the constitutional themes yet. What is more, it is not a sufficient instrument to shape local legal cultures at all. That being said, the international community of the Post-Westphalian values shares an international legal order with those who do not agree on the same values. In conclusion, an idea of constitutionalization in the international legal order is not of sufficient evidence yet.

On the other hand, in accordance with the economic and political globalism, constitutional principles and values are migrating as one of the most striking venues of contemporary constitutionalism, and this leads to a reduced differentiation between constitutional systems that share Post-Westphalian values at the same time. This fact would be considered as a basis for an inquiry of transnational constitutionalization. Therefore, the global constitutionalism discourse needs to be reconstructed in a horizontal dimension. This means that a constitutionalization in the global realm should be sought in the transconstitutional processes instead of the international institutionalization and codification processes.

6.3 Prospects for the Future of Global Constitutionalism

The interrogation about the viability of the idea of global constitutionalism in view of contemporary constitutionalism gains a new dimension at this point. The contributions to the global constitutionalism discourse mostly seek a vertical constitutionalization that may occur through the increase of integration and cooperation in international law. In a sense, these contributions strive to explain the cultural codes of a constitution in the international legal order. However, the fragmented structure of the international legal order prevents the rise of a constitutional meta-order. On the other hand, a burgeoning constitutional culture is observed in the global realm.[186] This newly emerging culture cannot be perceived without considering the

[186] As an underpinning idea, Gardbaum argues that an international constitutional law appears in various contexts, "mostly in the big-c sense," "but without the big-c constitution." Stephen Gardbaum, "The Place of Constitutional Law in the Legal System," in *The Oxford Handbook of Comparative Constitutional Law*, ed. Michel Rosenfeld and Andras Sajo (Oxford: Oxford University Press, 2012), 172. Global constitutional culture corresponds to what Gardbaum mentions as "the big-c sense."

role of transconstitutional relations that are medium to the migration of constitutional norms and values.

6.3.1 *Global Constitutionalism as a Matter of Transconstitutional Relations*

In view of global constitutionalism as a matter of transconstitutional relations, the fundamental claim here is that global constitutionalism should be considered a comparative law issue, rather than one of international law. In this regard, international law can be viewed as performing coordinative functions instead of the host of a constitutional reconstruction. Against this background, the main question arises as to whether the migration of constitutional norms and values through legal transplantations, transnational legal instruments and networkings can lead to a convergence of constitutional systems; and as a result, whether a common formation of constitutions can come into existence. It is evident that an inquiry for the answer of this question exceeds the borders of this research. However, this research will be able to achieve its aim by setting the ground for further research on this question. Therefore, under this narrower section, only a research problem can be proposed regarding the viability of the global constitutionalism discourse merely in the form of concluding remarks.

Petersmann draws attention to the fact that in the globally integrated world, domestic policies and foreign policies are much more permeable than in the past:

> Foreign policy measures (such as trade restrictions, monetary devaluations, development aid, military actions) tend to operate by taxing and restricting *domestic* citizens and are shaped through *domestic* policy-making processes ("all politics is local").[187]

This means that local domains are still very important, since they are the operational basis of global policies. On the other hand, as mentioned before, Friedman opines that mobility between legal cultures leads to a convergence through some specific fields, such as human rights. The knowledge of a general legal culture regarding a specific issue can be reached by gathering information from various legal cultures. A comparative study of legal cultures can be helpful in reaching these outcomes.[188] In this chapter, a special emphasis was placed on the cultural character of the global constitutionalism discourse. The main themes of global constitutionalism, such as global rule of law, integration, rights, world government etc. can hardly be dealt with by a focus on the black-letter law, as Schwöbel underscores, "there is a metaphysical dimension to constitutionalism, which seeks to foster a particular constitutional culture." This dimension is, in her point of view, the export of constitutional culture

[187] Petersmann, "How to Promote," 28. Emphasis belongs to the original text.

[188] Lawrence M. Friedman, "The Concept of Legal Culture: A Reply," in *Comparing Legal Cultures*, ed. David Nelken (Aldershot: Dartmouth, 1997), 35.

of imperial powers to the dominated actors.[189] This is indeed another way of expression of the main conclusion of this text. On the other hand, the cultural dimension does not only consist of the interaction of political cultures or the clash of different societal cultures. The meaning of constitutional norms depends on the context beyond their normative meanings. As underlined in the third chapter, constitution can be dealt with in its broader meaning that exceeds beyond normative meanings. This requires exploring its "meaning-in-use."[190] As Tushnet states, constitutions are "more used than defined, and understanding them means knowing how they are used."[191] At this point, constitutional practices generate the only context for further implications of constitutional substance beyond the formal validity area. Thereby, the interaction of legal cultures plays a key role in demonstrating the impact of constitutional migration.

As discussed in the third chapter, the character of contemporary constitutional texts is increasingly turning into a single one, that is to say, a rights-based legal constitution. As a major ground, rights have seized the role of the constituent powers of constitutions, and the impact of judicial reviews over constitutional matters has dramatically increased. The rights-based constitutions arose as the prevalent form of contemporary constitutions in this era. Transnational legal regulations helped the transmission of this new formation and standards. Being reminded of Slaughter's pertinent contributions, the transformation of international relations into transgovernmental networks also played a key role in the transmission of legal cultures.[192] The reconstruction of constitutionalism in this way can be depicted as a reflection of "global legal constitutionalism."[193] As a matter of fact, Bellamy deems this to be problematic in terms of democracy. The transnational legal systems strengthen legal constitutionalism, and as such, they mostly lead to the attenuation of democracy.[194] At the same time, this opinion challenges the opinions of Habermas on the deliberative democracy, which supposes that global legal constitutionalism may overcome the exclusion of people from the political processes.[195] On the other hand, the current restraints for participation in decision-making processes in the transnational domain, also disprove the thesis of Dworkin that a legal constitution is a must

---

[189] Schwöbel, *Global Constitutionalism*, 105.

[190] Antje Wiener, "Constitutionalism Unbound: A Practice Approach to Normativity" (Paper presented at 'Practice, Ethics and Normativity' at the Annual Millennium Conference 'Out Of The Ivory Tower - Weaving the Theories and Practice of International Relations', London School of Economics & Political Science, London, 22-23 October 2011, http://ssrn.com/abstract=2103049 or http://dx.doi.org/10.2139/ssrn.2103049), 15, last visit 11.04.2014.

[191] Mark Tushnet, "Constitution," in *The Oxford Handbook of Comparative Constitutional Law*, ed. Michel Rosenfeld and Andras Sajo (Oxford: Oxford University Press, 2012), 218.

[192] Slaughter, *A New World Order.*

[193] Richard Bellamy, *Political Constitutionalism: A Republican Defence of the Constitutionality of Democracy* (Cambridge: Cambridge University Press, 2007), 261.

[194] Ibid.

[195] Jürgen Habermas, *The Postnational Constellation* (Cambridge: Polity, 2001).

for a democracy. Evidently, the predictions of Dworkin for national democracies and constitutions do not work for the transnational level due to the underdevelopment of democratic mechanisms. However, this question is to be examined within a broader scope that deals with constitutionalism through its neighbouring disciplines and societal facts. Further empirical observations regarding constitutional and legal culture can provide this broader field of research.

As mentioned above, different constitutional traditions have developed in USA, the UK and the continental European countries (such as France and Germany). They generated the constitutional cultures that arose as major models for other cultures. Furthermore, as a very dynamic process, the migration of constitutional norms and values through the national and transnational realms, render this fact much more complex. In the global legal order, transnational and supranational centres are to be viewed as the transmitters of constitutional norms and values. However, the striking point is that such a transmission triggers the domestic domains; that is to say, the transnational and supranational domains remain as only the bearers in this process. In other words, the multilevel centres of the world legal system are far from establishing a foundational basis for constitutionalism for the reasons mentioned above. Domains of states remain an exception, although they come into play in many constitutional questions that are not to be resolved within only one centre.[196]

The circulation of constitutional rights and values throughout the world leads to an ongoing process of convergence or "dedifferentiation of constitutional norms."[197] However, while constitutional norms dedifferentiate, to what extent they generate dedifferentiated social, political and cultural outcomes is still problematic. Furthermore, this question is likely to be formulated as "to what extent the migration and dedifferentiation of constitutional norms (can) contribute to a global constitutional culture?" This question presupposes that beyond normative aspects, a constitutionalization process can be found embedded in the emergence of a constitutional culture.

This question has received various responses so far. For example, Tushnet argues that due to the effects of globalization, the exceptionalist traditions in constitutional law, particularly in the US Supreme Court, are likely to weaken over time.[198] He refers to two processes in the convergence of constitutional systems: Top-down (mainly through networking legal professionals, referring to Slaughter, or through transnational law), and bottom-up (economic globalization requires constitutional

[196] Marcelo Neves, *Transconstitutionalism*, trans. Kevin Mundy (Oxford and Portland Oregon: Hart Publishing, 2013), 148.

[197] As mentioned earlier, in modern society, the distinct legal orders are subordinated to the same binary code of legal/illegal. However, each legal order has its own structure, operations, legal procedures, and this situation creates a differentiation between these orders. Ibid., 74. Current facts in world constitutionalism, particularly through migration of constitutional values and norms between national, transnational and supranational legal orders give rise to an increasing vagueness of such differentiation. This is what is meant by a dedifferentiation in this realm.

[198] Tushnet, "The Inevitable Globalization," 987.

protection for markets).[199] Tushnet places an emphasis on the fact that this does not include an expectation for any further unity in the international legal order. In case of the convergence of legal systems, a striking potential problem is the clash of different cultural views or values in different legal systems. Gessner and Schade reflect a point of view that the conflicts between legal cultures can be overcome by virtue of "legal developments." Further, they argue that an international *ordre public* should be developed for the clash of divergent values.[200]

The idea of the convergence of legal cultures was contested for some reasons. As mentioned before, Legrand deems legal transplants to be impossible. According to Legrand, different legal cultures of host and exporting states create a barrier against a true transplantation.[201] He analyzed some functionalist views on the convergence of European legal systems which conclude that a new *jus commune* is in the making, by virtue of the developments through the EU Law and the Law of the CoE. The evidence taken by these views are "increasing reservoir of common rules, common concepts, common substantive and adjectival law, and common institutional bodies."[202] Legrand opposed these views by accusing them of adhering to legal propositions. According to Legrand, the rules cannot reflect the deeper structures of legal systems. In this regard, he states that common law and civil law systems cannot converge, particularly within the framework of European Law, since the unique character of cultures and the convergence of rules cannot mount to the convergence of cultures. Further, the differences between civil law and common law systems are epistemologically irreducible, as they reflect different legal mentalités.[203]

The inquiries about the phenomenon of convergence seeking a ground for a community are not new. For example, in the 1950s, Karl Deutsch argued from a culturalist perspective that the increasing communication between peoples creates a sense of community, which was developing towards an integration, and above all, towards a "security community." In this security community, people tend to solve disputes through peaceful changes.[204] This idea also complied with the federalist views, like

[199] Ibid., 988-994.

[200] Volkmar Gessner and Angelika Schade, "Conflicts of Culture in Cross-Border Legal Relations: The Conception of a Research Topic in the Sociology of Law," in *Global Culture,* ed. Mike Featherstone (London: Sage Publications, 1990), 265.

[201] Pierre Legrand, "European Legal Systems are not Converging," *International and Comparative Law Quarterly*, 45 (1996): 52-81. In this context, Merry draws attention to the role of local courts in adopting a new law from another nation and in constructing a new social order, by referring to studies on the meeting of secular laws with traditional cultures in Turkish and Ottoman history. Sally Engle Merry, "Anthropology, Law, and Transnational Processes," *Annual Review of Anthropology* 21 (1992): 370. Thus, as will be dealt with again in the following paragraphs, Merry's view can be regarded as opposite to Legrand's.

[202] Legrand, "European Legal Systems," 55.

[203] Ibid., 60 ff.

[204] Roger Eatwell, "Conclusion: Part One, Europe of the 'Nation States'? Concepts and Theories," in *European Political Cultures: Conflict or Convergence,* ed. Roger Eatwell (London: Routledge, 1997), 246.

Jean Monnet's in the 1950s.[205] An empirical research on the contemporary values of European political culture (including Eastern Europe and Russia) demonstrates that "democratic political systems," "market-oriented economic systems" and "extensive welfare systems" retain a widespread legitimacy in the countries concerned.[206] On the other hand, it is of note that the realist school of international relations retains a cynical approach to the European integration, since the leading powers of the EU, such as France and Germany, act in favour of the limitations on sovereignty. This is the case because the limitations provided greater gains for their further economic and political purposes at the same time.[207]

On the other hand, given the successful examples of the legal and constitutional transplants, the ideas of Legrand on the impossibility of legal migrations cannot be accepted. To be reminded of the example of Sally E. Merry for "vernacularization" of legal transfers, imported legal values or norms do not remain in the original forms, but they are adjusted to the culture of the importing legal system in good examples of legal transplants.[208] As the Women's Courts in India epitomized in Merry's explanation, this does not need a formal recognition by governments at all times; civic cultures can also automatically adopt foreign norms. That is to say, a cultural clash does not mean an eclectic instalment of foreign norms and values. At this point, it is of note that the convergence or dedifferentiation of law should also consider the fact of vernacularization. That is to say, as a matter of fact, the approach developed in this book does not view the communitarian purposes as the primary issues in the matter of convergence.

6.3.2 *Global Constitution as a Metonym*

The major conclusion of this book is that the global realm is not subject to a constitutionalization process in formal terms, but it is still of a constitutional culture. In a sense, this complies with the idea of Otto-Brun Bryde, as mentioned earlier, that the global realm cannot have a *Rechtstaat*, but could be governed by rule of law.[209] How does this paradox concern the global constitutionalism discourse? The answer is most likely to be that there is still room for a constitutionalization in the global realm. This constitution can be a consequence of the transconstitutional

---

[205] Ibid., 248.

[206] Ibid., 234.

[207] Ibid., 246.

[208] Merry, "What is Legal Culture?," 56. Also, Neves, *Transconstitutionalism*, 108.

[209] Brun-Otto Bryde, "Konstitutionalisierung des Völkerrechts und Internationalisierung des Verfassungsrechts," *Der Staat Bd.* 42 (2003), H. 1, 61-75 cited by Jürgen Habermas, "Does the Constitutionalisation of International Law Still Have a Chance?," in *Divided West*, ed. and trans. Cionan Cronin (Cambridge: Polity, 2006), 139

relations, not of a cosmopolitan drive, and it could be named a "global constitution as a metonym."[210]

To make it more clear, the historical development of modern constitutionalism proves that once a model of constitutionalism rises, it does not remain a property of its originating country, and becomes public as a part of a greater global political culture.[211] Given the success of German and Japanese constitutions imported from foreign models to a certain extent, the question arises whether or not the model of western liberal democratic constitutionalism can fit to every society as a universal phenomenon. The greatest challenge in this context is "to make these borrowed institutions relevant to unique national cultures and historical experiences."[212] As a matter of fact, this question also arises as the greatest challenge to the idea of global constitutionalism. The global constitutionalist ideas, as long as they do not adhere to an idea of a world government, should discuss about a constitutionalization process in the global realm without leaving national constitutions aside. At this point, national constitutions appear as one of the key points of this debate. In other words, the proponents of global constitutionalism should reformulate the main question in view of an option about whether or not a global constitutionalization process could come about through the dedifferentiation of different national constitutions. That is to say, would it be possible that all national constitutions would evolve to include the same norms and values? Would this be the main trend of contemporary constitutionalism? Will there be an invisible global constitution that will arise without any manifestation? A global constitution would arise as a "metonym" in this form since it represents every constitution, and at the same time it is embodied by every constitution. Oxford dictionaries define metonym as "[a] word, name, or expression used as a substitute for something else with which it is closely associated."[213] By this way, we can "use one part or aspect of an experience to stand for some other part (or the whole) of that experience."[214] In the daily language, these forms of expressions are used very frequently: e.g. Washington to refer to the US government, Brussels for the EU institutions, the Silicon Valley for the American high-tech industry, Picasso for a painting of Picasso and so forth. In the case of global constitution as a metonym, each national constitution has a metonymic relationship with global constitution. Each national constitution reflects global constitution. At the same

[210] Neves highlights that transconstitutionalism, in particular between state legal orders, is not to be understood as an overarching global legal order. Neves, *Transconstitutionalism*, 118. At this point it is of note that the main idea of this section shows parallelism with this opinion.

[211] Daniel Franklin and Michael Baun, "Political Culture and Constitutionalism: A Comparative Approach (Armonk: M.E. Sharpe, 1995), 224.

[212] Ibid.

[213] Oxford Dictionaries, http://www.oxforddictionaries.com/definition/english/metonym, last visit 17.11.2015.

[214] Penny Tompkins and James Lawley, "Metonymy and Part-Whole Relationships," http://www.cleanlanguage.co.uk/articles/articles/210/1/Metonymy--Part-Whole-Relationships/Page1.html, last visit 17.11.2015.

time global constitution represents each national constitution. This could be better explained by those words:

> In general the part differs from the whole.
> The part cannot totally contain the whole.
> But it always partially contains the whole.
> The part contains the whole to some degree.[215]

The idea of global constitution as a metonym relies on the fact that globalization has not yet achieved to sideline the importance and key positions of nation states. An inquiry for a transnational constitutionalism should not envisage an autonomous normative order emerging out of the borders of nation states.[216] In addition to that, the idea of global constitution as a metonym does not trigger the emergence of a transnational community. In other words, what is implied here is not a political integration of states. Instead, each constitution keeps its individual existence separately. It is rather the "intersection set" of all constitutions. Therefore, it does not resemble "total constitutions," like the German Basic Law, since it does not have a comprehensive character. It goes without saying that the "intersection set" consists of "rights," which is the central issue of the migration between contemporary constitutions. This idea prescribes a discursive constitution. This constitution would be cosmopolitan, as it follows a Kantian trajectory, but not communitarian.

The idea of the global constitution as a metonym can also be underpinned by the "IKEA Theory" of Günther Frankenberg. Günter Frankenberg defines the IKEA theory of constitutional transfer as follows:

> the global constitution is created by or rather emanates from processes of transfer and functions as a reservoir or, for that matter, a supermarket, where standardized constitutional items—grand designs as well as elementary particles of information—are stored and available, *prêtà-porter*, for purchase and reassemblage by constitution makers around the world.[217]

The national constitutions are the main reservoirs of the flow of the constitutional values and norms throughout the world. Constitutions retain their diatopical characters in this structure, and thereby create an opportunity for communication with other constitutions in the real sense. Constitutional culture creates a milieu for this communication, and it also provides the required energy sources for the flow of

---

[215] Bart Kosko, *Fuzzy Thinking: The New Science of Fuzzy Logic* (New York: Hyperion, 1993) cited by Ibid.

[216] Peer Zumbansen, "Carving Out Typologies and Accounting for Differences Across Systems: Towards a Methodology of Transnational Constitutionalism," in *The Oxford Handbook of Comparative Constitutional Law*, ed. Michel Rosenfeld and Andras Sajo (Oxford: Oxford University Press, 2012), 77.

[217] Günter Frankenberg, "Constitutional Transfer: IKEA Theory Revisited," *International Journal of Constitutional Law* 8, no. 3 (2010): 565.

constitutional values and norms. Therefore, the global constitution as a metonym is a product of constitutional culture, and it is essentially a cultural phenomenon.

However, it is of note that the major findings of this book on the convergence of constitutional cultures and the idea of a global constitution as metonym, should not be read as a prediction for the future of international relations or international law. Instead, as mentioned before, this research mainly suggests a new intellectual gateway in discussing the emergence of global law from the lens of constitutional law.

Chapter 7
Conclusion

Global constitutionalism appeared as one of the alternatives for inquiries on developing a new paradigm for global law. This book held global constitutionalism as a discourse that is contributed by varied ideas regarding a global constitution. Despite variations, the idea of global constitutionalism is most likely to be read as an inquiry for constitutional attributions to the increasing integration in the international legal order. The main contributions to the discourse mainly trigger this idea; some pursue it, and some others produce different claims by negating it.

It is evident that the most distinguishing trait of the global constitutionalism discourse is constitution itself. Global constitutionalism is of such an ambitious idea that the international domain undergoes an intense legalization, and this legalization is of the characteristics of a constitutionalization process. In this sense, global constitutionalism differs from other inquiries for global law, such as global administrative law and global legal pluralism, as it seeks a certain cosmopolitan output in the globalization of law. If so, what is a constitution then? Is constitution only a meta-law that subordinates other laws, is it an instrument to integrate a society, or is it a discursive object? At this juncture, it was fathomed in this book that various contributions to this debate dealt with different understandings of constitution as well as an international legal order. Therefore, this book did not adhere to a certain idea of constitution from the traditional constitutional theory, and reconstructed the meaning of contemporary constitution by diving into the integrative diversity of constitutional law.

It is a significant part of this research that constitutional law has seen serious transformations due to globalization and other enclosing societal facts. Constitution became a much more ambiguous concept due to the effects of globalization over

A. Atilgan, *Global Constitutionalism*, Beiträge zum ausländischen öffentlichen Recht und Völkerrecht, https://doi.org/10.1007/978-3-662-55647-4_7

established structures of legal systems.[1] Under these circumstances, how should contemporary constitution be identified? In a normative way, or in a discursive way? As a legal constitution, or a political constitution? While striving to identify the contemporary concept of constitution, could we deny the fact that such identification reflects a certain paradigm, or the *zeitgeist*? Different approaches to interpret the constitution, other than originalism, in the US Supreme Court were striking examples. On the other hand, beyond a normative reality, constitutions also reflect contextual meanings. A number of contexts that mark the contemporary meaning of constitution were identified. Above all, a norm or a value of modern constitution can no longer be considered as a property of a certain national constitutionalism. Since modern constitutions were born, they have been migrating. They have been an essential element of constructing a modern public power. Transnational law boosted this process. Within this fluid framework, rights appeared as the leading conductive element between constitutions. As a consequence of this inquiry, it was understood that rights arose as a historical actor in the structure of contemporary constitutions. They replaced the classical constituent power and became the major source of legitimacy for contemporary constitutions. Apart from a number of exceptions, such as the British constitutional tradition or the post-conflict states, rights became the common foundational and legitimating basis. Accordingly, the integrative function of constitution has also undergone a transformation. In this respect, it was proposed that constitutions can no longer reflect a motto of "We the People," but instead "We the Bearer of Rights."

Given these diverse meanings and various contexts, constitutions can hardly be framed within a normative typology. As Grimm's achievement criterion was employed, the result was that even commonalities of achieved constitutions do not comply with diverse situations, and they do not suffice to reflect contemporary contexts in which constitutions are most likely to be dealt with.

As seen from the distinction of political-legal constitution in the conventional constitutional law discourse, constitutions have been analyzed through two different essential readings. These readings have been termed as narrow-broad meanings of constitution, or small-c and big-c constitutions. The broader meaning of constitution, which is also likely to be termed as big-c constitution, refers to constitution along with its societal environment in wider contexts instead of the narrow meaning of constitution, in other words the normative body of a constitution. The unwritten and customary entity of the British Constitution is the most significant inspiring constitution for this idea. On the other hand, although the British Constitution epitomizes the idea of a broader meaning of a constitution very well, every constitution can be analyzed in broader terms. As a matter of fact, the global constitutionalism discourse reads modern constitution in this context. That is to say, an

[1] Peer Zumbansen, "Carving Out Typologies and Accounting for Differences Across Systems: Towards a Methodology of Transnational Constitutionalism," in *The Oxford Handbook of Comparative Constitutional Law*, ed. Michel Rosenfeld and Andras Sajo (Oxford: Oxford University Press, 2012), 92.

inquiry for a formal global constitution may not currently make sense depending on these methods to define a constitution; however, it turns into a fruitful inquiry when the emergence of a broader meaning of constitution is interrogated. At this juncture, the problem is that the traditional constitutional theory remains silent for an effective methodology. On the other hand, as a newly burgeoning discourse, constitutional cultural studies provide us with the facilities of the cultural paradigm, which has long appeared as a widespread way to understand the deeper meanings of law in socio-legal studies. Therefore, the main claim here was to depict the broader meaning of constitution through constitutional culture, and to interrogate the existence of the idea of global constitution through this way.

The concept of constitutional culture was analyzed by focusing on two dominating fields on this matter: constitutional culture as a legal culture and constitutional culture as a political culture. Thereby, two different sorts of potential dynamics of a global constitution were sought.

In the inquiry for a global constitutional culture as a legal culture, Friedman's idea of legal culture was at the core, which is basically marked by internal and external legal cultures. This book sought constitutional themes in these two trajectories of legal culture. At the end, it explored that constitutional themes already exist in global legal culture; or in other words, some certain developments within these frameworks are apt to be read as constitutional themes. However, these developments are not coherent. That is to say, international entities as the bearers of internal legal cultures do not respond to the same matter in the same dimension at all times; and the fragmentation of international legal order rises as a hindrance against the coherence sought here. On the other hand, it was even more incoherent in terms of the global, external legal culture. States, whose relations are increasingly being subject to networking activities besides diplomatic relations, were the central objects representing a public in international law in case of the external legal culture. The major output was that current global legal culture reflects the legal culture of a cluster of national legal systems, which are basically the legal systems of the leading western powers. This was raised as a legitimacy problem. Further, global external legal culture was problematic, since some states in particular may opt for bypassing international law in some cases; that is to say, treating international law as merely an unnecessary bulk of formalities. In terms of the external legal culture, it was more formidable to speak of constitutional themes. On the other hand, it should be noted that a tendency towards a common culture can be observed rather within internal legal culture, in particular in the fields of international criminal law, human rights and trade law, while this tendency is not supported by the external legal culture at all times. That is to say, states and the public are less inclined to act in line with the bearers of global internal legal cultures.

When it comes to the analysis of the global constitutional culture from the point of constitutional culture, the matter was dealt with in terms of some concepts that are very central to political culture in constitutional context. In this regard, consensus for a constitution appeared as a problematic issue in moral terms, on the ground that the international legal order was built relying on western values exceedingly. However, it was explored that an absolute consensus is not a must for a constitution to survive in all cases in view of the contemporary theories regarding consensus in diverse societies. The crucial point is to create a balance between diverse agreements for a constitution. Therefore, it cannot be concluded that a consensus is impossible in case of overweighing values of a certain community in a legal system. As to the legitimating sources of a constitution, this book placed an emphasis on the transformative facts about constituent power. The main difference is that the legitimating sources of constitutions have changed in the era of globalization. The new legitimating source of constitutions became rights in this era to a great extent. A striking point is that rights achieve this function by virtue of transnational law. In this respect, rights should be expected to be constituent powers of a global constitution, in case all requirements of a constitution are met. Rights can also provide the maintenance of a constitution. Last but not least, the book touched upon the idea of a global rule of law. Currently, the emergences of a global rule of law can be observed through the operation of various international organizations, in particular the dispute settlement bodies. However, as highlighted above, the current developments do not suffice to draw a frame of a full-fledged rule of law culture in international law. Further, it is a significant, unfavourable situation that the new relational rationality of international law mainly relies on networks, which act behind the closed doors in principle.

As discussed in the last chapter, the major conclusion of this research would be that the global realm does not have a formal constitution, and neither is a constitutionalization in progress. On the other hand, the global realm still has a constitutional culture, and this culture is developing continuously.

From this perspective, this book concurs on the idea that the fragmentation in the international legal order is the greatest obstacle for a unity. Against this background, the crucial point in the achievement of a constitution appears to remain on how to build "a unity in diversity," as it was achieved by the US Constitution through its motto "*E Pluribis Unum*."[2] The fragmentation prevents this unity in the international legal order. The constitutionalization processes came about as a result of certain societal developments, which were touched upon in various contexts in this text. As mentioned in the last chapter, the fragmented global order can hardly be analogized with the proto-constitutional orders of the Medieval era. Furthermore, the national constitutionalization processes followed an evolution from "society of individuals" to "society of networks," through "society of organizations." Compared to this development, the international legal order lacks such a presumption, that is to say, a parallel evolution. In addition, a legal constitutionalist construction of contemporary constitutionalism through constitutional jurisdiction is evident, and thus the viability of a constitutionalization beyond nation states remains questionable.[3]

[2] Michel Rosenfeld, "Constitutional Identity," in *Oxford Handbook of Comparative Constitutional Law*, ed. Michel Rosenfeld and Andras Sajo (Oxford: Oxford University Press, 2012), 774.

[3] Karl-Heinz Ladeur, "Ein Recht der Netzwerke für die Weltgesellschaft oder Konstitutionalisierung der Völkergemeinschaft," *Archiv des Völkerrechts* 49 (2011): 262.

Despite all, the major conclusion of this research is not that global constitutionalism is not a viable idea at all. Otherwise, this would mount to ignoring some of the most essential facts of contemporary constitutionalism. Above all, the global realm hosts a constitutional culture, although it is not a determinant and a coherent culture at all. In this regard, it could be argued that a global constitutional culture is hard to determine by virtue of a vertical inquiry. This means that the holistic approaches to global constitutionalism can hardly be proven from the cultural paradigm. Nevertheless, in this research, the alternative focus has arisen as the mobility of contemporary constitutional values and norms, that is to say, the horizontal stream of constitutions beyond national borders. This also determines the dimension for the stream of global constitutional culture. Therefore, the transconstitutional relations could be held as a ground for a global constitutionalization. As a matter of fact, this is the natural evolution line of modern constitutions, and sliding focus into this stream can help the global constitutionalism discourse gain a more realistic, theoretical ground. As a result of this process, a global constitution can come into being, not in a formal way, but as a metonym and in a discursive way. The reconstruction of this discourse in this dimension can help discussing these facts in a more realistic basis within the framework of contemporary constitutionalism.

Bibliography

Ackerman, Bruce. "The Rise of World Constitutionalism." Occassional Papers, Paper 4, 1996. http://digitalcommons.law.yale.edu/cgi/viewcontent.cgi?article=1005&context=ylsop_papers, last visit 11.10.2013.

Ackerman, Bruce. *We the People: Foundations*. Cambridge: Belknap Press of Harvard University Press, 1993.

Albert, Mathias. "World State: Brunkhorst's 'Cosmopolitan State' and Varieties of Differentiation." *Social & Legal Studies* 23(4) (2014): 517–531.

Allan, T. R. S. "Dworkin and Dicey: The Rule of Law as Integrity." *Oxford Journal of Legal Studies* 8 (2) (1988): 266–277.

Allott, Phillip. "The Emerging International Aristocracy." *NYU Journal of International Law and Politics* 35, no. 2 (2002): 309–338.

Alston, Philip. "The Myopia of the Handmaidens: International Lawyers and Globalization." *European Journal of International Law* 3 (1997): 435–448.

Alvarez, Jose E. "The New Treaty Makers." In *International Law: Classic and Contemporary Readings*, edited by Charlotte Ku and Paul F. Diehl, 3rd ed. 102–104. Boulder, Colo: Lynne Rienner Publishers, 2009.

Balkin, Jack M. "Framework Originalism and the Living Constitution." *Nortwestern University Law Review* 103 (2009): 1–93.

Banakar, Reza. "Who Needs the Classics? - On the Relevance of Classical Legal Sociology for the Study of Current Social and Legal Problems." 2012. http://ssrn.com/abstract=2140775, last visit 03.04.2014.

Barendt, Eric. *An Introduction to Constitutional Law*. Oxford: Oxford University Press, 1998.

Bates, Ed. *The Evolution of the European Convention on Human Rights: From Its Inception to the Creation of a Permanent Court of Human Rights*. Oxford: Oxford University Press, 2010.

Bauman, Zygmunt. *Globalization: The Human Consequences*. New York: Columbia University Press, 1998.

Baun, Michael J. "The Federal Republic of Germany." In *Political culture and constitutionalism: a comparative approach*, edited by Daniel P. Franklin and Michael Baun, 79–97. Armonk, NY: M.E. Sharpe., 1995.

Beatty, David M. *Constitutional Law: In Theory and Practice*. Toronto: University of Toronto Press, 1995.

Beck, Ulrich. *Cosmopolitan Vision*. Translated by Ciaran Cronin. Cambridge: Polity, 2006.

Bederman, David J. *Globalization and International Law*. New York: Palgrave Macmillan, 2008.

A. Atilgan, *Global Constitutionalism*, Beiträge zum ausländischen öffentlichen Recht und Völkerrecht, https://doi.org/10.1007/978-3-662-55647-4

Bellamy, Richard. "Constitutionalism." In *International Encyclopedia of Political Science*, edited by B. Badie, D. Berg-Scholsser and L. Morlino. IPSA/Sage 2010. http://ssrn.com/abstract=1676321, l, last visit 12.12.2014.

Bellamy, Richard. *Political Constitutionalism: A Republican Defence of the Constitutionality of Democracy*. Cambridge: Cambridge University Press, 2007.

Bellamy, Richard. "Political constitutionalism and the Human Rights Act." *International Journal of Constitutional Law* 94 (2011): 86–101.

Bellamy, Richard, and Dario Castiglione. "Constitutionalism and Democracy: Political Theory and the American Constitution." *British Journal of Political Science* 27, no. 4 (1997): 595–618.

Bendor, Ariel L., and Zeev Segal. "Constitutionalism and Trust in Britain: An Ancient Constitutional Culture, A New Judicial Review Model." *American University International Law Review* 17 (2001-2002): 683–722.

Benhabib, Seyla. *Another Cosmopolitanism*. Oxford: Oxford University Press, 2006.

Berman, Paul Schiff. "A Pluralist Approach to International Law." *The Yale Journal of International Law* 32, no. 2 (2007): 301–329.

Berman, Paul Schiff. "From International Law to Law and Globalization." University of Connecticut School of Law Articles and Working Papers, Paper 23, 2005. http://lsr.nellco.org/uconn_wps/23), last visit 11.07.2013.

Bianchi, Andrea. "Human Rights and the Magic of Jus Cogens." *European Journal of International Law* 19, no. 3 (2008): 491–508.

Broude, Tomer. "International Judicial Bodies as Sources of Normativity: The WTO Dispute Settlement System in Comparative Context." In *Governance and International Legal Theory*, edited by F. Dekker and Wouter G. Werner, 237–276. Leiden: Springer Science+Business Media, B.V. 2004.

Brunkhorst, Hauke. "Globalising Democracy Without a State: Weak Public, Strong Public, Global Constitutionalism." *Millennium – Journal of International Studies* 31 (2002): 675–690.

Brunkhorst, Hauke. "The Co-evolution of Cosmopolitan and National Statehood – Preliminary Theoretical Considerations on the Historical Evolution of Constitutionalism." *Cooperation and Conflict* 47, no. 2 (2012): 176–199.

Brunkhorst, Hauke. *Solidarity: From Civic Friendship to a Global Legal Community*. Translated by Jeffrey Flynn. Cambridge: The MIT Press, 2005.

Boyle, Alan E., and Christine M. Chinkin. *The Making of International Law*. Oxford: Oxford University Press, 2007.

Boyne, Roy. "Culture and the World-System." In *Global Culture: Nationalism, Globalization and Modernity, A Theory, Culture & Society*, edited by Mike Featherstone, 57–62. London: Sage Publications, 1990.

Brunnee Jutta and Stephen J. Toope. "International Law and Constructivism: Elements of an Interactional Theory of International Law." *Columbia Journal of Transnational Law* 39, no. 1 (2000-2001): 19–74.

Buergenthal, Thomas. "The Normative and Institutional Evolution of International Human Rights." *Human Rights Quarterly* 19, no. 4 (1997): 703–723.

Campbell, Kirsten. "The Making of Global Legal Culture and International Criminal Law." *Leiden Journal of International Law* 26 (2013): 155–172.

Cardozo, Benjamin N. *The Nature of the Judicial Process*. 13th ed. New Haven: Yale University Press, 1946.

Castiglione, Dario. "The Political Theory of the Constitution." In *Constitutionalism in Transformation: European and Theoretical Perspectives*, edited by Richard Bellamy and Dario Castiglione, 6–24. Oxford: Blackwell, 1996.

Caygill, Howard, and Alan Scott. "The Basic Law versus the Basic Norm? The Case of the Bavarian Crucifix Order." In *Constitutionalism in Transformation: European and Theoretical Perspectives*, edited by Richard Bellamy and Dario Castiglione, 93–104. Oxford: Blackwell, 1996.

Chesterman, Simon. "An International Rule of Law?" *The American Journal of Comparative Law* 56, no. 2 (2008): 331–361.

Choudry, Sujit. "Globalization in Search of Justification: Toward a Theory of Comparative Constitutional Interpretation." *Indiana Law Journal* 74 (1999): 820–892.

Choudry, Sujit. "Migration as a New Metaphor in Comparative Constitutional Law." In *The Migration of Constitutional Ideas*, edited by Sujit Choudry, 1–36. Cambridge: Cambridge University Press, 2006.

Cotterrell, Roger. "The Concept of Legal Culture." In *Comparing Legal Cultures*, edited by David Nelken, 13–32. Aldershot: Dartmouth, 1997.

Cotterrell, Roger. *The Sociology of Law: An Introduction*. London: Butterworths, 1984.

Craig, Paul. "Political Constitutionalism and the Judicial Role: A Response." *International Journal of Constitutional Law* 9, no. 1 (2011): 112–131.

Darian-Smith, Eve. *Laws and Societies in Global Contexts: Contemporary Approaches*. Cambridge: Cambridge University Press, 2013.

Delimatsis, Panagiotis. "A Global Law Perspective of the WTO." In *Reflections on Global Law*, edited by Shavana Musa and Eefje de Volder, 153–163. Leiden: Brill, 2013.

Denninger, Erhard. "Judicial Review Revisited: The German Experience." *Tulane Law Review* 59 (1984-5): 1013–1031.

Dicey, A.V. *Introduction to the Study of the Law of the Constitution*. 9th ed. London: Macmillan and Co., 1948.

Domingo, Rafael. *The New Global Law*. Cambridge: Cambridge University Press, 2010.

Donnelly, Jack. "Cultural Relativism and Universal Human Rights." *Human Rights Quarterly* 6 (1984): 400–419.

Donnelly, Jack. *Universal Human Rights: In Theory and Practice*. 3rd ed. Ithaca and London: Cornell University Press, 2013.

Doyle, Michael W. "The UN Charter – A Global Constitution?" In *Ruling the World? Constitutionalism, International Law, and Global Governance*, edited by Jeffrey L. Dunoff and Joel P. Trachtman, 113–132. Cambridge: Cambridge University Press, 2009.

Dworkin, Ronald. "Constitutionalism and Democracy." In *Constitutionalism and Democracy*, edited by Richard Paul Bellamy, 3–12. Aldershot, Hants: Ashgate, 2006.

Dworkin, Ronald. "Equality, Democracy and Constitution: We the People in Court." In *Constitutionalism and Democracy*, edited by Richard Bellamy, 13–36. Ashgate: Dartmouth, 2006.

Dworkin, Ronald. *Law's Empire*. Cambridge: The Belknap Press of Harvard University Press, 1986.

Dunoff, Jeffrey L. "The Politics of International Constitutions: The Curious Case of the World Trade Organization." In *Ruling the World? Constitutionalism, International Law and Global Governance*, edited by Jeffrey L. Dunoff and Joel P. Trachtman, 178–205. Cambridge: Cambridge University Press, 2009.

Dunoff, Jeffrey L., and Joel P. Trachtman, "A Functional Approach to Global Constitutionalism." Harvard Public Law Working Paper no. 08-57, 2008. http://ssrn.com/abstract=1311983, last visit 19.04.2015.

Eatwell, Roger. "Conclusion: Part One, Europe of the 'Nation States'? Concepts and Theories." In *European Political Cultures: Conflict or Convergence*, edited by Roger Eatwell, 252–269. London: Routledge, 1997.

Ehrlich, Eugen. *Grundlegung der Soziologie des Rechts*. Berlin: Duncker&Humblot, 1989.

Eisenstadt, S.N. "The Order-maintaining and Order-transforming Dimensions of Culture." In *Theory of Culture*, edited by Richard Münch and Neil J. Smelser, 68–87. Berkeley: University of California Press, 1992.

Elazar, Daniel J. "Globalization Meets the World's Political Cultures." Jerusalem Center for Public Affairs. http://www.jcpa.org/dje/articles3/polcult.htm, last visit 06.10.2015.

Ergil, Dogu. "The Kurdish Question in Turkey," *Journal of Democracy*. 11, (2000): 122–135

Ewing, K.D. "The Resilience of the Political Constitution." *German Law Journal* 14, no. 12 (2013): 2111–2136.

Falk, Richard A. *The Declining World Order: America's Imperial Geopolitics*. New York: Routledge, 2004.

Falk, Richard A., Robert C. Johansen, and Samuel S. Kim. "Global Constitutionalism and World Order." In *The Constitutional Foundations of World Peace*, edited by Richard A. Falk, Robert C. Johansen, and Samuel S. Kim. 3–12. Albany, NY: State University of New York Press, 1993.

Fassbender, Bardo. "Rediscovering a Forgotten Constitution: Notes on the Place of the UN Charter in the International Legal Order." in *Ruling the World? Constitutionalism, International Law, and Global Governance*, edited by Jeffrey L. Dunoff and Joel P. Trachtman, 133–148. Cambridge: Cambridge University Press, 2009.

Fassbender, Bardo. "Sovereignty and Constitutionalism in International Law." In *Sovereignty in Transition: Essays in European Law*, edited by Neil Walker, 115–144. Oxford: Hart Publishing, 2006.

Fassbender, Bardo. "The Meaning of International Constitutional Law." In *Transnational Constitutionalism: International and European Models*, edited by Nicholas Tsagourias, 307–328. Cambridge: Cambridge University Press, 2007.

Fassbender, Bardo. "The United Nations Charter as Constitution of the International Community." *Columbia Journal of Transnational Law* 36, no. 3 (1998): 529–619.

Ferejohn, John, Jack N. Rakove, and Jonathan Riley. "Editor's Introduction." In *Constitutional Culture and Democratic Rule*, edited by John Ferejohn, Jack N. Rakove, and Jonathan Riley. 1–40. Cambridge: Cambridge University Press, 2001.

Fine, Robert and Will Smith. "Jürgen Habermas's Theory of Cosmopolitanism." *Constellations* 10, no. 4 (2003): 469–487.

Fischer-Lescano, Andreas, and Gunther Teubner. "Regime-collisions: the Vain Search for Legal Unity in the Fragmentation of Global Law." *Michigan Journal of International Law* 25, no. 4 (2004): 999–1046.

Fischer-Lescano, Andreas. "Die Emergenz der Globalverfassung." *Zeitschrift für ausländisches öffentliches Recht und Völkerrecht* 63, no. 3 (2003): 717–760.

Fischer-Lescano, Andreas and Gunther Teubner. "Reply to Andreas L. Paulus, Consensus as Fiction of Global Law." *Michigan Journal of International Law* 25 (2003-2004): 1059–1073.

Franklin, Daniel. "American Political Culture and Constitutionalism." In *Political Culture and Constitutionalism: A Comparative Approach*, edited by Daniel Franklin and Michael Baun, 43–55. Armonk: M.E. Sharpe, 1995.

Franklin, Daniel P., and Michael J. Baun. "Introduction." In *Political Culture and Constitutionalism: A Comparative Approach*, edited by Daniel Franklin and Michael Baun, 1–9, Armonk: M.E. Sharpe, 1995.

Frankenberg, Günter. "Constitutional Transfer: IKEA theory revisited." *International Journal of Constitutional Law* 8, no. 3 (2010): 563–579.

Friedman, Lawrence M. "Borders: On the Emerging Sociology of Transnational Law." *Stanford Journal of International Law* 32 (1996): 65–90.

Friedman, Lawrence M. "Is There a Modern Legal Culture." *Ratio Juris* 7 (1994): 117–131.

Friedman, Lawrence M. *Law and Society: an Introduction*. New Jersey: Prentice Hall Inc., 1977.

Friedman, Lawrence M. "The Concept of Legal Culture: A Reply." In *Comparing Legal Cultures*, edited by David Nelken, 33–40. Aldershot: Dartmouth, 1997.

Friedman, Lawrence M. *The Legal System: A Social Science Perspective*. New York: Russel Sage Foundation, 1975.

Joyner, Christopher C., and John C. Dettling. "Bridging the Cultural Chasm: Cultural Relativism and The Future of International Law." *California Western International Law Journal* 20 (1989-1990): 275–314.

Galligan, Denis J. and Mila Versteeg, "Theoretical Perspectives on the Social and Political Foundations of Constitutions." In *Social and Political Foundations of Constitutions*, edited by Denis J. Galligan and Mila Versteeg, 3–50. Cambridge: Cambridge University Press, 2013.

Gardbaum, Stephen. "The Place of Constitutional Law in the Legal System." In *The Oxford Handbook of Comparative Constitutional Law*, edited by Michel Rosenfeld and Andras Sajo, 169–188. Oxford: Oxford University Press, 2012.

Gardner, James. "A Reply: What is a State Constitution?" *Rutgers Law Journal* 24 (1992-1993): 1025–1055.

Gessner, Volkmar, and Angelika Schade. "Conflicts of Culture in Cross-Border Legal Relations: The Conception of a Research Topic in the Sociology of Law". In *Global Culture*, edited by Mike Featherstone, 253–278. London: Sage Publications, 1990.

Gee, Graham. "The Political Constitutionalism of JAG Griffith." *Legal Studies* 28, no. 1 (2008): 20–45.

Gee, Graham and Grégoire C. N. Webber. "What is a Political Constitution?" *Oxford Journal of Legal Studies* 30, no. 2 (2010): 273–299.

Gillman, Howard. "The Collapse of Constitutional Originalism and the Rise of the Notion of the 'Living Constitution' in the Course of American State-Building." *Studies in American Political Development* 11 (1997): 191–247.

Goderis, Benedikt and Mila Versteeg. "Transnational Constitutionalism: A Conceptual Framework." In *Social and Political Foundations of Constitutions*, edited by Denis J. Galligan and Mila Versteeg, 103–133. Cambridge: Cambridge University Press, 2013.

Goldoni, Marco, and Christopher McCorkindale. "A Note From the Editors: The State of the Political Constitution." *German Law Journal* 14, no. 12 (2013): 2103–2110.

Goldsworthy, Jeffrey. "Constitutional Cultures, Democracy, and Unwritten, Principles." *University of Illinois Law Review* 2012, no. 3 (2012): 683–710.

Goldsworthy, Jeffrey. "Constitutional Interpretation." In *Oxford Handbook of Comparative Constitutional Law*, edited by Michel Rosenfeld and Andras Sajo, 689–717, Oxford: Oxford University Press, 2012.

Goldsworthy, Jeffrey. "Questioning the Migration of Constitutional Ideas: Rights, Constitutionalism and the Limits of Convergence." In *The Migration of Constitutional Ideas*, edited by Sujit Choudry, 115–141. Cambridge: Cambridge University Press, 2006.

Gosalbo-Bono, Ricardo. "The Significance of the Rule of Law and Its Implications for the European Union and the United States." *University of Pittsburgh Law Review* 72 (2010): 229–360.

Gözler, Kemal. *Anayasa Hukukunun Metodolojisi.* Bursa: Ekin Kitabevi Yayinlari, 1999.

Griffith, J.A.G. "The Political Constitution." *Modern Law Review* 42, no. 1 (1979): 1–21.

Griffith, J.A.G. "The Brave New World of Sir John Laws." *Modern Law Review.* 63 (2000): 159–176.

Griffith, J.A.G. *The Politics of the Judiciary*. London: Fontana, 1997.

Grimm, Dieter. "Does Europe Need a Constitution?" *European Law Journal* 1, no. 3 (1995): 282–302.

Grimm, Dieter. "Integration by Constitution." *International Journal of Constitutional Law* 3 (2005): 193–208.

Grimm, Dieter. "The Achievement of Constitutionalism and its Prospects in a Changed World." In *The Twilight of Constitutionalism?*, edited by Petra Dobner and Martin Loughlin. 3–22. Oxford: Oxford University Press, 2010.

Grimm, Dieter. "The Constitution in the Process of Denationalization." *Constellations* 12, no. 4 (2005): 447–463.

Grimm, Dieter. "Types of Constitutions." In *The Oxford Handbook of Comparative Constitutional Law*, edited by Michel Rosenfeld and Andras Sajo, 98–132. Oxford:Oxford University Press, 2012.

Guthrie, Douglas. "The Declining Significance of Guanxi in China's Economic Transition." *The China Quarterly* 154 (1998): 254–282.

Gwyn, William B. "Political Culture and Constitutionalism in Britain." in *Political Culture and Constitutionalism: A Comparative Approach*, edited by Daniel P. Franklin and Michael Baun, 13–42. Armonk: M.E. Sharpe, 1995.

Habermas, Jürgen. "Does the Constitutionalisation of International Law Still Have a Chance?" In *Divided West*, Jürgen Habermas, edited and translated by Cionan Cronin, 115–193. Cambridge: Polity, 2006.

Habermas, Jürgen. *The Postnational Constellation*. Cambridge: Polity, 2001.

Habermas, Jürgen. "Why Europe Needs a Constitution." in *Developing a Constitution for Europe*, edited by Erik Oddvar Eriksen, John Erik Fossum, Agustín Menéndez, 19–34. London: Routledge, 2004.

Hamann, Andrea and Hélène Ruiz Fabri. "Transnational Networks and Constitutionalism." *International Journal of Constitutional Law* 6, no. 3-4 (2008): 481–508.

Halmai, Gabor. "The Use of Foreign Law in Constitutional Interpretation." in *The Oxford Handbook of Comparative Constitutional Law*, edited by Michel Rosenfeld and Andras Sajo, 1328–1348. Oxford: Oxford University Press, 2012.

Halpin, Andrew, and Volker Roeben, ed. *Theorizing the Global Legal Order*. Oxford: Hart Publishing, 2009.

Hardin, Russel. "Why a Constitution?" In *Social and Political Foundations of Constitutions*, edited by Denis J. Galligan and Mila Versteeg, 51–72. Cambridge: Cambridge University Press, 2013.

Hart, H.L.A. *The Concept of Law*. 2nd edn. Oxford: Clarendon Press, 1994.

Helfer, Laurence R., and Anne-Marie Slaughter. "Toward a Theory of Effective Supranational Adjudication." *Yale Law Journal* 107 (1997): 273–391.

Henkin, Louis. "A New Birth of Constitutionalism: Genetic Influences and Genetic Defects." *Cardozo Law Review* 14, no. 3-2 (1992–1993): 533–547.

Hensel, Silke. "Constitutional Cultures in the Atlantic World During the 'Age of Revolutions'." In *Constitutional Cultures: On the Concept and Representation of Constitutions in the Atlantic World*, edited by Silke Hensel, Ulrich Bock, Katrin Dircksen and Hans-Ulrich Thamer, 3–20. Newcastle upon Tyne: Cambridge Scholars Publishing, 2012.

Heringa, Aalt Willem, and Philipp Kiiver. *Constitutions Compared: An Introduction to Comparative Constitutional Law*. 3rd ed. Cambridge: Cambridge University Press, 2012.

Hickman, Tom R. "In Defence of the Legal Constitution." *The University of Toronto Law Journal* 55, no. 4 (2005): 981–1022.

Hirschl, Ran. "On the Blurred Methodological Matrix of Comparative Constitutional Law." In *The Migration of Constitutional Ideas*, edited by Sujit Choudry, 39–66. Cambridge: Cambridge University Press, 2006.

Hirsh-Allen, Jake. "Bashir's Immunity: Arguments in Support of the Prosecution of an Incumbent Head of a Non-State Party by The International Criminal Court." 2008. http://jake.contemporaryfuture.com/docs/transystemicLaw/BashirsImmunity.pdf), last visit 12.09.2011.

Horan, Michael J. "Contemporary Constitutionalism and Legal Relationships between Individuals." *The International and Comparative Law Quarterly* 25, no. 4 (1976): 848–867.

Joyner, Christopher C. and John C. Dettling. "Bridging the Cultural Chasm: Cultural Relativism and The Future of International Law." *California Western International Law Journal* 20 (1989-1990): 275–314.

Kammerhofer, Jörg. *Uncertainty in International Law: A Kelsenian Perspective*. London: Routledge, 2011.

Kant, Immanuel. *Perpetual Peace: A Philosophical Sketch*. Translated by W. Hastie. Published by Slought Foundation, Philadelphia and the Syracuse University Humanities Center, 2010. http://perpetualpeaceproject.org/initiatives/publication.php, last visit 08.09.2014.

Kavanagh, Dennis. "Political Culture in Great Britain: The Decline of the Civic Culture." In *The Civic Culture Revisited*, edited by Gabriela A. Almond and Sidney Verba, 124–176. London: Sage Publications, 1989.

Kelsen, Hans. "The Function of a Constitution." Translated by Iain Stewart. In *Essays on Kelsen*. edited by Richard Tur and William Twinning, 109-119. Oxford: Clarendon, 1986.

Kelsen, Hans. "On the Basic Norm." *California Law Review* 47, no. 1 (1959): 107–110.

Kennedy, David. "The Mystery of Global Governance." In *Ruling the World: Constitutionalism, International Law, and Global Governance*, edited by Joel Trachtman, Jeff Dunoff, 37–68. Cambridge: Cambridge University Press, 2009.

Keohane, Robert O., and Joseph S. Nye Jr. "Introduction." In *Governance in a Globalizing World*, edited by Joseph S. Nye, and John D. Donahue, 1–43. Cambridge, Mass: Visions of Governance for the 21st Century, 2000.

Keohane, Robert O. and Joseph S. Nye, "Transgovernmental Relations and International Organizations," *World politics: A Quarterly Journal of International Relations* 27, no. 1 (1974): 39–62.

King, Michael. "Comparing Legal Cultures in the Quest for Law's Identity." In *Comparing Legal Cultures*, edited by David Nelken, 119–134. Aldershot: Dartmouth, 1997.

Kingsburry, Benedict. "The Concept of 'Law' in Global Administrative Law." *The European Journal of International Law* 20, no. 1 (2009): 23–57.

Kingsbury, Benedict, and Megan Donaldson. "Global Administrative Law." Max Planck Encyclopedia of Public International Law, last updated: April 2011. http://opil.ouplaw.com/view/10.1093/law:epil/9780199231690/law-9780199231690-e948?rskey=jtGmdz&result=1&prd=EPIL, last visit 10.05.2015.

Kingsbury, Benedict, Nico Krisch, and Richard B. Stewart. "The Emergence of Global Administrative Law." *Law and Contemporary Problems* 68, no. 3/4 (2005): 15–47.

Kizilcelik, Sezgin. *Sosyoloji Teorileri.* Cilt 1. Konya: Nüve Kültür Merkezi, 1994.

Kjaer, Poul. *Constitutionalism in the Global Realm: A Sociological Approach.* London: Routledge, 2014.

Klabbers, Jan. "Constitutionalism Lite." *International Organizations Law Review* 1 (2004): 31–58.

Klabbers, Jan. *International Law.* Cambridge: Cambridge University Press, 2013.

Kleingeld, Pauline. "Six Varieties of Cosmopolitanism in Late Eighteenth-Century Germany." *Journal of the History of Ideas* 60, no. 3 (1999): 505–524.

Koch, Charles H. Jr. "Envisioning a Global Legal Culture." *Michigan Journal of International Law* 25 (2003): 1–76.

Koh, Harold Hongju. "The 1994 Roscoe Pound Lecture: Transnational Legal Process." *Nebraska Law Review* 75, no. 1 (1996): 181–207.

Kommers, Donald P. "German Constitutionalism: A Prolegomenon." Scholarly Works Paper no. 98, 1991. http://scholarship.law.nd.edu/law_faculty_scholarship/98, last visit 14.04.2014.

Koskenniemi, Martti. "Constitutionalism as Mindset: Reflections on Kantian Themes about International Law and Globalization." *Theoretical Inquiries in Law* 9 (2007): 9–36.

Koskenniemi, Martti. *From Apology to Utopia: The Structure of International Legal Argument; With a New Epilogue.* Cambridge: Cambridge University Press, 2005.

Koskenniemi, Martti. "The Politics of International Law: 20 Years Later." *European Journal of International Law* 20, no. 1 (2009): 7–19.

Koskenniemmi, Martti. "The Fate of Public International Law: Between Technique and Politics." *The Modern Law Review* 70, no. 1 (2007): 1–30

Kratochwil, Friedrich. "Leaving Sovereignty Behind? An Inquiry into the Politics of Post-Modernity." In *Legality and Legitimacy in Global Affairs*, edited by Richard Falk, Mark Juergensmeyer, Vesselin Popovski, 127–148. New York: Oxford University Press, 2012.

Krisch, Nico. *Beyond Constitutionalism: The Pluralist Structure of Postnational Law.* Oxford: Oxford University Press, 2010.

Ku, Charlotte. *International Law, International Relations and Global Governance.* London: Routledge, 2012.

Kumm, Mattias. "Democratic Constitutionalism Encounters International Law: Terms of Engagement." In *The Migration of Constitutional Ideas*, edited by Sujit Choudry, 256–293. Cambridge: Cambridge University Press, 2006.

Kymlicka, Will. *Contemporary Political Philosophy: An Introduction.* 2nd ed. Oxford: Oxford Books, 2002.

Ladeur, Karl-Heinz. "Ein Recht der Netzwerke für die Weltgesellschaft oder Konstitutionalisierung der Völkergemeinschaft." *Archiv des Völkerrechts* Bd. 49 (2011): 246–275.

Ladeur, Karl-Heinz. "Governance, Theory of." Max Planck Encyclopedia of Public International Law, last updated: September 2010. http://opil.ouplaw.com/view/10.1093/law:epil/9780199231690/law-9780199231690-e940?rskey=8nhhTc&result=5&prd=EPIL, last visit, 01.11.2014.

Ladeur, Karl-Heinz. "Globalization and Public Governance – A Contradiction?" In *Public Governance in the Age of Globalization*, edited by Karl-Heinz Ladeur, 1–24. Aldershot: Ashgate, 2004.

Ladeur, Karl-Heinz. "ICANN and the Illusion of a Community Based Internet: Comments on Jochen von Bernstorff." In *Transnational Governance and Constitutionalism*, edited by Christian Joerges, Inger-Johanne Sand, Gunther Teubner, 283–286. Portland: Hart Publishing, 2004.

Ladeur, Karl-Heinz. "The Emergence of Global Administrative Law and Transnational Regulation." Institute for International Law and Justice Working Paper, no. 2011/1, Finalized 04.04.2011. http://www.iilj.org/publications/the-emergence-of-global-administrative-law-and-transnational-regulation-2/), last visit 19.12.2013.

Ladeur, Karl-Heinz. "The Role of Contracts and Networks in Public Governance: The Importance of the 'Social Epistemology' of Decision Making." *Indiana Journal of Global Legal Studies* 14, no. 2 (2007): 329–351.

Ladeur, Karl-Heinz. "The State in International Law." Comparative Research in Law & Political Economy Research Paper no. 27, 2010. http://digitalcommons.osgoode.yorku.ca/cgi/viewcontent.cgi?article=1094&context=clpe, last visit 21.04.2013.

Ladeur, Karl-Heinz. "The Theory of Autopoiesis as an Approach to a Better Understanding of Postmodern Law- From the Hierarchy of Norms to the Heterarchy of Changing Patterns of Legal Inter-relationships." EUI Working Paper Law no. 99/3, 1999. http://cadmus.eui.eu/bitstream/id/943/law99_3.pdf), last visit 13.04.2014.

Ladeur, Karl-Heinz. "Towards a Legal Theory of Supranationality: The Viability of Network Concept." *European Law Journal* 3 (1997): 33–54.

Ladeur, Karl-Heinz. "'We, the European People…'-Relache?" *European Law Journal* 14, no. 2 (2008): 147–167.

Law, David S., and Mila Versteeg. "The Evolution and Ideology of Global Constitutionalism." *California Law Review* 99 (2011): 1163–1254.

Legrand, Pierre. "Comparative Legal Studies and The Matter of Authenticity." *Journal of Comparative Law* 1 (2006): 365–460.

Legrand, Pierre. "European Legal Systems are not Converging." *International and Comparative Law Quarterly* 45 (1996): 52–81.

Lerner, Hanna. "Constitution-writing in Deeply Divided Societies: The Incrementalist Approach." *Nations and Nationalism* 16, no. 1, 2010, 68–88.

Lindahl, Hans. "Legal Order and the 'Globality' of Global Law." In *Reflections on Global Law*, edited by Shavana Musa and Eefje de Volder, 36–44. Leiden: Brill, 2013.

Linklater, Andrew. *The Transformation of Political Community: Ethical Foundations of the Post-Westphalian Era*. Columbia: University of South Carolina Press, 1998.

Loughlin, Martin. "Ten Tenets of Sovereignty." In *Sovereignty in Transition: Essays in European Law*, edited by Neil Walker, 55–86. Oxford: Hart Publishing, 2006.

Loughlin, Martin. "The Concept of Constituent Power." *European Journal of Political Theory*, 13, no. 2 (2013): 218–237.

Loughlin, Martin. *The Idea of Public Law*. Oxford: Oxford University Press, 2003.

Loughlin, Martin. "What is Constitutionalisation." In *The Twilight of Constitutionalism?*, edited by Petra Dobner and Martin Loughlin, 47–72. Oxford: Oxford University Press, 2010.

Ludwikowski, Rett R. "Constitutional Culture of the New East-Central European Democracies." *Georgia Journal of International and Comparative Law* 29 (2000): 1–29.

Luhmann, Niklas. "Globalizaton or World Society: How to Conceive of Modern Society?" *International Review of Sociology: Revue Internationale de Sociologie* 7, no. 1 (1997): 67–79.

Luhmann, Niklas. *A Sociological Theory of Law*. Translated by Martin Albrow and Elizabeth King-Utz, edited by Martin Albrow. Florence: Routledge, 2013.

Luhmann, Niklas. "The Unity of the Legal System." In *Autopoietic Law: A New Approach to Law and Society*, edited by Gunther Teubner, 12–35. Berlin: Walter de Gruyter, 1988.

Mattheis, Clemens. "The System Theory of Niklas Luhmann and the Constitutionalization of the World Society." *Göttingen Journal of International Law* 4, no. 2 (2012): 625–647.

Mautner, Menachem. "Three Approaches to Law and Culture." *Cornell Law Review* 96 (2011): 839–867.

Mazzone, Jason. "The Creation of a Constitutional Culture." *Tulsa Law Review* 40 (2005): 671–698.

McDougal, Myres S. and W. Michael Reisman. "International Law in Policy-oriented Perspective." In *The Structure and Process of International Law: Essays in Legal Philosophy, Doctrine and Theory*, edited by R. St. J. Macdonald and Douglas M. Johnston, 103–130. The Hague: Nijhoff, 1983.

, McIlwain Charles Howard . *Constitutionalism: Ancient and Modern*. Indianapolis: Liberty Fund, 2007.

Mégret, Frédéric. "Globalization." Max Planck Encyclopedia of Public International Law, last updated: February 2009. http://opil.ouplaw.com/view/10.1093/law:epil/9780199231690/law-9780199231690-e939?prd=EPIL, last visit 19.06.2014.

Menyhart, Russel. "Changing Identities and Changing Law: Possibilities for a Global Legal Culture." *Indiana Journal of Global Legal Studies* 10 (2003): 157–199.

Merry, Sally Engle. "Anthropology, Law, and Transnational Processes." *Annual Review of Anthropology* 21 (1992): 357–379.

Merry, Sally Engle. "Legal Pluralism." In *The Globalization on International Law*, edited by Paul Schiff Berman, 29–60. Aldershot: Ashgate, 2005.

Merry, Sally Engle. "What is Legal Culture? An Anthropological Perspective." *Journal of Comparative Law* 5 (2010): 40–58.

Mezey, Naomi. "Law As Culture." In *Law and Societies in Global Contexts: Contemporary Approaches*, edited by Eve Darian-Smith, 57–73. Cambridge: Cambridge University Press, 2013.

Miller, Arthur Selwyn. "Notes on the Concept of the Living Constitution." *The George Washington Law Review* 31, no. 5 (1963): 881–918.

Minkkinen, Panu. "Political Constitutionalism versus Political Constitutional Theory: Law, Power, and Politics." *International Journal of Constitutional Law* 11, no. 3 (2013): 585–610.

Moran, Mayo. "Inimical to Constitutional Values: Complex Migrations of Constitutional Rights." In *The Migration of Constitutional Ideas*, edited by Sujit Choudry, 233–255. Cambridge: Cambridge University Press, 2006.

Musa Shavana and Eefie de Voider. "Interview with Professor Neil Walker Global Law: Another Case of the Emperor's Clothes?" In *Reflections on Global Law*, edited by Shavana Musa and Eefje de Volder, 3–20. Leiden: Brill, 2013.

Mutua, Makau W. "Savages, Victims and Saviors: The Metaphor of Human Rights." In *Laws and Societies in Global Contexts: Contemporary Approaches*, edited by Eve Darian-Smith, 84–96. Cambridge: Cambridge University Press, 2013.

Münch, Richard. "Constructing a European Society by Jurisdiction." *European Law Journal* 14 (2008): 519–541.

Münch, Richard. *Die Struktur der Moderne: Grundmuster und differentielle Gestaltung des institutionellen Aufbaus der modernen Gesellschaften*. Frankfurt am Main: Suhrkamp, 1984.

Münch, Richard. *Understanding Modernity: Toward a New Perspective Going Beyond Durkheim and Weber*. New York: Routledge, 2010.

Nagan, Winston P., and Garry Jacobs. "New Paradigm for Global Rule of Law." *Cadmus* 1, no. 4 (2012): 130–146.

Nelken, David. "Towards a Sociology of Legal Adaptation." In *Adapting Legal Cultures*, edited by David Nelken and Johannes Feest, 7–54. Portland: Hart Publishing, 2001.

Nelken, David. "Using the Concept of Legal Culture." UC Berkeley, Papers Presented in the Center for the Study of Law and Society Bag Lunch Speaker Series, 2004. http://escholarship.org/uc/item/7dk1j7hm, last visit 09.05.2013.

Neves, Marcelo. "Comparing Transconstitutionalism in an Asymmetric World Society: Conceptual Background and Self-Critical Remarks." Adam Smith Research Foundation Working Papers Series no. 02, 2005. http://www.gla.ac.uk/media/media_401302_en.pdf), last visit 1.3.2015.

Neves, Marcelo. *Transconstitutionalism*. Translated by Kevin Mundy. Oxford and Portland Oregon: Hart Publishing, 2013.

Nye, Joseph S., and David Welch. *Küresel Catisma ve Isbirligini Anlamak*. Translated by Renan Akman, Istanbul: Is Bankasi Kültür Yayinlari, 2010.

Oder, Bertil Emrah. *Avrupa Birligi'nde Anayasa ve Anayasacilik*. Istanbul: Anahtar Kitaplar, 2004.

Oeter, Stefan. "Global Constitutionalism: Fundamental Norms, Contestation and the Emergence of Constitutional Quality." In *Peace Through Law: Reflections on Pacem in Terries from Philosophy, Law, Theology and Political Science*, edited by Heinz-Gerhard Justenhoven and Marry Ellen O'Connell, 83–108. Baden-Baden: Nomos, 2016.

Oeter, Stefan. "Regime Collisions from a Perspective of Global Constitutionalism." In *Contested Regime Collisions: Norm Fragmentation in World Society*, edited by Kerstin Blome, Andreas Fischer-Lescano, Hannah Franzki, Nora Markard, Stefan Oeter, 21–48. Cambridge: Cambridge University Press, 2016.

Oeter, Stefan. "Theorizing Global Legal Order-An Institutionalist Perspective." In *Theorizing the Global Legal Order*, edited by Andrew Halpin and Volker Roeben, 61–84. Oxford: Hart Publishing, 2009.

Parsons, Talcott. "Order and Community in the International Social System." In *International Politics and Foreign Policy*, edited by J.N. Rosenau, 120–129. New York: Free Press of Rosenau, 1961.

Parsons, Talcott. *Politics and Social Structure*. New York: Free Press, 1969.

Paulus, Andreas L. "International Legal System as a Constitution." In *Ruling the World?: Constitutionalism, International Law, and Global Governance*. edited by Jeffrey L. Dunoff and Joel P. Trachtman, 69–109. Cambridge: Cambridge University Press, 2009.

Perry, Michael J. "What is 'the Constitution'? (and Other Fundamental Questions)." In *Constitutionalism: Philosophical Foundations*, edited by Larry Alexander, 99–151. Cambridge: Cambridge University Press, 1998.

Peters, Anne. "Compensatory Constitutionalism: The Fundamental Function and Potential of Fundamental International Norms and Structures." *Leiden Journal of International Law* 19 (2006): 579–610.

Peters, Anne. "Conclusions." In *The Constitutionalization of International Law*, edited by Jan Klabbers, Anne Peters, Geir Ulfstein, 342–352. Oxford: Oxford University Press, 2009.

Peters, Anne. "Fragmentation and Constitutionalization." In *The Oxford Handbook of the Theory of International Law*, edited by Anne Orford and Florian Hoffmann, 1011–1031. Oxford: Oxford University Press, 2016.

Peters, Anne. "Global Constitutionalism Revisited." *International Legal Theory* 11 (2005): 39–68.

Peters, Anne, and Klaus Armingeon. "Introduction: Global Constitutionalism from an Interdisciplinary Perspective." *Indiana Journal of Global Legal Studies* 16, no. 2 (2009): 385–395.

Peters, Anne. "The Merits of Global Constitutionalism." *Indiana Journal of Global Legal Studies* 16, no. 2 (2009): 397–411.

Peters, Anne. "The New Arbitrariness and Competing Constitutionalisms: Remarks on ECtHR Grand Chamber Al-Dulimi." EJIL: Talk, June 30, 2016. http://www.ejiltalk.org/the-new-arbitrariness-and-competing-constitutionalisms-remarks-on-ecthr-grand-chamber-al-dulimi/?, last visit 03.03.2017.

Petersmann, Ernst-Ulrich. "Constitutionalism and International Organizations." *Northwestern Journal of International Law & Business* 17, no. 2-3 (1996-1997): 398–469.

Petersmann, Ernst-Ulrich. "How to Promote the International Rule of Law? Contributions by the World Trade Organization Appellate Review System." *Journal of International Economic Law* 1 (1998): 25–48.

Petersmann, Ernst-Ulrich. "Multilevel Trade Governance in the WTO Requires Multilevel Constitutionalism." In *Constitutionalism, Multilevel Trade, Governance and International Economic Law*, edited by Christian Joerges and Ernst-Ulrich Petersmann, 5–58. Oxford: Hart Publishing, 2011.

Petersmann, Ernst-Ulrich. "The WTO Constitution and Human Rights." *Journal of International Economic Law* 3 (2000): 19–25.

Poole, Thomas. "Tilting at Windmills? Truth and Illusion in The Political Constitution." *The Modern Law Review* 70 (2007): 250–277.

Post, Robert C. "Foreword: Fashioning the Legal Constitution: Culture, Courts, and Law." *Harvard Law Review* 117 (2003): 4–112.

Post, Robert C., and Reva B. Siegel. "Originalism as a Political Practice: The Right's Living Constitution." Faculty Scholarship Series no. 171, 2006. http://digitalcommons.law.yale.edu/fss_papers/171, last visit 19.01.2014.

Pound, Roscoe. "Law in Books and Law in Action." *American Law Review* 44 (1910): 12–36.

Powell, Emilia Justyna, and Sara McLaughlin Mitchell. "The International Court of Justice and the World's Three Legal Systems." *The Journal of Politics* 69, no. 2 (2007): 397–415.

Preuss. Ulrich K. "Disconnecting Constitutions From Statehood: Is Global Constitutionalism a Viable Concept?" In *The Twilight of Constitutionalism*, edited by Petra Dobner and Martin Loughlin, 23–46. Oxford: Oxford University Press, 2010.

Preuß, Ulrich K. "Equality of States – Its Meaning in a Constitutionalised Global Order." *Chicago Journal of International Law* 9, no. 1 (2008-2009): 17–49.

Raz, Joseph. "On the Authority and Interpretation of Constitutions: Some Preliminaries." In *Constitutionalism: Philosophical Foundations*, edited by Larry Alexander, 152–193. Cambridge: Cambridge University Press, 1998.

Rehnquist, William H. "The Notion of a Living Constitution." *Harvard Journal of Law & Public Policy* 29, no. 2 (2006): 401–415.

Reisman, W. Michael, Siegfried Wiessner, and Andrew R. Willard. "The New Haven School: A Brief Introduction." *Yale Journal of International Law* 32 (2007): 575–582.

Reisman, W. Michael. "The View from the New Haven School of International Law." Faculty Scholarship Series, Paper 867, 1992. http://digitalcommons.law.yale.edu/fss_papers/867/, last visit 09.08.2014.

Robertson, Roland. "Mapping the Global Condition: Globalization as the Central Concept." In *Global Culture: Nationalism, Globalization and modernity, A Theory, Culture & Society*, edited by Mike Featherstone, 15–30. London: Sage Publications, 1990.

Rosenfeld, Michel. "Constitutional Identity." In *Oxford Handbook of Comparative Constitutional Law*, edited by Michel Rosenfeld and Andras Sajo, 756–776. Oxford: Oxford University Press, 2012.

Rosenfeld, Michel. "Is Global Constitutionalism Meaningful or Desirable?" *The European Journal of International Law* 25, no. 1 (2014): 177–199.

Ruskola, Teemu. "Legal Orientalism." In *Laws and Societies in Global Contexts: Contemporary Approaches*, edited by Eve Darian-Smith, 74–83. Cambridge: Cambridge University Press, 2013.

Samuel, Geoffrey. *An Introduction to Comparative Law Theory and Method*. Oxford: Hart Publishing, 2014.

Samuel, Geoffrey. "Comparative Law and Its Methodology." In *Research Methods in Law, edited by* Dawn Watkins and Mandy Burton, 100–118. London: Routledge, 2013.

Sands, Philippe. "Turtles and Torturers: The Transformation of International Law (Pinochet and Shrimp/Turtle cases)." *New York University Journal of International Law and Politics* 33, no. 2 (2001): 527–559.

Santos, Boaventura de Sousa. "Towards a Multicultural Conception of Human Rights." In *Global Culture: Nationalism, Globalization and Modernity, A Theory, Culture & Society*, edited by Mike Featherstone, 214–229. London: Sage Publications, 1990.

Santos, Boaventura de Sousa. *Toward a New Legal Common Sense: Law, Globalization, and Emancipation*. London: Butterworths, 1995.

Sassen, Saskia. "Neither Global Nor National: Novel Assemblages of Territory, Authority and Rights." In *Laws and Societies in Global Contexts: Contemporary Approaches*, edited by Eve Darian-Smith, 23–38. Cambridge: Cambridge University Press, 2013.

Sassen, Saskia. *Territory, Authority, Rights: From Medieval to Global Assemblages*. Updated Edition. Princeton: Princeton University Press, 2008.

Schauer, Frederick. "On the Migration of Constitutional Ideas." *Connecticut Law Review* 37 (2004-2005): 907–919.

Schneider, Cornelia. "The Constitutional Protection of Rights in Dworkin's and Habermas' Theories of Democracy." *UCL Jurisprudence Review* (2000): 101–121.

Schneiderman, David. "Banging Constitutional Bibles: Observing Constitutional Culture in Transition." *University of Toronto Law Journal* 55, no. 3 (2005): 833–852.

Schneiderman, David. "Property Rights and Regulatory Innovation: Comparing Constitutional Cultures." *International Journal of Constitutional Law* 4, no. 2 (2006): 371–391.

Schwöbel, Christine E. J. *Global Constitutionalism in International Legal Perspective*. Leiden: Nijhoff, 2011.

Scott, Paul. "(Political) Constitutions and (Political) Constitutionalism." *German Law Journal*, 14, no. 12 (2013): 2157–2184.

Siegel, Reva B. "Constitutional Culture, Social Movement Conflict and Constitutional Change: The Case of the De Facto ERA." Faculty Scholarship Series no. 1097, 2006. http://digital-commons.law.yale.edu/fss_papers/1097), last visit 19.01.2014.

Silbey, Susan S. "Legal Culture and Cultures of Legality." In *Handbook of Cultural Sociology*, edited by John R. Hall, Laura Grindstaff, and Ming- Cheng Lo, 470–479. London and New York: Routledge, 2010.

Silbey, Susan S. "Legal Culture and Legal Consciousness." In *International Encyclopedia of Social and Behavioral Science*, edited by Neil J. Smelser and Paul B. Baltes, 8623–8629 Amsterdam: Elsevier, 2001.

Simma, Bruno and Philip Alston. "The Sources of Human Rights Law: Custom, Jus Cogens and General Principles." *Australian Yearbook of International Law* 12 (1988-9): 82–108.

Slaughter, Anne-Marie. *A New World Order*. Princeton: Princeton University Press, 2004.

Smith, Anthony D. "Towards A Global Culture?" In *Global Culture: Nationalism, Globalization and Modernity, A Theory, Culture & Society*, edited by Mike Featherstone, 171–192. London: Sage Publications, 1990.

Snyder, Francis. "The Unfinished Constitution of the European Union: Principles, Process and Culture." In *European Constitutionalism Beyond the State*, edited by J.H.H. Weiler and Marlene Wind, 55–73. Cambridge: Cambridge University Press, 2003.

Specter, Matthew G. *Habermas: Entelektüel Bir Biyografi*. Istanbul: Iletisim Yayinlari, 2012.

Starke, J. G. "Elements of the Sociology of International Law." *Australian Year Book of International Law* 1 (1965): 119–136.

Sterio, Milena. "The Evolution of International Law." *Boston College International and Comparative Law Review* 31, no. 2 (2008): 213–256.

Stone-Sweet, Alec. "What is a Supranational Constitution? An Essay in International Relations Theory." *The Review of Politics* 56, no. 3 (1994): 441–474.

Sunstein, Cass. "Incompletely Theorized Agreements in Constitutional Law." Public Law and Legal Theory Working Paper no. 147, 2007. http://chicagounbound.uchicago.edu/cgi/viewcontent.cgi?article=1149&context=public_law_and_legal_theory), last visit 11.07.2015.

Teitel, Rutti G. "Humanity's Law: Rule of Law for the New Global Politics." *Cornell International Law Journal* 35, no. 2 (2002): 355–389.

Teubner, Gunther. *Constitutional Fragments: Societal Constitutionalism and Globalization*. Translated by Gareth Norbury. Oxford: Oxford University Press, 2012.

Teubner, Gunther. "Global Private Regimes: Neo-Spontaneous Law and Dual Constitution of Autonomous Sectors?" In *Globalization and Public Governance*, edited by Karl-Heinz Ladeur, 71–88. Ashgate: Aldershot, 2004.

Thierry, Hubert. "The European Tradition in International Law: The Thought of Georges Scelle." *European Journal of International Law* 1 (1990): 193–209.

Thirlway, Hugh. *The Sources of International Law*. 1st ed. Oxford: Oxford University Press, 2014.

Thornhill, Chris. "A Sociology of Constituent Power." *Indiana Journal of Global Legal Studies* 20, no. 2 (2013): 551–603.

Thornhill, Christopher J. A. *Sociology of Constitutions: Constitutions and State Legitimacy in Historical-sociological Perspective*. Cambridge: Cambridge University Press, 2011.

Thornhill, Chris. "Contemporary Constitutionalism and the Dialectic of Constituent Power." *Global Constitutionalism* 1, no. 3 (2012): 369–404.

Thornhill, Chris. "Niklas Luhmann and the Sociology of the Constitution." *Journal of Classical Sociology* 10, no. 4 (2010): 315–337.

Thornhill, Chris. "Rights and Constituent Power in the Global Constitution." *International Journal of Law in Context* 10, no. 3 (2014): 357–396.

Tomkins, Adam. "Constitutionalism." In *The Oxford Handbook of British Politics*, edited by Matthew Flinders et al., 239–261. Oxford: Oxford University Press, 2009.

Tomkins, Adam. *Our Republican Constitution*. Oxford: Hart, 2005.

Tomkins, Adam. *Public Law*. Oxford: Oxford University Press, 2003.

Tomkins, Adam. "The Role of the Courts in the Political Constitution." *University of Toronto Law Journal* 60 (2010): 1–22.

Tomkins, Adam. "What's Left of the Political Constitution?" *German Law Journal* 14, no. 12 (2013): 2275–2292.

Tompkins, Penny and James Lawley. "Metonymy and Part-Whole Relationships." http://www.cleanlanguage.co.uk/articles/articles/210/1/Metonymy--Part-Whole-Relationships/Page1.html, last visit 17.11.2015.

Tomuschat, Christian. "Obligations Arising for States Without or Against Their Will." *Recueil des Cours* 241, no. 4 (1993): 195–374.

Trachtman, Joel P. "Constitutional Economics of the World Trade Organization." In *Ruling the World? Constitutionalism, International Law and Global Governance*, edited by Jeffrey L. Dunoff and Joel P. Trachtman, 206–232. Cambridge: Cambridge University Press, 2009.

Treves, Tullio. "Customary International Law." Max Planck Encyclopedia of International Law, 2006, 17. http://opil.ouplaw.com/view/10.1093/law:epil/9780199231690/law-9780199231690-e1393?prd=EPIL, last visit 14.11.2014.

Tully, James. *Strange Multiplicity: Constitutionalism in an age of Diversity*. Cambridge: Cambridge University Press, 2007.

Tushnet, Mark. "Constitution." In *The Oxford Handbook of Comparative Constitutional Law*, edited by Michel Rosenfeld and Andras Sajo, 217–232. Oxford: Oxford University Press, 2012.

Tushnet, Mark. "The Inevitable Globalization of Constitutional Law." *Virginia Journal of International Law* 49 (2008-2009): 985–1006.

Tushnet, Mark. "The Relation Between Political Constitutionalism and Weak-Form Judicial Review." *German Law Journal* 14, no. 12 (2013): 2249–2264.

Twining, William. *Globalisation and Legal Scholarship*. Tilburg Law Lectures Series, Montesquieu seminars 4. Nijmegen: Wolf Legal Publishers, 2009.

Twining, William. "Implications of 'Globalisation' for Law as a Discipline." In *Theorizing the Global Legal Order*, edited by Andrew Halpin and Volker Roeben, 39–59. Oxford: Hart Publishing, 2009.

Viellechner, Lars. "Verfassung als Chiffre." *Zeitschrift für ausländisches öffentliches Recht und Völkerrecht* 1 (2015): 233–258.

Von Bogdandy, Armin. "Constitutionalism in International Law: Comment on a Proposal from Germany" *Harvard International Law Journal* 47, no. 1 (2006): 223–242.

Vorländer, Hans. "Integration durch Verfassung? Die symbolische Bedeutung der Verfassung im politischen Integrationsprozess." In *Integration durch Verfassung*, edited by Hans Vorländer, 9–42. Wiesbaden: Westdeutscher Verlag, 2002.

Vorländer, Hans. "What is 'Constitutional Cultures'?" In *Constitutional Cultures: On the Concept and Representation of Constitutions in the Atlantic World*, edited by Silke Hensel, Ulrich Bock, Katrin Dircksen and Hans-Ulrich Thamer, 21–42. Newcastle upon Tyne: Cambridge Scholars Publishing, 2012.

Wacks, Raymond. *Understanding Jurisprudence: An Introduction to Legal Theory*. Oxford: Oxford University Press, 2009.

Walker, Luke A. "ICANN's Uniform Domain Name Dispute Resolution Policy." *Berkeley Technology Law Journal* 15 (2000): 289–311.

Walker, Neil. "Making a World of Difference? Habermas, Cosmopolitanism and the Constitutionalization of International Law." EUI Working Papers, Law No. 17, 2005. http://cadmus.

eui.eu/bitstream/handle/1814/3762/WPLAWNo.200517Walker.pdf?sequence=1, last visit 11.10.2013.

Walker, Neil. "Postnational Constitutionalism and the Problem of Translation." In *European Constitutionalism Beyond the State*, edited by J.H.H. Weiler and Marlene Wind. 27–54. Cambridge: Cambridge University Press, 2003.

Walker, Neil. Universalism and Particularism in Human Rights: Trade-Off or Productive Tension? Edinburgh School of Law Research Paper no. 2012/10, 2012. http://ssrn.com/abstract=2021071, last visit 13.04.2015.

Wallerstein, Immanuel. "Culture as the Ideological Battleground of the Modern World-System." In *Global Culture: Nationalism, Globalization and Modernity, A Theory, Culture & Society*, edited by Mike Featherstone, 63–66. London: Sage Publications, 1990.

Wallerstein, Immanuel. *European Universalism: The Rhetoric of Power*. New York: New Press, 2006.

Walter, Christian. "International Law in a Process of Constitutionalization." In *New Perspectives on the Divide Between National and International Law*, edited by Janne Nijman and Andre Nollkaemper, 191–215. Oxford: Oxford University Press, 2007.

Weiler, J.H.H. and M. Wind. "Introduction." In *European Constitutionalism Beyond the State*, edited by J.H.H. Weiler and Marlene Wind, 1–6. Cambridge: Cambridge University Press, 2003.

Wendt, Alexander. "Why a World State is Inevitable." *European Journal of International Relations* 9, no. 4 (2003): 491–542.

Wenzel, Nikolai. "From Contract to Mental Model: Constitutional Culture as a Fact of the Social Sciences." *Review of Austrian Economy* 23 (2010): 55–78.

Wieland, Joachim. "Germany in the European Union - The Maastricht Decision of the Bundesverfassungsgericht." *European Journal of International Law* 5 (1994): 259–266.

Wiener, Antje. "Constitutionalism Unbound: A Practice Approach to Normativity." Paper presented at 'Practice, Ethics and Normativity' at the Annual Millennium Conference 'Out Of The Ivory Tower - Weaving the Theories and Practice of International Relations', London School of Economics & Political Science, London, 22-23 October 2011. http://ssrn.com/abstract=2103049 or http://dx.doi.org/10.2139/ssrn.2103049), last visit 11.04.2014.

Wiener, Antje. "Constructivism: The Limits of Bridging Gaps." *Journal of International Relations and Development* 6, no. 3 (2003): 252–275.

Wiener, Antje. "Global Constitutionalism: Mapping an Emerging Field." Paper presented at the Conference "Constitutionalism in a New Key? Cosmopolitan, Pluralist and Public Reason-Oriented," WZB and Humboldt University, Berlin, 28-29 January 2011. http://cosmopolis.wzb.eu/content/programs/ conkey_Wiener_Mapping-Field.pdf), last visit 10.01.2014.

Wiener, Antje. *The Invisible Constitution of Politics: Contested Norms and International Encounters*. Cambridge: Cambridge University Press, 2008.

Yunker, James A. *The Idea of World Government: From Ancient Times to the Twenty First Century*. London: Routledge, 2011.

Zangl, Bernhard. "Is There an Emerging International Rule of Law?" In *Transformations of the State*, edited by Stephan Leibfried and Michael Zürn, 73–91. New York: Cambridge University Press, 2005.

Zervaki, Antonia. *Resetting the Political Cultural Agenda: From Polis to International Organization*, Cham: Springer, 2014.

Zumbansen, Peer. "Carving Out Typologies and Accounting for Differences Across Systems: Towards a Methodology of Transnational Constitutionalism." In *The Oxford Handbook of Comparative Constitutional Law*, edited by Michel Rosenfeld and Andras Sajo, 75–97. Oxford: Oxford University Press, 2012.

Zumbansen, Peer. "Transnational Law." In *Elgar Encyclopedia of Comparative Law*, edited by Jan M. Smits, 738–755. Cheltenham: Edward Elgar, 2006.

Max-Planck-Institut für ausländisches öffentliches Recht und Völkerrecht

Beiträge zum ausländischen öffentlichen Recht und Völkerrecht

Hrsg.: A. von Bogdandy, A. Peters

Bde. 27–59 erschienen im Carl Heymanns Verlag KG Köln, Berlin (Bestellung an: Max-Planck-Institut für Völkerrecht, Im Neuenheimer Feld 535, 69120 Heidelberg); ab Band 60 im Springer-Verlag GmbH

---

275 Aydin *Atilgan*: **Global Constitutionalism.** 2018. xx, 312 Seiten. Geb. € 114,99 zzgl. landesüblicher MwSt.

274 Andreas *Kolb*: **The UN Security Council Members' Responsibility to Protect**. 2018. XXI 624 Seiten. Geb. € 199,99 zzgl. landesüblicher MwSt.

273 Matthias *Goldmann*, Silvia *Steininger* (eds.): **Democracy and Financial Order: Legal Perspectives**. 2018. xx, 222 Seiten. Geb. € 114,99 zzgl. landesüblicher MwSt.

272 Jochen *Rauber*: **Strukturwandel als Prinzipienwandel.** 2018. XXXIV, 970 Seiten. Geb. € 159,99

271 Anja *Höfelmeier*: **Die Vollstreckungsimmunität der Staaten im Wandel des Völkerrechts.** 2018. XX 356 Seiten. Geb. € 89,99

270 Rudolf *Bernhardt*, Karin *Oellers-Frahm*: **Das Max-Planck-Institut für ausländisches öffentliches Recht und Völkerrecht.** 2018. XII, 344 Seiten. Geb. € 89,99

269 Philine *Wehling*: **Wasserrechte am Nil.** 2018. XVI, 349 Seiten. Geb. € 84,99

268 Katharina *Berner*: **Subsequent Agreements and Subsequent Practice in Domestic Courts.** 2018. XLV, 298 Seiten. Geb. € 114,99 zzgl. landesüblicher MwSt.

267 Josephine *Asche*: **Die Margin of Appreciation.** 2018. XII, 255 Seiten. Geb. € 84,99

266 Nele *Yang*: **Die Leitentscheidung.** 2018. XI, 362 Seiten. Geb. € 84,99

265 Roya *Sangi*: **Die auswärtige Gewalt des Europäischen Parlaments.** 2018. XV, 179 Seiten. Geb. € 69,99

264 Anna *Krueger*: **Die Bindung der Dritten Welt an das postkoloniale Völkerrecht.** 2018. XII, 434 Seiten. Geb. € 89,99

263 Björnstjern *Baade*: **Der Europäische Gerichtshof für Menschenrechte als Diskurswächter.** 2017. XVIII, 543 Seiten. Geb. € 99,99

262 Felix *Lange*: **Praxisorientierung und Gemeinschaftskonzeption.** 2017. XIV, 403 Seiten. Geb. € 94,99

261 Johanna Elisabeth *Dickschen*: **Empfehlungen und Leitlinien als Handlungsform der Europäischen Finanzaufsichtsbehörden.** 2017. XIX, 277 Seiten. Geb. € 84,99

260 Mohamed *Assakkali*: **Europäische Union und Internationaler Währungsfonds.** 2017. XV, 516 Seiten. Geb. € 99,99

259 Franziska *Paefgen*: **Der von Art. 8 EMRK gewährleistete Schutz vor staatlichen Eingriffen in die Persönlichkeitsrechte im Internet.** 2017. XV, 220 Seiten. Geb. € 69,99

258 Tim René *Salomon*: **Die internationale Strafverfolgungsstrategie gegenüber somalischen Piraten.** 2017. XXXII, 743 Seiten. Geb. € 129,99

257 Jelena *Bäumler*: **Das Schädigungsverbot im Völkerrecht.** 2017. XIX, 379 Seiten. Geb. € 89,99

256 Christopher *Peters*: **Praxis Internationaler Organisationen - Vertragswandel und völkerrechtlicher Ordnungsrahmen.** 2016. XXVIII, 498 Seiten. Geb. € 99,99

255 Nicole *Appel*: **Das internationale Kooperationsrecht der Europäischen Union.** 2016. XVIII, 608 Seiten. Geb. € 109,99

254 Christian *Wohlfahrt*: **Die Vermutung unmittelbarer Wirkung des Unionsrechts.** 2016. XIX, 300 Seiten. Geb. € 84,99

253 Katja *Göcke*: **Indigene Landrechte im internationalen Vergleich.** 2016. XVII, 818 Seiten. Geb. € 139,99

252 Julia *Heesen*: **Interne Abkommen.** 2015. XXI, 473 Seiten. Geb. € 94,99

251 Matthias *Goldmann*: **Internationale öffentliche Gewalt.** 2015. XXIX, 636 Seiten. Geb. € 109,99

250 Isabelle *Ley*: **Opposition im Völkerrecht.** 2014. XXIII, 452 Seiten. Geb. € 94,99

249 Matthias *Kottmann*: **Introvertierte Rechtsgemeinschaft.** 2014. XII, 352 Seiten. Geb. € 84,99

248 Jelena *von Achenbach*: **Demokratische Gesetzgebung in der Europäischen Union.** 2014. XVI, 522 Seiten. Geb. € 94,99

247 Jürgen *Friedrich*: **International Environmental "soft law"**. 2014. XXI, 503 Seiten. Geb. € 94,99 zzgl. landesüblicher MwSt.

246 Anuscheh *Farahat*: **Progressive Inklusion.** 2014. XXIV, 429 Seiten. Geb. € 94,99

245 Christina *Binder*: **Die Grenzen der Vertragstreue im Völkerrecht.** 2013. XL, 770 Seiten. Geb. € 119,99

244 Cornelia *Hagedorn*: **Legitime Strategien der Dissensbewältigung in demokratischen Staaten.** 2013. XX, 551 Seiten. Geb. € 99,99

243 Marianne *Klumpp*: **Schiedsgerichtsbarkeit und Ständiges Revisionsgericht des Mercosur.** 2013. XX, 512 Seiten. Geb. € 94,99

242 Karen *Kaiser* (Hrsg.): **Der Vertrag von Lissabon vor dem Bundesverfassungsgericht.** 2013. XX, 1635 Seiten. Geb. € 199,99

241 Dominik *Steiger*: **Das völkerrechtliche Folterverbot und der "Krieg gegen den Terror".** 2013. XXX, 821 Seiten. Geb. € 139,99

240 Silja *Vöneky*, Britta *Beylage-Haarmann*, Anja *Höfelmeier*, Anna-Katharina *Hübler* (Hrsg.): **Ethik und Recht - Die Ethisierung des Rechts/Ethics and Law - The Ethicalization of Law.** 2013. XVIII, 456 Seiten. Geb. € 94,99

239 Rüdiger *Wolfrum*, Ina *Gätzschmann* (eds.): **International Dispute Settlement: Room for Innovations?** 2013. XIV, 445 Seiten. Geb. € 94,95 zzgl. landesüblicher MwSt.

238 Isabel *Röcker*: **Die Pflicht zur rahmenbeschlusskonformen Auslegung nationalen Rechts.** 2013. XXIII, 410 Seiten. Geb. € 89,95

237 Maike *Kuhn*: **Die Europäische Sicherheits- und Verteidigungspolitik im Mehrebenensystem.** 2012. XIII, 325 Seiten. Geb. € 79,95

236 Armin *von Bogdandy*, Ingo *Venzke* (eds.): **International Judicial Lawmaking.** 2012. XVII, 509 Seiten. Geb. € 94,95 zzgl. landesüblicher MwSt.

235 Susanne *Wasum-Rainer*, Ingo *Winkelmann*, Katrin *Tiroch* (eds.): **Arctic Science, International Law and Climate Change.** 2012. XIX, 374 Seiten. Geb. € 84,95 zzgl. landesüblicher MwSt.

234 Mirja A. *Trilsch*: **Die Justiziabilität wirtschaftlicher, sozialer und kultureller Rechte im innerstaatlichen Recht.** 2012. XIX, 559 Seiten. Geb. € 99,95

233 Anja *Seibert-Fohr* (ed.): **Judicial Independence in Transition.** 2012. XIII, 1378 Seiten. Geb. € 169,95 zzgl. landesüblicher MwSt.

232 Sandra *Stahl*: **Schutzpflichten im Völkerrecht - Ansatz einer Dogmatik.** 2012. XXX, 505 Seiten. Geb. € 94,95

231 Thomas *Kleinlein*: **Konstitutionalisierung im Völkerrecht.** 2012. XLII, 940 Seiten. Geb. € 149,95

230 Roland *Otto*: **Targeted Killings and International Law.** 2012. XVIII, 661 Seiten. Geb. € 109,95 zzgl. landesüblicher MwSt.

229 Nele *Matz-Lück*, Mathias *Hong* (Hrsg.): **Grundrechte und Grundfreiheiten im Mehrebenensystem - Konkurrenzen und Interferenzen.** 2012. VIII, 394 Seiten. Geb. € 89,95

228 Matthias *Ruffert*, Sebastian *Steinecke*: **The Global Administrative Law of Science**, 2011. IX, 140 Seiten. Geb. € 59,95 zzgl. landesüblicher MwSt.

227 Sebastian *Pritzkow*: **Das völkerrechtliche Verhältnis zwischen der EU und Russland im Energiesektor.** 2011. XXIV, 304 Seiten. Geb. € 79,95

226 Sarah *Wolf*: **Unterseeische Rohrleitungen und Meeresumweltschutz.** 2011. XXIII, 442 Seiten. Geb. € 94,95

225 Clemens *Feinäugle*: **Hoheitsgewalt im Völkerrecht.** 2011. XXVI, 418 Seiten. Geb. € 89,95

224 David *Barthel*: **Die neue Sicherheits- und Verteidigungsarchitektur der Afrikanischen Union.** 2011. XXV, 443 Seiten. Geb. € 94,95

223 Tilmann *Altwicker*: **Menschenrechtlicher Gleichheitsschutz.** 2011. XXX, 549 Seiten. Geb. € 99,95

222 Stephan *Bitter*: **Die Sanktion im Recht der Europäischen Union.** 2011. XV, 351 Seiten. Geb. € 84,95

221 Holger *Hestermeyer*, Nele *Matz-Lück*, Anja *Seibert-Fohr*, Silja *Vöneky* (eds.): **Law of the Sea in Dialogue.** 2011. XII, 189 Seiten. Geb. € 69,95 zzgl. landesüblicher MwSt.

220 Jan *Scheffler*: **Die Europäische Union als rechtlich-institutioneller Akteur im System der Vereinten Nationen.** 2011. XXXV, 918 Seiten. Geb. € 149,95

219 Mehrdad *Payandeh*: **Internationales Gemeinschaftsrecht.** 2010. XXXV, 629 Seiten. Geb. € 99,95

218 Jakob *Pichon*: **Internationaler Strafgerichtshof und Sicherheitsrat der Vereinten Nationen.** 2011. XXVI, 399 Seiten. Geb. € 89,95

217 Michael *Duchstein*: **Das internationale Benchmarkingverfahren und seine Bedeutung für den gewerblichen Rechtsschutz.** 2010. XXVI, 528 Seiten. Geb. € 99,95

216 Tobias *Darge*: **Kriegsverbrechen im nationalen und internationalen Recht.** 2010. XXXV, 499 Seiten. Geb. € 94,95

MIX
Papier aus verantwortungsvollen Quellen
Paper from responsible sources
FSC® C105338

If you have any concerns about our products,
you can contact us on
ProductSafety@springernature.com

In case Publisher is established outside the EU,
the EU authorized representative is:
Springer Nature Customer Service Center GmbH
Europaplatz 3, 69115 Heidelberg, Germany

Printed by Libri Plureos GmbH
in Hamburg, Germany